Exchange 2000 Server Administration: A Beginner's Guide

ABOUT THE AUTHORS

Bill English, MCSE, MCT, CTT, is the coauthor of *Exchange 2000 Server Administrator's Companion* and *MCSE Readiness Review Exam 70-224: Installing, Configuring, and Administering Microsoft Exchange 2000 Server*, both from Microsoft Press. He is the owner of Networknowledge (www.networknowledge.com), a consulting and training firm offering services to small- and medium-sized businesses. Bill is the Senior Exchange Technologist for MindSharp Learning Center in Minneapolis. He also teaches Windows 2000 and Exchange 2000 courses at Crown College in St. Bonifacious, Minnesota.

Nick Cavalancia, MCSE, MCT, MCNE, MCNI, is Director of Training and Consulting for Comsphere (www.comsphere.com) and specializes in high-end Exchange 2000 and Windows 2000 infrastructure designs. Nick has worked as a Microsoft and Novell trainer, consulted on large-scale Exchange 5.*x* and Exchange 2000 projects supporting 2,000–150,000 users, and edited and contributed to numerous books. He also speaks regularly at conferences, including the Microsoft Exchange Conference 2000.

Exchange 2000 Server Administration: A Beginner's Guide

BILL **ENGLISH**
& NICK **CAVALANCIA**

Osborne/**McGraw-Hill**

New York   Chicago   San Francisco
Lisbon   London   Madrid   Mexico City
Milan   New Delhi   San Juan
Seoul   Singapore   Sydney   Toronto

Osborne/**McGraw-Hill**
2600 Tenth Street
Berkeley, California 94710
U.S.A.

To arrange bulk purchase discounts for sales promotions, premiums, or fund-raisers, please contact Osborne/**McGraw-Hill** at the above address. For information on translations or book distributors outside the U.S.A., please see the International Contact Information page immediately following the index of this book.

Exchange 2000 Server Administration: A Beginner's Guide

234567890 CUS CUS 01987654321

ISBN 0-07-213119-5

Publisher
    Brandon A. Nordin
Vice President & Associate Publisher
    Scott Rogers
Senior Acquisitions Editor
    Jane Brownlow
Project Editor
    Jenn Tust
Acquisitions Coordinator
    Ross Doll
Copy Editor
    Karyn DiCastri

Proofreader
    Linda Medoff
Indexer
    Jack Lewis
Computer Designers
    Elizabeth Jang, Carie Mahnekoff
Illustrators
    Beth E. Young, Lyssa Sieben-Wald
Cover Design
    Amparo Del Rio
Series Design
    Peter F. Hancik

This book was composed with Corel VENTURA™ Publisher.

To Ed and Mary Jane English, my parents, who taught me
how to work hard and have fun. —*BE*

To Linda Hackett and in memory of Michael Burnside.
These two saw me for what I could be, pushed me,
and showed me I could become more. —*NC*

AT A GLANCE

CONTENTS

Part II

Administration Deployment

Part III

Exchange 2000 Server Architecture

Part IV

Advanced Administration

Part V

Client Administration

ACKNOWLEDGMENTS

As with most books, by the time you're finished writing it, you realize that you could not have finished it without the assistance of many people. This one is no exception. First and foremost, I'd like to thank my coauthor, Nick Cavalancia, who jumped in at midstream and did a great job writing his chapters. It's good to work with a coauthor who you know will write quality material. Nick, thanks for your work on this book and for being willing to take on this project with little notice.

I'd also like to thank Jane Brownlow, the acquisitions editor and an all-around great gal. Jane, you took the ebb and flow of life's unexpected turns with grace and calmness. Thanks for your flexibility, understanding, and professionalism throughout this project. I've had a good experience working with you, and I am looking forward to doing it again.

Jenn Tust and Ross Doll made sure that the chapters kept moving through the various stages and even put up with some lateness on my part. Thanks for not hounding me when I got behind on some of my chapters and for gently pushing me to get back on schedule. I appreciate your professionalism.

I also want to thank Neil Salkind, my agent, and the folks at StudioB, who helped keep this project going and gave me excellent advice as the book unfolded. Neil, as always, you're great to work with.

Here in Minnesota, I'd like to thank my wife, Kathy, for letting me work some nights and weekends and for supporting me in this project. Honey, you're the best wife a guy could ever want. I'd also like to thank my brother-in-law, Bruce Powers, who directed me toward the computer field several years ago. Bruce, your advice was some of the best I've ever received.

I want to thank Dave Fletcher and Mary Texer at MindSharp Learning Center in Minneapolis for working with my schedule and giving me the time needed to write this book. Thanks for your flexibility.

Finally, I'd like to thank Jesus Christ, who gave me the talent and the opportunity to coauthor this book and without whom I would be lost forever.

—Bill English

This being my first go as an author, I am keenly aware of all the work others have put into the success of this book. To Jane Brownlow, Jenn Tust, Ross Doll, Beth Young, Lyssa Sieben-Wald, and the rest of the folks at Osborne, I want to tell you how truly appreciative I am of your dedication to this book. Without your efforts, all of this would simply be but a few pages of text sitting on a computer screen somewhere....

A great big thanks goes to my coauthor, Bill. Thank you for the opportunity to work with you on this book. It was a great honor for me to be asked to help you finish it. The jump from being a technical editor to author was a challenging one but was also filled with fun. I'm especially glad I got to work on this book with you. I think we both learned from our last book together (and this one) that it's not what you work on, but who you work with.... I consider you not just a colleague and coauthor, but also my friend.

I want to thank my wife, Jenay, who never complained even once (yes honey, I noticed!) about the crazy schedule this book sometimes had. J, thanks for believing in me and my decision to take on this project. Without your support, I would never get *anything* done. I also would like to thank my sons Colin and Nicholas. You both are my constant reminder of what's truly important in life. Without the two of you, nothing in this world would be worth doing.

To my mom, thanks for being one of my best friends.

To my dad (who shares my name), now you can brag to your friends that you wrote a book, too!

To "my biggest fan" Fernando, your belief in me is powerful enough to sail a thousand ships! Your friendship and encouragement are greatly treasured.

To Jerry, who first taught me Exchange and now calls me with Exchange questions, thanks for being my best friend.

Last (but not least), I'd like to thank God who gave me the opportunity, the desire, and the ability to coauthor this book.

—Nick Cavalancia

INTRODUCTION

Microsoft Exchange 2000 Server represents a significant step forward in messaging software. With the advent of Windows 2000 and its architectural improvements, Exchange 2000 Server is now more flexible and scalable than ever before. These advances will dramatically change your administrative tasks, file management, and database maintenance.

Exchange 2000 Server is now one of the foundational programs that will directly integrate with at least two of the new .NET server platforms: Mobile Information Server (MIS) and SharePoint Portal Server (SPS). Among other things, MIS will leverage the monitoring tools of Exchange 2000 Server to gather presence information on the wireless devices that are considered part of your network. Users will soon be able to install a small Outlook client on a cell phone and use that device to send and receive e-mail. This is already being done with pagers, and MIS will be the liaison between your LAN-based users and your wireless users. But you'll need Exchange 2000 to run MIS on your network.

SPS will tightly integrate with Exchange public folders, allowing you to create workspaces in which documents can be profiled, categorized, published, and approved. SPS will also offer a much improved and advanced search and indexing feature, which allows users to regularly have searches conducted in the background for certain topics at specified locations, such as public folders, file shares, and Web sites. To do all this, you'll need Exchange 2000 to run SPS on your network.

By now, it should be clear that Exchange 2000 Server is the future, and those who are running another messaging system will be, at a minimum, integrating Exchange 2000 Server into their present environment if they want to be compatible with the future.

Exchange 2000 Server is a knowledge-management program, providing secure methods of making information available to knowledge workers at any time, from any place, and using any client, including cell phones, personal digital assistants, computers, and other new products.

WHO SHOULD READ THIS BOOK

Exchange 2000 Server Administration: A Beginner's Guide is written for the person who knows little or nothing about Exchange. If you have managed Exchange 5.*x* Servers and now want a brief primer on Exchange 2000 Server, this book will be helpful to you. If you're brand new to Exchange and know nothing about Exchange 5.5 Server then this book will be a great start in your journey to become an Exchange administrator. However, if you have worked with Exchange 2000 Server since the beta releases or consider yourself to be an advanced Exchange administrator, you might just want to use this book as a refresher course and hopefully you'll learn a thing or two. Our goal in this book is not to rewrite the *Exchange 2000 Resource Kit* or to give you all the details about this program. (That task has been accomplished with the *Exchange 2000 Server: The Complete Reference*, which is also published by Osborne.) Instead, our goal is to introduce Exchange 2000 Server to you and the many others who will be asked to install and administrate this powerful product without any formal training.

We do assume that you have some Windows 2000 background, and we do refer to general Active Directory (AD) concepts without always taking the time to explain them in depth. You may want to purchase a copy of the *Windows 2000 Resource Kit* and have that nearby when you read this book. At times, we'll mention a concept and then refer you to the resource kit for further information.

WHAT'S IN THIS BOOK

Exchange 2000 Server Administration: A Beginner's Guide is organized into five parts.

The three chapters in Part I, "Migration and Coexistence," are targeted toward folks who need to do a migration from Exchange 5.5 Server to Exchange 2000 Server. A good understanding of this material will provide you with a foundation for good administration. Chapter 1 illustrates one method of upgrading from Exchange 5.5 Server to Exchange 2000 Server. It also outlines some of the other methods that are available for migration. Since the majority of Exchange installations are in environments with fewer than four Exchange Servers, we've chosen to illustrate how to migrate in a smaller environment. Chapter 2 discusses the coexistence issues between these two platforms and how they can work together to provide a seamless environment for your users while the migration is under way. Chapter 3 examines how Exchange 2000 integrates with Windows 2000.

Part II, "Administration Deployment," is aimed at readers who want to get going on administration and deployment of Exchange 2000 Server. It includes six chapters that are essential reading for those who are in a multi-routing group environment. Chapter 4 discusses how to install Exchange 2000 Server in more depth than was covered in Chapter 1. In Chapter 4, we explore some of the options and features in the installation/migration process that were not covered previously. Chapter 5 examines creating and managing recipients while concentrating on how to manage mail-enabled objects in Active Directory Users and Computers. Chapter 6 discusses public folder replication as well as how to create and manage public folders. Chapter 7 takes a look at storage groups, when you want to create multiple storage groups and how to plan for and administrate them. Chapter 8 focuses on planning for and administering routing groups. We also discuss system policies for Exchange Servers and illustrate how to implement both a Public Store Policy and a Mailbox Store Policy. Chapter 9 finishes our section on administration by focusing on the Routing Group Connectors (RGCs).

Part III, "Exchange 2000 Server Architecture," is our two-chapter architecture section. This is for the real geeks who want to know how the Exchange 2000 platform is put together. Chapter 10 discusses the storage and database architecture. We explain the new streaming file and how the Extensible Storage Engine (ESE) and transaction logs work, and then we illustrate the genius of the new Exchange Installable File System. Chapter 11 looks at the new routing architecture, including connector costs, the link state table, and the link state algorithm. We also discuss how to route messages between groups and to foreign e-mail systems.

"Advanced Administration" is the main topic of our four-chapter Part IV. For this part, we assume that you already know a few things about administering Exchange 2000 and Windows 2000. Chapter 12 illustrates how to configure security for the Exchange platform. Certificate Services and the Key Management (KM) Server are discussed in depth. Chapter 13 provides an overview of how to monitor Exchange 2000 services and servers using the new Exchange monitoring tools. Chapter 14 provides an in-depth look at disaster recovery and backup procedures. *Be sure to read this chapter if data recovery is important to you.* Chapter 15 walks through some of the key points for performance monitoring of Exchange 2000 Server. Key performance counters are discussed with tips on how to use them in your environment.

Part V, "Client Administration," is the last section, and it takes a brief look at the two main client interfaces for Exchange 2000 Server. Chapter 16 briefly discusses the various messaging clients for Exchange 2000 Server and then dives into the Outlook 2000 client illustrating some of the more interesting features of Outlook 2000. And wrapping up the book is Chapter 17, which outlines how to implement instant messaging (IM) in your environment. IM is a tool that most users will want to utilize; be sure to read this chapter before you try to deploy IM in your environment.

Sections of the first draft of this book were written on the RC2 version of Exchange 2000 Server. However, all chapters have been edited against the final code for Exchange 2000 Server, which was released in the early fall of 2000. As is true with most books, some readers like to communicate with the author(s). If you would like to send an e-mail to ask a question or to offer a suggestion, you may do so to Bill English at benglish@networknowledge.com or to Nick Cavalancia at nickc@comsphere.com.

We hope you enjoy reading this book and using it as a reference in your activities as an Exchange 2000 Server Administrator.

PART I

Migration and Coexistence

CHAPTER 1

Upgrading to Exchange 2000 Server

Migrating to Exchange 2000 Server and ensuring coexistence with Exchange 5.5 Server is going to be one of your most prominent challenges. This chapter details how to make the transition smooth and ensure that messaging traffic flows uninterrupted, and it also gives you a road map to follow when performing the migration and points out problems to avoid. Even though this is a beginner's book on Exchange 2000, we'd like to help you avoid beginner mistakes.

Before doing an upgrade to Exchange 2000, you must first perform an upgrade to Windows 2000 Server on at least one server that will be hosting Exchange 2000 Server. Before installing Exchange 2000 Server, you must have Active Directory (AD) up and running. We will not discuss in depth in this book how to plan for and perform a migration to Windows 2000 Server from Windows NT 4.0 Server. If you need to learn more about that, please consult the following books:

▼   *Microsoft Windows 2000 Server Resource Kit*, Microsoft Press.

▲   *Windows 2000 Administration*, by George Spalding, Osborne/McGraw-Hill.

Even though we're not going to outline how to perform a migration from Windows NT 4.0 Server to Windows 2000 Server, there are a few principles that need to be mentioned here about a Windows 2000 upgrade in order to paint the backdrop for our Exchange migration discussions.

First, you will upgrade your Primary Domain Controller (PDC) that holds at least one of your main user account databases to Windows 2000 Server. During this installation process, the contents of the Windows NT security accounts database are copied into Active Directory (AD). As part of this upgrade process, dcpromo.exe is automatically run so that the PDC can still perform its functions with the downstream Backup Domain Controllers (BDCs). Because of this, AD will be created running in mixed mode. If at all possible, plan out your domain structure and migrate all of your PDCs to Windows 2000. This will help minimize the possibility of having duplicate accounts later on.

Also, try to get to a single domain model in NT 4.0 Server before migrating to Windows 2000 Active Directory. While there are tools available to help conduct a smooth migration from a multiple-domain model to AD, it is easiest and best to migrate from a single domain.

Upgrading the PDC has several considerations. The first is the partition size on your current PDC. If you were like most administrators, you probably created a 2GB partition for the operating system. In Windows 2000, the basic installation often consumes at least 1GB of disk space; this leaves little room for other necessities, such as the pagefile.sys or programs that must be installed in the system root directory. Hence, the best practice in this scenario is to create a new NT 4.0 Server with a 4GB partition and install it as a BDC. Then promote it to PDC, and run the upgrade to Windows 2000 on this new server. This is preferable to using a third-party partition program to rearrange current partition sizes on your current PDC. Of course, if you don't want to migrate your existing Windows NT security accounts database to AD, you can use the Active Directory Migration Tool (ADMT) to copy user accounts from the Windows NT PDC to AD.

You will want to take a good, hard look at your current hardware and make sure that it will provide enough resources to run Windows 2000, Exchange 2000, and any other BackOffice products or .NET server platforms that you plan to run in the next three to five years. In most companies today, except for the smallest of environments, the minimum hardware being purchased are dual PIII/800 with a minimum of 512MB RAM. In many cases, 1GB of RAM is being ordered to ensure that there are enough server-side resources to meet the increasing demand from the users.

The first PDC that is upgraded to a Windows 2000 domain controller (DC) will hold all five operation master roles, including the PDC Emulator role. This role allows the Windows 2000 domain controller to look and feel like a PDC to existing BDCs on the network. You can still use the former PDC to create new security principles, such as user, group, and workstation accounts, in AD and have these new accounts replicated to the BDCs. At the BDC, these new objects will look like NT 4.0 security principles, not AD objects. Cool, eh?

NOTE: If, at this point, the Windows 2000 domain controller that is operating as the PDC Emulator goes offline, you can promote a Windows NT 4.0 BDC to PDC. This will neither interrupt network operations nor adversely affect your security accounts database.

Once you've upgraded your PDC to Windows 2000 AD, you can go ahead and migrate the BDCs, though this really isn't necessary. However, it is always a best practice to take one BDC offline during this process, in case you need to failback to your Windows NT 4.0 domain. Once your domain controllers and members servers that are going to host Exchange 2000 Servers have been migrated to Windows 2000, it's time to begin looking at migrating to Exchange 2000 Server.

PLANNING YOUR EXCHANGE 2000 MIGRATION

What we are going to discuss now is how to plan for your Exchange 2000 migration. *Do not skip reading this section and do not perform your migration without first making sure you have done due diligence in this planning area.* Failure to fully plan out your Exchange 2000 migration *will* lead to problems in administering and operating your new Exchange 2000 organization.

In addition, this chapter will illustrate how to migrate from a single domain model to AD. We realize that there are other, more complicated scenarios, but space limitations prohibit us from detailing additional scenarios. Keep in mind that the majority of Exchange 5.5 installations are in a single domain environment with only a few Exchange 5.5 Servers.

Reliance on Windows 2000

Exchange 2000 Server relies heavily on Windows 2000 in three main areas: the directory, transport, and name resolution. Previous versions of Exchange included a separate directory of objects that was distinct from the security accounts database managed by the PDC. In Windows 2000, we use a single database that performs both functions with the same set of objects. Windows 2000 manages this database and Exchange 2000 Server leverages its features. One example of this is the Global Address List (GAL), which is really a listing of all the mail-enabled objects in AD.

After Windows 2000 is installed, the transport stacks, such as Simple Mail Transfer Protocol (SMTP) and Network News Transfer Protocol (NNTP), are placed inside the inetinfo.exe process (Internet Information Services or IIS) and run as separate transport stacks. Windows 2000 and Exchange 2000 will use these stacks for both messaging and overhead functions, such as directory replication. When Exchange 2000 Server is installed, it extends these stacks with additional command verbs and an advanced routing component, the link state protocol, to ensure that you enjoy an enterprise-class messaging and collaboration system.

The Exchange 2000 development team wrote both versions of the messaging protocol stacks. By decoupling these protocols from the information store services and placing them inside IIS, it allows both Windows 2000 and Exchange 2000 to use common protocol architecture.

Collaborative applications and messaging functionality both require name resolution. The Domain Name System (DNS) is now the preferred method of name resolution for Exchange 2000, and this function is offered by Windows 2000 Dynamic DNS. Any service resolution that was performed by the Windows Internet Naming Service (WINS) in Windows NT 4.0 has been moved over to DNS as the primary service to the IP resolution process. If you are running any specialized applications that run inside an Exchange public folder and that rely on WINS resolution, you should plan to have that application updated to work with Windows 2000 DNS. Until then, be sure to run WINS on your network.

DSAccess and Global Catalog (GC) Usage

DSAccess is a new shared Application Programming Interface (API) between Exchange 2000 and AD that performs several functions. It is used by the store.exe process, IIS protocols, and Outlook Web Access (OWA). DSAccess is a shared memory cache that increases performance for messaging operations and provides access to both configuration and recipient data from AD to Exchange services and Outlook users.

One of the main functions of DSAccess is to scan AD to ensure that Exchange services has knowledge of the various GCs available. Both the Exchange Server and Outlook clients access the GC to locate recipients across all domains and to make routing decisions across all Windows 2000 sites. In essence, Exchange 2000 Server relies heavily on GC services, and the best practice is to make sure you have no more than one GC for every four Exchange 2000 Servers, per site and per domain.

DSAccess will detect and keep a list of usable GC Servers. Preferred GC Servers are those located in the same Windows 2000 site as the Exchange 2000 Server. User requests for e-mail addresses are load balanced across all GC Servers in the site. Should all the GC Servers in the site become unavailable, DSAccess will scan AD for new GC Servers and then add those servers to its list.

Extending the Schema

When the first Exchange 2000 Server is installed into AD, the schema will be extended. Because this represents over 1000 changes to the schema, Microsoft has provided a switch, /ForestPrep, which can be run with the Setup program to extend the schema to include Exchange 2000 objects without installing any of the Exchange services.

This command, along with the /DomainPrep command, was introduced for larger organizations that were dividing their networking administration and Exchange administration between two teams. In larger installations, it is preferable to have one person, or team, extend the schema (which is considered a network administrative function) and a different person, or team, install Exchange 2000 Server.

NOTE: In smaller environments, where one or two people perform all administrative functions, running this command is not necessary since the setup.exe program will automatically run both the /ForestPrep and /DomainPrep commands as part of the installation of the first Exchange 2000 Server.

Be sure to plan for enough time to allow the schema to replicate throughout your forest. If you have deeply nested child domains, you'll need to wait for the schema to fully replicate to that domain before you'll be able to install Exchange 2000 into it. Because this potentially represents a large amount of replication traffic among all your domain controllers, the best practice would be to either extend the schema early in your forest development so that new domain controllers inherit the fully extended schema or, if your forest is fully populated with many domain controllers, extend the schema at the beginning of a long period of downtime when network traffic will be relatively light—like on a Friday night.

Moreover, you will need direct network connectivity to the Schema Master, which is, by default, the first domain controller installed into your forest. If you don't have this type of connectivity, then you should extend the schema on the Schema Master itself.

Microsoft has placed the fully extended schema on the Exchange 2000 Server CD-ROM in text form for manual inspection. You may use it to discern what changes will need to be made to your schema before you run the /ForestPrep switch, which you do by opening each Lightweight Directory Access Protocol (LDAP) Data Interchange Format (LDIF) file in Notepad and printing the file for manual inspection.

Deployment Options

Exchange 2000 Server will have two different ways to install. First, there will be a wizard-based setup that can be used for local server-based installations and through Terminal Services. The ability to install Exchange 2000 Server inside of Terminal Services means that remote locations won't require you to send a person on site just to do the installation. To learn more about how to use Terminal Services, please consult the Windows 2000 Server Resource Kit.

Exchange 2000 Server can also be installed using the silent, or batch, installation method. This method, which does not use Terminal Server, allows for remote installations of Exchange 2000 Server and has its questions answered from an *.ini file, similar to how unattended installations have been performed for Windows NT 4.0 and Windows 2000 Servers. One nice feature about the silent installation method is that you can create the *.ini file at your desktop by driving the Exchange 2000 Server setup user interface (UI) through a mock installation. During the installation, you can choose to create the *.ini file, which will then be used for the unattended installation of Exchange 2000. When the silent install is performed, it will run exactly as it did when you performed the mock install on your desktop.

Exchange 5.x Sites Versus Administrative and Routing Groups

In Exchange 5.x, you have been working inside sites, which has defined both your routing and administrative boundaries. In planning for your new Exchange 2000 organization, you'll be able to divide these functions so that your routing topology is not required to mirror your administrative topology. An *administrative group* is, essentially, a collection of Exchange objects, like servers, that can be administered as a group. A routing group defines the boundaries between permanent, high-bandwidth connectivity and slower, less reliable connectivity. Obviously, servers that enjoy permanent, high-bandwidth connectivity will be placed in the same routing group, whereas servers that do not will be placed in different routing groups. By the way, you get to decide what is considered "permanent, high-bandwidth" in your environment.

This different way of dividing up administrative functions could potentially have profound implications for how your Exchange 2000 organization is managed. For instance, it is now possible to put one person, or a group of people, in charge of managing just the routing connectors while assigning the management of the Exchange 2000 Servers to another person, or group of people.

In most organizations, this will carry political and interpersonal consequences. How your administrative functions will be apportioned among team members needs to be fully discussed and resolved before Exchange 2000 is introduced into your network.

Also, it is during the installation of an Exchange 2000 Server that you will choose which administrative and routing group combination the server will reside in. While it is possible to move servers between routing groups, this can only be done if the routing groups exist in the same administrative group and if the organization is in native mode. Therefore, the best practice would be to create all of these groups after the installation of the first Exchange 2000 Server, but before subsequent installations or migrations of other Exchange 2000 Servers. Be sure to plan for this function at this juncture in your migration. These groups should ultimately reflect the exact administrative model you intent to implement.

Mixed Mode Versus Native Mode

At some point, you will have migrated all your Exchange 5.*x* Servers to Exchange 2000. Once this is accomplished, you will be able to move your Exchange organization into native mode. You should plan for when to do this and who will perform the function.

Mixed mode simply means that there are still some Exchange 5.*x* Servers on your network with which you need interoperability. Mixed mode also means that you can be interoperable with Exchange 4.*x* and 5.*x*, even if all your Exchange Servers are running 2000. If you think that there is even a remote possibility that you will need interoperability with Exchange 5.*x* Servers in the future, you should stay in mixed mode. Plan for this and consider every possibility, even if it seems rather off the wall. Doing so will enable you to be legacy compatible in the future, if it is ever required.

If you know that, after migrating all your Exchange 5.*x* Servers to 2000, you will not need to be compatible with Exchange 5.*x* Servers, then go ahead and move your organization into native mode. Once you do so, you'll be able to divide up functionality between the administrative and routing groups. As long as you are in mixed mode, your Exchange 2000 organization must look and function like an Exchange 5.*x* organization to maintain 5.*x* compatibility. This means that administrative groups in 2000 will function like 5.*x* sites. By the way, moving into native mode is a one-way, one-time conversion.

NOTE: Once the organization has been moved to native mode, it cannot be moved back to mixed mode.

Planning for Groups in Exchange 2000 Server

If you are working in a single-domain environment, you may skip this section. However, if you're working in a multiple-domain environment with messaging occurring between users in different domains, then you should read on.

When working in a multiple-domain environment, it is important to remember that messages sent to a group of users in another domain must first have the group's membership list enumerated by the sending Exchange 2000 Server. When crossing domain boundaries, the GC Server is consulted to obtain a group's member list.

Now, global groups are listed in the GC, but their membership is not. Hence, if a message is sent to a global group, the GC will be queried by the sending Exchange 2000 Server for the global group's membership. Since the GC Server doesn't have that list, it will return a Null response because there are no users in the list to send a message to. The trick with this is that the Exchange 2000 Server will not return an error message to the message's originator nor will a Non-Delivery Report (NDR) be generated. In essence, once the Null response is received by the Exchange 2000 Server, it will basically drop the message, and that will be the end of it.

So, the best practice is to always use Universal Groups for distribution lists in a multiple-domain environment because a Universal Group's membership is enumerated in the GC and, therefore, will be available for use across domain boundaries. And remember that you must have a Windows 2000 native mode domain in order to create Universal groups. It may be necessary to create a Windows 2000 native mode domain specifically for this purpose.

Deployment Components

Because you will be working with two different directories for a period of time, you'll need to understand the deployment components, what they can do for you, and how to plan for them. The three components that will be of most interest to you are the Active Directory Connector (ADC), the Connection Agreement (CA), and the Site Replication Services (SRS). All three of these components ensure that your 5.*x* information is replicated to AD.

The AD Connector

Many companies have amassed large amounts of data in their 5.*x* directory that would be very costly to re-create in Exchange 2000. Hence, the AD connector allows you to upload current information into AD and also to create new user accounts at the same time. The connector can run on a scheduled or continual basis.

Inside the connector, you will create one or more CAs. Suffice it to say for now that you will need to plan out *exactly* which connectors you want to set up *before* you implement any of them.

The ADC uses LDAP to transport data from the old Exchange directory to AD. Since Windows 2000 and Exchange 2000 use the latest version of LDAP, your Exchange Directory Service (XDS) must be version 5.5. If you are running either Exchange 5.0 or 4.*x*, you should first plan to upgrade your Exchange Servers to 5.5 and then upgrade them again to Exchange 2000.

Objects with similar semantics will be merged in AD. Mailboxes in Exchange 5.5 will become mail-enabled users in AD, custom recipients will become mail-enabled contacts, and distribution lists will become distribution groups.

Before you can upgrade your Exchange 5.5 organization to Exchange 2000, you must install the ADC with a CA between your Exchange 5.5 organization and Windows 2000 AD.

Connection Agreements (CAs)

There are two types of CAs: User CAs and Configuration CAs (ConfigCA). As you administer a mixed environment, you will become most familiar with the User CA.

A User CA is always created between a recipient container in the 5.5 directory and an organization unit (OU) in AD. It defines the schedule, authentication method, and direction that synchronization should take. Moreover, it provides you with granular control over when and how objects are replicated between the two directories.

For instance, if your Exchange 5.5 organization was set up so that all recipients—including mailboxes, custom recipients, and public folders—were created in the default recipient's container, then you'll have the opportunity to replicate those objects based on their class to different organization units. This will allow you to create a cleaner recipient structure in AD without having to re-create all the objects and folders.

Be sure to plan your OU structure before you install Exchange 2000 Server. You'll need to take into consideration how non-mail-enabled objects will be organized in AD and then plan accordingly. Since the OU structure is entirely there to ease administrative effort, be sure to use the OU structure to your advantage.

Site Replication Services (SRSs)

This is probably the most confusing component you'll work with. SRS is a service that lives on an Exchange 2000 Server and that looks like an Exchange 5.5 directory to 5.5 Servers. What SRS does is make a Directory Replication Bridgehead Server that has been upgraded to Exchange 2000 look like an Exchange 5.5 Directory Replication Server to other 5.5 Directory Replication Bridgehead Servers.

And just like a User CA replicates user and group information to the domain partition in AD, the SRS uses the ConfigCA to replicate site and physical information of your Exchange 5.5 organization to the configuration partition in AD.

The SRS uses the same Extensible Storage Engine (ESE) database design. When communicating with Exchange 5.5 Servers, it incorporates the Exchange 5.5 replication engine and uses mail-based messaging for intersite replication and Remote Procedure Call (RPC)–based communications for intrasite replication. SRS supports both LDAP and Exchange Directory Services (XDS) as access protocols. The Message Application Programming Interface (MAPI), however, is disabled so that Exchange 5.5 clients don't use this database for regular data access. The SRS databases are designed to be a holding tank for replication traffic between the two directories.

SRS supports the Knowledge Consistency Checker (KCC), which allows the SRS to write to both naming contexts—the Windows 2000 and the Exchange 5.5 context. Also, in Exchange 5.5, the KCC is limited to writing inside the site context. This limitation is removed for the SRS, so it can write to the directory in any Exchange 5.5 site.

The Site Consistency Checker (SCC) is a decision-analysis component of the SRS, and its function is to make sure that all the existing Exchange 5.5 sites are represented in the existing connection agreements. This is especially helpful if you introduce Exchange 2000 into a large Exchange 5.5 organization and then, later on, introduce other Exchange 5.5 sites into the organization, even though you're steadily migrating existing servers to Exchange 2000. The SCC will analyze the current 5.5 topology and ensure this topology is represented in the CAs. Without adding these sites to existing connection agreements, the information in those sites won't make it into AD. So, the SCC's role is very important during a migration of a dynamic Exchange 5.5 organization that is also performing a migration to Exchange 2000.

Planning at this stage is obviously important because you can still add Exchange 5.5 Servers and new 5.5 sites even though you've already started an Exchange 2000 migration. This would come in very handy in a situation in which your company desires to move forward with Exchange 2000 but is considering purchasing another company at the same time. The SRS, SCC, KCC, ADC, and CAs allow you to go ahead with your migration, stay in mixed mode, and incorporate a new messaging system.

Client-Side Implications

When planning a move to Exchange 2000 Server, you might think that you need to simultaneously upgrade your clients as well. This is not the case. While all Exchange 2000 clients require access to a GC Server, Exchange 2000 will work with Outlook 97, Outlook 98, and Outlook 2000 clients differently to help them achieve this goal. However, at the server end, be sure that your Exchange 2000 Servers and the GCs are in close proximity to each other because Exchange 2000 conducts numerous GC lookups. Unless you have a real good reason to do otherwise, the best practice would be to have two GCs per Windows 2000 site that will host at least one Exchange 2000 Server. By doing this, you ensure that Exchange 2000 will not need to cross a slow WAN link in order to perform a GC lookup, and if one GC goes offline, there is a second one available to serve; the Exchange 2000 requests.

Planning for your clients should take the direction to Outlook 2000 or better, but it isn't necessary and can be conducted independent of the server upgrades.

Merging Legacy Directories with Exchange 2000

The question we need to look at here is how you can upgrade existing legacy directories into a single way to begin thinking about this is that you'll have multiple data sources with a single target database. The multiple data sources will have accounts and attributes on those accounts, like the user's name, address, and phone. But each account in AD will have a SIDHistory attribute which will retain the old, Windows NT 4.0 SID. When these multiple data sources are replicated to AD, multiple accounts will be created. So Microsoft wrote the Active Directory Accounts Cleanup Wizard (ADCLEAN), which looks at the SIDHistory attribute of each AD object and where it finds matches in the SIDs, it attempts to merge these objects into a single object. Thus, ADCLEAN provides the merging of twin objects in AD.

When planning in this area, be sure to include the use of ADCLEAN. This is an area that could cause you considerable headaches, so be sure to conduct careful planning of how the accounts will be merged in AD. We demonstrate how to use ADCLEAN in the section "Upgrading in Other Scenarios," later in this chapter.

So, you're really faced with two migration choices. First, completely upgrade your Windows NT 4.0 domain to AD. This is by far the easiest method and completely removes the possibility of having twin accounts created in AD because the CA will match up the Exchange 5.5 mailboxes with the Windows 2000 user account and the merge will be complete. However, in many environments, this simply won't be possible.

Second, you can upgrade Exchange 5.5 to AD while there are still Windows NT 4.0 domains that contain user accounts on your network. In larger organizations, some with over 200 domains, this is the likely scenario. Hence, administrators in these environments will need to use ADCLEAN to clean up twins after a later Windows NT 4.0 upgrade to AD.

In addition, there will be the need to use the Active Directory Migration Tool (ADMT), which allows for the migration of user accounts from one directory to another.

A Handy Planning Summary

Here are the main issues that you should address and be ready for *before* starting your Exchange 2000 migration:

▼ Confirm that AD is installed on your network.

■ Make sure that the server upon which you run /ForestPrep is either the Schema Master (recommended) or that it is a Windows 2000 domain controller that has direct IP connectivity to the Schema Master.

■ Give yourself sufficient time to extend the schema and to have those extensions migrated to all the domain controllers in your forest before proceeding with the Exchange 2000 migration.

■ If you need to perform remote installations of Exchange 2000, then be sure to either install Terminal Services or create the necessary *.ini files to perform the installation in silent mode.

■ Discuss and resolve any political issues surrounding the new administrative model that you will enforce once you have moved to native mode. Remember that the division of your routing topology and administrative topology could represent significant role changes for key IT administrators. This must be discussed and resolved in advance to maintain a good team dynamic.

■ After installing your first Exchange 2000 Server, be sure to create all the planned administrative and routing groups to reflect your new Exchange 2000 administrative model so that other Exchange 2000 Servers can be installed directly into these groups.

■ Determine how long you will need legacy compatibility and then plan to switch to native mode only after this time period has passed. Decide who will perform the switch to native mode so that it isn't done prematurely by another administrator. The best practice would be to have a server-by-server list detailing the order and time when each server will be migrated.

■ Plan out your ADC connection agreements, especially if you have multiple Exchange 5.5 sites with multiple servers in each site.

- Plan out when your clients will be upgraded to Outlook 2000 or newer software and what that will entail. Remember that a client upgrade is not necessary, but it should be done, either as a separate plan or as part of the overall migration.

▲ Detail which directories the user accounts will be migrated from. Also, if possible, try to perform a trial migration on an isolated network to learn what the ramifications are before doing this in a production environment. Read up on ADCLEAN, and be prepared to use it.

This tool will come in handy when you want to migrate your user accounts to a new AD without upgrading a Windows NT 4.0 PDC. To learn more about the ADMT, please consult the Windows 2000 Resource Kit.

In planning your upgrade, if at all possible, try to first move all your user accounts to one domain in NT 4.0. While this might require some adjustments that could prove costly or time consuming, it would also make the migration to Windows 2000 go more smoothly. Also, we would not recommend moving forward with an Exchange 2000 migration without first knowing in which domain all the existing Windows NT 4.0 user accounts reside and checking whether there is a way to first migrate those domains to AD. Energy put into this part of the planning process will likely make your migration easier and more seamless.

MIGRATING TO EXCHANGE 2000 SERVER

Now that we've covered planning issues, let's see how this is actually done. What we will be doing here is running through a standard upgrade of a network for a fictitious company, TrainsByDave. Their Windows NT 4.0 domain name is trainsbydave, and their Web site is **trainsbydave.com**. They currently have four offices in Sacramento, Tucson, Minneapolis, and Indianapolis. The PDC is in Minneapolis. Sacramento and Indianapolis each have one BDC, and Tucson has one member server. All four servers are running Windows NT 4.0 Server, Service Pack 6a, and Exchange 5.5, Service Pack 3.

The Exchange organization name is, not surprisingly, trainsbydave. Each server is in its own site, named after its state: California, Arizona, Minnesota, and Indiana. Each site is connected by a Site Connector, and there is a linear topology for Directory Replication connectors so that the Directory Replication path is California > Arizona > Minnesota > Indiana. This illustration shows the initial organization topology inside the Exchange Administrator:

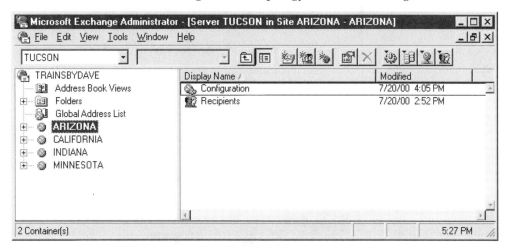

Next, we upgraded Minneapolis to Windows 2000 and installed AD as a part of the upgrade. After that, Tucson was upgraded to Windows 2000 as a member server in AD. So, as we begin our discussion, we have four servers, one is running Windows 2000 AD in mixed mode, two are NT 4.0 BDCs, and the fourth is a Windows 2000 member server in the AD domain, trainsbydave.com.

Installing the ADC Service

Before running the /ForestPrep command, we must first install the ADC service on Minneapolis. This is necessary to accomplish if you intend to upgrade your 5.5 organization to Exchange 2000, as is the recommended method by Microsoft. This will allow the ConfigCA to be installed by the SRS when the time comes.

To install the ADC, run Setup from the ADC folder located on the Exchange 2000 Server CD-ROM. Click Next on the Welcome screen and choose both check boxes: Microsoft Active Directory Connector Service component and Microsoft Active Directory Connector Management components, shown next. Selecting the former will install the ADC Server. Selecting the latter will install the ADC Microsoft Management Console (MMC) snap-in.

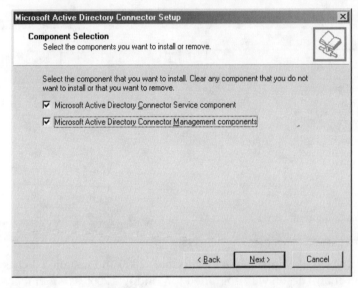

The next screen will give you a choice as to where you would like the service installed. The default is c:\program files\MSADC. Thereafter, you'll need to enter a service account name and password under which you would like the ADC service to run. We recommend creating a separate account for this service, because, in terms of security, it is best to have different accounts for different services. After entering the name and password, the service installs and you've finished.

The installation of the ADC service extends the schema, but not to the extent that the /ForestPrep command does. Figure 1-1 shows what the schema looks like after the ADC service has been installed. Notice that there are only nine Exchange object classes. After running the /ForestPrep command, there are well over 100 Exchange object classes.

Installing the ADC service will also create security groups: the Exchange Domain Servers global group and the Exchange Enterprise Servers domain local group.

The Exchange Domain Servers global group is given read permissions to Exchange configuration container objects and will contain all the Exchange 2000 Servers in the domain. The Exchange Enterprise Servers domain local group will have permissions to modify properties on all recipients and Exchange configuration objects and will contain all the Exchange Domain Servers groups from all the domains. The Exchange and ADC service accounts will automatically be made members of these two groups.

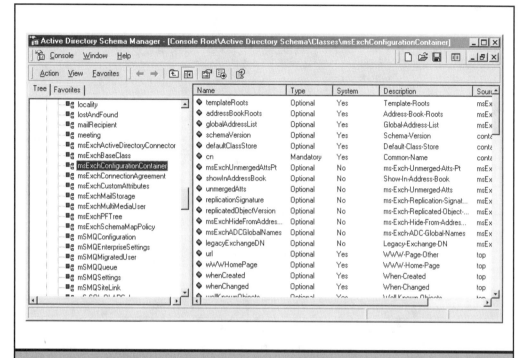

Figure 1-1.   The AD schema after the ADC service is installed

TIP: One very nice thing that the Exchange development team did was to make sure that if, at each point in the Setup program, something isn't configured just right, the Setup program will halt and give you a message indicating the problem and, sometimes, the solution. If you receive an error message at any point during your migration process, be sure to pay attention to it. It is put there to make sure you don't do something that you'll later regret.

Before you run the /ForestPrep command, you can first set up a connection agreement so that the 5.5 account information can be replicated to AD. Chapter 2 will go over how to set up a CA in detail, so please refer to that chapter for an in-depth discussion on what each configuration option means. Here, we will cover only the necessary details needed to set up the CA.

First, open up the Active Directory Connector Manager, right-click the ADC object, point to New, and select Recipient Connection Agreement. In the General tab, as shown in Figure 1-2, you should input a descriptive name for the CA to uniquely identify what this connector is going to do. We've named ours "Minnesota 5.5 site to AD" to signify

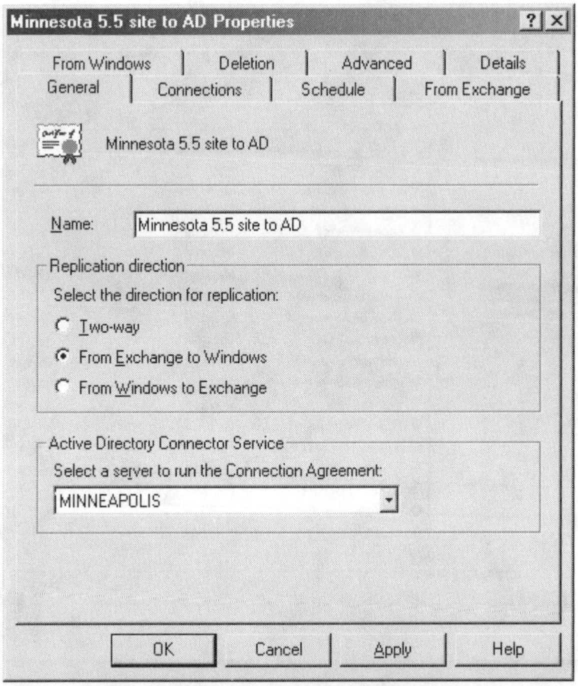

Figure 1-2. The General tab for creating a new connection agreement

that the objects in the Minnesota site will be replicated to AD using this connector. In a multiple-site environment, it is not necessary to create a CA for each site to AD before running the /ForestPrep command. However, it is necessary that at least one site have a CA created.

On the Connections tab, shown in Figure 1-3, you'll need to enter the user account and password that will have sufficient rights to write to each directory. It need not be the same account and, frankly, most likely won't be. Generally, you should be able to use the Active Directory Administrator user account for writing to AD, and the Exchange service account for writing to and reading from the Exchange 5.5 directory.

Figure 1-3.   The Connections tab in creating a new connection agreement

Now, if you don't change the port number in the Exchange 5.5 Administrator to something other than 389, which is the default LDAP number, then you will get the error message shown here:

What this means is that there is a port number conflict since both the Exchange 5.5 directory and AD will want to read and write using the same port number. To avoid this error message and get the CA working, you'll need to change the port number for LDAP services in the Exchange Administrator. Most administrators choose port 390, as shown in Figure 1-4. Then stop and start your Exchange services. This should eliminate the error message.

After resolving the port number conflicts, you'll then need to choose at least one recipient container to synchronize to AD. At this point, you can do a number of things to fix your container structure or synchronize different object classes to different organiza-

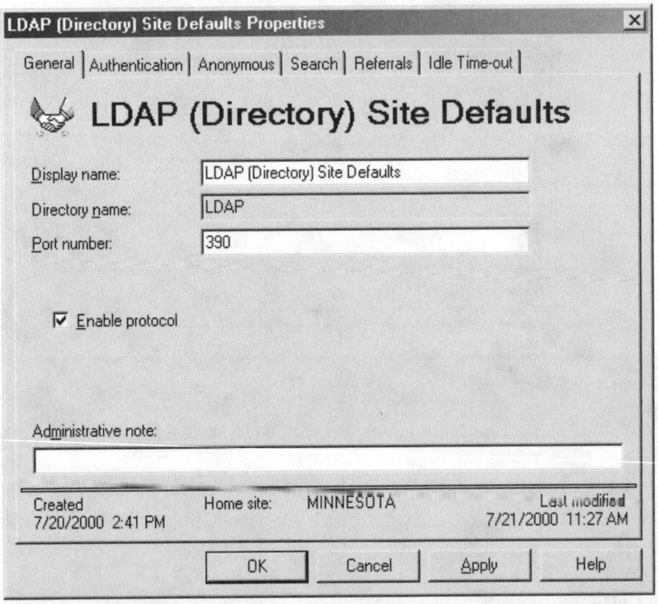

Figure 1-4.   Changing the LDAP port number in the Exchange Administrator

tional units. You'll really have loads of flexibility here. For instance, you can choose to synchronize all the distribution lists to one OU and all the mailboxes to another OU. If these objects are already quarantined in their own recipients container in the 5.5 directory, then you can synchronize recipient containers with OUs in AD. The big picture here is to think about which OUs should hold which type of recipients, and then synchronize accordingly.

We've chosen to replicate the default recipient's container to the User's OU. The next illustration shows the Choose A Container selection box:

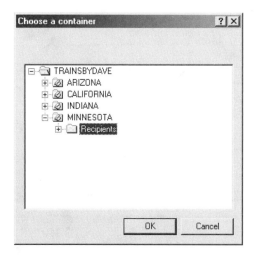

Figure 1-5 shows how this will look on the From Exchange tab. You'll also need to choose at least one organization unit to which objects should be replicated by choosing the Modify button.

At this point, we're able to create the CA and move on to running /ForestPrep.

Running /ForestPrep

Since we have an AD that is not yet extended to include all the Exchange 2000 Server objects, we must prepare the schema to accept the impending Exchange 2000 installations. This is accomplished by running setup.exe on the server CD-ROM with the /ForestPrep

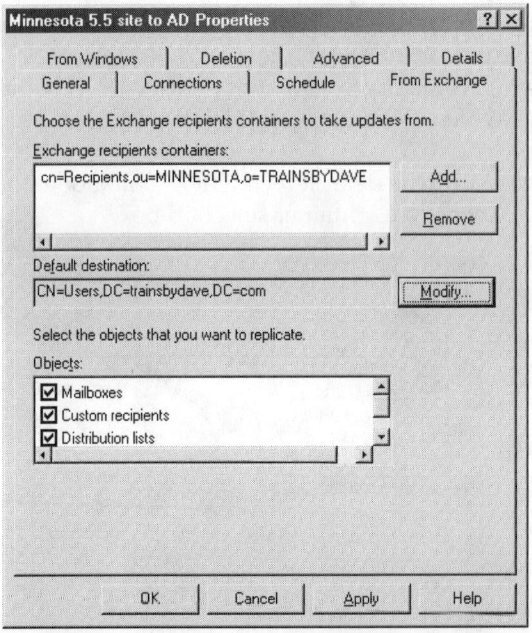

Figure 1-5. The From Exchange tab in creating a new connection agreement

switch. To show how the schema is extended by this action, Figure 1-6 shows the schema without any extensions installed for Exchange, including both the /ForestPrep and the ADC service extensions.

The Setup program will start as normal with the welcome and licensing screen being the first to be presented. After agreeing with the license agreement (have you ever seen a licensing agreement you *didn't* agree with?), you'll be asked to enter the product key on the next screen. Then, you'll be presented with the component selection screen,

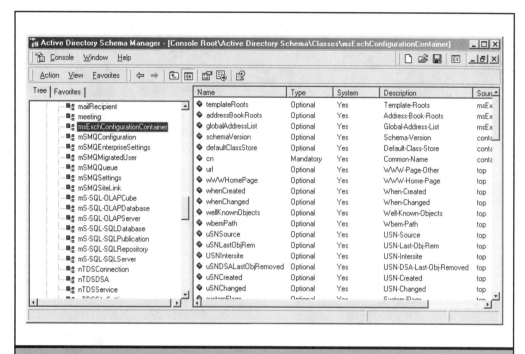

Figure 1-6. The AD schema before running the /ForestPrep and ADC setup

and the only option will be to select Forestprep, as illustrated in Figure 1-7. However, if you are running this command from a Windows 2000 member server or a domain controller that is unable to discern which site it belongs in, you won't be able to proceed. The latter scenario is usually caused by not creating the appropriate sites in Active Directory Sites and Services.

NOTE: Also, remember that you must be logged on as a member of both the Enterprise Admins and the Schema Admins.

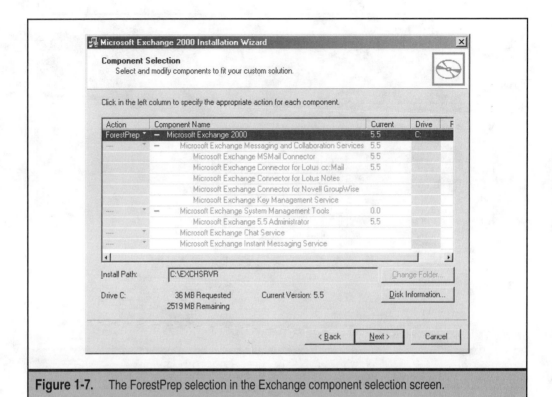

Figure 1-7.   The ForestPrep selection in the Exchange component selection screen.

If, at this point, you receive an error message indicating that the /ForestPrep action cannot be conducted because "You must be an Exchange Full Administrator to run Setup. You must use an account that has been granted Full Exchange Administrator role using the Exchange Administrative Delegation Wizard," then you should be sure to add the user account you are logged on with to the Enterprise Admins group, as this is the only group, by default, that has full permissions to the Exchange organization object.

NOTE: The /ForestPrep switch not only extends the schema, but it also creates the Exchange organization and subcontainers in AD. If you choose to upgrade the Exchange 5.5 organization when running the /ForestPrep command, it will use the directory information from the Exchange 5.5 organization to create the new organization in AD. If you choose to create a new organization and then later want to move your 5.5 objects into AD, you must use the same organization name in both directories.

Now comes the fun part. In Figure 1-8, you'll see the next screen in our setup process. At this point, we must choose whether to create a new Exchange organization or join/upgrade an existing Exchange 5.5 organization. You will make the selection based on your

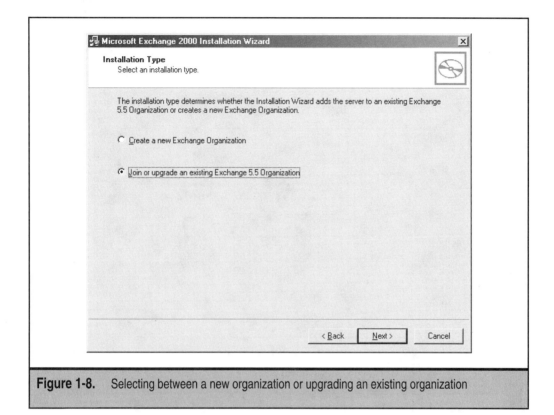

Figure 1-8.   Selecting between a new organization or upgrading an existing organization

plan. If you want to create a new organization, then the first selection is the correct one. If you'd like to upgrade your Exchange 5.5 organization, then choose the second selection. Choosing the upgrade option means that the ADC service needs to be previously installed and is the recommended method.

Keep in mind the following:

▼ If you choose to upgrade your Exchange 5.5 site, the next screen will ask for the name of the Exchange 5.5 Server to which it will read directory information.

▲ If you install the ADC and then run /ForestPrep and choose to upgrade the 5.5 site, it will then let you extend the schema and instantiate the Exchange organization objects in the AD using information from the 5.5 directory. Later on, when the SRS is installed during the server upgrade, it will need the ADC running to install the ConfigCA.

If you run /ForestPrep and choose to create a new organization, you won't need the ADC service installed. However, it will still create the organization name you input and other Exchange 2000 objects in AD. Also, as Figure 1-9 shows, you may receive a message

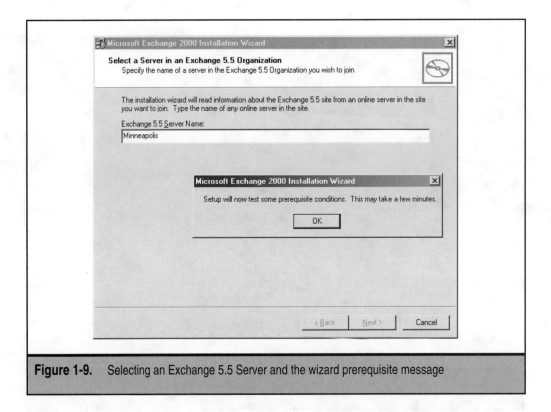

Figure 1-9. Selecting an Exchange 5.5 Server and the wizard prerequisite message

from the Installation Wizard saying that some prerequisite conditions will be tested. What this means is that the system will check for the existence of the ADC service, and, if it is installed, you'll be allowed to move forward. If not, then you'll need to exit the Setup program and install the ADC service as outlined previously.

Also, at this point, you might receive an error message indicating that AD was unable to bind to the Exchange 5.5 directory because it is "an unexpected type." This message means that you need to change the default port number for the LDAP in the Exchange 5.5 Administrator from port 389 to some other port. Most administrators choose port 390. You'll then need to stop and restart the Exchange 5.5 services to bind the LDAP protocol to the new port. Thereafter, this error message should not appear.

We chose to upgrade our Exchange 5.5 organization; so after selecting to upgrade our Exchange 5.5 organization, we were prompted (as illustrated in Figure 1-10) to

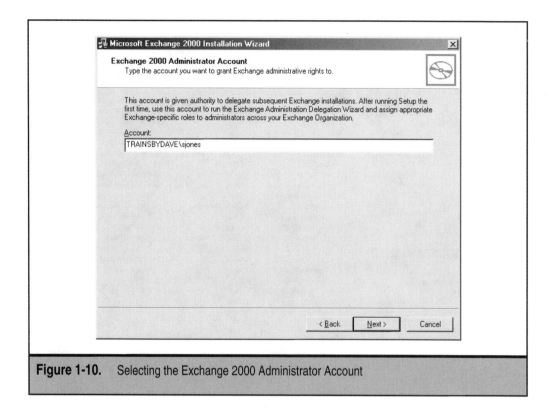

Figure 1-10.   Selecting the Exchange 2000 Administrator Account

supply the user account that will be given authority to delegate administrative authority to other user accounts. Essentially, this account will decide who has what level of administrative permissions in your Exchange organization. Make sure that you select this account carefully, because it gives high-level, broad permissions to your entire Exchange 2000 organization.

You then must input the Exchange service account password on the next screen. When you click Next, the schema will be extended. Depending on the resources of your server, this could take anywhere from ten minutes to over an hour to complete.

Figure 1-11 shows what the new, updated schema will look like. Even though you can't see it fully in the graphic, there were approximately 155 new object classes created along with approximately 820 new attributes. In addition, around 270 new attributes were marked for replication in the GC.

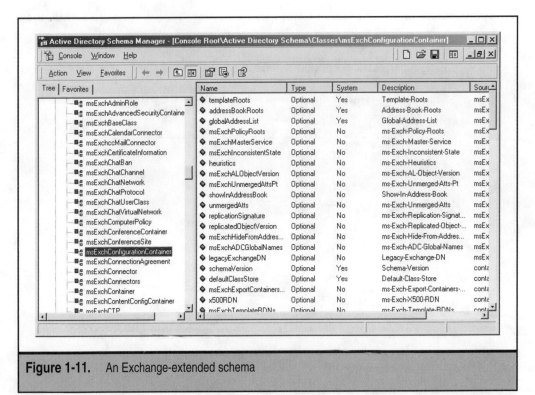

Figure 1-11. An Exchange-extended schema

By using the Active Directory Service Interface (ADSI) tool, you can see that the top-level Exchange 2000 objects were created in the configuration partition, as shown in Figure 1-12.

Now, we need to run the Setup program again, this time using the /DomainPrep switch. This needs to be done for each domain in your forest that will host an Exchange 2000 Server or that will host mail-enabled users or groups.

To run setup with this switch, you must have Domain Admin–level permissions in the current domain. This means that the domain administrator can run this command—it need not be done by an Enterprise Administrator. Like the /ForestPrep switch, this is a command-line operation that can be performed either from the command prompt or from the Run command in the Start menu.

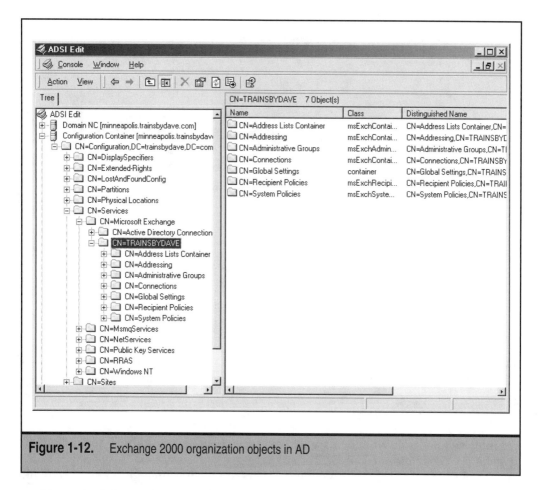

Figure 1-12. Exchange 2000 organization objects in AD

Figure 1-13 shows that the DomainPrep command is entered into the Action column. All you'll need to do is select Next, and the setup program will move to the Component Progress screen. If your domain is identified as an insecure domain, as shown here,

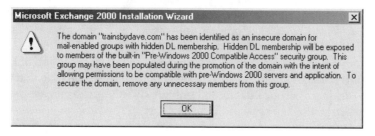

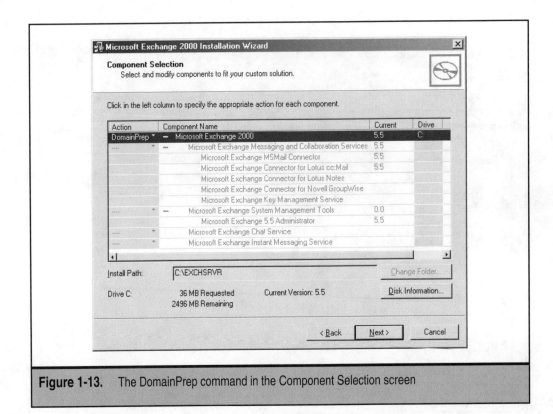

Figure 1-13.   The DomainPrep command in the Component Selection screen

the informational note will pop up with the Component Progress screen reminding you that hidden Distribution List (DL) membership will be exposed to members of the built-in "Pre-Windows 2000 Compatible Access security group and to remove any unnecessary members from this group."

This means that when the server was promoted to domain controller, the option to "weaken permissions" was selected. Choosing to weaken permissions means that an NT Remote Access Server (RAS) can properly authenticate logon requests using what's known as a *Null* session. The reason this carries a security risk is that if the Everyone group is in "Pre-Windows 2000 Compatible Access," anybody can read any attribute of any user. This could be a security risk.

A couple of items should be noted. First, if this is a new installation of Exchange 2000 Server into AD instead of upgrading a 5.5 organization, this is the time that the Exchange-specific global and local groups discussed previously in this chapter are created. Second, this is usually a much faster process than the /ForestPrep process.

Finally, we're ready to upgrade the first Exchange 5.5 Server to Exchange 2000. To upgrade the first server, we need to run the Exchange 2000 Setup program again and move through the welcome, licensing, and product key screens as we did when we ran the /ForestPrep and /DomainPrep switches.

Then we'll choose to upgrade the Exchange 5.5 Server to Exchange 2000. At this point, as in all installations, the Setup program does an internal check of the system's configuration to ensure that it is all set up properly. If it isn't, an information message box will appear, indicating actions that need to be performed or problems that need to be resolved before setup can continue. If you receive an error message that Setup cannot continue because the objects in the Exchange 5.5 directory have not finished replicating to AD, you should go back to the ADC service and either manually create a connection agreement to migrate the 5.5 directory information into AD, or make sure your CAs are working properly. For information on how to create a CA, see Chapter 2.

You cannot install additional components during the upgrade of an Exchange 5.5 Server. For instance, if you want to install the Instant Messaging Service, you'll need to rerun the Setup program and install that component in a separate administrative act. This is shown in Figure 1-14, where our only choices are to upgrade the Exchange 5.5 installed components.

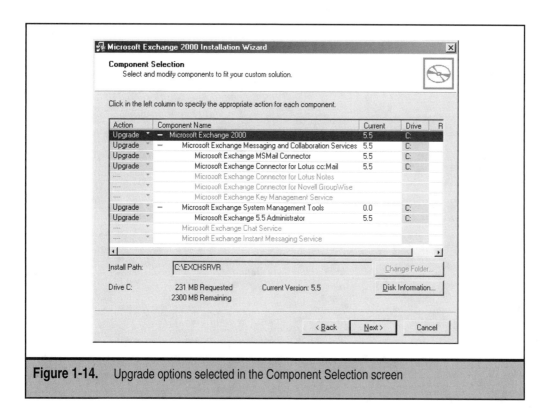

Figure 1-14.   Upgrade options selected in the Component Selection screen

After clicking Next, you'll need to type in the Exchange service account password on the next screen, accept the defaults given to you in the Component Summary screen (Figure 1-15), and then watch Exchange upgrade from 5.5 to 2000. After the upgrade is completed, you'll need to reboot the server. Until it is rebooted, Exchange services will be unavailable to users from that server. So plan to perform upgrades of your Exchange

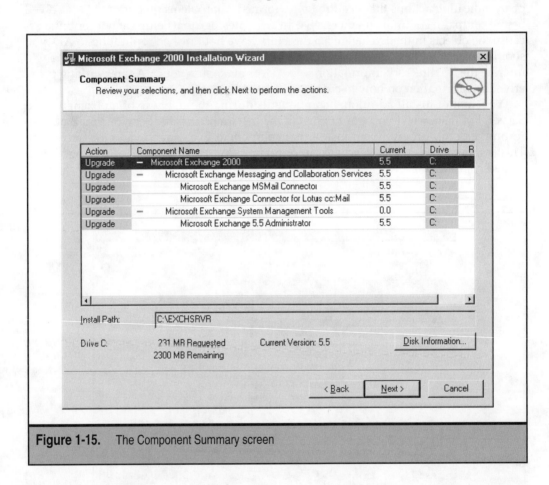

Figure 1-15. The Component Summary screen

Servers during business hours only if it isn't a big deal in your company to reboot a server during those hours.

During the upgrade process, the Exchange 5.5 databases are converted to Exchange 2000. The most prominent feature here is that the databases are now comprised of two files, the *.stm and the *.edb file. In Exchange 5.5, we only had the *.edb file. For a more complete discussion on databases in Exchange 2000 Server, see Chapter 11.

Also, the ConfigCA is automatically installed to pass site information from the Exchange 5.5 directory service to AD. After upgrading Minneapolis, Figure 1-16 shows the automatically installed connection agreement.

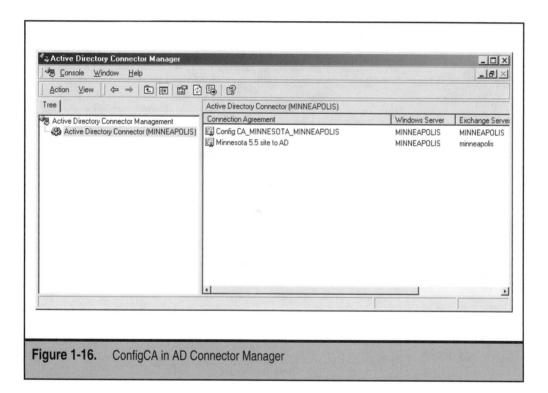

Figure 1-16.   ConfigCA in AD Connector Manager

You'll also find, as shown next, that there are several additional menu choices given to you under the Microsoft Exchange common group, including ADCLEAN and both the 5.5 Administrator and the Exchange 2000 System Manager. Microsoft grouped these menu choices together so that you wouldn't need to navigate around your entire desktop to open up the administrative utilities that would most often be used.

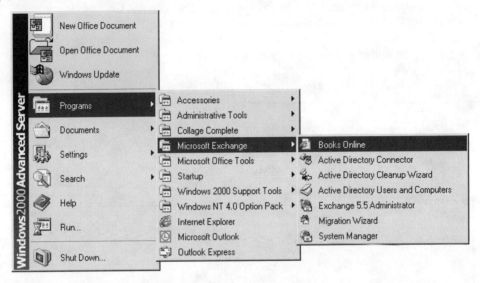

After the upgrade is complete, one of the interesting things you'll find is that all the objects in the Exchange Administrator are colored in and available for manipulation (Figure 1-17). However, in System Manager, only the Exchange 2000 Server objects are colored in. Exchange 5.5 objects appear transparent, but they are still available for admin-

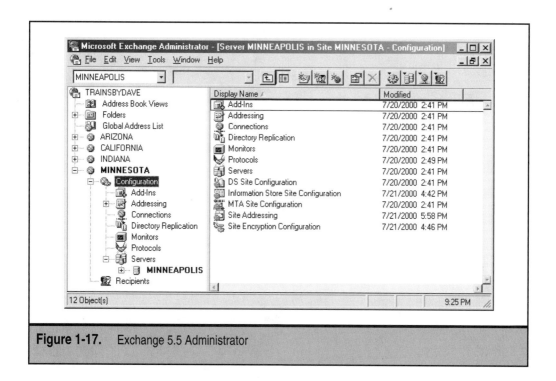

Figure 1-17. Exchange 5.5 Administrator

istrative manipulation (Figure 1-18). Also, additional container objects that are specific to Exchange 2000 will appear under the Exchange 2000 administrative group. Furthermore, you'll note that each Exchange 5.5 site appears as a separate administrative group in the

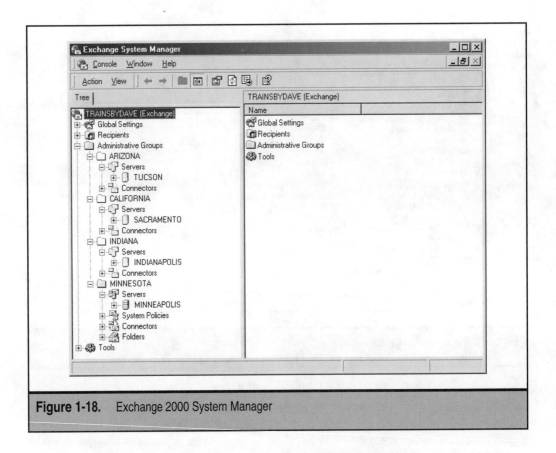

Figure 1-18.   Exchange 2000 System Manager

System Manager. In the next chapter on coexistence, we'll dive into how to administrate a mixed network of Exchange 5.5 and Exchange 2000 Servers.

Now, one thing is missing. Did you notice it? Neither Figure 1-17 nor 1-18 shows a routing group, which is how the message routing topology is created. Interestingly enough, System Manager will show the messaging connectors under a Connectors container, but not the routing group container.

Furthermore, if we open up Active Directory Services Interface (ADSI), shown in Figure 1-19), we can see that the connector objects themselves are under the routing

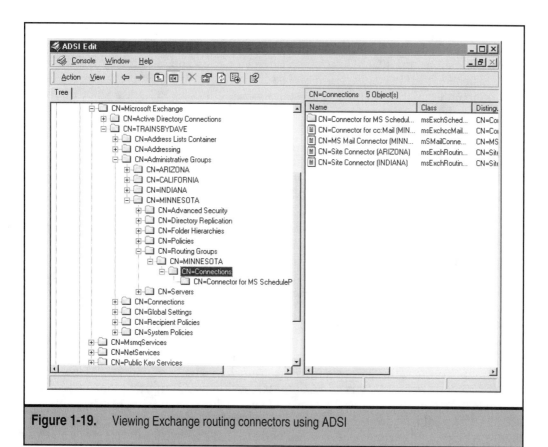

Figure 1-19.   Viewing Exchange routing connectors using ADSI

groups' container. This means that the view in System Manager is meant to help the Exchange 5.5 administrator's transition to Exchange 2000 Server a bit more smooth visually. These objects will rearrange themselves after all the Exchange 5.5 Servers have been migrated to Exchange 2000.

Notice that what once were Site Connectors are now routing group Connectors (RGC). We'll cover these connectors more in detail in Chapter 9; but for now, suffice it to say that an RGC is going to be the most commonly and widely used connector when passing messages between two Exchange routing groups. It uses SMTP as its native transport protocol and is more tolerant of low-bandwidth environments. To an Exchange 5.5 Server, the RGC looks like a Site Connector and will communicate using RPCs instead of SMTP. Hence, it is a bit of a con artist. It can communicate using either method in either platform and will present itself as either an RGC or a Site Connector, depending on the platform it wants to communicate with.

Upgrading an Exchange 5.5 Server on a Windows 2000 Member Server

In this section, we want to highlight a few differences when upgrading an Exchange 5.5 Server on a Windows 2000 Server that is a member of an AD domain. First, bear in mind that Exchange 2000 Server must have access to AD services. This is easily accomplished if all the Exchange 2000 Servers are installed on AD domain controllers. However, a Windows 2000 member server doesn't hold a local copy of AD, so an Exchange 2000 Server installed on a member server will generate additional network traffic when it needs to interact with AD and will need direct, high-speed connectivity to at least one domain controller.

Second, remember that since this is a member server, the /ForestPrep and /DomainPrep commands need not be run. Those are only for the domain controllers.

Third, the Exchange services domain account must be a member of local Administrator's group. You can add this account to the group by using the Computer Management utility. Navigate to Local Users and Computers inside the Computer Management utility, open up the Administrator's group, and click Add. Then be sure to select your AD domain in the Look in: drop-down list. Select the Exchange services account, as shown in Figure 1-19 (called "Exchange" in my test network), and then click OK.

Finally, be sure that you have run the Delegation of Control Wizard on the Exchange 2000 organization object so that you are logging on as a user that has Full Exchange Permissions to the entire organization in order to perform the upgrade. You must log onto the domain, not the local computer, to successfully run Setup to upgrade the Exchange Server.

Steps for Upgrading from Exchange 5.5 to Exchange 2000

1. Make sure to do due diligence in your planning of this migration effort.

2. Install Service Pack 3 for Exchange 5.5 Server on each Exchange Server before upgrading the server.

3. Upgrade at least one PDC to Windows 2000 Server so that you have an AD which an Exchange 2000 organization can be created.

4. Install the ADC service and configure a connection agreement between the Exchange 5.5 directory and AD.

5. Log on as a user who is a member of both the Schema Admins and Enterprise Admins security groups before running /ForestPrep.

6. Add the ADC service account to the local Administrator's built-in security group.

7. Run the /ForestPrep command and extend the schema. Make sure to allow enough time for the schema to replicate to all the domain controllers in your forest before proceeding.

8. Run the /DomainPrep command in each domain that will either host an Exchange 2000 Server or host mail-enabled objects.

9. Run the Setup command and upgrade your first Exchange 5.5 Server to Exchange 2000.

10. Upgrade the other Exchange 5.5 Servers to Exchange 2000 according to your plan.

UPGRADING THE REMAINING EXCHANGE 5.5 SERVERS

Once the first Exchange 5.5 Server has been upgraded to Exchange 2000, you are now ready to upgrade the rest of the servers. Several factors will influence which servers will be upgraded and the order in which they are upgraded. For instance, there is a very large number of companies that are using Exchange for their messaging platform, and that operate on only one or two Exchange Servers in a single Exchange 5.5 site at a single geographical location. For this group, its pretty easy to know which servers will be upgraded and in what order. There isn't a great deal of planning that needs to be done.

However, for other companies, there are multiple sites hosting multiple servers. The order and way in which these servers are upgraded becomes extremely important. So, what we will discuss now is how these servers are upgraded and some potential problems you should think about before performing additional upgrades.

On our test network, we've chosen to upgrade Sacramento next. We were able to make an arbitrary choice because we have nothing riding on a bad decision at this point. However, you will probably find yourself in a different situation. So, please consider the following issues when making your choice.

User Impact   During the upgrade process, Exchange services are unavailable. Plan the upgrade of each Exchange Server during a time that will minimize downtime for your users.

Message Flow   Upgrading a Directory Replication Bridgehead Server (DRBHS) before upgrading other Exchange Servers in a given site may or may not be the correct choice of action. Each DRBHS will use SMTP to communicate with other Exchange 2000 Servers, so you'll need to consider the bandwidth between your Exchange 5.5 sites. For instance, if you are working over a 56Kbps leased line (not frame relay) that is sometimes prone to saturation and sometimes is not, then you most likely chose to consider that as a slow or unreliable WAN link for Exchange 5.5 sites and placed your Exchange 5.5 Servers on either side of the leased line in different sites. Furthermore, you probably set up an X.400 connector to pass messages between the two sites.

In Exchange 2000 Server, SMTP is the default message transport service. SMTP is much more forgiving of low-bandwidth and/or high-latency environments. This means that you might actually be able to place all your servers on either side of the leased line in the same routing group. You could effectively tie together your Exchange 5.5 sites, in this scenario, by first upgrading the DRBHSs and placing them in the same routing group. Then, messages would be passed via RPCs between the remaining Exchange 5.5 Servers and the Exchange 2000 Servers, but passed over SMTP between the two Exchange 2000 Servers. Thus, the X.400 connector could be eliminated and the Exchange 2000 Servers could act as a backbone over the leased line.

Location   Sometimes, the geographical location of a server will determine when you can upgrade it. If you need to physically visit each server, then this will be a huge factor in determining when you can perform an upgrade of the server.

MIGRATION AND DEPLOYMENT CONSIDERATIONS

In this section, we'll both look at upgrading from a broader perspective and consider the effects an upgrade has on AD.

How the Upgrade Process Changes AD

Earlier in the chapter, we discussed the two types of information that needs to be synchronized with AD—namely, Exchange 5.5 site information, which needs to be synchronized with the AD configuration partition, and Exchange 5.5 user and mailbox information, which needs to be synchronized with the Domain partition in AD. It is the Active Directory Connector (ADC), a service that runs on your Windows 2000 Server, that will handle these replication activities.

The ADC will handle CAs for both partitions, but the CA for each partition is not installed at the same time. Table 1-1 outlines the order in which these services should be installed and what their effect will be on your AD.

It is a good idea to place your Exchange 2000 Servers close to a GC Server, preferably on the same segment. In smaller companies where there are not many changes to AD, you can probably get away with running both GC Services and Exchange 2000 Services on the same physical box. Be sure to conduct solid capacity planning on your servers before implementing this topology.

UPGRADING IN OTHER SCENARIOS

What we have described so far is how to perform an upgrade to Exchange 2000 Server from Exchange 5.5 Server when you only have one domain. In addition, we have assumed that you were able to upgrade the PDC first and convert all the user accounts to AD.

Action	Command	Effect
Install the ADC	Run Setup from the ADC folder on your Exchange 2000 Server CD-ROM. This is covered in Chapter 3.	A number of schema changes will be made and replicated to all domain controllers in the forest because these changes occur in the configuration partition in AD and all domain controllers in the forest have a complete copy of the configuration partition. In addition, because the partial attribute set is changed, all Global Catalog (GC) Servers replicate partial replicas from other domains. Depending on your topology, this could mean significant replication traffic. You'll also need to manually configure CAs between each Exchange 5.5 site and AD for the domain partition synchronization.
Run /ForestPrep	Setup.exe /ForestPrep	More schema changes are made and replicated to all the domain controllers in the forest. Here, the partial attribute set does not change, so the GC Servers do not replicate a second time.
Run /DomainPrep	Setup.exe /DomainPrep	Very small changes are made to the domain partition, and these changes are replicated to the other domain controllers in this domain.
Run Setup for Exchange 2000 Server	Setup.exe	When the first Exchange 2000 Server is installed, a ConfigCA is automatically created by the SRS. Exchange 5.5 site information is replicated to the configuration partition in AD; and this information is, in turn, replicated to all the Windows 2000 domain controllers in the entire forest.

Table 1-1.   Upgrade Actions and Their Effects on AD

While this is the preferred and most simple solution, sometimes this migration path cannot be implemented.

It might be that in your environment, you'll need to create a new Windows 2000 AD and then migrate all the user accounts to the directory instead of upgrading the PDC. If this is the case, then you'll need to use the Active Directory Migration Tool (ADMT) to migrate the user accounts. Then, when the Active Directory Connector (ADC) is installed and mailbox accounts are migrated to AD, you'll find that two instances of each account might appear in the directory. In this scenario, you'll then need to use ADCLEAN to merge these duplicate accounts into one mail-enabled user account in AD. We discuss ADCLEAN in detail in the next chapter.

While it is impossible to cover every migration scenario in this book, we can give you some basic paths to follow, and these are outlined in Table 1-2. These scenarios are also illustrated in the Blueprints in the middle of the book.

TIP: To learn more about these scenarios and how to use them in your deployment, consult Chapter 6 and Microsoft Press' Exchange 2000 Server Resource Kit.

The best practice would be to test this migration several times in a lab environment and then perform the migration in your production environment.

Scenario	Tools Needed
Perform an in-place upgrade of your Windows NT 4.0 account domains and use the ADC to synchronize Exchange 5.5 information to AD.	ADC
Run ADC, upgrade the account domains at a later time, and then run ADCLEAN	ADC ADCLEAN
Run ADC and clone the user accounts at a later time using Active Directory Migration Tool (ADMT).	ADC ADMT
Run ADMT with SIDHistory and then run ADC to synchronize Exchange 5.5 information to AD	ADC ADMT
Run the ADMT without SIDHistory, re-create the ACLs, and then run ADC to synchronize Exchange 5.5 information to AD.	ADC ADMT

Table 1-2.   Outline of Deployment Scenarios with Required Tools

SUMMARY

In this chapter, you learned how to do an upgrade from Exchange 5.5 Server to Exchange 2000 Server for both a domain controller and a member server. You also learned the steps that are involved in performing a seamless upgrade. In the next chapter, we'll cover how to manage the coexistence of Exchange Servers. We'll take a look at the ADC, ADCLEAN, and other administrative activities that you'll need to perform.

CHAPTER 2

Coexistence with Exchange 5.5 Server

In the previous chapter, you learned how to migrate from Exchange 5.5 Server to Exchange 2000 Server. Now it's time to discuss how these two systems will coexist until you're ready to flip the switch to native mode and close the door on the possibility of ever running anything older than Exchange 2000 Server.

If you're working in a smaller company with only one or two Exchange Servers, this chapter may not be that relevant for you because upgrading two servers can be accomplished rather quickly, and there is little need to coexist with an Exchange 5.5 Server for weeks or months.

However, if you're in a larger company—one that has 20, 30, or more servers—chances are they won't be migrated at the same time. Hence, the issue of how to provide seamless services to your users during the migration period is extremely important.

You'll be happy to know that coexistence between Exchange 5.5 and Exchange 2000 can exist for any length of time. The only drawback will be the inability to use all the features of Exchange 2000 Server until you can move it into native mode, which means that there are no more legacy Exchange 5.5 Servers on your network. After Exchange 2000 Server is installed, regardless of whether it is a new installation or an upgrade of Exchange 5.5 Server, it is automatically installed in *mixed mode*, which means that Exchange 2000 Server can interoperate with an Exchange 5.5 Server. It does this because mixed mode assumes you need compatibility between the two systems. If you are migrating to Exchange 2000 Server for all its bells and whistles, you won't get them as long as you're in mixed mode—which assumes you either have or will have a need to integrate with Exchange 5.5 and, therefore, must impose Exchange 5.5's limits on all Exchange 2000 Servers.

One of these limitations is that routing groups must correspond to administrative groups, except when all of the servers in an administrative group have been upgraded to Exchange 2000 Server. Thereafter, you can create additional routing groups, but they are still limited to working inside one administrative group. New routing groups cannot cross administrative group boundaries unless Exchange 2000 Server is running in native mode.

The single largest source of pain for you when administrating coexistence will be integrating directories and making sure that you don't create multiple instances of the same object in either directory. That's why, in this chapter, we'll mainly discuss directory coexistence issues and look at the Active Directory Connector (ADC) Service and the Site Replication Service.

DIRECTORY COEXISTENCE WITH EXCHANGE 5.5 SERVER

When you have a mixed environment of Exchange 5.5 and Exchange 2000 Servers, what you really have are two directories that must be integrated if you are going to maintain any sense of a seamless environment. Getting these two directories to synchronize their information—to ensure that no objects are left out or are accidentally duplicated in both directories—is no small task.

Happily, Microsoft has provided several services to make this task much simpler. The ADC Service synchronizes user objects and information between the two directories. Microsoft also has written a new service to synchronize site information with the Active Directory (AD) configuration partition called the Site Replication Service (SRS). As we learned in the previous chapter, we don't do anything to install this service. It installs automatically whenever a Directory Replication Bridgehead Server (DRBHS) or the first Exchange 5.5 Server in a site is upgraded to Exchange 2000. And Microsoft has written the Recipient Update Service (RUS), a service that updates new information about recipients to the target directory. These three services work in tandem with the Connection Agreements (CAs) that you set up in the ADC service to ensure that there is complete and accurate directory synchronization.

Let's first take a closer look at the SRS, the ADC, and the various ways that CAs can be created, and then we'll discuss the RUS in detail.

Site Replication Service (SRS)

You'll recall that the SRS is installed on the Exchange 2000 Server whenever a DRBHS is upgraded to Exchange 2000 Server or when the first Exchange 2000 Server is installed into an Exchange 5.5 site. The SRS makes the Exchange 2000 Server look and feel like an Exchange 5.5 directory service to the other 5.5 Servers in the site, and it runs on the Exchange 2000 Server to replicate site and configuration information between the 5.5 Servers and AD. It will participate in directory replication with the other 5.5 Servers and use RPCs to communicate with them. If there are other Exchange 2000 Servers in the site, it will use Simple Mail Transport Protocol (SMTP) to communicate with them. The SRS is also responsible for making the AD look like a 5.5 directory to the other 5.5 Servers.

By the same token, the SRS is able to communicate with AD and translate AD replication calls to the 5.5 site. You can think of the SRS as the liaison between these dissimilar directories. Hence, it is able to communicate both directions, between both directories.

When the SRS is initially installed, the Exchange 2000 Setup Wizard analyzes your Exchange 5.5 organization and builds the appropriate ConfigCAs that are needed to replicate Exchange 5.5 site information with the configuration partition in AD. The automatic configuration agreements are called ConfigCAs and cannot be modified after they are created.

For example, you might recall that our network has four servers—Indianapolis, Minneapolis, Tucson, and Sacramento—that are hosting in four sites—Indiana, Minnesota, Arizona, and California. All but Tucson are domain controllers; Tucson is a member server. When the first server, Minneapolis, was upgraded to Exchange 2000, only one ConfigCA was created between the Exchange 5.5 organization and AD. This agreement was for the Minnesota site only and is illustrated in Figure 2-1. However, all the site objects in the organization were replicated to AD.

NOTE: The Active Directory Connection service is more fully discussed in the next section, "Active Directory Connector Service."

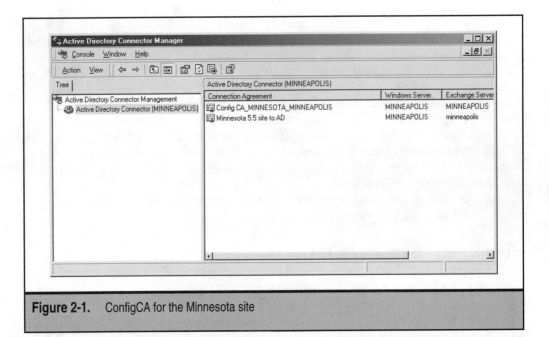

Figure 2-1.   ConfigCA for the Minnesota site

When the Indianapolis Exchange Server was upgraded to Exchange 2000, another ConfigCA was created to replicate the Indiana site information to the configuration partition in AD. This is shown in Figure 2-2.

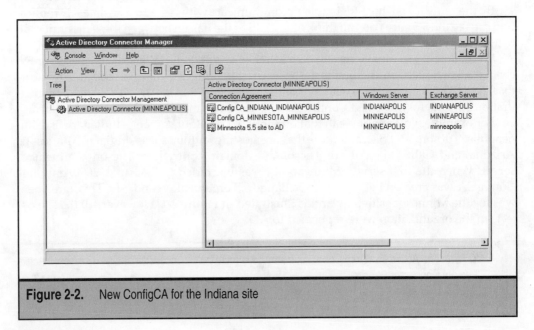

Figure 2-2.   New ConfigCA for the Indiana site

When the Active Directory Services Interface (ADSI) Edit program is opened up, we can see that all four sites are represented in AD. They appear as administrative groups, as shown in Figure 2-3. This is because the directory service has replicated these site objects around the 5.5 organization and, in turn, the SRS replicated this information into the configuration partition in AD. Since two of the servers, Minneapolis and Indianapolis, have been upgraded at this point, what you're really seeing are two administrative groups and two Exchange 5.5 sites. In addition, each ConfigCA is also listed as a separate service in the System Manager snap-in indicating which server the service is running on (see Figure 2-4).

Now it stands to reason that if the SRS is looking like a regular directory replication service to the other Exchange 5.5 servers, you would be able to find and administrate the 5.5 directory replication connector. Well, this is true, but you won't find this connector in the System Manager snap-in. You will see its existence in ADSI Edit (see Figure 2-5). However, you can't administrate this connector from this tool. You must go back to the Exchange 5.5 Administrator to change configuration properties on this connector.

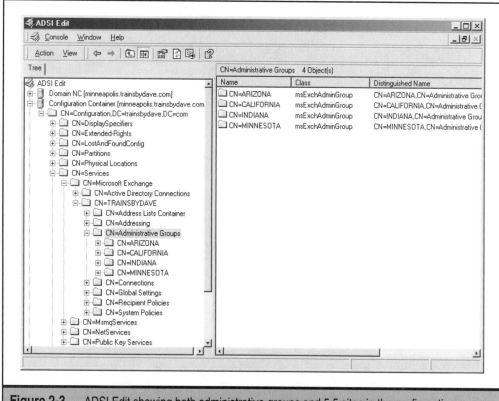

Figure 2-3. ADSI Edit showing both administrative groups and 5.5 sites in the configuration partition of AD

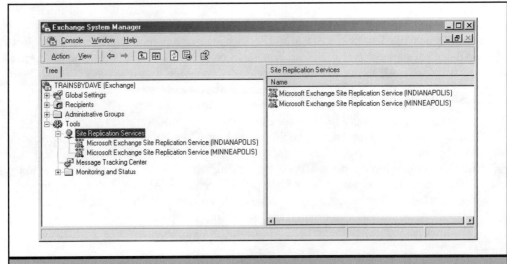

Figure 2-4. The Minneapolis and Indianapolis Site Replication Services

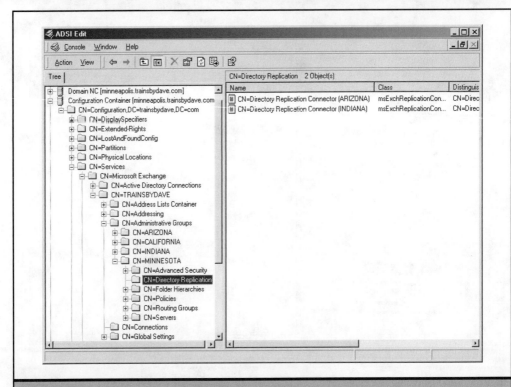

Figure 2-5. The Directory Replication Connector object in the configuration partition

Now, let's discuss a hypothetical situation in which there are multiple servers in three different sites with directory replication connectors and then glean some principles by which to manage the SRS. Figure 2-6 shows our fictitious organization.

Let's assume that Servers 2, 4, and 8 are the DRBHSs for these three sites and that we have upgraded Server 1 in Site 1 to Exchange 2000. Since this is the first server to be upgraded in the site, the SRS will be installed and activated. This is illustrated in Figure 2-7.

Now, if Server 3 in Site 1 is upgraded to Exchange 2000, its SRS will be installed but will remain disabled because an active SRS is installed and running on Server 1. This is shown in Figure 2-8. Without another Exchange 5.5 Server in Site 1, Server 2 cannot participate in intrasite directory replication. As the number of 5.5 Servers decreases in a site, either through upgrading them to Exchange 2000 or by taking them offline entirely, it stands to reason that the number of servers participating in 5.5 replication decreases.

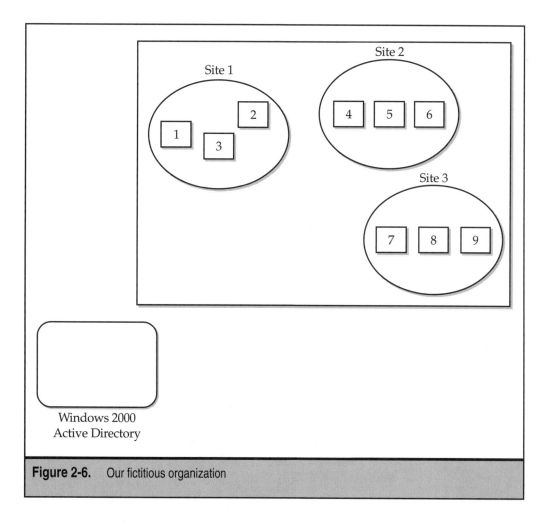

Figure 2-6.   Our fictitious organization

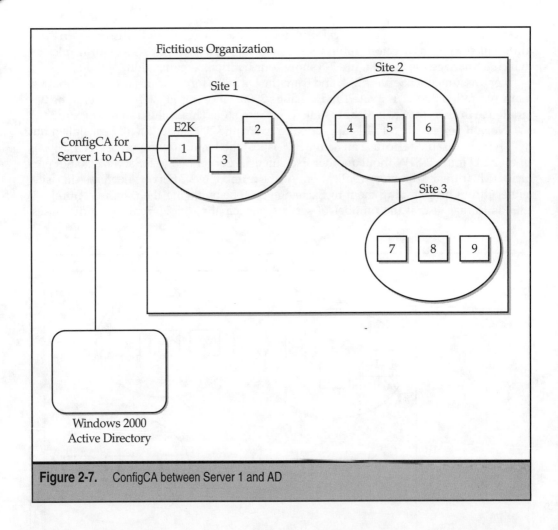

Figure 2-7. ConfigCA between Server 1 and AD

When there is only one 5.5 Server left in the site, it has no other 5.5 Server with which to replicate directory information. The best practice would be to upgrade the last two 5.5 Servers at the same time.

However, when Server 2 is upgraded to Exchange 2000 Server, its SRS will be installed and activated because it is a DRBHS. This server will continue to allow replication messages to be passed between Sites 1 and 2. Also, a second ConfigCA is installed in the ADC service for this site. And, a special version of the Knowledge Consistency Checker (KCC), called the Super Knowledge Consistency Checker (SKCC), will handle the coordi-

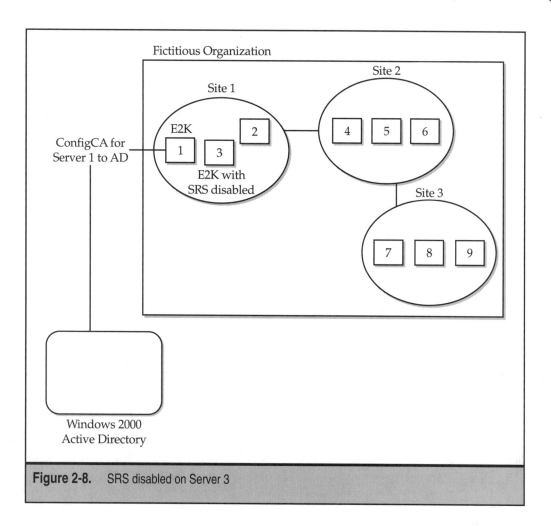

Figure 2-8. SRS disabled on Server 3

nation of these multiple ConfigCA to establish the best replication path. This is illustrated in Figure 2-9.

If the first Exchange 2000 Server is also the DRBHS, there will be only one SRS installed and activated. All the other servers will have the SRS installed when they are upgraded, but their services will be disabled.

If you already have user CAs in the site, you will need to either move them to another Exchange 5.5 Server in the site or delete them in the ADC Manager before you upgrade or decommission the 5.5 Server to which they are connected. The best thing to do is to create

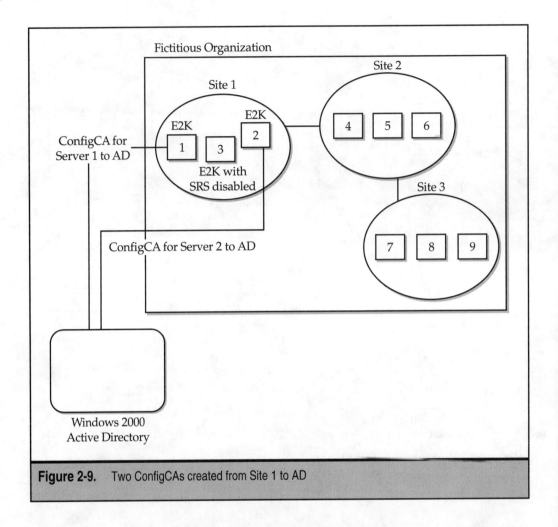

Figure 2-9.   Two ConfigCAs created from Site 1 to AD

your user CAs to a server with an active SRS. Then you will not need to move them again; you'll only need to delete them once you're ready to go into native mode.

So, we have upgraded the three servers in Site 1, but the other servers in Sites 2 and 3 are still running Exchange 5.5. When you upgrade servers from multiple sites, additional ConfigCAs are installed to replicate site information to the AD.

Let's say we decide to upgrade Server 6 in Site 2. When this occurs, the SRS will be installed and activated since it is the first server in the site with Exchange 2000 installed. A ConfigCA is created between Server 6 and AD to replicate site information about Site 2 to AD, as shown in Figure 2-10.

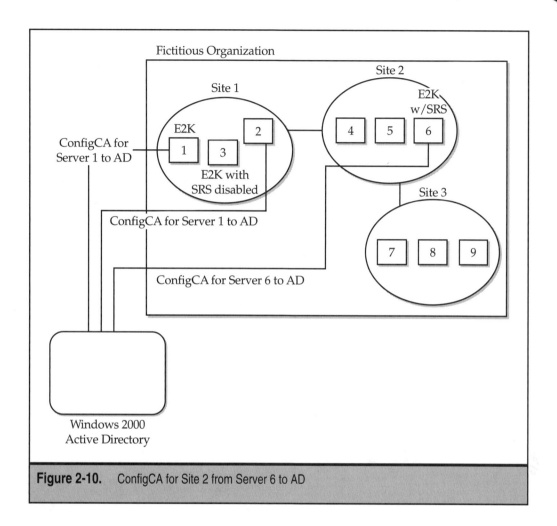

Figure 2-10. ConfigCA for Site 2 from Server 6 to AD

The SKCC will handle configuration changes in the site and will arbitrate which ConfigCA will be responsible for replicating site information changes about Site 3 to AD, and vice versa. When faced with a decision about which site should take responsibility for a third 5.5 site that has no ConfigCA installed into it, the SKCC selects the site with the closest alphabetical name. There is no interface to the SKCC; it just does its job.

Now, if the DRBHS in Site 2 is upgraded to Exchange 2000, as shown in Figure 2-11, another ConfigCA will be created, and there will be four ConfigCAs replicating site and configuration information between the two directories.

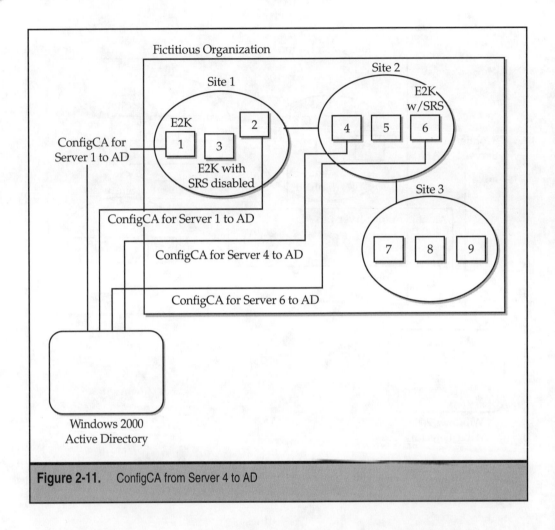

Figure 2-11. ConfigCA from Server 4 to AD

If similar actions were committed in Site 3, there would be six ConfigCAs to manage. It has probably become clear at this point that there are two different things to do.

First, if at all possible, upgrade your DRBHSs first in each 5.5 site. This will eliminate the creation of additional ConfigCAs by the ADC service if the DRBHS is not the first server in the site upgraded to Exchange 2000 Server.

Second, upgrade the last two Exchange 5.5 Servers to Exchange 2000 at approximately the same time so that the last 5.5 Server's directory information doesn't become too old or out of synchronization with the other server's information in its site.

Once all of your Exchange 5.5 Servers have either been upgraded to Exchange 2000 Server or have been taken offline, you can switch to native mode. This action will negate the need for the SRS; and, thereafter, you can delete all your ConfigCAs and user CAs, and then remove the ADC service from all your machines. But keep in mind that going to native mode means that you cannot run any older messaging system from Microsoft than Exchange 2000 Server.

Active Directory Connector Service

The Active Directory Connector (ADC) Service, a service that is installed on one or more Windows 2000 domain controllers, manages both configuration and user CAs. These two types of agreements correspond to two of the three AD partitions. A user's CA will replicate user information between the 5.5 directories and the domain partition in AD. The ConfigCA will replicate 5.5 site information to the configuration partition in AD.

NOTE: To learn more about the three partitions in AD and what types of information they hold, please see *Windows 2000 Administration* by George Spalding, Osborne/McGraw-Hill, 2000.

When a CA is configured, it synchronizes user objects in the 5.5 directory to the domain partition in AD. Since many organizations have rich directory information that would be costly and time consuming to re-enter into AD, this tool allows for this information to be uploaded from the 5.5 directories to AD.

This is accomplished by having the ADC service match the Exchange 5.5 objects with equivalent AD objects. For example, Exchange 5.5 mailboxes are translated into AD mail-enabled users. Chapter 3 discusses the various objects in both directories and how they match up.

Currently, there are two versions of the ADC service: one that ships with Windows 2000 and one that ships with Exchange 2000. As we discussed in Chapter 1, you should always use the Exchange 2000 Server version since it will also replicate site information to the configuration partition and user information to the domain partitions. The version with Windows 2000 Server will only replicate user information to the domain partition. In the future, the only version that will be available will come with Exchange 2000 Server.

The actual association that is used in the CA is between containers in both directories. For instance, the default Recipients container for an Exchange 5.5 site might be associated in the CA with a custom organization unit in AD. If a two-way CA is created, the objects in each container will be replicated to the other container. You do have the flexibility to choose to create one-way agreements so that replication between two containers flows in only one direction.

Lightweight Directory Access Protocol (LDAP) is used to perform the synchronization. Remember that if you plan to run Exchange 5.5 on a Windows 2000 domain controller, you'll need to change the port number for LDAP services in Exchange 5.5. For more information on this topic, refer to Chapter 1.

Creating a CA is rather painless, though there are several tabs that will need to be configured. The real difficulty with this tool is one of its largest features: it allows you to implement nearly any connection topology that you desire. We'll first take a look at how to create a CA, and then we'll discuss, at length, the different ways that CAs can be implemented.

To create a CA, open up the ADC Manager snap-in; right-click the ADC object in the left pane; point to New; and select Recipient Connection Agreement, as illustrated in Figure 2-12.

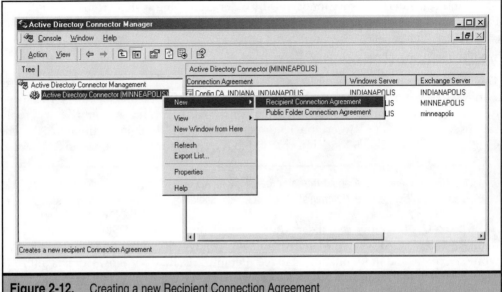

Figure 2-12. Creating a new Recipient Connection Agreement

The Properties dialog box will then appear, and the first thing you'll need to do is name your CA. We suggest that the name be descriptive, since it will indicate which type of CA is inside the ADC Manager snap-in. We've named ours "Two-way between Sacramento and AD for Custom Recipients" (see Figure 2-13). Remember that Sacramento is still running NT 4.0 and Exchange 5.5 at this point in the book to indicate that this connector will synchronize newly created objects to both directories. When I select the Two-Way radio button, a message will pop up, as shown next, indicating that the CA will need to write to the Exchange directory and that the account used to connect to the Exchange 5.5 container will need write permissions on the Exchange 5.5 directory.

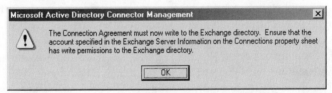

If you have more than one server that has the ADC service installed, you'll be able to select which server you wish to manage this CA by clicking the drop-down list under Select A Server To Run The Connection Agreement, as shown in Figure 2-13.

After naming the CA, you'll move to the Connections tab (see Figure 2-14), where you'll specify which AD domain controller and Exchange 5.5 Server will participate in this CA. The AD domain controller is specified in the Windows Server Information box. You can choose which type of authentication you wish to perform: the default is Windows Challenge/

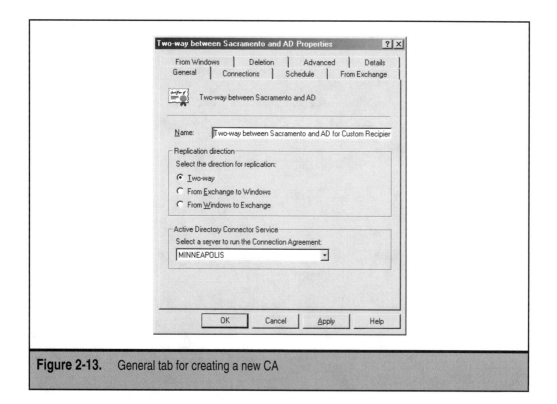

Figure 2-13. General tab for creating a new CA

Response. You'll also need to have the CA connect as a user account that has permissions to write to the AD. Do not choose the default Administrator account here. We prefer to choose the Exchange services account, since it has permissions to write to the directory.

You'll then need to specify the Exchange 5.5 Server under the Exchange Server Information box. You'll also need to choose the port number for LDAP services to use. This number should match the number specified in the LDAP protocol for the Exchange 5.5 Server. To learn how to change this port number, consult Chapter 1. Notice that we chose port 390 for LDAP services since LDAP services in Windows 2000 has already locked the default port of 389 for its own use.

Choose the Exchange 5.5 service account to connect to the Exchange 5.5 directory, since it has the ability to write to the 5.5 directory.

The Schedule tab is where you can configure when the CA will fire (Figure 2-15). We've selected Always, which means every 15 minutes. The Replicate The Entire Directory The Next Time The Agreement Is Run check box allows you the option to force the entire directory to replicate the next time the agreement is run by the ADC service. Only select this check box if you're sure you want the entire directory to replicate at the next replication interval. In large environments, this could represent substantial replication traffic and could consume more or all of your bandwidth during the replication process.

Figure 2-14.   Connections tab for the new CA

The From Exchange tab is where you will designate which Exchange 5.5 containers will be source containers for user object replication into AD. Click the Add For The Exchange Recipients containers box, and you'll see the Choose A Container box appear, as shown here:

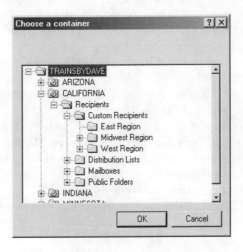

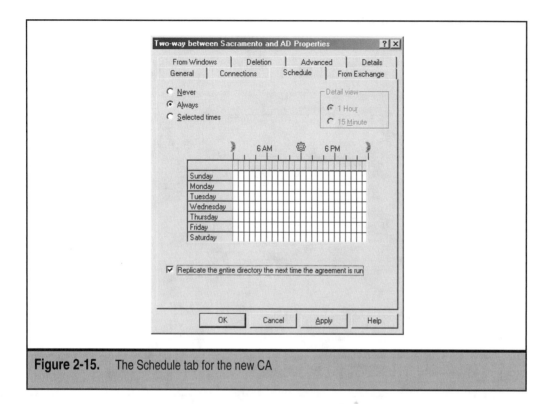

Figure 2-15.   The Schedule tab for the new CA

For the sake of illustration, we've chosen to synchronize only the objects between the custom Recipients container to the mail-enabled contacts organizational unit, as shown in Figure 2-16. Notice that under the Objects selection box, we've only selected the Mailboxes check box. This means that only mailbox objects inside the custom Recipients container and mail-enabled contacts in the mail-enabled contacts organizational unit will be synchronized between the two containers.

Use the From Windows tab to perform the exact same functions as the From Exchange tab, except that you reverse the roles of your containers. We'll cover how to customize this tab for various purposes a bit later in this chapter. Figure 2-17 shows how to configure this CA to enable synchronization for objects that need to be synchronized to the Exchange 5.5 custom Recipients container.

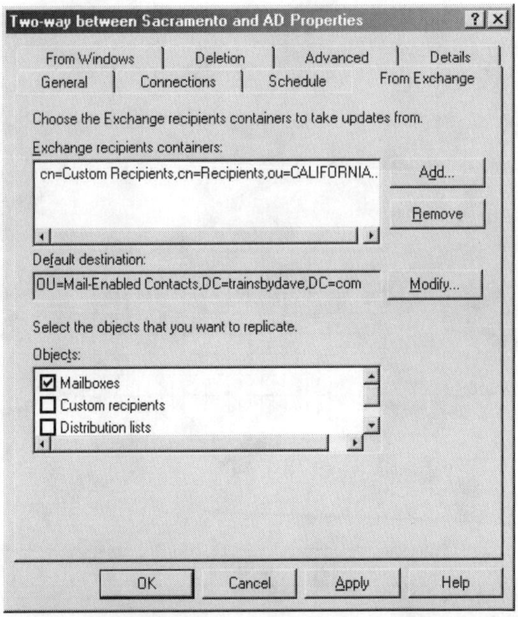

Figure 2-16.   The From Exchange tab in creating a new CA

Use the Deletion tab (see Figure 2-18) to choose how to handle object deletions. Essentially, you can choose to have the object deleted in the target container if it has been deleted in the source container; or you can choose to have it deleted in the source container and have that action recorded in a file, but leave the object in the target container intact.

If you want to have the object deleted in the target container, choose the corresponding Delete radio buttons. Notice that you can have objects deleted in one target container but not the other. You'll also notice that the file types that record the deletions are the types that are used by both platforms to import new information into the directory. By ussng these files, you can accumulate deletion information in the file and then, at a later time, import the information and choose to have the objects deleted as part of the importation process.

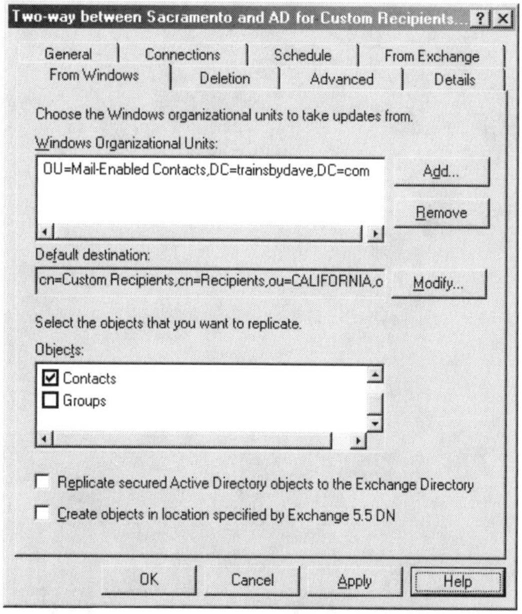

Figure 2-17. The From Windows tab in creating a new CA

The Advanced tab is one of the more important tabs to pay attention to when creating a new CA (Figure 2-19). In the Paged Results area, you can specify how many objects are replicated in each batch. (In LDAP terms, this batch is referred to as a *page*, but this term should not be confused with how it is used in Word or general discourse. "Page" means a series of changes, grouped together and then sent as one replication message.) Increasing the size reduces the number of pages being replicated between the two directories, but it requires more memory per page to complete the process. The default is 20 changes per page.

If you want this CA to be a primary CA, then choose the This Is A Primary Connection Agreement For The Connected Exchange Organization check box. Every ADC service must have at least one primary CA to each directory from which it wishes to replicate

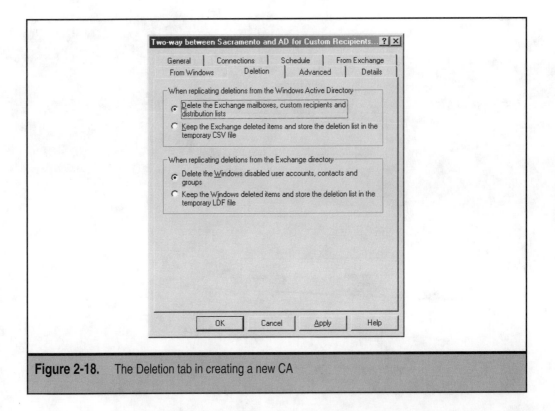

Figure 2-18.   The Deletion tab in creating a new CA

objects. Primary agreements will create new directory objects in the target container if needed, nonprimary agreements will not. You will see that this check box is selected by default. Since this is a two-way CA, both primary check boxes are selected, so that newly created objects in either source directory can be created in the target directory.

The This Is An Inter-Organization Connection Agreement check box allows objects to be synchronized between two different organizations. For instance, if, during the upgrade, you chose to create a new Exchange organization, then you'll need to select this check box to allow for object synchronization between your Exchange 5.5 organization and the new Exchange 2000 organization.

The bottom part of this tab has two important configurations. First is the When Replicating A Mailbox Whose Primary Windows Account Does Not Exist In The Domain

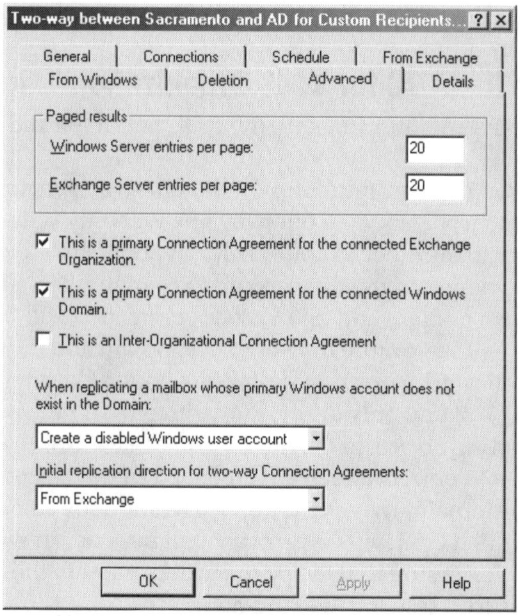

Figure 2-19.   The Advanced tab in creating a new CA

selection drop-down list. What you are doing here is telling the ADC service how to behave when the mailbox in the Exchange 5.5 directory is being replicated to AD and there is no corresponding primary Windows user account in AD with which to associate the mailbox. You'll have three choices.

▼   **Create A Disabled Windows User Account**   This action will create a user account that will not permit logons.

■   **Create A New Windows User Account**   This action will create a new user account in AD that includes the membership groups and permissions for the user.

▲   **Create A Windows Contact**   This action will create an account that points to an external SMTP address that is outside your Exchange 2000 organization.

Second, you can choose which directory will go first, either Exchange 5.5 or AD. The default is to start the replication process by replicating new objects in AD from the Exchange 5.5 directory.

The Details tab is a place where you can input administrative notes. It also displays the date the CA was created and the last date it was modified.

How to Configure the ADC for Your Organization

Now, let's discuss the ins and outs of using the ADC Service and the various possibilities the CAs afford us.

You'll recall that you can configure the CA for one-way synchronization in either direction or two-way synchronization. A one-way CA will only write changes in one direction: from one directory to the other as you specify, as shown in Figure 2-20. It is a common topology to configure one-way agreements from Exchange 5.5 to AD; and in most smaller companies that have one domain and one Exchange site, this will be all that is required.

In companies that will have more than one AD domain and more than one site, things start to get more complicated. You should plan to define at least one CA per site and AD domain as a primary CA. If you only define one primary CA per site and AD domain, this will help avoid duplicating objects in the forest. You can use nonprimary CAs to help replicate attribute changes to objects already established in the target directory. Figure 2-21 illustrates what a two-domain, two-site topology would look like.

How you define which CAs will be primary will depend on where the user accounts should ultimately reside. Be sure that the primary CAs point to the destination where you want your user objects to reside for the long haul.

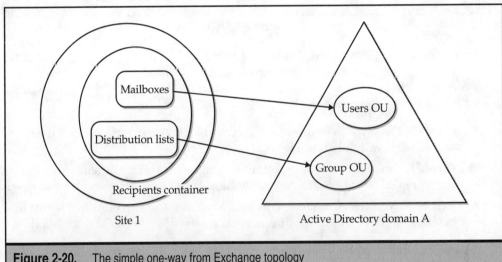

Figure 2-20. The simple one-way from Exchange topology

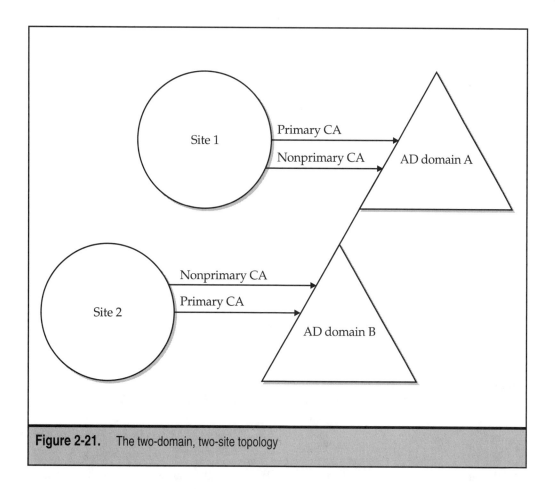

Figure 2-21. The two-domain, two-site topology

You'll recall that in Exchange 5.5, by default, all the recipient objects are created inside the Recipients container. Now, many Exchange administrators really didn't pick up on the fact that multiple subcontainers could be created so that a large, monolithic list of all the site's recipients didn't appear under the Recipients container, but instead were grouped into subcontainers intended to hold only one type of recipient. Figure 2-22 shows how these subcontainers could be created in the Microsoft Exchange Administrator.

Since many administrators either didn't know about this feature or didn't take advantage of it, many have multiple types of recipients under the default Recipients container,

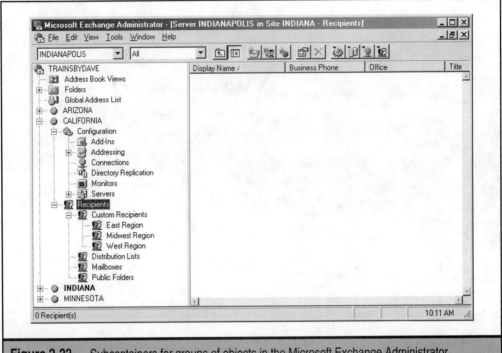

Figure 2-22.   Subcontainers for groups of objects in the Microsoft Exchange Administrator

such as mailboxes, distribution lists, and public folders. Mixing different object types inside the same container is generally not a good administrative practice.

With the ADC, you can fix this by creating multiple CAs that will replicate user objects to different OUs in AD. This is accomplished by doing two things:

▼ Choosing the correct user object to replicate, such as mailboxes, custom recipients, or distribution lists (see Figure 2-23), and

▲ Choosing the correct target OU to which to replicate these objects.

Let's assume that you have four types of recipients in your default Recipients container, but you would like to group each type of recipient into a separate OU in Windows 2000. No problem. Just create four different CAs, each one coming from the same

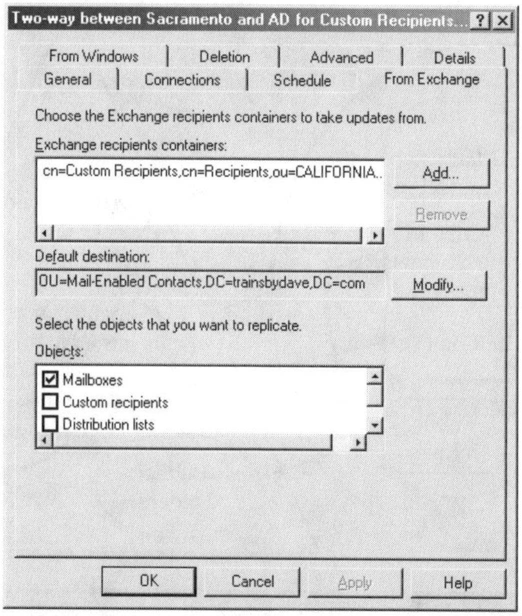

Figure 2-23.   Choosing the correct object to replicate in the From Exchange tab of a CA

source Recipients container in Exchange 5.5 but targeting a different OU for each object type (see Figure 2-24).

You could target these objects to go to different domains so that your public folders would all reside in a native mode domain that utilized universal security groups.

Creating a Public Folder Connection Agreement

As you'll notice in Figure 2-23, there is not a choice to select the public folder recipient and replicate it to an OU in Windows 2000. In all likelihood, you're going to want to migrate your public folders into Windows 2000 so there is a CA that can be created just for public folders. Let's take a closer look at this CA.

First, you'll open up the ADC Manager and choose to create a new Public Folder Agreement instead of a new Connection Agreement. Figure 2-25 shows that the General

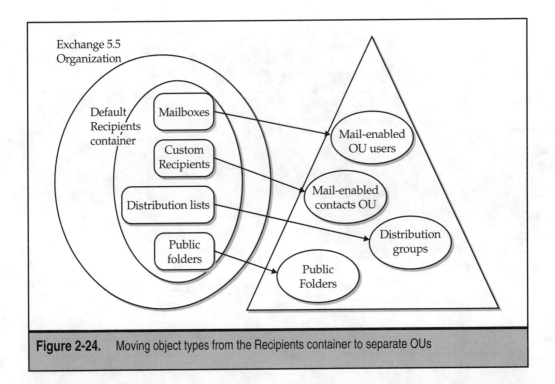

Figure 2-24. Moving object types from the Recipients container to separate OUs

tab will look the same as a user CA, but that your only choice will be a Two-Way agreement because the other two options will be grayed out.

The Connections and Schedule tabs will work the same as in a user CA. However, the From Exchange and From Windows tabs will have a different look and feel. Your only administrative act on these two tabs will be to ensure that the Public Folders check box is selected. The Source and Target containers will be selected for you and unavailable for modification. On the From Windows tab, you'll also be able to select to replicate secured objects, just as you could in the user CA. Figures 2-27 and 2-28 shows what these two tabs should appear as.

Use the Deletions tab to choose to delete objects in the target container if they have been deleted in the source container. You will not have the option to record deleted objects to a file. On the Advanced tab, you'll probably want to leave this at default, unless you already have a primary CA for public folders; then you could deselect that particular box.

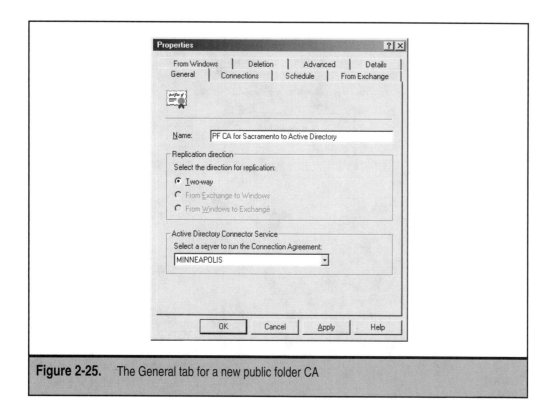

Figure 2-25.   The General tab for a new public folder CA

So, really, the main part of creating a public folder CA is to give a name and input the accounts that will be used to read and write from each directory. Thereafter, you'll find that the CA will work on its own and replicate the public folder information to the default public folder tree.

Replicating User Accounts from Foreign Exchange 5.5 Organizations

The ADC can be used to replicate directory information from multiple, foreign Exchange 5.5 directories to a single AD, but there are limitations and issues that you should understand if you are charged with such a task. A *foreign* 5.5 directory would be one in which there is no replication path between AD and the 5.5 directory.

First, Microsoft does not support the Windows 2000 version of the ADC, under any circumstances, when it is used to connect different Exchange 5.5 directories to the same AD. Make sure to use the Exchange ADC for this work; otherwise, Microsoft Product Support will not support you.

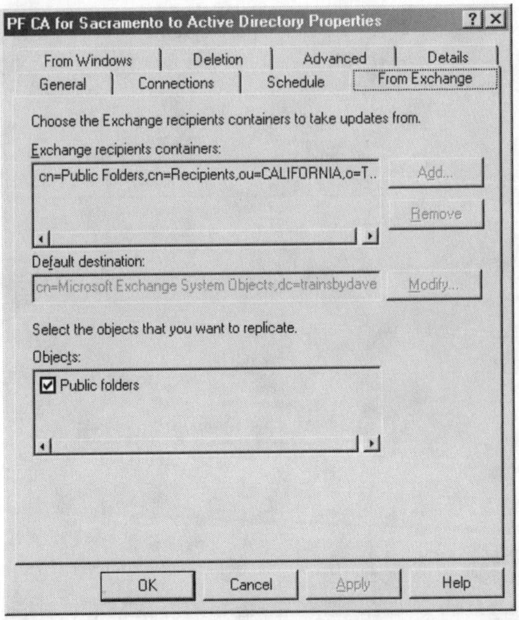

Figure 2-26. The From Exchange tab in creating a new public folder CA

Second, the Exchange 2000 version of the ADC is not supported by Microsoft under any circumstances unless you have either first deployed Exchange 2000 in the AD forest or run the /ForestPrep setup command to extend the schema *before* you create an inter-organizational CA to indicate the Exchange organization for the AD forest.

Third, after you have created an inter-organizational CA between AD and the 5.5 forest, all subsequent CAs must be configured as inter-organizational CAs, otherwise, the ADC Service will assume the CA is an intra-organizational CA. You must tell the ADC Service that the source directory (i.e., the Exchange 5.5 Directory) is not connected to any of your Exchange 2000 Servers, and that its directory information is coming from a directory with whom the AD does not have replication privileges.

Fourth, if you create an inter-organizational CA, a process is initiated that cannot be reversed. As an inter-organizational CA, it begins linking objects in the AD forest with objects in the source directory to facilitate inter-organizational synchronization. *Clearing the This Is An Inter-Organizational Connection Agreement check box will not roll back any changes made in AD.* In addition, neither deleting and re-creating objects in the AD nor

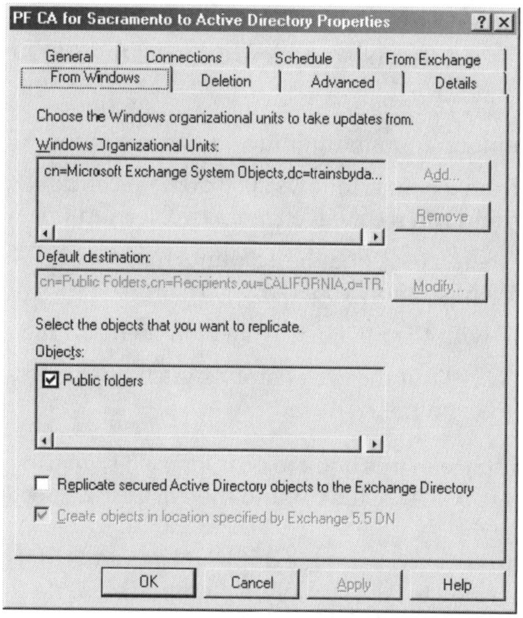

Figure 2-27.   The From Windows tab in creating a new public folder CA

deleting the CA will roll back the changes. Hence, once the objects are linked and replicated, you cannot roll back changes made to the AD, short of restoring an old version of your AD as an authoritative restore. Microsoft does not offer any tested, documented, or supported procedures to undo changes made to the AD as a result of running an inter-organizational CA.

Fifth, it is by design that proxy addresses for objects replicated to AD from a foreign 5.5 directory will not be replicated into AD. This is not a problem, technically speaking, but it may represent a significant headache for you if you need those addresses. An inter-organizational CA only replicates the primary address of an Exchange 5.5 object into the AD.

Active Directory Account Cleanup Wizard

The only way to get user account information into AD from an Exchange 5.5 Server is to use the ADC. The most straightforward method of uploading this information is to do an in-place upgrade of the NT 4.0 Primary Domain Controller (PDC) to Windows 2000 AD, and then follow that by upgrading the Exchange 5.5 Servers to Exchange 2000 Server. However, not all will be able or willing to do it this way.

There are actually five different scenarios for using the ADC to migrate accounts to Windows 2000:

▼ Conduct an in-place domain upgrade and then run the ADC

■ Run the ADC from a new Windows 2000 domain controller, upgrade your PDC to the new AD, and run the Active Directory Cleanup Wizard (ADCLEAN)

■ Run the ADC, then later clone the accounts from the NT 4.0 PDC using the Active Directory Migration Tool (ADMT)

■ Run the ADMT with the SIDHistory switch, then run the ADC

▲ Run the ADMT without the SIDHistory switch, re-create all the Access Control Lists (ACLs), and run the ADC.

There isn't enough space in this book to go over each scenario in depth; so in this section we'll describe how to use ADCLEAN, and then in the next section we'll describe how to use the ADMT.

ADCLEAN is a tool designed to merge duplicate accounts that are created when multiple directories are migrated to AD. Usually, a common scenario that produces duplicate accounts is when a PDC is upgraded to join an existing AD after previously installing an ADC to an Exchange 5.5 Server in that domain.

When you install Exchange 2000 Server, ADCLEAN is automatically installed. To start this program, use the shortcut in the Exchange menu. The first screen that you will see is a Welcome screen. After clicking Next, you will be presented with the Identify Merging Accounts screen, as shown in Figure 2-28.

There are three ways to identify duplicate accounts. ADCLEAN works with each method. You can use ADCLEAN to search for duplicate accounts, select duplicate accounts manually, or import a list of accounts.

Using ADCLEAN to Search for Duplicate Accounts   By default, ADCLEAN searches the entire forest for duplicate accounts. You can limit the search, however, by selecting certain containers and subcontainers in which you want the wizard to search. Referring back to Figure 2-28, if you want the search to encompass the entire forest, then do nothing, because the Search Entire Directory Or Selected Containers check box is automatically selected. If you don't add any specific containers, it assumes you want to search the entire directory. To search specific containers or OUs, click the Add button and make your selection.

This is also the screen where you can choose to import a list of merging accounts from a file. Select the check box and specify the file you wish to have imported.

If you want to base the search for duplicate accounts only on objects that were created in AD by the ADC, be sure to leave the default, Search Based On Exchange Mailboxes

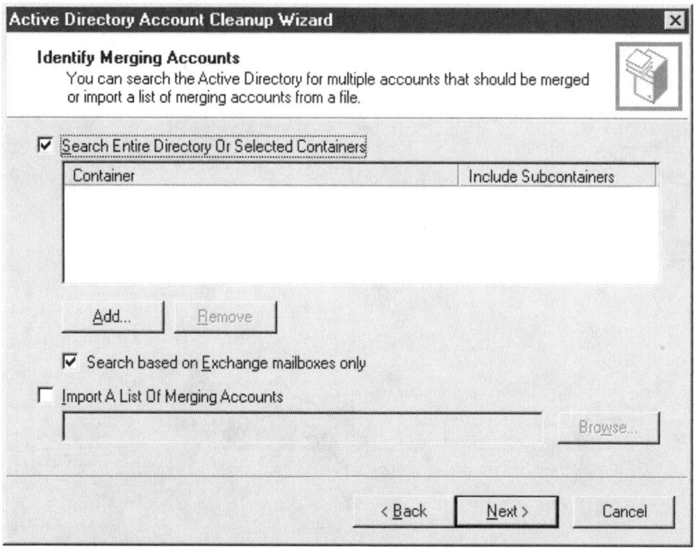

Figure 2-28.   The Identify Merging Accounts screen in ADCLEAN

Only check box, selected. If you want all sources of object creation to be included, such as a mail connector or other tools, clear this check box.

After you have made your choices, click Next. The directory will be searched and a Review Merging Accounts screen will appear, as shown in Figure 2-29. From this screen, you can click on an account to get account information or just click Next and the accounts will be merged.

If you click the Add button, you'll be presented with the Select Merging Accounts box. This presents to us the second way to merge duplicate accounts.

Manually Merging Duplicate Accounts   The Select Merging Accounts screen lets you manually select two different user accounts and then merge them into one account. However, you can't just willy-nilly select accounts and merge them. There are some restrictions that must be followed. First, the target object must be an active user. You cannot merge two accounts into an inactive user account.

Second, the source object cannot be mail-enabled. If it is, then the merge can't proceed because this utility doesn't merge mailboxes, just user accounts.

Third, objects from different forests cannot be merged even if there is a trust relationship between them. And fourth, both accounts must belong to the same Windows 2000 domain and that domain must be operating in native mode. As long as you're operating in mixed mode, you won't be able to merge both accounts.

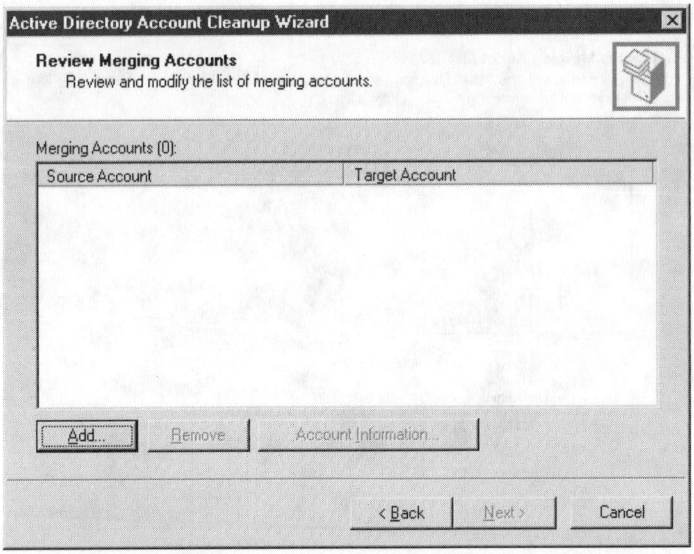

Figure 2-29. The Review Merging Accounts screen in ADCLEAN

The requirement to be in native mode in order to merge accounts will present some interesting issues to consider if you plan to have a long-term coexistence with Windows 2000 and Windows NT 4.0 Servers. This requirement of native mode to run ADCLEAN argues in favor of a couple of things. First, if at all possible, move all your accounts into one domain before performing an upgrade to Windows 2000. The thinking here is that if you can eliminate multiple sources for user accounts, you'll have a much higher chance of not needing to run ADCLEAN at all. Second, if you must have multiple source-account databases for your migration to Windows 2000 Server, then get all the accounts cleaned up before migrating to Exchange 2000 Server.

Importing a List of Accounts   To import a list of accounts, simply select the .csv file that contains the names, and then let ADCLEAN review the accounts and follow the wizard as needed. Refer to Figure 2-30 to see where to specify a file to be used by ADCLEAN.

Active Directory Migration Tool (ADMT)

The ADMT is designed to migrate user, group, and computer accounts from Windows NT 4.0 domains to AD, between AD forests and between domains in a single AD forest. This tool offers the flexibility to take certain NT 4.0 domains and migrate the user, group, and computer account information without the need to upgrade the operating system itself.

Select Merging Accounts   ☒

Source account:
William English/Users/trainsbydave.com   Browse...

Display Name: William English

Logon ID: wenglish

E-Mail:

Title:

Target account:
Bill English/Users/trainsbydave.com   Browse...

Display Name: Bill English

Logon ID: benglish

E-Mail:

Title:

                              OK   Cancel

Figure 2-30.   Selecting two accounts to merge in the trainsbydave.com domain

NOTE: At the time of this writing, you must go to the downloads section of **http://www. microsoft.com/exchange** to get this tool. Once downloaded, you can double-click the file and it will self-extract and run through the installation wizard on the machine it is saved on. Once the tool is installed, a shortcut is placed in the Administrative Tools menu called Active Directory Migration Tool.

Using ADMT, you can restructure your domain design at any stage to better meet the needs of your organization. Most often, the results of using this tool are fewer domains and better management of your user, group, and computer accounts. Generally, you'll install a new forest and then use this tool to migrate accounts to the forest to achieve a better layout of these accounts.

A domain upgrade, sometimes called an *in-place upgrade*, involves upgrading each domain's PDC to Windows 2000, and either upgrading or decommissioning all the Backup Domain Controllers (BDCs) as well. This means that all the Windows NT domains are upgraded directly into the Windows 2000 forest and that your current domain structure is retained. After upgrading all your Windows NT domains, you'll use ADMT to migrate the upgraded domains to a new forest. In essence, you'll be creating a temporary forest into which the Windows NT domain structure will be migrated, and then you'll create a new structure in the permanent forest into which accounts will be migrated.

If you're planning to consolidate or migrate accounts between domains in the same forest, then you'll be working with several concepts—including a source domain, target domain, and agents, which are installed from the computer upon which ADMT is running to other computers. Once installed, these agents run as a service using the local system security credentials.

The ADMT allows for test runs to be performed, similar to how the Gateway Services for Netware Tool in Windows NT allowed for test migrations of user accounts before performing the actual migration. After running the test migration, you can review the log files and reports to determine if there are any problems that might need fixing.

Once you have determined that there are no problems in your test migration, you can use the ADMT to migrate users, groups, and computer accounts. Then you'll want to use the Security Migration Wizard (SMW) to update the ACLs on the target computers.

PUBLIC FOLDER COEXISTENCE

How public folders apply permissions is one area in which there are distinct, fundamental differences between Exchange 5.5 and Exchange 2000. Exchange 2000 Server uses user and security groups from AD to guard access to a public folder. Exchange 5.5 employed Exchange objects, such as mailboxes and distribution lists, for this purpose.

So, in order to apply permissions to public folders in Exchange 2000 similar to those that existed in Exchange 5.5, AD must have an equivalent object to an Exchange 5.5 distribution list. This object is a universal security group, which is only available when Windows 2000 is running in native mode.

The way to make this work is to have at least one native mode domain in your Windows 2000 forest. Then, you'll want to configure a CA between the 5.5 directory and the native mode domain to synchronize the groups between them, and move the public folders to that domain. When the synchronization occurs, any 5.5 distribution lists will become universal security groups in the native mode domain, and their membership will be published in the Global Catalog. Once published, these groups can be used to secure the public folders with permissions similar to those of Exchange 5.5 Server.

If, for some reason, you choose not to set up a native mode domain and you are using distribution lists to apply permissions to a public folder, you will lose this group permission ability in Exchange 2000 when the public folders are replicated. This means you'll need to use (and possibly create new) AD objects to assign permissions to public folders. The best thing to do is to create a native mode domain and assign permissions using the universal security group feature.

SUMMARY

We've focused in this chapter on the Site Replication Service, which replicates site and configuration information between both platforms, and the Active Directory Connector Service, which replicates user information between both platforms and public folder co-existence. If you are going to run a truly mixed environment of Exchange 5.5 and Exchange 2000 Server, then you will not be able to live without these services.

In this chapter we've discussed the tools that allow Exchange 5.5 and Exchange 2000 Server to run together; and in the next chapter, we'll shift our focus away from Exchange 5.5 and discuss how Exchange 2000 and Windows 2000 integrate to provide a lean, mean messaging machine. We'll look at specific points where the two platforms integrate and detail how Exchange 2000 needs Windows 2000 to run properly.

CHAPTER 3

Exchange 2000 Server Integration with Windows 2000 Server

W ith the tight integration of Exchange 2000 Server and Windows 2000 Server, it is essential for good administration of Exchange 2000 to have a solid understanding of the points of integration between these two platforms. This chapter provides insight into how your administrative activities will impact both systems. Moreover, you'll be able to use the symmetry to your advantage and, hopefully, reduce your administrative effort. The first part of the chapter will focus on how these two systems integrate and the specific points at which Exchange 2000 relies on Windows 2000. Some planning tips will be covered later in this chapter.

Exchange 2000 Server interacts with Windows 2000 Server in a number of ways. Let's take a look at each one individually.

DIRECTORY INTEGRATION WITH WINDOWS 2000 SERVER

The first and most prominent point of integration is Active Directory (AD). The Exchange 2000 and Windows 2000 Servers use the same database for account directory information. What remains in Exchange 2000 Server is the administration of messaging and collaborative services. Hence, you'll use the Active Directory Users and Computers snap-in to manage user accounts and the System Manager snap-in to manage the Exchange organization objects, such as servers, routing groups, or recipient policies.

You might recall that in Exchange 5.5 Server, a separate pair of databases—the priv.edb and the pub.edb—were used to hold messaging and public information. Windows NT 4.0 Server had a separate database for security accounts (called *security principles* in Windows 2000) that enjoyed only marginal integration with the Exchange 5.5 directory objects. This division of databases and duplication of user information has been eliminated in Exchange 2000. For instance, Windows 2000 will hold all user information; and if you want to create a mailbox for a particular user, the mailbox itself will be created in a different database to hold the messages, but the directory information about that mailbox will be little more than additional attributes on the user object in the Windows 2000 AD database.

Hence, a user object can be *mail-enabled*, meaning that it has a mailbox in an Exchange 2000 store (a *store* is the name for an Exchange 2000 database) and that the account is able to send and receive messages. Mail-enabling objects is pervasive in Windows 2000 and Exchange 2000, and Table 3-1 lists the Exchange 5.x directory objects and their equivalent AD objects.

Let's take a few minutes to discuss each of these objects in detail. How to administer users, groups, and contacts is discussed in detail in Chapter 5.

Exchange 5.5 Directory Object	Active Directory Object	Additional Information
Mailbox	Mailbox-enabled User	AD user account that has additional properties to hold messaging-specific information. This account can send and receive messages. This object can be used in Access Control Lists (ACLs) to assign permissions.
	Mail-enabled User	This is an AD user account that can authenticate in your domain and has a foreign e-mail address instead of a local mailbox.
Custom Recipient	Mail-enabled Contact	AD object that has a Simple Mail Transport Protocol (SMTP) address to which messages can be sent. This object cannot be used in the ACLs to assign permissions. 5.x
Distribution List	Mail-enabled Group	Group object in AD that has additional properties to receive messages. Both security and distribution groups can be mail-enabled. Any group scope can be set on a mail-enabled group. Using groups from AD eliminates the need to create redundant account lists.
Public Folder	Public Folder	This object is created in System Manager or Outlook, not through the standard Active Directory Users and Computers snap-in.

Table 3-1. Comparison of AD and Exchange 5.5 Directory Objects

Users

Windows 2000 user objects are created in the domain partition of AD, and are fully replicated to each domain controller in the domain and partially replicated to each Global Catalog (GC) server in the forest. This means that each domain controller in the domain will contain a full, read-write copy of the object, whereas each GC server will contain a read-only copy of the object with a limited set of attributes for the object. In AD, a user object is referenced by its Lightweight Directory Access Protocol (LDAP) context, which is also known as its Distinguished Name (DN).

TIP: The LDAP protocols and an object's DN are described in the X.500 standard, along with other directory terms and concepts. The X.500 standard can be obtained from the International Telecommunications Union at **http://www.itu.org**.

When a user object is mail-enabled, several things happen. First, two e-mail addresses are generated for the user object, an X.400 and an SMTP address. Second, a mailbox is created in an Exchange store just for the user account. This is where this user's e-mails will be held. Finally, the GC is updated so the user will appear in the Global Address List.

The administration of this object can be accomplished totally within the Active Directory Users and Computers tool. This snap-in is also provided as a standard Exchange menu choice after Exchange 2000 is installed.

Groups

Groups are a way to take multiple user accounts and place them into one administrative unit for bulk e-mail or security purposes. Smart use of groups will greatly diminish the number of administrative points in AD. Exchange 2000 uses groups as distribution lists, thus nullifying the need to create an identical but separate list of users in Exchange for large messaging delivery that already exists in Windows 2000.

There are two types of groups: *security* and *distribution*. Security groups can be added to an object's ACL (Access Control List) for permission's assignment. Distribution groups are created only for the purpose of sending a bulk e-mail to multiple recipients.

As well as having two types of groups, there are three group scopes: global, domain local, and universal.

Global Group   A global group can contain users and computers from the local domain only, but it can be used anywhere in the forest by being placed inside either a domain local, global, or universal group. The group itself is replicated to the GC server, but its membership is not. The Security Identifier (SID), a unique number assigned to each object in the AD, is made a part of the user's access token.

Global groups can be converted to universal in scope as long as they do not contain other global groups as members and Windows 2000 Server is running in native mode.

Domain Local Group   Domain local groups can contain members from any domain, including users, groups, and computers, but they can only be used in the domain in which they were created. The existence of a domain local group is replicated to the GC, but its membership is not.

As long as this type of group doesn't contain another domain local group as a member, it can be converted to universal in scope. Of course, Windows 2000 Server must be running in native mode in order to accomplish this.

Universal Group   Universal groups can contain members from any domain, including users, groups, and computers, and they can be used anywhere in the forest. Both the existence of a universal group and its membership is replicated to the GC server, and membership in a group is determined at the point of log on. What this means is that if you add a user to a universal group, the user will need to log off and log on again in order to apply the new group membership to his or her access token.

Universal groups can be either security or distribution in type, but AD must be in native mode in order to have the security type available for a universal group.

Group Membership Expansion   When a group is configured to be a distribution group, a copy of the message is sent to every member of the group. The SMTP service does the expansion of the group, which means that the group's membership is delineated and the message is attached to each recipient individually. Membership for domain local and global groups is obtained from a local domain controller. Membership for a universal group is obtained from a GC server. There are several items to note here.

First, if the global or universal group resides in a remote domain, then you'll have two choices for expansion:

▼   Forward the message to the remote domain and let it be expanded there; or

▲   Expand the membership locally by making LDAP calls to a domain controller in the remote domain to obtain the group's membership. To do this, you'll need to have direct IP connectivity to at least one domain controller in the other domain from the local expanding server.

Either option generates additional network traffic. The question is, which one will generate the least traffic? You may need to do some capacity planning to figure that out, and then configure your server's SMTP service accordingly.

Second, setting the expansion server is done on the group's property pages. Open up Active Directory Users And Computers | View | Advanced Features. Right-click the group you wish to configure and select Properties. Figure 3-1 shows what the Exchange Advanced tab will look like. This tab will not appear unless you have first chosen the Advanced Features view for the snap-in. Under the Expansion Server drop-down list, the default will be Any Server In The Organization. However, you may use this list to select a specific server in the Exchange organization to expand messages sent to this group. The list that appears here will cross domain boundaries, so you can choose a server in the list's remote domain and force messages originating in your domain to be forwarded to the selected server in the remote domain for expansion.

Group membership should be limited to 5,000 members, regardless of the type of group. While this number is not enforced in the user interface by Windows 2000, Microsoft recommends that you consider this a hard limit to work with, because the design specifications for Windows 2000 guarantee replication of group membership for only up to 5,000 users. Unpredictable results could occur if you use more than this number. To place more than 5,000 members in a single group, nest other groups inside the desired group.

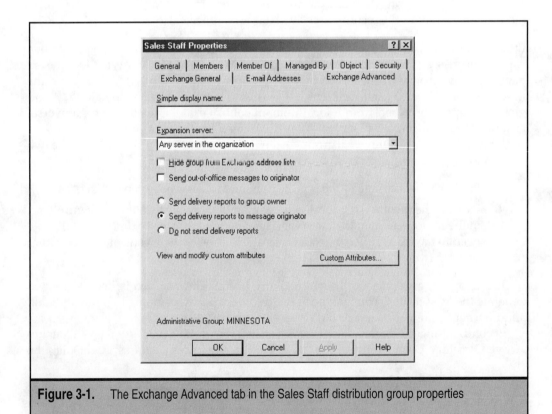

Figure 3-1.   The Exchange Advanced tab in the Sales Staff distribution group properties

Action Points for Mail-Enabling Groups

When mail-enabling groups to act as distribution lists, you should keep the following points in mind.

▼   **Group membership stability**   Don't use a universal group if membership changes frequently, because each change forces a replication of the entire group's membership to each GC server. The exception to this is when you are operating in a multidomain environment. See Chapter 5 for more details.

■   **The number of AD domains**   Single domain environments need not worry about GC replication, whereas multiple domains and sites do. Since it is best to have at least one GC in each domain and site, make sure you understand how GC replication works and what will happen when you change membership to a universal group, or when you create a new global or domain local group

▲   **Usability of the group outside your domain**   If bulk messages need to be sent to users who reside in multiple domains, it is best to use universal groups. Messages will not be sent to the users and error messages or Non-Delivery Reports (NDR) won't be generated if you use a global group across domain boundaries.

Active Directory Naming Contexts and Exchange 2000

The AD is actually comprised of three different database partitions: configuration, domain, and schema. This division in the AD can be most clearly seen when the Active Directory Service Interface (ADSI) Edit is first opened, as shown in Figure 3-2. You'll notice that right off the bat, the utility divides AD into three parts. (This tool is available under the Support folder on your Windows 2000 Server CD-ROM.) Most of Exchange 2000's information is held in the configuration partition. These partitions are also called *naming contexts*. In this section, we'll look at the three naming contexts and how Exchange 2000 interacts with them.

Configuration Partition   Most of the administrative information is held in this partition, including data about the routing groups, administrative groups, and bridgehead servers. When an Exchange 2000 Server needs to plan a routing path for a message, it consults with a local domain controller to read the configuration partition in AD.

Since the configuration partition is replicated to all domain controllers in the forest, each domain controller in the forest will have access to the same information, unless there is a temporary latency in replication of new or changed data for this partition. Figure 3-3 shows the configuration partition in ADSI Edit.

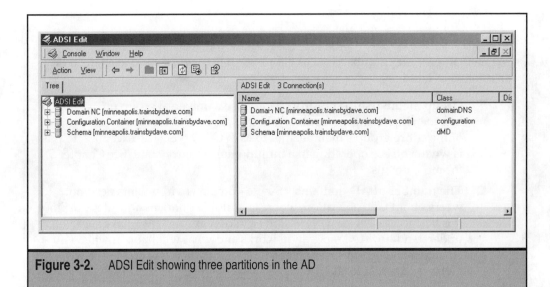

Figure 3-2.   ADSI Edit showing three partitions in the AD

Domain Partition   All the user objects reside in the domain partition. If those objects are mail-enabled, then Exchange will need to consult with this partition for that information. This includes security attributes that define permissions to Exchange objects. Public folder information is also held in the domain partition, including its security information, such as who has access to the folder contents. Of course, only mail-enabled public folders will appear as objects in the domain partition of AD. In addition, public folder tree information is held in the configuration parition in AD.

Domain information is only replicated to the local domain controllers, it is not replicated forest wide. Instances of each object are automatically replicated to the GC, which will have a subset of each object's attributes. The GC, by default, is on the root domain controller of the forest. You, the administrator, decide which other servers will be GC servers by manually configuring them in Active Directory Sites and Services.

Schema Partition   The schema defines the object classes and their attributes that make up the directory. When Exchange 2000 is installed, it must extend the schema to include object classes and attributes that are Exchange specific. This action represents close to 1,000 changes to the schema. For a more detailed discussion on extending the schema, consult Chapter 1.

Global Catalog

The GC is a read-only copy for all domain objects in the forest; however, it doesn't contain all the attributes for each object. Hence, when a new object is created in one of the domains, a copy of that object is automatically sent to the GC with only the attributes. It is the GC that provides the address book lookup services to Exchange 2000 Servers and clients.

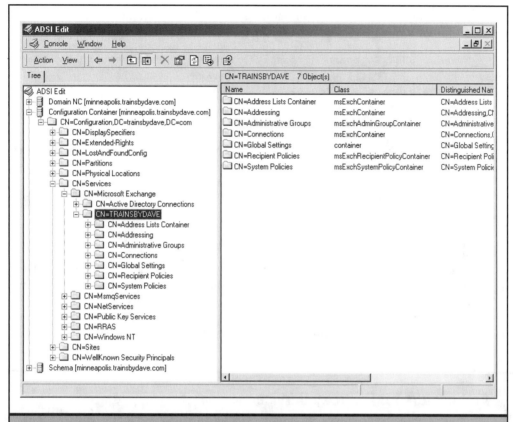

Figure 3-3.   Configuration partition in ADSI Edit

Address book lookups are facilitated by the *DSProxy* (DSPROXY.DLL) service. To Outlook 97 and 98 clients, this service imitates the Named Service Provider Interface (NSPI) that is inherent in the directory service of Exchange 5.*x* and earlier versions. These clients were written to interface with this protocol. When these clients generate a request for an address book item, DSProxy will capture the request and forward the packets to the nearest GC for resolution. The GC will return the results to the DSProxy service for passage back to the client. Since DSProxy doesn't even open the packets when they are being sent back and forth, this is a very fast proxy process.

For Outlook 2000 clients, the DSProxy service will refer them directly to the local GC server for future requests. This referral happens the first time an Outlook 2000 client re-quests an address book lookup function, and the referral remains active until the Outlook 2000 client's session is terminated with the server or the GC server goes offline.

The referral from the DSProxy service enters the following in the user's Message Application Programming Interface (MAPI) profile:

```
HKEY_CURRENT_USER\Software\Microsoft\WindowsNT\CurrentVersion\Windows
Messaging System\Profiles\profile name\dti8934....2fe194
        Value name:   001e6602
        Value type:   String
Value data:   \\insertyourownDirectoryServername.domain
```

If you wish to preclude DSProxy from sending a referral to Outlook 2000 and later clients, you should edit the following registry key:

```
HKEY_LOCAL_MACHINE\System\CurrentControlSet\Services\MSExchangeSA\Parameters
        Value name:   No RFR Service
        Value type:   DWORD
        Value data:   0x1
```

When an Exchange 2000 Server boots up, it queries the Domain Name System (DNS) to find the most appropriate domain controller for the DSProxy service to use in performing name resolution, and it will pass that name to the DSProxy service. Then, when a client needs a referral to a GC for address book lookups, the DSProxy service will query the DNS server for a GC, and then proxy the client request to the GC sever.

Architecture for DSProxy Service

When a client, such as Outlook 98, attempts to perform a lookup in the address book, the following communications occur.

1. One packet is sent to the Exchange 2000 Server with the name it wishes to look up in the Global Address List (GAL).

2. Exchange 2000's DSProxy service proxies the request to the nearest GC server.

3. The GC returns a result to the DSProxy service.

4. Exchange 2000 returns the result to the client.

5. The client sends an acknowledgement back to the Exchange 2000 server.

6. Exchange 2000 proxies the acknowledgment to the GC server.

It is possible to explicitly set the server that DSProxy will use. You can accomplish this by editing the following registry keys:

```
HKEY_LOCAL_MACHINE\System\CurrentControlSet\Services\MSExchangeSA\Parameters
            Value name:   NSPI Target Server
            Value type:   String
            Value data:   GC-Server-Name
HKEY_LOCAL_MACHINE\System\CurrentControlSet\Services\MSExchangeSA\Parameters
            Value name: RFR Target Server
            Value type: String
            Value Data: GC-Server-Name
```

If the GC server being used by the DSProxy service fails, a call-back to the Exchange System Attendant (SA) service occurs and the SA issues a new server name to DSProxy to use in the future. This activity by the SA is known as *retargeting*.

Obviously, it would be best if all this traffic occurred between domain controllers that operated in the same Windows 2000 site. Forcing this type of traffic over a WAN link could prove to be troublesome, depending on the amount of available bandwidth and its reliability.

DSProxy works over TCPIP, IPX/SPX, and AppleTalk protocols. It does not work over Netbios because Netbios lacks a network layer in its architecture.

Internet Information Services

In Exchange 5.5 Server, the information store itself hosted the server end of many messaging protocols, including Post Office Protocol version 3 (POP3), Internet Message Access Protocol version 4 (IMAP4), and MAPI. Hosting the message transport protocols directly by the information store led to scalability problems. For instance, most Exchange Servers couldn't host more than a few thousand users, and there was no good way to create an Exchange farm of servers so that implementations could scale into the millions of users.

In Exchange 2000, these protocols have been decoupled from the information store and placed inside of Internet Information Services 5.0 (IIS), with the exception of MAPI. Essentially, IIS now acts as the messaging transport protocol engine with each messaging protocol stack residing independently inside of IIS. More important, these protocols can be run on different servers than those housing the store databases, creating the possibility that a bank of front-end servers can be created, which will capture user requests for Exchange 2000 services and proxy those requests to a bank of back-end servers hosting the services and databases.

Outlook Web Access   Exchange 2000 uses IIS for Outlook Web Access (OWA), which provides a browser-based interface to basic messaging functions and to expose the *Web store*, which is a repository for any type of document that can be accessed by both LAN and Internet protocols.

Inside of IIS, you'll find that when OWA is installed, several virtual directories are also installed in the default Web site (Figure 3-4). These virtual directories act as the liaisons between the Exchange Server and the browser client.

OWA is invoked at the client end by entering the URL, **http://domainname/ exchange**, as shown in Figure 3-5.

SMTP   Exchange 2000 also relies heavily on the SMTP that is managed by the inetinfo.exe process (IIS). This protocol stack is essential to nearly all Exchange Server communications and user-initiated messages.This SMTP virtual server is discussed in depth in Chapter 9.

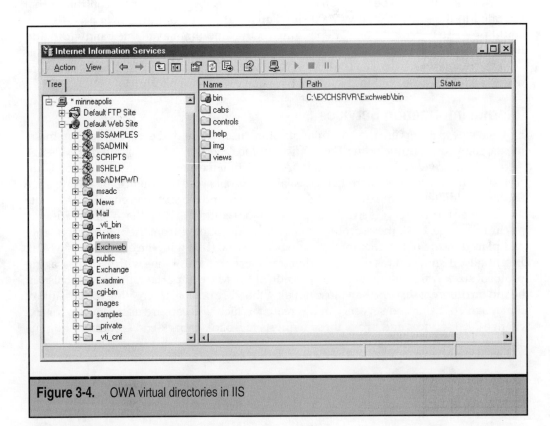

Figure 3-4.   OWA virtual directories in IIS

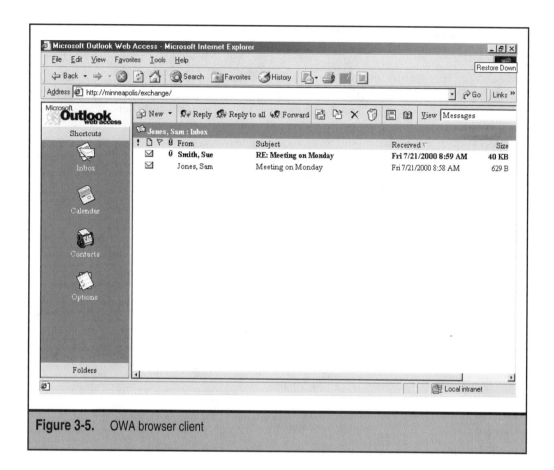

Figure 3-5.   OWA browser client

Instant Messaging and Conferencing   Instant Messaging (IM) is a new Exchange 2000 Real-Time Collaboration (RTC) service that allows users to see presence information for other users and provide a mechanism for instant communication between them. This service requires the use of a Web site and operates over port 80. Thus, Exchange 2000 is very reliant on the HTTP protocol inside IIS to make IM work properly.

Conferencing is another new RTC product being offered as an extension to Exchange 2000 Server. This service allows users to host virtual conferences that combine the transference of data, voice, video, and chat messages. Clients join a conference by connecting to a conference URL in their browsers; and, after successful authentication, clients are passed to the appropriate conference server and IIS is no longer involved. Thus, Exchange 2000 relies on IIS services to ensure that users can join a conference.

Conferencing services are going to become the normal way to conduct meetings for geographically dispersed users. This will become a heavily used technology as bandwidth availabilities increase. You should plan to become proficient at conferencing technologies in the coming months.

Network News Transfer Protocol (NNTP)   NNTP also runs inside IIS. When a newsgroup is set up or pulled into the Exchange 2000 organization, the news articles must be posted to a public folder. Exchange 2000 needs IIS to manage this protocol and client connections to the newsgroups being hosted in the public folders.

NNTP is, in our estimation, the most under-utilized protocol on most LANs. Any time you have users who need to collaborate on projects or engage in ongoing discussions, and who cannot meet face-to-face, NNTP would be an excellent choice to meet their needs.

For instance, let's assume that you have six managers, spread out over six different cities. These managers have been given the task of completing a project plan for upper management. They need to collaborate and have ongoing discussions about how to plan for several eventualities. Instead of flying them to one location to meet, they could collaborate using an internal newsgroup and access that newsgroup using Outlook Express (OE). Then, if they needed to meet, their meetings would be about making decisions, not about learning new information. The newsgroup can be secured to require a password so that only those six users can access the newsgroup. OE is easy to use and painless to set up.

NNTP, in Exchange 5.5, was installed using the Windows NT 4.0 Option Pack. Because this protocol has been moved under IIS in Windows 2000, it is now installed through the Add/Remove Programs icon in the Control Panel as a subcomponent for IIS services, as shown in Figure 3-6.

Once installed, you can create one or more NNTP virtual server in the Exchange System Manager that will host one or more newsgroups. Passage of news articles in and out of an Exchange NNTP newsgroup is handled by the NNTP protocol stack inside IIS. When Exchange 2000 Server is installed, the NNTP protocol is extended to allow newsgroup management inside the Exchange System Manager.

Integration with DNS

It is no understatement to say that Exchange 2000 Server is heavily reliant on DNS for name resolution. Happily, Microsoft has updated its DNS to be dynamic, meaning that records in the DNS database can be updated without manual intervention. However, some of the records used by Exchange are not dynamically updated; and, hence, you will need to perform some manual functions in the DNS snap-in. So, first, let's take a look at some basic information about DNS records and how that relates to Exchange 2000 Server.

Each server in DNS should have an *Address* or *A* entry. This entry is nothing more than a mapping of the server's host name to its IP address. Figure 3-7 shows the DNS tables for trainsbydave.com.

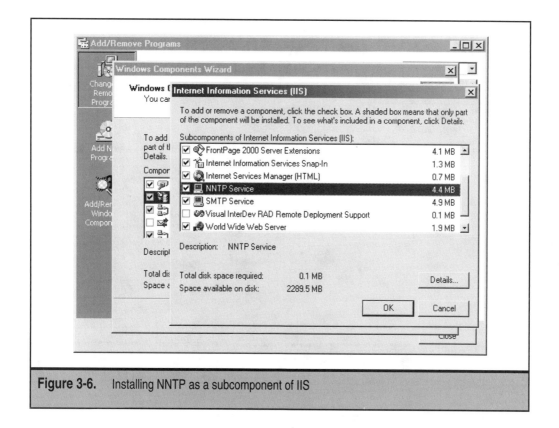

Figure 3-6.   Installing NNTP as a subcomponent of IIS

You'll notice that the Minneapolis server is listed as a host with an IP address of 192.168.2.200. Furthermore, you'll notice that www is listed as an alias to Minneapolis. This entry references Minneapolis's Fully Qualified Domain Name (FQDN), which is the server name plus its entire domain name.

If you know the name of a server, you can ping (Packet Internet Groper) the server name to obtain its IP address and FQDN. This is illustrated in Figure 3-8.

Now, notice what happens when we ping "WWW." Because it is aliased to the Minneapolis name, we will get the same results, as illustrated in Figure 3-9.

Referring back to Figure 3-7, you can see the existence of four folders inside of trainsbydave.com. These folders represent where the service records (SRV) are held in DNS. Figure 3-10 has expanded the _tcp folder to reveal which services are currently being offered over TCP in the trainsbydave.com domain. You can see that global catalog, kerberos, password, and LDAP services are available.

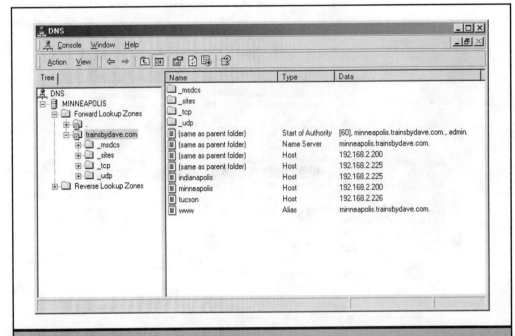

Figure 3-7.   DNS tables for trainsbydave.com

```
Microsoft Windows 2000 [Version 5.00.2195]
(C) Copyright 1985-1999 Microsoft Corp.

C:\>PING MINNEAPOLIS

Pinging minneapolis.trainsbydave.com [192.168.2.200] with 32 bytes of data:

Reply from 192.168.2.200: bytes=32 time<10ms TTL=128
Reply from 192.168.2.200: bytes=32 time<10ms TTL=128
Reply from 192.168.2.200: bytes=32 time<10ms TTL=128
Reply from 192.168.2.200: bytes=32 time<10ms TTL=128

Ping statistics for 192.168.2.200:
    Packets: Sent = 4, Received = 4, Lost = 0 (0% loss),
Approximate round trip times in milli-seconds:
    Minimum = 0ms, Maximum = 0ms, Average = 0ms

C:\>_
```

Figure 3-8.   Results of pinging the Minneapolis server name

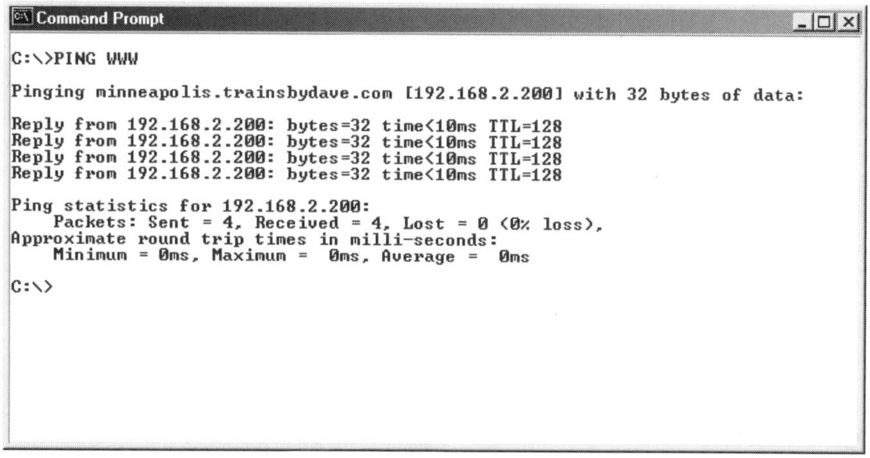

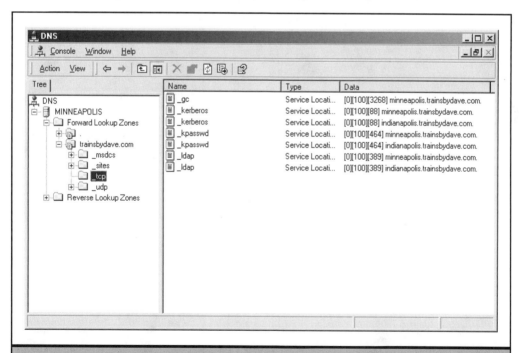

Figure 3-9.   Resolving WWW to the Minneapolis server

Figure 3-10.   SRV records for trainsbydave.com

Now SMTP doesn't resolve to an A record by default. When SMTP needs to find another SMTP server, its queries DNS for a Mail Exchange (MX) record and then attempts to make a TCP port 25 connection to the IP address recorded in the DNS tables.

MX records can be added with ease by right-clicking the domain name in DNS and selecting New Mail Exchanger from the context menu. Once you have done this, the New Resource Record dialog box will appear. Enter the Exchange Server's FQDN under Mail Server, and assign it a preference value. This is illustrated in Figure 3-11.

You can see in Figure 3-12 how the record will appear.

The preference value tells SMTP which server to attempt connection to first if more than one record exists for any one SMTP server. This is a very common practice. Let's assume that the IP address for the SMTP server for trainsbydave.com is 192.168.2.200. As long as the appropriate MS entries exist in DNS, any other SMTP server on the Internet can make a TCP port 25 connection to this IP address and send the commands to transfer mail.

However, what happens if the SMTP Server for trainsbydave.com is unavailable? Well, with a second entry to the ISP's SMTP Server in DNS, mail will be transferred there

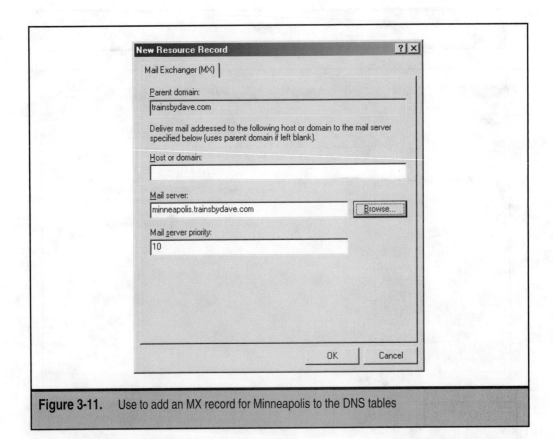

Figure 3-11.   Use to add an MX record for Minneapolis to the DNS tables

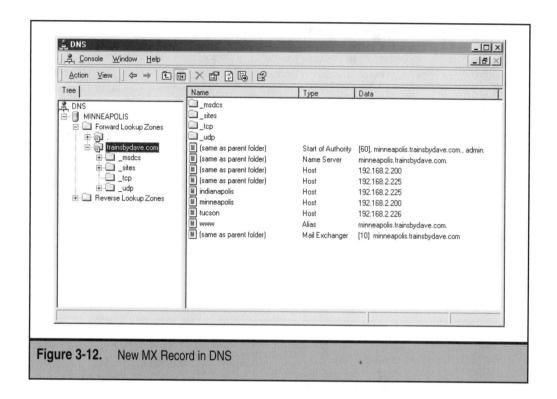

Figure 3-12.   New MX Record in DNS

and held until the SMTP Server for trainsbydave.com comes online and downloads the waiting message from the ISP.

Preference values tell the connecting SMTP Servers to first try to connect to the server with the lowest value and then, if it isn't available, to connect to the next server with the next lowest value until one is found that messages can be transferred to. So, the MX record for the SMTP virtual server for the trainsbydave.com domain would have a preference value lower than any other SMTP server, such as the ISP's SMTP server for trainsbydave.com.

Because of the way Microsoft wrote its DNS services for Windows 2000, there is a pecking order in which resolution occurs when SMTP attempts to find another SMTP server. First, it will query DNS for an MX record for the destination server that it is looking for. If no such record exists, it will query DNS for an A record for the server's host name; and if one is found, it will attempt a TCP port 25 connection to that server, even though it was using the A record and not the MX record. And if neither an MX or an A record exists in DNS, the Exchange will default to the Netbios name resolution process, which means that it will attempt resolution at a WINS server and if no WINS server exists, then it will perform a Netbios broadcast.

GC Services and Exchange 2000 Server

By default, there is only one GC in the forest—the root domain controller in the root domain. All other GC servers must be manually instantiated. To create a GC server, open up the Active Directory Sites and Services snap-in, and navigate to your server object and expand it; then right-click the NTDS Settings object and select Properties. Figure 3-13 shows that all you need to do is select the GC check box, and this server will become a GC server.

The GC server resolves all address book lookups. As we discussed earlier in the section "Global Catolog," the DSProxy Server refers address book lookups from clients to the nearest GC server. Where you place the GC servers is immensely important, because you must balance user needs to have fast address book lookups against the amount of replication traffic that will occur between the GC servers. This is where you must do some capacity planning to determine how much bandwidth is being consumed with GC replication traffic and how much would be consumed if additional GC servers were added.

If at all possible, you should really attempt to place GC servers near each Exchange 2000 Server. In smaller companies that operate inside of one domain and fewer servers, consider the possibility of placing your Exchange Server on a Windows 2000 domain controller that is also a GC server.

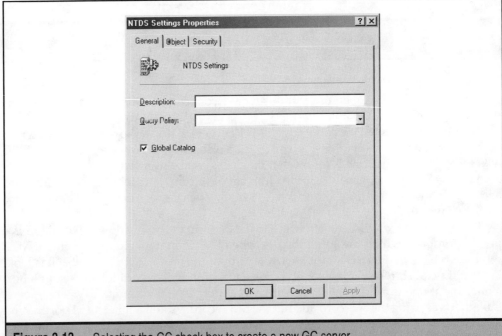

Figure 3-13.   Selecting the GC check box to create a new GC server.

Now I know that some of you are flinching at this suggestion—putting Exchange, domain controller, and GC services on the same box. And in larger organizations, this would not be a good idea. But in smaller companies whose directory information changes infrequently, and that are operating in a single site and a single domain, one could very well house these services on a single server. While this solution is not for everyone, it can be a plausible scenario for companies that are smaller in size and location.

However, regardless of your size, you should have, at a minimum, two GC servers per Windows 2000 site and domain that will house an Exchange 2000 Server or mail-enabled objects. Having two GCs provides fault tolerance as well as choices to your Exchange servers when GC services are needed.

Windows 2000 Security and Exchange 2000 Server

The basis of Windows 2000 security is derived partly from the NTFS file system and its ability to place an ACL to each object, file, and folder. And, unlike Windows NT 4.0, ACLs are created not only for the object, but also for every attribute for each object. This provides you, the administrator, with granular control over who can access the attributes and the objects.

Public folders now have ACLs, unlike Exchange 5.5 Server, because they are now objects in the AD. You can now use Windows 2000 security to lock your public folders. As Figure 3-14 illustrates, you can use AD security principles to assign various levels of permissions to a public folder. Open the folder's properties, navigate to the Permissions tab, and select Directory Rights.

You can also set Administrative rights for public folders by clicking the Administrative Rights button and configuring the groups and permissions as necessary; see Figure 3-15.

ACLs can also be used by clicking the Mailbox Rights button in the user's object properties in the Active Directory User and Computers snap-in; see Figure 3-16.

Windows 2000 Administration and Exchange 2000

If you've been working in a company in which network and messaging administration has a sharp division of labor, you'll need to consider changing your administrative models to accommodate the changes that Exchange 2000's integration with Windows 2000 represents.

This is perhaps the most obvious point of integration and one that might cause the most internal stress in your organization, because the traditional division of labor between the network and exchange teams will likely change. For instance, unlike Windows NT 4.0 and Exchange 5.5, where two accounts are created for each user, only one is created in AD. Moreover, when a user account is mail-enabled, additional attributes are added and filled in to the user object; a new user object is not created. Hence, larger organizations will need to decide who will be creating the new user accounts and who will be mail-enabling the accounts.

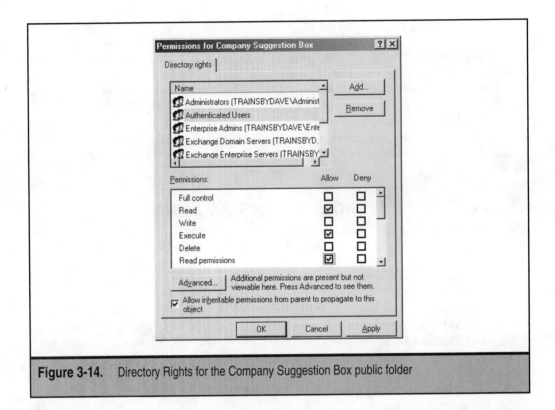

Figure 3-14.   Directory Rights for the Company Suggestion Box public folder

User account administration is accomplished fully through the Active Directory Users and Computers snap-in. How this is accomplished and what the administrative techniques are in creating and managing users is discussed in Chapter 5.

Active Directory Connector (ADC) and Exchange 2000 Server

The ADC is used by Exchange 2000 Server to synchronize information between its directories and AD in Windows 2000. It is a replication and mapping engine that moves objects between the Exchange 5.5 directory and AD. The ADC provides the framework in which one or more CAs can be created to define how and when objects will be replicated to the other directory. For more information about the ADC, see Chapter 2.

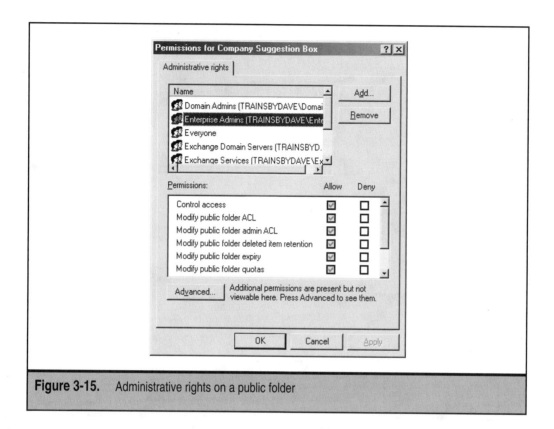

Permissions for Company Suggestion Box   ? X

Administrative rights

Name	
🏿 Domain Admins (TRAINSBYDAVE\Domai	**Add...**
🏿 Enterprise Admins (TRAINSBYDAVE\Ente	**Remove**
🏿 Everyone	
🏿 Exchange Domain Servers (TRAINSBYD.	
🏿 Exchange Services (TRAINSBYDAVE\Ex	

Permissions: Allow   Deny

	Allow	Deny
Control access	☑	☐
Modify public folder ACL	☑	☐
Modify public folder admin ACL	☑	☐
Modify public folder deleted item retention	☑	☐
Modify public folder expiry	☑	☐
Modify public folder quotas	☑	☐

Advanced... | Additional permissions are present but not viewable here. Press Advanced to see them.

OK   Cancel   Apply

Figure 3-15.   Administrative rights on a public folder

SUMMARY

In this chapter, you learned about the various points of integration between Exchange 2000 Server and Windows 2000 Server. You learned that the integration is tight and that there are many daily functions for which Exchange 2000 relies on Windows 2000. These two products are so tightly integrated that Exchange 2000 cannot even be installed without the existence and availability of the AD to the new Exchange 2000 Server.

In Chapter 4, we'll discuss not only what is needed to install Exchange 2000 Server, but also the various ways to do this. And, we'll look at some of the hardware requirements for Exchange 2000 and discuss how to troubleshoot a failed installation.

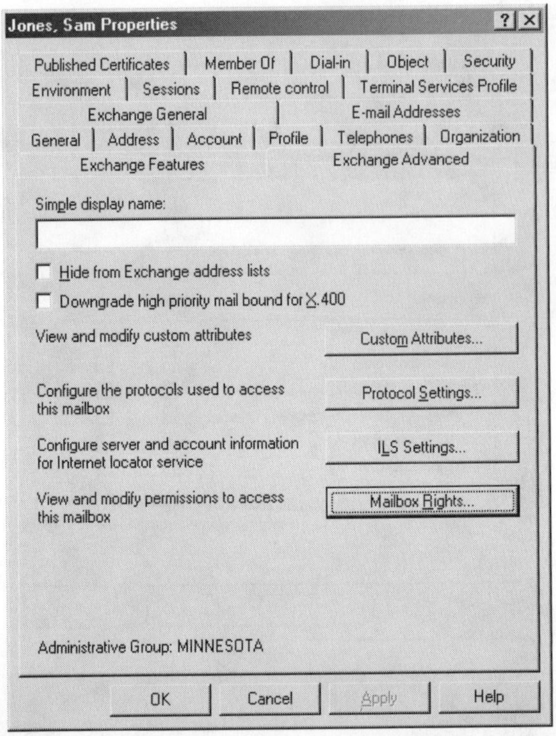

Figure 3-16. The Mailbox Rights button in the user account properties

PART II

Administration
Deployment

CHAPTER 4

Installing Exchange 2000 Server

In Chapter 1, we discussed one way to migrate from Exchange 5.5 to Exchange 2000. By necessity, we also discussed how to install Exchange 2000 Server—at least from the viewpoint of performing a migration.

In this chapter, we'll discuss how to install Exchange 2000 Server by focusing on the practical steps and actions you'll need to perform in order to install it. This chapter is not intended to be a planning chapter to help you determine when the methods presented here should be employed, though we will mention some planning tips.

Let's first take a look at what Exchange 2000 Server requires before it can be installed, then we'll look at how to perform a manual installation and an unattended (silent) installation. Finally, we'll outline the different e-mail migration paths that can be performed from foreign e-mail systems.

REQUIREMENTS TO INSTALL EXCHANGE 2000 SERVER

Here's what you must have to install Exchange 2000 Server:

▼ An available Windows 2000 Server with Active Directory (AD) and Windows 2000 Service Pack 1 installed.

■ A Windows 2000 Server that is either a domain controller or a member server for the local server installation.

■ Network News Transfer Protocol (NNTP) must also be installed locally on the server that is going to host Exchange.

■ If this is a reinstallation, the Mdbdata folder must be empty.

■ A Domain Name System (DNS) must be available.

■ At least 500MB of free disk space.

■ A minimum of 256MB RAM.

▲ A Pentium 300 or greater processor.

Now, looking at the processor and RAM requirements, you'll probably think that these are a bit silly. However, there are reasons for these requirements, not the least of which is that Microsoft is an international corporation and must consider the general hardware capacities of their customers in countries other than the United States. In many locations, hardware capacity is much less than it is in the United States, and Microsoft's platforms must be written to accommodate this variance.

A quick review of Microsoft's platforms will give you a better indication of how much processing power and RAM capacity you'll likely need.

While you could install all these operating systems on their minimum hardware platforms, it's pretty obvious that you wouldn't ever do it. Hence, even though we recommend a minimum set of hardware resources, we also know that in most installations, you'll be working with hardware that is far more powerful than the minimums given.

Operating System	Minimum Hardware Requirements	Could You?	Would You?
DOS	8086/8088; 64Kbps RAM	Yes	No
Windows 3.x	286; 1MB RAM	Yes	No
Windows 95	386/25; 4MB RAM	Yes	No
Windows 98	486DX/66; 16MB RAM	Yes	No
Windows NT 4.0 Workstation	486DX/66; 12MB RAM	Yes	No
Windows NT 4.0 Server	486DX/66; 16MB RAM	Yes	No
Windows 2000 Professional	P/133; 64MB RAM	Yes	No
Windows 2000 Server	P/166; 64MB RAM	Yes	No
Exchange 2000 Server	P/200; 64MB RAM	Yes	No

Table 4-1. Minimum Hardware Requirements for Microsoft's Operating Systems

So, how much hardware do you need? Our advice is to err on the side of buying (seemingly) too much. Microsoft has released a white paper, "Deploying the Active Directory Connector within Microsoft," which describes their current hardware platforms for all of their Exchange 2000 Servers (see Table 4-2). Suffice it to say that they rarely purchase single processor equipment and they always have Redundant Arrays of Independent Disks (RAID5) hardware.

Number of Users	CPU	RAM	Hard Drive
Fewer than 500 users	1 at 200 Mhz or faster	256MB	25Gb RAID array, redundant controllers
500–1,000 users	4 at 200 Mhz or faster	512MB	125Gb RAID array, redundant controllers
1,000–3,000 users	8 at 550 Mhz or faster	4Gb	600Gb RAID array, cluster technology
Public Folder Server	2 at 200 Mhz or faster	512MB	50Gb RAID array, redundant controllers

Table 4-2. Microsoft's Published Internal Hardware Requirements for Exchange 2000 Server

When consulting, it is common to ask customers to think back three to five years to what they were purchasing for hardware back then. At the time of this writing, going back three years, generally they were purchasing Pentium MMX processors operating around 233 Megahertz (P/233) with 128MB RAM; or, if they were really adventurous, they were purchasing Pentium II (PII) processors. It is then helpful to ask them where they think hardware will be in three to five years, and what they will do if a new software package is released that requires higher-powered hardware.

Even for small companies (under 25 users), it is generally an unwise decision to purchase less than dual processors with less than 512MB RAM for an Exchange 2000 Server. This might seem like overkill, but in three years you will be glad you purchased this machine. Buying now what seems like overkill for hardware capacity will make the machine usable for a much longer time.

INSTALLING EXCHANGE 2000 SERVER

There are several ways to install Exchange 2000 Server. The most common, straightforward, method is to perform a new installation of the program. Another way to install Exchange 2000 Server is to perform an upgrade from Exchange 5.5. This method has its own pitfalls and challenges and is outlined in detail in Chapter 1. A third method of installing Exchange 2000 Server is to perform an unattended installation, also called a *silent* installation, which you'll find in the "Performing a Silent Installation" section, later in this chapter.

Performing a New Installation of Exchange 2000 Server

There are several decision points that you need to plan for during the installation. Here is a grocery list of these points:

- ▼ Name of your new Exchange 2000 organization
- ■ Name and password of the Exchange 2000 service account
- ■ Specific components you wish to install
- ■ Location of your Exchange files and databases
- ▲ User account that will be granted Delegation Authority Control

We strongly suggest that these decisions be made before you start the installation process. There are a couple of no-return decisions—the name of the organization and the account granted Delegation Authority Control—that are particularly important to plan out.

Once the name of the organization is set in AD (Active Directory), it cannot be changed without uninstalling and then reinstalling Exchange 2000 Server. That isn't a fun thing to do because the databases cannot be ported to the new installation. Also, the user account that is granted the authority to delegate control of Exchange objects to other users cannot be changed once the installation program is underway. The only way to change it after the installation is complete is to log on with that account and change permissions on the organization object.

To start the installation, run setup.exe from the i386 folder on your Exchange 2000 Server CD-ROM, or you can just insert the server CD-ROM into the CD-ROM drive and it will autostart with the Exchange 2000 Server splash screen. Select to install Exchange 2000 Server, and you'll see the Welcome screen for the installation program; see Figure 4-1.

After clicking Next, Setup will copy some files to your hard drive, and then it will present you with the licensing agreement screen. You must agree with the license before you can proceed; see Figure 4-2.

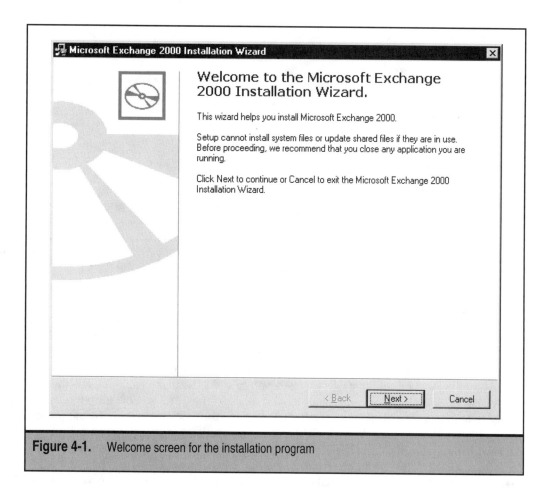

Figure 4-1.   Welcome screen for the installation program

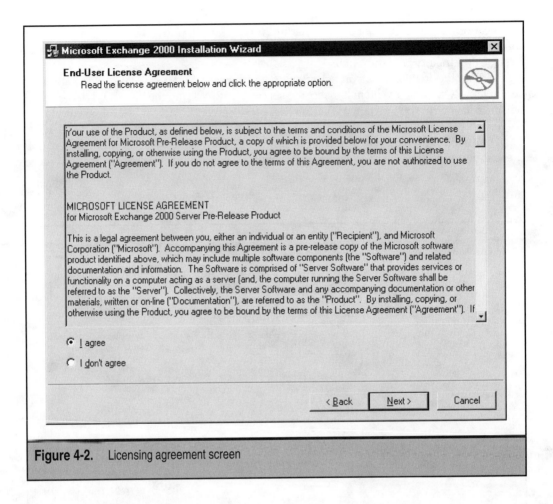

Figure 4-2. Licensing agreement screen

Once you have agreed to the license, you'll need to input the product key code and click Next. After that, you'll be presented with the Component Selection screen (Figure 4-3).

On this screen, under the Action menu next to the Microsoft Exchange 2000 object, you can choose to perform a Typical, Minimum, or Custom installation. A Typical installation will install the messaging databases for both public and private stores, as well as the System Manager. Selecting Custom will allow you to select the exact mix of components that you wish to install. The Minimum installation removes the System Manager from the components selected and installs only the databases, transaction logs, and Exchange Services. For the purpose of our discussion in this section, we'll perform a Typical installation.

After choosing your installation action, you'll be given a choice as to where in the Exchange organization you wish to install your new server. If this is the first server of a new installation, then the default will be First Administrative Group/First Storage Group. Remember that the first server installed creates the Exchange organization if the

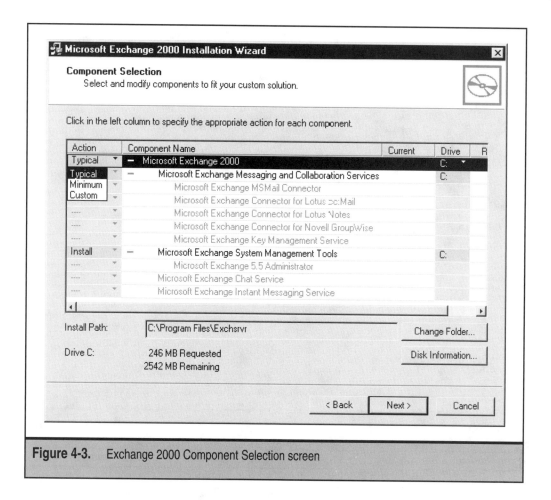

Figure 4-3. Exchange 2000 Component Selection screen

/ForestPrep or Active Directory Connector (ADC) service setup has not been run. If this is an additional server, and if you have already set up your administrative and routing groups, then you can choose which administrative and routing group into which you wish to install the new Exchange 2000 Server. This is illustrated in Figure 4-4.

After choosing the administrative and routing group, you will then need to input the correct password for the Exchange account. Files will then start to be copied, and services will subsequently be installed.

The file-copy and service-installation phase is, by far, the longest part of the installation process. Once Exchange 2000 has been installed, you'll be ready to create user's mailboxes and let messaging begin.

There are more than a few switches that can be used in conjunction with the Setup command. If you type in the Setup command at the Run command with the /? Switch, you'll receive a list of all the available switches, as shown in Figure 4-5.

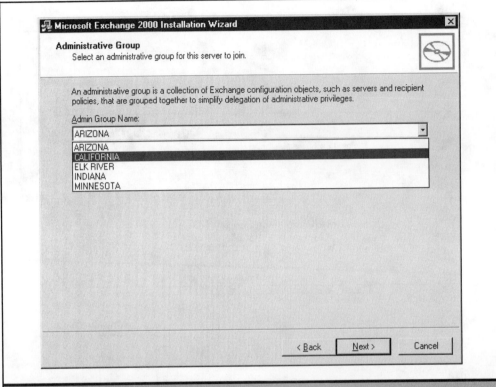

Figure 4-4. Selecting the administrative and routing group in which to install a new Exchange 2000 Server

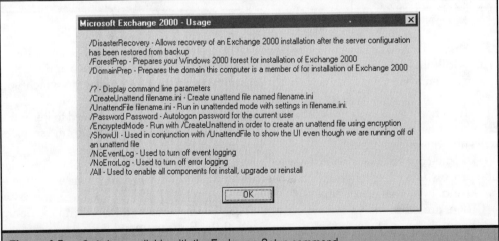

Figure 4-5. Switches available with the Exchange Setup command

Each of the switches in Figure 4-5 is used at a specific point. For example, the /CreateUnattend filename.ini switch creates a file by which you can then perform other unattended installations of Exchange 2000 Server. If you want to encrypt the unattend file, use the /EncryptedMode switch, which will encrypt the filename.ini file so that its contents cannot be seen or modified by the wrong people before being used by Setup. If you want to follow the progress of a silent installation, you can use the /ShowUI switch, which will show the screens while the installation is proceeding, even though no user interaction is required.

Notice that you cannot use the switches to select certain components for installation—that must be done at the Component Selections screen. The only exception to this is the /All switch, which is used to enable all components for installation.

Now, depending on which components you selected during the installation, there are up to 18 services added to Windows 2000 by Exchange 2000. In addition, certain folders are automatically shared. This is outlined in Table 4-3.

When Exchange 2000 Server is installed, a very long list of folders is created under the Exchsrvr folder. Table 4-4 outlines each of these folders and the data they will hold.

Believe it or not, sometimes an installation doesn't work. So we've put together some of the more common issues for troubleshooting a bad Exchange 2000 installation. If you're having problems installing Exchange 2000 Server, first make sure that you are meeting all of the minimum requirements, then check Table 4-5 to see if your problem is outlined. If it isn't, find your error message(s) in TechNet or online at **msnews. microsoft.com** in one of the Exchange newsgroups.

TIP: TechNet is a monthly subscription from Microsoft that contains knowledge-base articles, resource kits in electronic form, service packs, utilities, and seminars on disk. This is a very valuable resource that you should have if you're going to administer an Exchange 2000 network. More information about TechNet may be found at **http://www.microsoft.com/technet**.

Directory	Shared As	Permissions
Exchsrvr\Address	Address	Administrators and Site Services account—Full Control
		Everyone—Read
	Tracking.log	Administrators and Site Services account—Full Control
		Everyone—Read

Table 4-3. Summary of Share-Point Permissions

Folder	Contents of Folder
Address	Address proxy Dynamic Link Libraries (DLLs). The default installation will contain DLLs for Microsoft Mail and AppleTalk networks, Lotus cc:Mail, SMTP, and X.400. These DLLs generate the addresses for each new recipient.
Bin	Binary files for the Exchange 2000 program and the System Manager.
CCMCdata	The directory structure that serves as the temporary location that the Lotus cc:Mail connector uses to store messages during transit.
Conndata	MS Mail connector.
Conferencing	Videoconferencing files.
Connect	Components for Exchange 2000 connectors.
Dxadata	Default location where the directory synchronization databases between Microsoft Mail and Exchange 2000 are located, along with their transaction logs.
Exchweb	Outlook Web Access (OWA) information.
ExchangeServer_ *servername*	Data for MSSearch and context indexing support.
Mdbdata	Default location for the store databases (Priv1.stm/Priv1.edb/ Pub1.stm/Pub1.edb) and their transaction logs.
Mtadata	Default location for the MTA's configuration, template database, and log files.
Res	Holds other types of files, such as the logs for the Event Viewer and the Windows 2000 Performance Monitor.
Schema	OLE EDB schema.
Srsdata	Site Replication Service (SRS) data.
Servername.log	Holds the tracking logs that enable the message tracking feature of Exchange 2000 to work.

Table 4-4. Default File Location and Structures

Performing a Silent Installation

Performing a silent installation means that, without manual intervention, you supply the answers that Setup needs in order to complete. This is done through the creation of a common text file. We usually call this an *unattend file*. To create this file, run the Setup program with the /createunattend switch and specify the name of the file, such as Setup /CreateUnattend filename.ini.

Problem	Error message (If Applicable)	Solution
You suspect that the /ForestPrep command didn't work.		Ensure the account that is performing the /ForestPrep command has permissions in the Schema Admins and Enterprise Admins groups, and Local Administrator rights to the server.
You suspect that the /DomainPrep command didn't work.		Ensure the account that is performing the /DomainPrep command has permissions in the groups Domain Admins and local Administrator rights to the server.
Network connection fails during a network installation.		Restart the server, turn off any running Exchange Services, and rerun Setup.
	Setup was unable to bind to the Exchange Server.	This is the error message that you'll receive if the account you used to start the Exchange 2000 Setup does not have the correct permissions for the target server's Exchange 5.5 directory. The solution is to give this account Administrator permissions at the Site and Configuration levels of your Exchange 5.5 organization.
You install Exchange 2000 Server into a child domain and Setup ceases to work the first time with this error message.	The Directory Service is busy.	This is a named pipe transport problem. When Exchange 2000 starts, the server side creates a pipe to be used by clients. The first time a client attempts to use a pipe, that first pipe will be used. Subsequent client connection attempts will require additional pipes to be created on the server side. If a client attempts to connect to the server before another pipe can be created, the server will appear busy and it will not accept the connection. The client will then receive this error message. When installing Exchange 2000 into a domain, it acts like a client to the directory service running on Windows 2000. The solution is to rerun the Exchange 2000 Setup and install the components that didn't install during the first installation.

Table 4-5.   Common Installation Problems and Solutions

Problem	Error message (If Applicable)	Solution
Setup fails during the installation.	Error 0xC103798A	If any component of Exchange 5.5 Server doesn't completely uninstall, there will be a DLL version conflict for the exchmem.dll file. The solution is to rename the exchmem.dll file exchmem.old, and then Exchange 2000 will copy the appropriate exchmem.dll file during setup.
Setup fails while trying to join an existing Exchange 5.5 site that also has a large number of servers or sites.		On the LDAP properties' Search tab in the Exchange 5.5 Administrator, configure the value for Maximum Number of Search Results Returned to a value that is equal to or greater than the total number of servers in the Exchange 5.5 organization. You need to perform this for each site in your Exchange 5.5 organization.
When attempting to join an Exchange 5.5 site, setup fails if it is being run on a Windows 2000 domain controller.		This is due to a port number conflict. Before you run Exchange 5.5 on a Windows 2000 domain controller, you must install Exchange 5.5 Service Pack 3 and change the port number in the Exchange Administrator for LDAP Services to a port other than 389 (usually 390). Restart your Exchange 5.5 services.
During and after setup, you receive false alerts in Exchange 5.5, which attempts to start services that are no longer in existence.		This occurs because the server you are upgrading is also being monitored by another Exchange 5.5 Server. Disable monitoring services for that server.

Table 4-5.   Common Installation Problems and Solutions *(continued)*

Now, the Setup wizard will run through its screens as if it is going to do a real setup. And if you're running this command on a server that already has Exchange 2000 Server installed, you'll need to select the Reinstall action and then proceed through the screens as if you're going to reinstall Exchange 2000 Server.

However, Setup will *not* run the full Setup program, but instead it will create the unattend file and give you a splash screen (Figure 4-6) indicating the location of the file that was just created. Figure 4-7 shows what a portion of the text file looks like in Notepad.

Other Installation Considerations

It is important to understand that the Exchange 2000 Server Setup program will use the Exchange 5.5 Server Service Pack 3 to extract site information from an Exchange 5.5 Server for the configuration partition in AD. Without Exchange 5.5 Server running Service Pack 3, the upgrade process will fail.

After you have tied together your two directories—AD and Exchange 5.5—with the connection agreements, you then need to consider moving at least one AD domain into native mode. This is due to the use of distribution lists in Exchange 5.5 to assign permissions

Figure 4-6. Final screen in the setup program when creating an unattend file

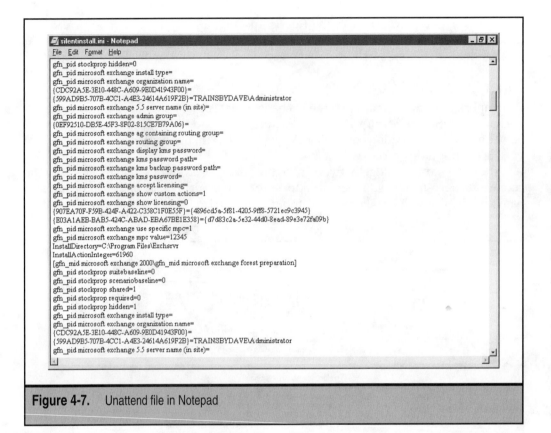

```
silentinstall.ini - Notepad                                                                    _ 8 X
File  Edit  Format  Help
gfn_pid stockprop hidden=0
gfn_pid microsoft exchange install type=
gfn_pid microsoft exchange organization name=
{CDC92A5E-3E10-448C-A609-9E0D41943F00}=
{599AD9B5-707B-4CC1-A4E3-24614A619F2B}=TRAINSBYDAVE\Administrator
gfn_pid microsoft exchange 5.5 server name (in site)=
gfn_pid microsoft exchange admin group=
{0EF92510-DB5E-45F3-8F02-815CE7B79A06}=
gfn_pid microsoft exchange ag containing routing group=
gfn_pid microsoft exchange routing group=
gfn_pid microsoft exchange display kms password=
gfn_pid microsoft exchange kms password path=
gfn_pid microsoft exchange kms backup password path=
gfn_pid microsoft exchange kms password=
gfn_pid microsoft exchange accept licensing=
gfn_pid microsoft exchange show custom actions=1
gfn_pid microsoft exchange show licensing=0
{907EA70F-F59B-424F-A422-C358C1F0E55F}={4896cd5a-5f81-4205-9ff8-5721ec9c3945}
{E03A1AEB-BAB5-424C-ABAD-EBA67BE1E358}={d7d83c2a-5e32-44d0-8ead-89e3e72fa09b}
gfn_pid microsoft exchange use specific mpc=1
gfn_pid microsoft exchange mpc value=12345
InstallDirectory=C:\Program Files\Exchsrvr
InstallActionInteger=61960
[gfn_mid microsoft exchange 2000\gfn_mid microsoft exchange forest preparation]
gfn_pid stockprop suitebaseline=0
gfn_pid stockprop scenariobaseline=0
gfn_pid stockprop shared=1
gfn_pid stockprop required=0
gfn_pid stockprop hidden=1
gfn_pid microsoft exchange install type=
gfn_pid microsoft exchange organization name=
{CDC92A5E-3E10-448C-A609-9E0D41943F00}=
{599AD9B5-707B-4CC1-A4E3-24614A619F2B}=TRAINSBYDAVE\Administrator
gfn_pid microsoft exchange 5.5 server name (in site)=
```

Figure 4-7.   Unattend file in Notepad

to one or more public folders. In Exchange 5.5, you could use a distribution list to assign permissions to a public folder, but Windows 2000 places an Access Control List (ACL) on each public folder, and uses its own users and groups to assign permissions. Windows 2000 cannot use a distribution list to assign permissions.

In addition, in Exchange 5.x, distribution lists could include user accounts from any site in the organization. The equivalent for this in Windows 2000 is a universal security group, which is only available in a native mode domain. Thus, if you want to continue securing one or more public folders in Exchange 2000 as you did in Exchange 5.5, you'll need to place those public folders in a Windows 2000 native mode domain and use a universal security group to assign permissions to those folders.

This means that you may need to create a special domain in which to place the public folders until such time as you move other Windows 2000 domains into native mode. At that point, you can migrate your public folders to another domain and decommission the temporary domain that was created to hold the public folders.

Coexistence with Other Systems

Exchange 2000 Server ships with connectors for transparent operation with foreign e-mail systems. These connectors include

- ▼ Lotus Notes
- ■ Lotus cc:Mail
- ■ Novell GroupWise
- ■ Microsoft Mail
- ■ A Free/Busy connector for Microsoft Schedule +
- ▲ X.400 connector

These connectors can transfer messages over LANs, X.25, and asynchronous packet-switching networks.

In addition, Microsoft has provided a Migration Wizard to enable migration to Exchange 2000 from any of the following:

- ▼ Lotus Notes 3.*x*, 4.0, and 4.1
- ■ Lotus Domino 4.5 and 4.6
- ■ Microsoft Mail 3.*x*
- ■ Lotus cc:Mail, database versions DB6 and DB8
- ■ Novell GroupWise 4.*x* and 5.*x*
- ■ Collabra Share 1.*x* and 2.*x*
- ■ Internet Message Application Programming version 4 (IMAPv4)–compliant Internet messaging systems
- ▲ LDAP-compliant Internet directory services

You may want to consult Technet and other documentation about these connectors to learn more about how they work.

SUMMARY

In this chapter, you have learned how to install Exchange 2000 Server, how to perform a silent installation, and what some of the installation considerations are. In the next chapter, we'll move from installation issues to administrative issues once the server is installed.

CHAPTER 5

Creating and Managing Recipients

Once Exchange 2000 Server is installed and your user accounts and mailboxes have been migrated from an Exchange 5.5 Server, it's time to get down to the business of managing your Exchange 2000 environment.

One of the main functions in managing an Exchange 2000 environment is the creation and configuration of recipient objects. Now, lest we be fooled here, this involves much more than just mail-enabling a user account or public folder. Once enabled, there are a host of configuration parameters that need to be considered. In addition, the types of recipients have changes from Exchange 5.5 and now include mail-enabled user accounts, contacts, groups, and public folders.

Since all of these configurations are held in Active Directory (AD), the primary tool for creating and managing recipients is Active Directory User and Computers. In this chapter, we'll illustrate how to create and configure each of these recipient types. Thereafter, we'll look at how to create and manage customized address lists for your users.

CREATING AND MANAGING RECIPIENTS

Let's start out by looking at how to create a user account, how to mail-enable the account, and how to configure a mail-enabled user account.

Creating a New User Account

To create a new user account, open up Active Directory Users And Computers, right-click the object in which you want to create the user account, point to New, and then select User, as shown in Figure 5-1.

The New Object – User screen will appear, and you can fill it in with the appropriate information. Once filled in, click Next, and you can input the user's password and other password-specific configuration information.

Click Next after entering the password information, and you'll be prompted to create a mailbox for this user (Figure 5-2). On this screen, you can deselect the Create An Exchange Mailbox check box if you don't want to create a mailbox for the user while creating the account. This should be done if there is one team of administrators responsible for creating user accounts and another team that is responsible to mail-enable these accounts.

The Alias input box is where you can customize the Simple Mail Transport Protocol (SMTP) alias that will be used for this account. For example, in larger organizations, log-on names might be something like "US456723," while the SMTP alias might be a concatenation of their name, such as "benglish" for "Bill English." By default, the alias that is presented here is the same as the log-on name from the first screen in this wizard (refer to Figure 5-2). But if you change the alias on this screen, you'll find the log-on name will not change with it.

You also have your choice of which Exchange Server and mailbox store you want the user's mailbox to be created in. Using the drop-down arrows, select the appropriate server/mailbox store combination, and click Next.

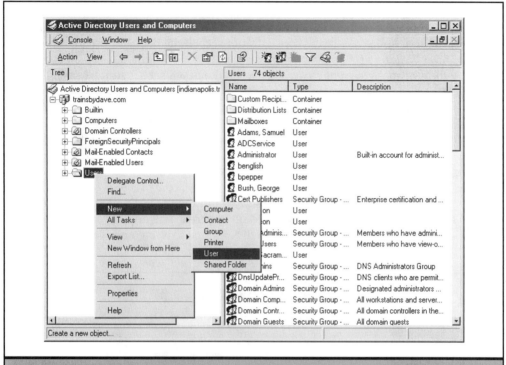

Figure 5-1.   Selecting a new user account in Active Directory Users and Computers

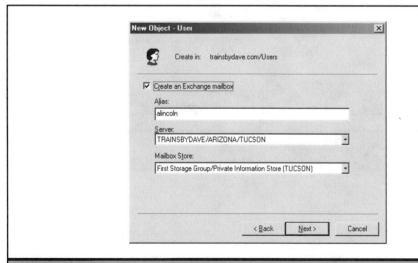

Figure 5-2.   Creating a mailbox for a new user account

The final screen (Figure 5-3) outlines the particulars of the object that will be created. This is the one place where you can see what all your choices were in the wizard. If you need to make changes to any of the configurations, click the Back button and make your changes. After clicking Finish, the new user account will be created.

If you didn't choose to create a mailbox when the new user account was created, you can still mail-enable the account in Active Directory Users And Computers by right-clicking the user's account, and then selecting Exchange Tasks (Figure 5-4).

This wizard enables you to perform several functions, including creating and deleting a mailbox for a recipient, moving a mailbox to another server or mailbox store, and enabling Instant Messaging for the user account. When you choose this task, the Welcome To The Exchange Task Wizard splash screen will come up. If you don't want to keep seeing this screen, select the Do Not Show This Welcome Page Again check box.

After clicking Next, the Available Tasks screen in the wizard will appear. Highlight Create Mailbox, and click Next. The Create Mailbox screen will appear, and you can enter the user's alias and location where you wish the mailbox to be created. The Tasks In Prog-

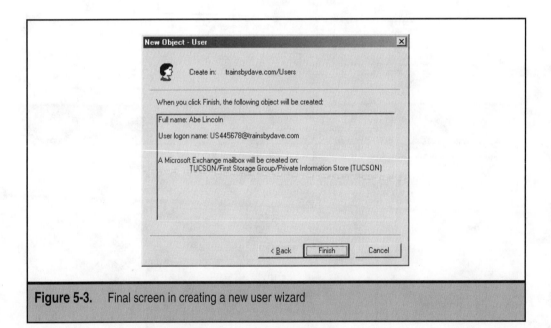

Figure 5-3.   Final screen in creating a new user wizard

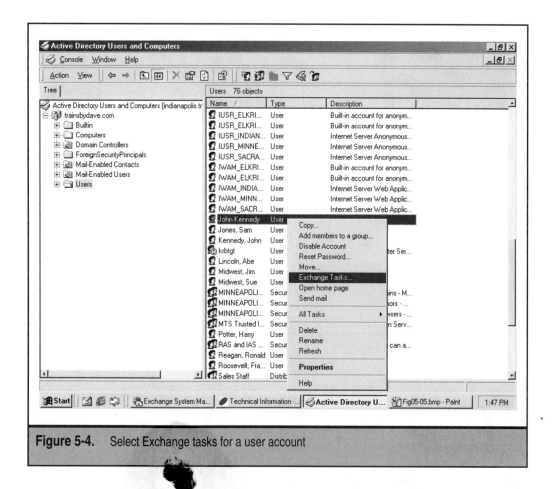

Figure 5-4.   Select Exchange tasks for a user account

ress screen will appear briefly, informing you that the mailbox is being created; and then the Final screen will appear, giving a summary of the actions that were taken (Figure 5-5).

Using this same wizard, you can move a mailbox by selecting the Move Mailbox item on the Available Tasks screen. Once selected, you'll be presented with the Move Mailbox screen (Figure 5-6). Here, you can choose which server (in the same administrative group) you want to move the mailbox to, along with the specific mailbox store. After

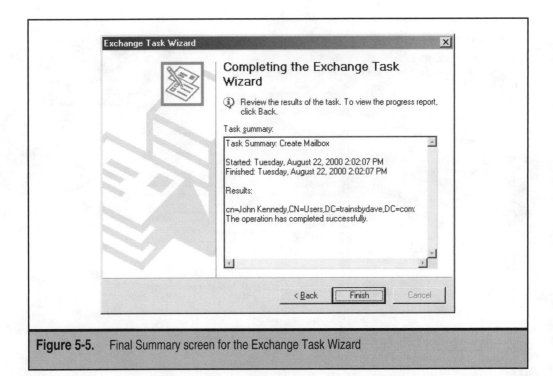

Figure 5-5.   Final Summary screen for the Exchange Task Wizard

making your selections, click Next, and the Tasks In Progress screen will appear and track the move of the mailbox in real time; then the Final summary screen will appear where you can click Finish to end the wizard.

Configuring Mail-Enabled User Accounts

Now that you know how to create a new user account and mail-enable it, it's time to look at how to configure the account. To start the configuration process, right-click the user account in Active Directory User And Computers; then click Properties. The user's account properties should appear.

Interestingly enough, if, in the View menu, you do not have Advanced Features selected, then the Exchange Advanced tab, along with several others, will not appear. So be sure to have Advanced Features selected before working with a user's configuration so that you can see all of the options available to you.

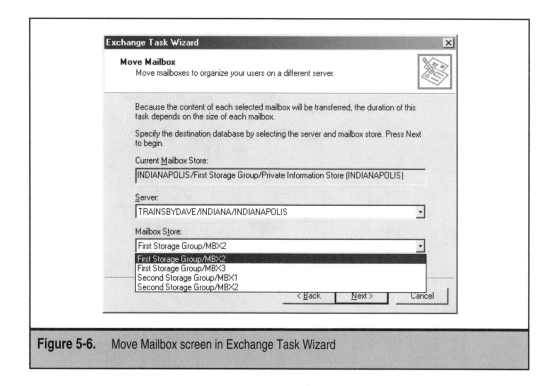

Figure 5-6. Move Mailbox screen in Exchange Task Wizard

There are four main tabs of interest for our discussions: General, Features, Addresses, and Advanced. On the Exchange General tab (Figure 5-7), you can learn where the user's mailbox is presently stored and what alias the user is using. There are also three buttons that provide additional configuration options.

The Delivery Restrictions button allows for restrictions to be placed on messages based on outgoing or incoming size. Furthermore, restrictions can be created based on the originator of the message, as shown in Figure 5-8. This provides flexibility in deciding who can send messages to a particular recipient.

The Delivery Options button allows for the configuration of who can send mail on behalf of this user: whether there is to be a forwarding address, whether messages should be delivered to both the forwarding address and the local mailbox, and what the maximum number of recipients can be for any outgoing message.

Now the Send On Behalf Of configuration can be created at either the client or the server side. On the server side, simply click the Add button and choose the account

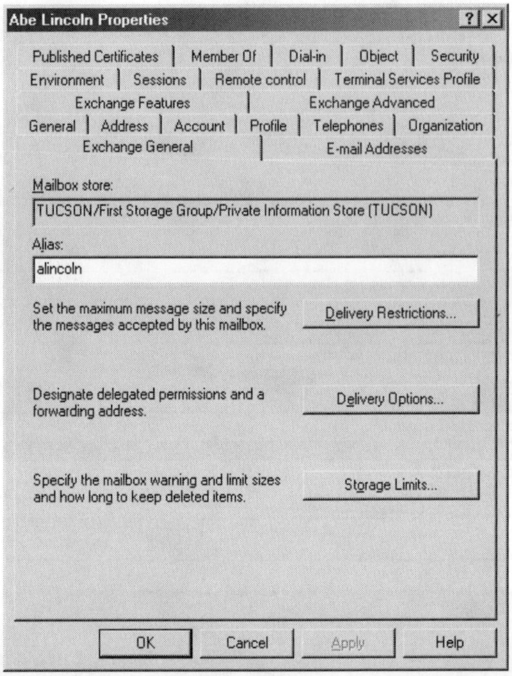

Figure 5-7. Exchange General tab in Abe Lincoln's properties

within the forest that will have Send On Behalf Of permissions for this account. At the client side, in Outlook 2000, navigate through the Tools/Options menu and select the Delegates tab. Once you choose a user account to have Send On Behalf Of permissions, you'll be presented with a host of choices, as shown in Figure 5-9, which can granularly define what this user can do on behalf of the configured user. If necessary, a message summarizing the new permissions can be sent to the delegate by selecting the Automatically Send A Message To Delegate Summarizing These Permissions check box.

The Storage Limits button is where you can set limits on the amount of data that a user can hold in his or her mailbox. This can be set on a per-mailbox basis by deselecting the

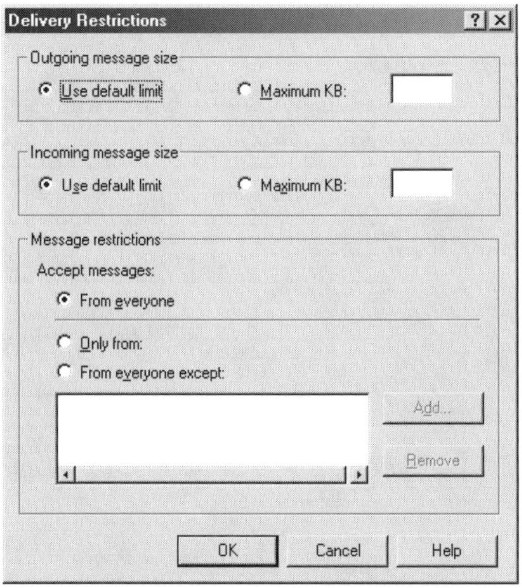

Figure 5-8.   Delivery Restrictions for user's account

User mailbox store defaults check box. To set storage limits for all users, leave this check box selected and configure the mailbox store properties. To learn more about how to do this, consult Chapter 7.

Moving to the E-mail Addresses tab (Figure 5-10), we find the various addresses that have been created for this user account and mailbox. You'll notice that there is a cc:MAIL, an MS, two SMTPs, and an X.400 address. You'll also notice that by leaving the Automatically Update E-mail Addresses Based On Recipient Policy check box selected, you can have these e-mail addresses updated without ever having to physically visit each user account.

Each user account can have multiple SMTP addresses, which comes in handy if you want mail addressed to more than one recipient to appear in the same mailbox. For example, if you are the administrator for your Web site, you'll have one internal SMTP address that coworkers will use to send you mail. But you could also have the postmaster and

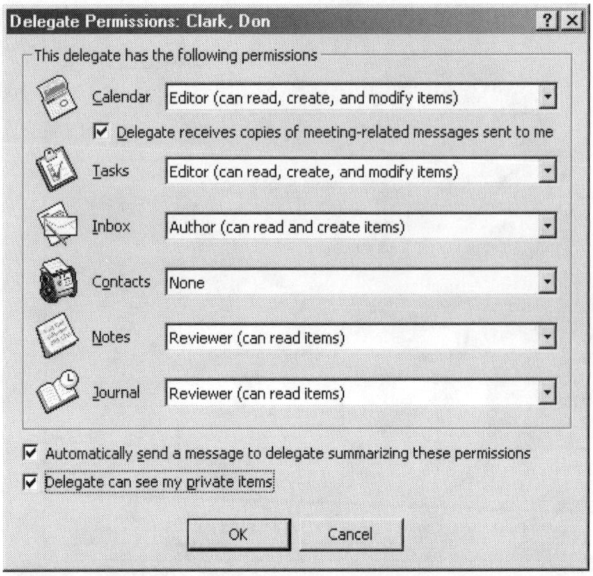

Figure 5-9. Configuration options in Outlook 2000

Webmaster e-mail addresses assigned to your mailbox so that visitors on the Internet who send mail to the Webmaster will have their messages routed to your in box.

This feature can also be used if some of your users have names that are difficult to spell. For example, a female user named "Gale" could have her first name misspelled as "Gayle" or "Gail." Adding SMTP addresses to Gale's account that include the various misspellings of her name will reduce the number of Non-Delivery Report (NDRs) returned to the message originators and increase her chances that she will receive messages sent to her, even if her name is misspelled.

Now, you might be wondering how to make certain addresses go away or make others appear. For instance, you might want to remove the cc:MAIL and MS Mail addresses and have another customized address applied to each mailbox. There are a couple of things to consider here. For every connector that is installed, there will be a corresponding address created for each mailbox. Now, because the Indianapolis server was upgraded from Exchange 5.5, and because the MS Mail and Lotus cc:Mail connectors were

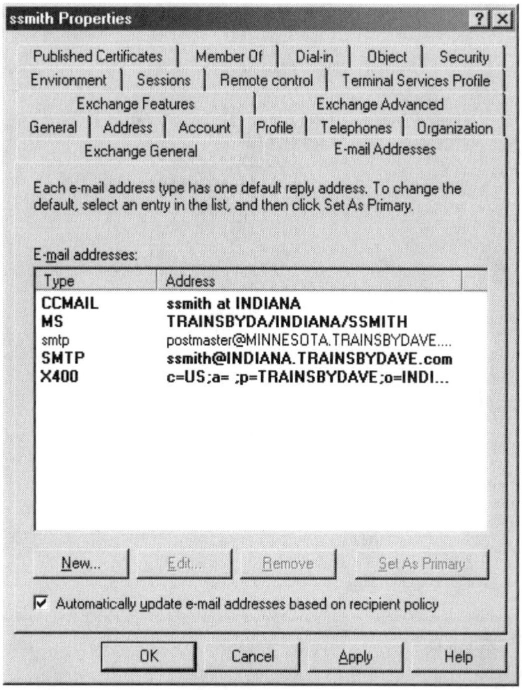

Figure 5-10.   E-mail Addresses tab in user properties

initially installed in 5.5, even though the connectors themselves were not installed with the upgrade, the address generations of these two platforms were migrated to maintain address generation integrity with the accounts that were also migrated. So, it is possible to have addresses being generated for which there are no installed connectors.

If you need to see what default addresses are being generated for mailbox recipients in your forest, navigate to the Recipients container in System Manager, find the Default Recipient Policy under the Recipient Policies container, and open up its properties. Figure 5-11 illustrates what you should see.

To remove an address proxy generation, simply deselect the box and the address will be removed from the user's properties. Allow time for this change to replicate to all the domain controllers in your domain.

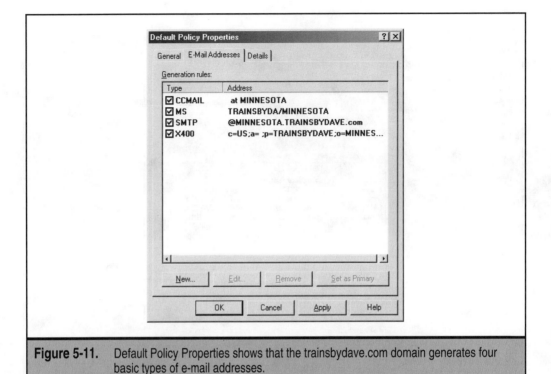

Figure 5-11.   Default Policy Properties shows that the trainsbydave.com domain generates four basic types of e-mail addresses.

If you want to create a new address type for your users, click the New button. You'll be presented with a list of address types from which you can choose:

▼ Custom Address

■ X.400 Address

■ Microsoft Mail Address

■ SMTP Address

■ cc:Mail Address

■ Lotus Notes Address

▲ Novell GroupWise Address

Select which address type you wish to create and then input the correct information in the following screens. Once created, a new address will be created for each user in your organization and should appear in the properties after directory replication has completed.

If you have more than one type of address, such as multiple SMTP addresses, you'll need to select one to be the *primary* address, which will act as the Reply To address when e-mail is originated using this account. To select such an address, highlight the desired address in the user's properties; then click the Set As Primary button, as shown in Figure 5-12.

Looking at the Exchange Features tab, we can see in Figure 5-13 that there is really more of a listing of the additional Exchange services, such as Instant Messaging, that this account is engaging in. We'll look at how to configure the Instant Messaging client in Chapter 10.

The Exchange Advanced tab offers a potpourri of configuration options, many of which will only concern you if you are engaged in very specific activities. Let's discuss them individually.

First, as you can see in Figure 5-14, there is a place to enter a Simple Display Name. Use this input box to enter a name for this account that a foreign e-mail system will recognize if it doesn't recognize the default naming conventions. On this same tab, you can also hide this recipient from the Global Address List by selecting the Hide From Exchange Address Lists check box. If you want to force e-mail that will be transported over an X.400

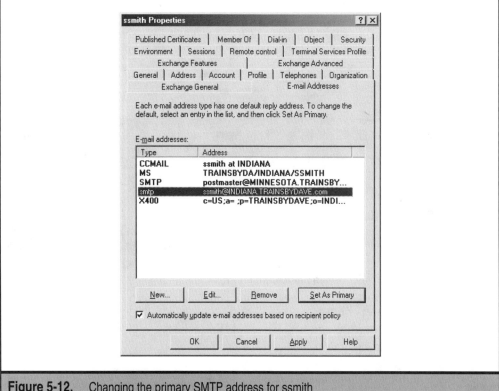

Figure 5-12.   Changing the primary SMTP address for ssmith

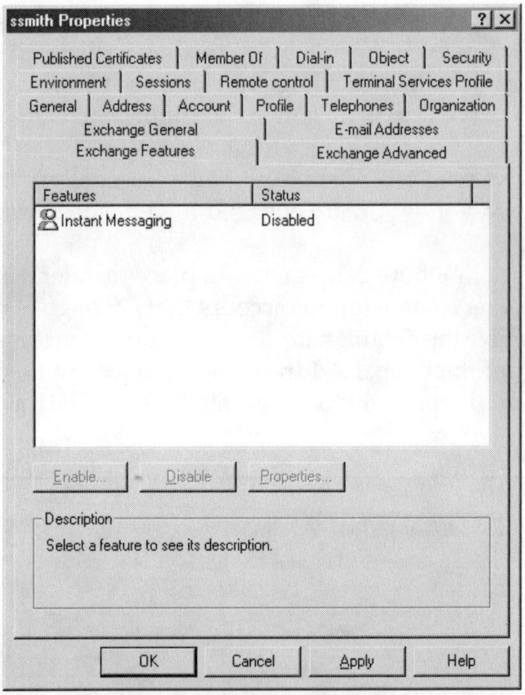

Figure 5-13.   Exchange Features tab in user properties

connector to be downgraded from high priority to normal priority, then select the Down-grade High Priority Mail Bound For X.400 check box.

The Custom Attributes button is the location where you can enter company-specific information on a user, such as an employee number, hire date, or location of cubicle. These attributes are defined in the properties of a public folder, which we will discuss in Chapter 6. Figure 5-15 shows the Exchange Custom Attributes screen for a user's properties.

The Protocol Settings button is the location where you can enable or disable HTTP, Internet Message Access Programming version 4 (IMAP4), or Post Office Protocol version 3

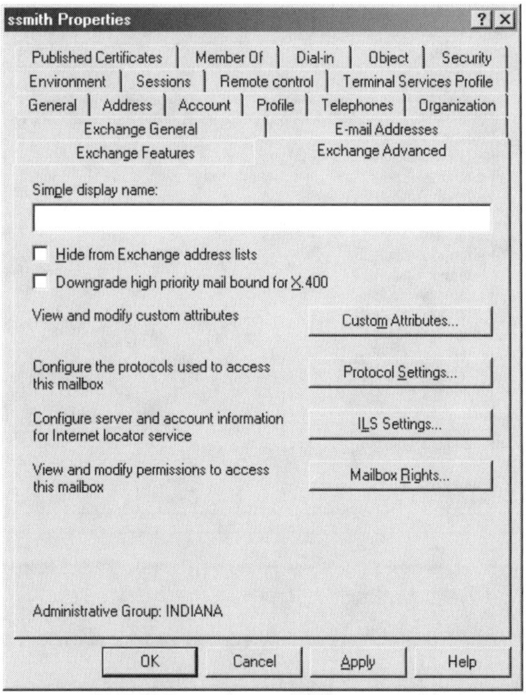

Figure 5-14.   Exchange Advanced tab in user's properties

(POP3) services for this user's mailbox. For example, if you disable HTTP for a user, that user will not be able to view e-mail using Outlook Web Access (OWA).

As you can see in Figure 5-16, for IMAP4 and POP3 clients, you can customize their Multipurpose Internet Mail Extensions (MIME) settings, specify a default character set, and configure other options as well. These options are not available for the HTTP protocol.

The Internet Locator Server (ILS) Setting button is used to configure a user's ILS and account for Net Meeting services. And the Mailbox Rights button is used to view and

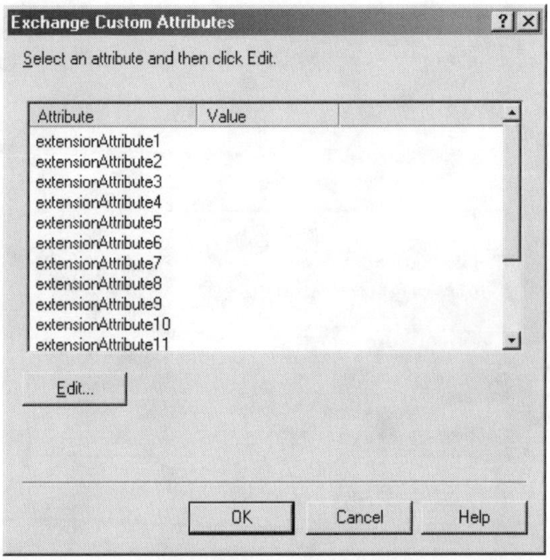

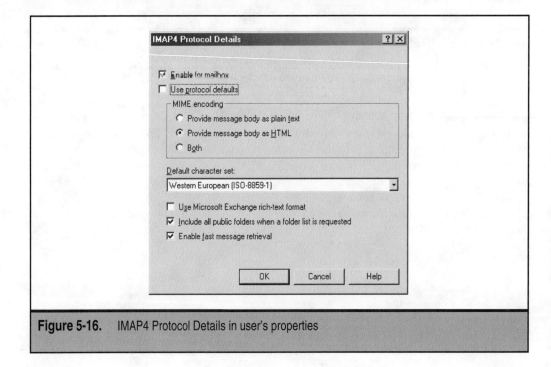

Figure 5-15. Exchange Custom Attributes screen in user's properties

Figure 5-16. IMAP4 Protocol Details in user's properties

modify permissions on the mailbox, not on the user account. To change permissions on the user's account, use the Security tab.

Creating and Configuring Contacts

A contact is an account that is created in AD that has two main features. First, it can neither be used to authenticate a user on the network nor to assign permissions to objects in the directory, so creating these accounts doesn't represent a security threat. Second, the account is created to send messages to a foreign e-mail account, usually an SMTP account, and does not represent a human user on your network.

Generally speaking, it is a good idea to create a different organizational unit in which to house your contacts, especially if you're going to have more than a few of them. In some companies, where contractors are used on a regular basis, this becomes even more important. So consider creating an organizational unit (OU) for your contacts.

To create a contact, right-click the OU, point to New, and then select Contact. You'll be able to enter the contact's name and display the name on the first screen. On the next screen, you can either mail-enable the contact (Figure 5-17) or choose not to mail-enable the contact.

The default is to make the contact mail-enabled. If you leave it as such, you'll need to click the Modify button, select the type of address that should be applied to this contact,

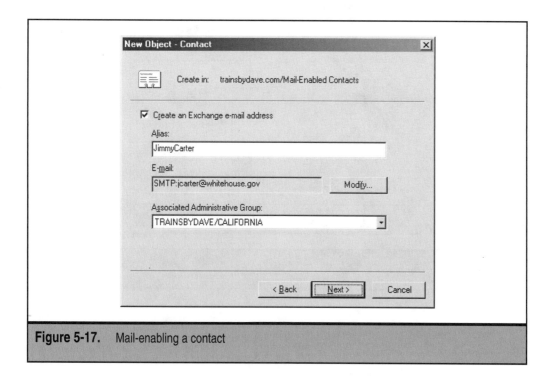

Figure 5-17.   Mail-enabling a contact

and fill in the appropriate information. You can also choose which administrative group this contact should be associated with for administrative purposes.

The next screen will summarize your actions, and you'll need to click Finish to create the new contact. Now, to configure the contact, you'll need to right-click the contact's object in Active Directory Users And Computers and open its properties. There, you'll find a host of configuration options that can help you organize and sort your contacts based on your needs.

Most of the tabs and input boxes are self-explanatory, so we won't go through them in great detail. However, on the Exchange Advanced tab (Figure 5-18), you can force messages sent to this contact to be in the form of MAPI rich text. Select this, if appropriate.

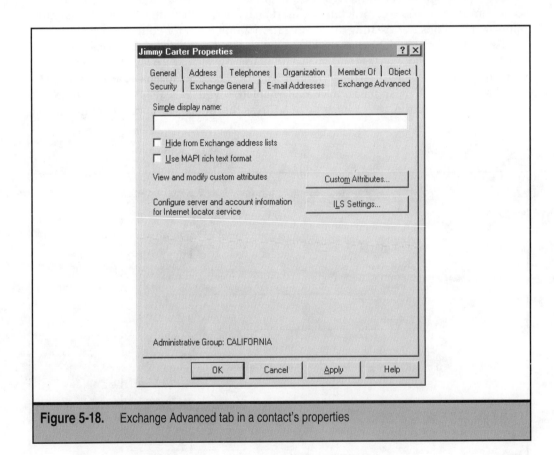

Figure 5-18.   Exchange Advanced tab in a contact's properties

Creating and Configuring Distribution Groups

In this section, we will be discussing how to mail-enable groups in AD. Unlike Exchange 5.5, we do not set up a separate group for security purposes and another for e-mail distribution. These activities can be combined in one administrative unit, called a *mail-enabled group*. So, in Exchange 2000 Server, all we need to do is to take user groups that have already been created in AD and mail-enable them.

To create a new group, right-click the OU, point to New, and select Group. In this dialog box, you can create the new group and mail-enable it at the same time, by choosing its Scope and then selecting Distribution as the Group Type.

After clicking Next, you can mail-enable the group by selecting the Create An Exchange E-mail Address check box. Doing so allows the group to act as a recipient and work like distribution lists in Exchange 5.5. It is generally recommended that you use universal groups as distribution groups, unless you are working in a single-domain environment, in which case you can use global groups.

Once a group is mail-enabled, you can send messages to it, and it will act like a distribution list. The message will be expanded and then sent to each recipient in the group. The nice

Why Use Universal Groups?

You might be wondering why we are recommending the use of universal groups in a multidomain environment. The answer has to do with how groups are enumerated in the Global Catalog (GC). Domain local and global group memberships are not enumerated in the GC, whereas universal group memberships are. Also, keep in mind that the organization's Global Address List is generated by the GC. So, even though a global group appears in the GC, the GC will not know *who* is a member of that group. If a message is sent to a mail-enabled global group in a remote domain, the GC will not be able to send the message to the group's members because the GC doesn't know who the group's members are. And the real interesting thing is that the message will appear to have been sent—no NDR or error messages are generated in this instance. However, if a message is sent to a universal group in a remote domain, the GC will know the members of that group and will work with the SMTP Server to send a message to each user in the list. The problem we're outlining here is only relevant in a multidomain environment. In a single-domain environment, messages can be sent to a global group because the domain controller will be able to give the group's membership to the SMTP Server who will, in turn, send the message to each user.

thing about this is that you can minimize administrative effort by using user groups that were created for assigning permissions to resources to also act as distribution lists for those members who are mail-enabled. Of course, a mail-enabled group need not be a security group, but these two functions can be accomplished with the same AD object.

Once the group is created, you can open up its properties to see that there are a number of configuration options. Since many of them are self-explanatory, we'll only mention a few here.

First, on the Members tab, individual users, other groups, and mail-enabled public folders can be added. This means that a single distribution group can be used to send messages to every type of recipient available in Exchange 2000: mailboxes, groups, contacts, and public folders. On the Member Of tab, this group can, itself, become a member of another distribution group. When used correctly, it allows for the nesting of distribution groups to ease administrative effort.

For example, let's assume you have an overall distribution group called Customers. However, inside this group, you have three other distribution groups as members, each divided along your three product lines. Now, if you want to send an e-mail message to those in product line number one, you could send the message to the product line one group. However, if you had a more general message for all of your customers, such as a grand opening for a new location, then you could send the message to the Customers distribution group, and that message would, in turn, be sent to all three product line distribution groups. By nesting your distribution groups, you can efficiently select the scope of your e-mail message based on its purpose.

On the Exchange General tab, you can specify a unique alias for the distribution group. This is especially helpful if the group's name is long and you don't want to force users to type in such a long name. Also, message size limits can (and should) be set on this tab, as well as from whom it will accept messages.

Now, there are a couple of things to keep in mind. First, the wider or broader the scope of the distribution group, the more tightly message originators should be controlled. For instance, you don't want to leave the default Accept Messages From Everyone for the All Company Users Distribution list. Can you see it now? A disgruntled employee is on his way out the door and spams everyone in the company with pornographic images. Not a good thing, right? So increasingly tighten who can send messages to a distribution group as the group's scope widens.

Second, you'll want to limit the message size. One of the book's authors once worked in company where the owner himself would spam everyone in the company (80 users in three cities) with unzipped scanned images of magazine articles about the company. When dialing in over a 56.6Kbps connection, it took over 20 minutes to download the e-mail because he didn't identify it in the subject line as an e-mail with a large attachment.

While such situations might be politically difficult to manage, they need our attention as administrators. We should be very attentive to how message size affects our remote users, and, therefore, we should be diligent about enforcing message size limitations.

With the Single Instance Storage (SIS) feature of Exchange 2000 Server (SIS is discussed in detail in Chapter 11), we don't need to be as concerned about our databases growing out of control because of large message spamming; however, we should be concerned about bandwidth usage that large message spamming consumes. Be careful to perform regular capacity planning for your network, and ensure that you have set the message size limits at the largest, but optimal, setting possible.

On the Exchange Advanced tab, as illustrated in Figure 5-19, you'll need to decide if a specific expansion server needs to be specified. This is done by using the Expansion Server drop-down list box.

The purpose of the expansion server is to specify which server will expand the membership list of the distribution group, and perform its routing and selection process to send the message to each group member. This is both a RAM- and a processor-intensive activity. For small lists of under 50 or 75 members, this is not a big deal and can be performed on any server in the administrative group.

But if the list contains several hundred or even several thousand members, it might be wise to dedicate a server to this function. Expanding even a simple message and then

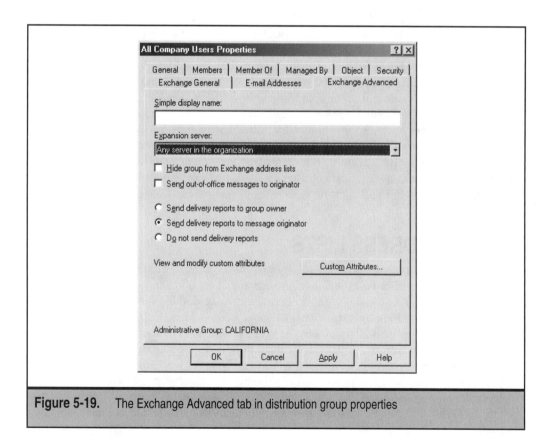

Figure 5-19.   The Exchange Advanced tab in distribution group properties

running each user through the routing and selection process, could take hours. Dedicating a server to this function, in such a scenario, just makes sense.

On the Exchange Advanced tab, you can also specify how delivery reports should be handled and whether out-of-office messages from recipients should be sent to the originator of the message. Generally, you'll want to leave this check box unselected; but there might be certain kinds of distribution groups, such as time-sensitive messages or mission-critical groups, where having an out-of-office message sent to the originator would be a wise course of action.

TIP: Send your company-wide e-mail messages using the BCC field instead of the To field. If the message is sent using the To field, then anyone can use the Reply To All and send their response to everyone in the company. By using the BCC field, the originator's name will appear as being the originator of the message. Therefore, if a user uses the Reply To All function, the message will only come back to the originator of the message.

Creating and Configuring Mail-Enabled Public Folders

There might be times when you'll want a public folder to act as a mail-enabled recipient. All public folders can receive e-mail messages if they are first mail-enabled. To do this, navigate to the public folder in System Manager, right-click the folder, point to All Tasks, and select Mail Enable. You'll be presented with a question from the Exchange System Manager asking if you really want to mail-enable this public folder. Click Yes, and you're done.

After mail-enabling a public folder, you can open its properties and find that there are three additional tabs added to this object, including the E-mail Addresses, Exchange Advanced, and Exchange General tabs. All of these tabs have configurations that are similar, if not identical, to configuration options on other Exchange recipients, so we won't go into detail about them again. Suffice it to say that after mail-enabling a public folder, it can be used as any other recipient type.

MANAGING ADDRESS LISTS

Address lists are managed under the Recipients folder in System Manager. Address lists are created by using filter rules—rules that search AD and find objects that match a predefined set of criteria. Once all the objects are accumulated, a list is built and becomes an address list. Figure 5-20 shows the default Global Address List Rule filter.

You'll notice in Figure 5-20 that there is a Preview button, which can be used to preview what the list will return from AD. Clicking this button forces the rules to filter AD and return a result set. This set is then displayed in the Address List Preview. This feature can be used to shape and sculpt a set of rules so that only the desired objects are placed in the list.

Default rules are provided for All Contact, All Groups, All Users, and Public Folders. Additional rule sets can be created by right-clicking the All Address Lists container,

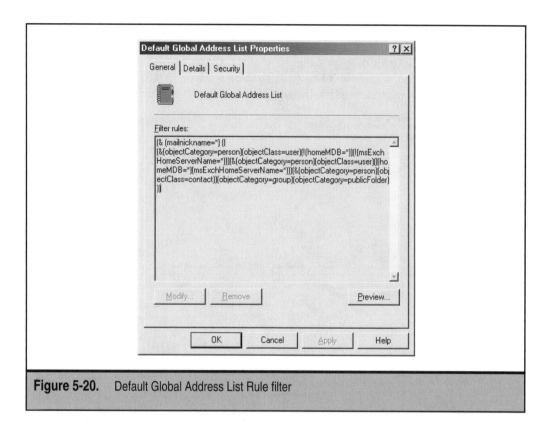

Figure 5-20.   Default Global Address List Rule filter

pointing to New, and selecting New Address. When you do this, you'll need to give it a name, click Next, create the rules, and click Finish.

Interestingly enough, you really don't need a developer to create these rules. What they did was to take the Advanced Find feature out of Active Directory Users And Computers and use that utility here to give us a graphical front end for rule creation, shown here:

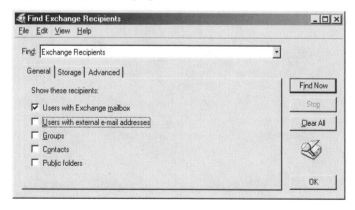

To illustrate this point, we created an address list called Indianapolis Employees and configured the Advanced Find utility to show only Users With Exchange Mailbox on the General tab. We then specified the Indianapolis server on the Storage tab, selected the Mailboxes on this server radio button, and clicked Finish. The rule was created, and the results were accurate by showing only two users in the Indianapolis area, as illustrated here:

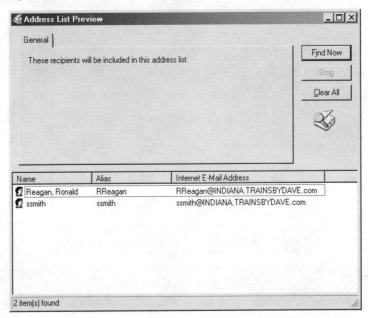

The newly created address list will appear in the Outlook 2000 client as another available address list, as shown here:

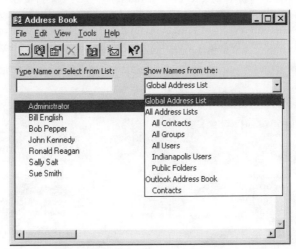

The fact that AD enables object centralization means that we can now leverage the same information for multiple purposes. Running a filter rule against the objects in AD is a prime example of how the directory will change how we manage information.

There is no limit to the number of unique address lists that can be created, but on a practical scale, you should keep them to a minimum to reduce search times for users.

An address list is another object in the directory, so it will have an Access Control List (ACL) for security purposes. This means that you can create an address list, and then specify who can access the list by assigning permissions to the list using users and groups in AD. Some address lists, such as top corporate executives or those who hold sensitive positions, may not want their e-mail addresses available to everyone. Use the ACL to limit who can see sensitive address lists. By default, the Everyone group is not given any access and the Authenticated Users group is only given List Contents permissions.

After an address list is created, it will not update immediately. If you need it to update immediately, or if you just want to force an address list to update because new users have been added to AD, find the Recipient Update Services (RUS) the Recipients container, right-click the RUS, and select Update Now.

Offline Address Lists

If you need certain kinds of offline address lists, then you'll need to create them under the Offline Address Lists folder under the Recipient's folder. They are created in the same manner as other address lists. Unfortunately, you cannot copy and post an address list from one container to another. So if you need to create an intricate set of address lists that are available both on the LAN and by remote, you'll need to create these lists twice—one time under the All Address Lists container and a second time under the Offline Address Lists folder.

SUMMARY

In this chapter, you learned how to create and manage mailbox, public folder, distribution group, and contact recipients. You also learned how to create and manage address lists. This was a big "how to" chapter and should get you going on the basics of managing mailboxes in your environment.

In the next chapter, we'll take a look at how public folders are created and managed. This is a more complex topic, but just as necessary to performing good day-to-day Exchange administration. Public folders will become more centralized in our administrative activities as we move forward in this industry, so don't skip reading the next chapter.

CHAPTER 6

Creating and Managing Public Folders

Microsoft Exchange information can basically be divided conceptually into two types: private and public. Private information is generally thought of as messages stored in the mailbox that is only available to an individual or delegated user. Other types of private information can include tasks, journal entries, personal contacts, and notes. Public information is generally thought to reside in public folders and is available to a wider audience than private information. Public information can take any form, including audio clips, graphics, text files, and spreadsheets.

Public folders are intended to share information across organizations or across the Internet. They provide an ideal foundation for sharing data and working with collaborative applications. Whenever your organization has files and documents that must be available to multiple users, you can use public folders to distribute the information.

Probably the simplest public folder to create is a Contacts public folder. In such a folder, contact information can be entered once, but then be made available and used by everyone in the organization. If you publish the folder on the Internet, the information can be made available to people worldwide. Other basic types of public folders would be public journals, in which managers can track activities of individual team members; public calendars, in which employees can find out about events or resource availabilities; or public discussion forums, in which users can asynchronously engage in public conversations.

This chapter will introduce you to public folders and demonstrate how to create and manage them. In addition, we'll look at replication issues and strategies for managing your public folder hierarchies.

PUBLIC FOLDER INTRODUCTION

Public folders provide the foundation for the Exchange 2000 Server collaborative system. Inside these folders, users can share information. More important, customized applications can be used as the default form into which users can enter information that is then transferred to a database in SQL Server or Oracle Server.

Each public folder can be exposed on the Web and has an automatic URL associated with it. Exchange also creates a default HTML page for each folder, which can be replaced or customized. In addition, the URL for a folder can be redirected to a different URL if needed.

Public folder information is held in an Exchange database that is managed by the store.exe process. This database is exactly the same as that of a mailbox store and enjoys the benefits of transaction logging and other Extensible Storage Engine (ESE) features (these features are covered in Chapter 11).

Public folders are really the power of Exchange 2000. They comprise the framework in which collaborative applications can be created and leveraged for the Digital Nervous System. So let's take a few pages to outline how public folders work.

Public Folder Referrals

Within a routing group, users will access local public folders. However, if there is no copy of a public folder in the local routing group then they can be (and by default, will be) referred to Exchange 2000 Servers in other routing groups. This is because public folder referrals are enabled by default on the routing group connector. If you select the Do Not Allow Public Folder Referrals check box, in Figure 6-1, users will be prevented from accessing public folders in remote routing groups.

Internet Publishing

Public folders can be published on the Internet; and information retained inside them can be accessed using Hypertext Transfer Protocol (HTTP), and modified using Web Development and Author Versioning (WebDAV). However, not only does the folder itself have a unique URL, but also each item inside the folder. These URLs are dynamically generated by Exchange 2000 and are constructed using the path to the folder and the Subject line of the item.

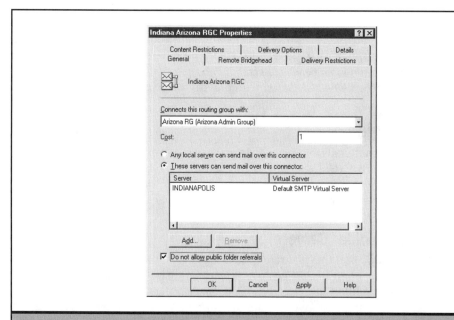

Figure 6-1.   The Do Not Allow Public Folder Referrals check box on the General tab of the routing group connector

Full-Text Indexing

The Microsoft Search service is now a part of the information store service in Exchange 2000. This allows the contents of a public folder to be indexed, which, in turn, allows Outlook 2000 clients the option of locating Office documents and message attachments through full-text searches. Unlike Exchange 5.5, Exchange 2000 is fast becoming a great platform for document management.

Public Folder Hierarchy

The hierarchy for public folders is held in one or more trees. There is one default Public Folder tree that is created when the first Exchange 2000 Server is installed into Active Directory (AD). This tree is automatically replicated to all the Exchange 2000 Servers in the organization.

If any additional trees are needed, they must be manually created and their replication must be manually configured. Exchange 2000 supports multiple public folder trees, which are also known as *hierarchies*, to give you better administrative control over work-flow solutions.

On each server, you can only associate one public folder tree with a public store. Therefore, architecturally speaking, you can only associate one public folder tree per store, per server. For example, if you have four public folder trees that require replication to one Exchange 2000 Server, then you must create four public stores, one for each tree. It doesn't matter, in terms of our discussion here, if these stores are in the same storage group or not. The important thing to remember is that each tree can only be associated with one store on each server, and each store can only be associated with one tree on each server.

Public Folder Strategies

There are advantages and disadvantages to using a single or multiple public folder strategy. When designing your Exchange 2000 organization, you'll need to design a public folder strategy. There are two basic types of strategies: Standalone public folder strategy and Replicated public folder strategy.

Standalone Public Folder Servers

While you might conclude that this is not the best strategy for your organization, it is the default for public folders when Exchange 2000 is initially installed. The main advantage of not replicating your public folders is that no replication traffic is incurred. Furthermore, any changes to content in a given folder are immediately available to other users. Finally, a single folder strategy is both easier to manage and less expensive, since multiple, physical servers are not necessary. It is also the only strategy available for a single-server installation, which is a high number of Exchange deployment environments.

However, one of the largest disadvantages of this strategy is that a single point of failure exists. This isn't so much a load-balancing issue as it is one of fault tolerance. If this single server goes down for some reason, there is no other place on the network to which users can be referred for public folder information.

A single folder strategy is usually best under the following two situations:

▼   Small LANs with few servers

▲   No time-critical or mission-critical information is held in a public folder

Replicated Public Folder Servers

This strategy replicates public folders and their content between two or more public folder servers. These servers can be either dedicated public folder servers, or dual-purpose servers providing both public folder and messaging functions.

The main advantage of replicating public folders between servers is that fault tolerance is achieved. If one of the servers become unavailable, users can still access the content on the other server. While both servers are up and running, you can load-balance public folder requests between servers. Users can work with both replicas and make changes when needed. Exchange can also send notifications when there is a conflict in changed data.

The main disadvantage of having multiple public folder servers is the bandwidth that is consumed for replication of data. This becomes a more important issue if replication must occur over a slow or unreliable WAN link. One other downside is that there is latency between modified content in a folder and when that modification is replicated to the other public folder servers. This means that there will be moments in time when users will be working with outdated information. Fortunately, you can set the replication schedule as needed on a per-folder basis. This is covered more fully later in "Administering Public Folders."

CREATING PUBLIC FOLDERS AND PUBLIC FOLDER TREES

Public folders can be created using the Exchange System Manager. In order to create a new public folder, you will need to have created a public folder container in your administrative group (this container is already created by default for the First Administrative Group) and at least one public folder tree.

Additional public folder trees should be created if

▼   You need tighter security on a group of folders.

■   Your default public folder tree is becoming too large.

■   You want to quarantine projects into their own set of folders.

▲   You want easier management of public folders.

154

Exchange 2000 Server Administration: A Beginner's Guide

To create a new public folder tree, right-click the public folder container; input the name of the new tree (Figure 6-2); and if any public folder stores are available that have not yet been associated with a tree on this server, make that association on this tab as well.

Notice that this is a General Purpose tree, meaning that its contents can only be accessed either by Network News Transfer Protocol (NNTP) or (HTTP), but not by the Outlook 2000 client. After the tree has been built, you'll need to create a new public store to associate with the tree if there wasn't a store available when the tree was created. To create a new public store, right-click the storage group in which you want the store created, point to New, and select Public Store. Once you've entered the name of the store, click the Browse button for the Associated public folder tree input box and choose the new tree. This is shown here:

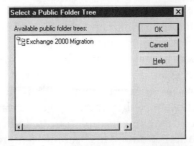

Once the new tree is associated with a public store, it's time to create a new folder using System Manager. Right-click the public folder tree, point to New, and select Public Folder.

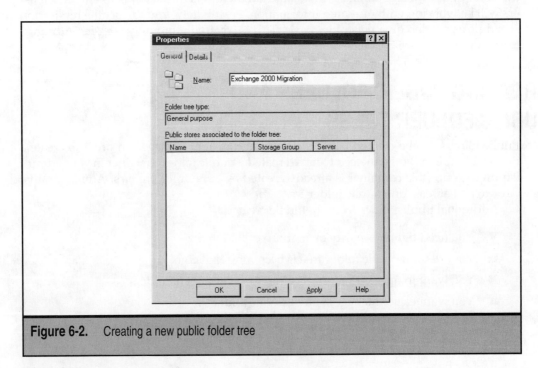

Figure 6-2. Creating a new public folder tree

Figure 6-3 shows that you'll need to enter the folder's name and, if needed, a description. Exchange will automatically fill in the Path when the folder is created.

Either during the folder's creation or after it is done, you can configure its properties. The Replication tab (Figure 6-4) is the place where other servers are designated as servers that will hold replicas of the public folder. Notice that you're not forced into replicating an entire tree; instead, you can choose to replicate an individual folder. This allows for maximum administrative control and flexibility in deciding where to place public folders on your network.

Figure 6-5 shows that the Limits tab can be used to automatically expire messages that have become too old to be useful in the folder, or to send warnings to the folder owner if the contents begin to exceed a predetermined volume.

For all three settings, you can either use the public store defaults or specify values individually for the folder. The best practice is to use the public store default values unless there are specific reasons to adjust the limits.

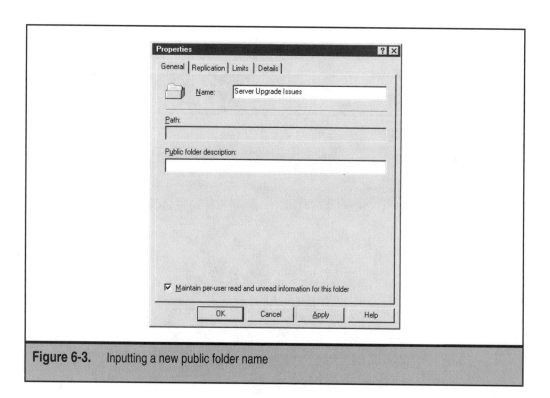

Figure 6-3. Inputting a new public folder name

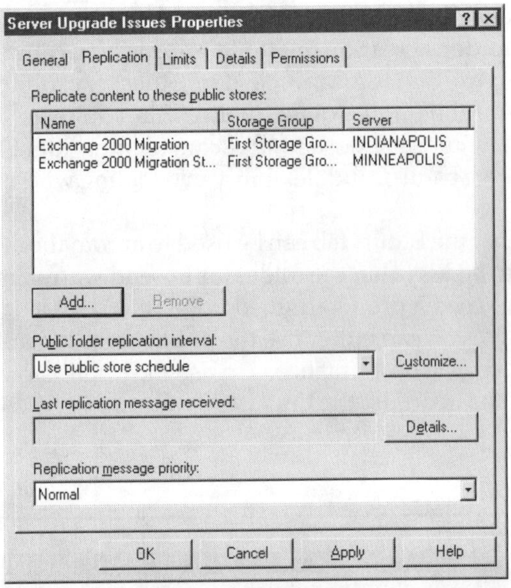

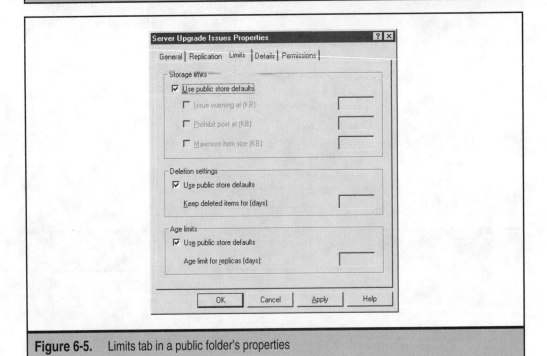

Figure 6-4. Replication tab in a public folder's properties

Figure 6-5. Limits tab in a public folder's properties

DELETING PUBLIC FOLDER AND PUBLIC FOLDER TREES

Public folder trees can be deleted only when they no longer contain any objects and their association with a public store has been severed. So, before you try to delete a tree, you must first delete all the folders in the tree and then disassociate the tree from all the public stores in the organization. Thereafter, you can right-click the tree and select Delete. By the same token, public folders cannot be deleted until they, too, are empty.

NOTE: Once a public folder or a public folder tree has been deleted, it cannot be recovered except by restoring it from tape backup. However, to do the restore, you'll need to restore the administrative group where the tree or container was created, which will overwrite changes that might have been made to other items in the group. Do not delete a public folder or public folder tree unless you know that you won't need it in the future.

ADMINISTERING PUBLIC FOLDERS

There are many features of Exchange that will aid your administration of public folders. In this section, we'll discuss how to control public folder replication, propagate configuration settings on a public folder, move public folders to another tree, maintain the Organizational Forms Library, and set public folder affinities.

Public Folder Replication

Public folders can be replicated, either on an individual basis or as a batch by replicating an entire tree or a subset of the folders in the tree. Schedules can be set and modified as needed; and if you need to make folder replication available between organizations, there are ways to accomplish this, too. When managing public folder replication, you'll first need to select which folders to replicate, assign a schedule for replication, and then set the replication message priority.

The internal component that manages replication between public folders is the Public Folder Replication Agent. The store.exe process manages this agent. Its responsibilities include tracking changes, sending and receiving replication messages from other public folder servers, and maintaining state information for each item in each folder.

Replication is conducted at the item level, meaning that if there is a change to a public folder item, the entire item is replicated. Also, you cannot schedule the replication of an individual item to another folder. The most granular level of replication can be set only at the folder level.

NOTE: Before a public folder can be replicated to another server, that server must have a public store associated with the source tree. However, the association, in itself, does not mean that any of the tree's folders will be replicated. You must configure the folders themselves for replication.

To set a folder to replicate, right-click the folder, open its properties, and then use the configuration options on the Replication tab to add more stores (refer to Figure 6-4). If you need to remove a replica of a folder, simply remove the server from the list on the folder's Replication tab.

When scheduling replication of public folders, you'll need to consider how often information in the folders will change and how fast those changes need to be made available to everyone in the organization. For example, a public folder for company memos that is updated with new memos every two hours throughout the day would need a more aggressive replication schedule than a public folder that hosts the company employee manual, which might be updated once a month or so. Time-critical information will need a more frequent replication schedule than other types of information.

The schedule can be set so that replication occurs during times when WAN bandwidth usage is less. Using nonpeak hours for replication of less-critical information is smart administration and should be considered if this represents a plausible solution for your environment.

Replication can be set on a per-folder or per–public store basis. Schedules set at the folder level override the replication schedule set on the public store. To set replication for a single folder, navigate to the Replication tab in the folder's properties, click the Customize button, and set the schedule needed for this public folder, as shown here:

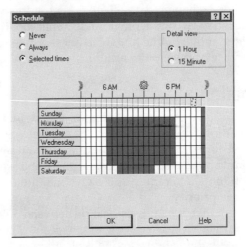

You may want to set replication schedules for all the folders in the tree, and then set special replication schedules for time-critical folders. To ensure that those folders that don't require a special replication schedule are replicated according to the public store's schedule, use the folder's properties to choose the store's default schedule (refer to Figure 6-4).

To set the same replication schedule for all folders in a tree, use the public store's properties (Figure 6-6) to set the replication schedule for all the folders in the store. If you

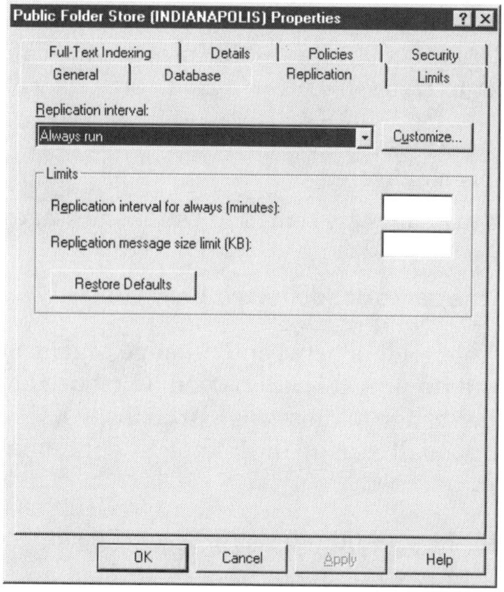

Figure 6-6.   Replication tab in public store's properties

click the Replication interval drop-down list, you'll find that there are several prebuilt replication schedules, including

▼ Always Run

■ Never Run

■ Run every hour

■ Run every 2 hours

■ Run every 4 hours

▲ Use custom schedule

If one of the prebuilt schedules doesn't fit your needs, choose Use Custom Schedule, click the Customize button, and enter the needed schedule in the Schedule box. You'll notice that as you make different selections in the Replication interval drop-down list, the schedule is automatically updated in the Schedule box.

Replication message priorities can be established for certain public folders. The priority determines the order in which messages are sent by the Exchange system. Urgent messages are delivered first. You would want to set priorities for those folders that have time-critical replication messages. To create priority for replication messages, choose the level of priority needed in the Replication Message Priority drop-down box on the folder properties Replication tab (refer to Figure 6-4). You'll have three choices:

▼ **Not Urgent**   These messages are sent last, after the Normal and Urgent messages have been delivered.

■ **Normal**   These messages are sent after Urgent messages but before Not Urgent messages.

▲ **Urgent**   These messages are delivered first.

If you need to replicate folders between Exchange organizations, use the InterOrg Replication Utility. Before running this utility, you'll first need to create a user account, mailbox-enable it, and then assign permissions to it on the two servers that will be sending and receiving the information. To set up the InterOrg Replication Utility, you must complete these steps:

1. Prepare the publishing (sending) server.
2. Prepare the subscribing (receiving) server.
3. Set up the Replication Agent.
4. Create a configuration file.
5. Set up the replication service.

Preparing the Publishing Server

The publishing server hosts the source folders and makes them available to one or more subscribing servers. The publishing server controls the direction of replication. Preparing the publishing server means first creating a new Windows 2000 user account that the Replication Agent will use for authentication. This account must also be mailbox-enabled and then must be configured as an Owner for each folder so that the folder's permissions can be replicated to the receiving server. This means that in order to replicate Anonymous permissions that have been assigned to a source folder, the Replication Agent must be an Owner of that folder in order to replicate those permissions to the receiving server.

One last thing you must do in preparing the server is to create a new public folder on the publishing server named *ExchsyncSecurityFolder*. Grant the Replication Agent user account Folder Visible permission to this folder, and do not specify any Default or Anonymous permissions to this folder.

Preparing the Subscribing Server

The subscribing server is located in a different Exchange organization, and it will receive replicated content from the publishing server. Modifications to content can be made on the subscribing server and replicated back to the publishing server if the publishing server allows it. Similar to the publishing server, you must create a Windows 2000 account on the subscribing server for the Replication Agent and mailbox-enable that account. Then you must create a root folder for every part of the hierarchy that is to be replicated to the subscribing server. Top-level folders are not automatically created by this replication process, but subfolders are. Then add the Replication Agent user account as Owner for every folder that is to receive replicated content. Create an ExchsyncSecurityFolder on the subscribing server, grant the Replication Agent account Folder Visible permissions to this folder, and do not specify any Default or Anonymous permissions.

Setting Up the Replication Agent

The Replication Agent is another Windows 2000 computer that is logically placed between the publishing and subscribing servers. This machine performs its duties by logging on to both the publisher and the subscriber. Often, the Replication Agent is also the publishing server, but that is not a requirement. The Replication Agent must be a member of the Windows 2000 domain for either the publishing or subscribing server, and it must have Outlook and Exchange 2000 installed.

   The agent will need a directory called Exchsync on both the publishing and subscribing servers. After creating this directory, you'll need to copy the Exscfg.exe and Exssrv.exe files from the Exchange Server CD to this directory on both servers.

NOTE: Exscfg.exe is the replication configuration program and Exssrv.exe is the replication utility.

Creating the Configuration File

The Replication Agent will use a single file to record its replication sessions. To create this file, use the Exscfg.exe program on both servers. Under the Session menu, click Add. Then add a file for public folder replication, and save the file. Do the same for a Free/Busy folder replication.

Set Up the Replication Service

To set up this service, double-click the Exssrv.exe program that is saved on both servers. Click Install, and then type in a domain account for the service to authenticate with when it starts. The account can reside in either the publishing or subscribing domain. If you choose to use an account in a different domain, then use the *domain\username* convention to specify the account.

   After typing in the password for the account, specify the path and filename of the configuration file you created earlier. Accept the defaults, exit the utility, and double-click the utility to run it again. When it starts again, click Start to run the service.

NOTE: If you are going to replicate free/busy information between organizations, then for each mailbox on the source server, you must create a corresponding mail-enabled contact on the target server. It is the SMTP address of these objects that is used to pair them up, so be sure that these addresses are identical in both organizations.

Propagating Public Folder Settings

Folder properties can be propagated down a hierarchy so that changing a single configuration option for each folder need not involve opening the properties of each folder. Properties that are set for a parent folder can be applied to all subfolders, but properties set on a subfolder cannot be applied to peer or parent folders.

To propagate folder settings to all subfolders, right-click the parent folder, point to All Tasks, and select Propagate setting. Select the settings you want to apply to the subfolders.

Moving Public Folders

Sometimes, there will be situations in which you'll need to move a public folder to a new location within the same folder tree. This can be done using simple cut-and-paste methods. Individual folders or groups of folders can be moved in this manner, as long as they are within the same tree. You cannot move, copy, or paste a folder from one tree to another.

Managing the Organizational Forms Library

An Organizational Forms Library is a repository of forms accessed by users in a company. Often, these forms allow users to enter or view information in a database. Common forms include supply requests, mileage input forms, or telephone message forms.

You can create forms in System Manager or in the Outlook client. After the form is created, it is saved in the Organizational Forms Library. This library is a special type of public folder that is listed under the system folders. A language must be assigned to it, and you can have only one library per language.

Setting Public Folder Limits

Setting limits on public folders is the best way to ensure that folder content stays current and that the size of a public folder doesn't grow unchecked. As you can see in Figure 6-7, there are three configuration settings: Storage Limits, Deletion Settings, and Age Limits.

Storage Limits

This area is used to control the size of the public folder and its contents. By default, storage limits are set on the public store; and if the Use Public Store Defaults check box is selected, then the public folder will inherit the settings from the public store. However, if you'd like different settings for a particular public folder, deselect this check box, and you can set the parameters individually.

NOTE: If you choose to accept the store defaults, be sure to enter limit values on the store itself. Failure to do this could result in one public folder consuming all remaining disk space.

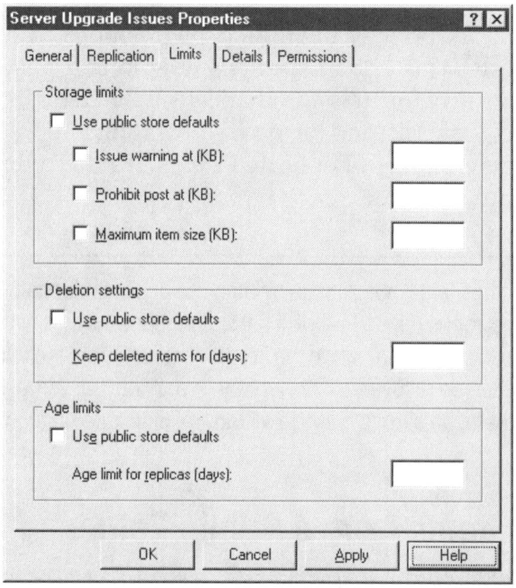

Figure 6-7. Limits tab of a public folder's properties

The Issue Warning At (KB) setting means that when the folder reaches the specified size, a warning message is sent to the administrator. Acceptable values range from 0–2097151KB for all three of these settings.

The Prohibit Post At (KB) setting means that when the folder reaches the specified size, users can no longer post to the folder. This value represents the maximum KBs that the public folder can hold.

The Maximum Item Size (KB) represents the largest allowable size for a post. Postings larger than this are returned to the user with an error message indicating that the post exceeded the size limit on the public folder.

Deletion Settings

This setting has time as its focus, whereas the Storage Limits setting has size as its focus. In the Deletion Settings area, you can specify the length of time deleted items are allowed to remain in the public folder before they are removed from the public folder by Exchange. Again, you can allow the folder to inherit the public store settings or they can be set individually for each folder. Configure the Keep Deleted Items For (Days) setting as needed.

Age Limits

This setting also has time as its focus; but unlike the Deletion settings, this area is focused on active, available posts. This option specifies how long a post may be in the public folder and available for use before it is automatically deleted by Exchange. Configure the Age Limit For Replicas (Days) setting to specify how long a replicated item may remain in the folder before being deleted. Replicated items are tracked separately from items posted directly to the public folder.

NOTE: Remember that items must first be deleted in a public folder and then removed. The time period between when the item is deleted—which basically means that it is marked as hidden and stripped of its permissions—and the point at which the item is removed from the folder represents a window in which a deleted item can be recovered if necessary. If you find that some items are being deleted and you wish to recover them, be sure to create a window of time long enough to allow for the recovery of deleted items.

Recovering Deleted Items from a Public Folder

Deleted items in a public folder can be recovered as long as you've set a deleted item retention time for the public folder store from which the items were deleted, and the retention period for the data hasn't expired. Assuming both of these things are true, you can recover deleted items by performing the following steps:

1. In Outlook 2000, access the public folder from which you want to recover the item.
2. Navigate to the Tools menu and select Recover Deleted Items. The Recover Deleted Items From dialog box appears.
3. Select the item(s) you wish to recover and click Recover Selected Items.

You'll note that deleted items can only be recovered using the Outlook client. Since Outlook can only access the default public folder tree, recovery of deleted items from folders residing in other trees is not possible.

ACCESSING PUBLIC FOLDERS

Public Folders can hold all types of information, including media clips, text documents, and spreadsheets. Given that a variety of information can be held in these folders, it stands to reason that a variety of clients should be able to access them, including Outlook 97/98/2000, Internet mail clients, newsreaders, Windows Explorer, Web browsers, and Office applications such as Word or Excel.

The component that makes this all happen is the Exchange Installable File System (ExIFS). This kernel-mode component provides a front-end file system interface to the public folder's streaming file where data is held in raw mode. ExIFS has the ability to present the information held in the public folder as a file system and accept file system calls from various applications. This means that the same information, such as a graphics file, can be made available to a variety of clients.

To illustrate this point, refer to Figures 6-8 through 6-11. You'll notice that the same set of documents is available whether viewing the documents through Windows Explorer, the native application, Outlook Web Access (OWA), or Outlook.

To access documents in a public folder using Windows Explorer, use the M: drive, which is the default drive mapping to the ExIFS driver, and navigate to the public folder, shown in Figure 6-8.

These documents can also be opened using their native application. In Figure 6-9, we've illustrated that the M: drive can be used to find a Word document residing in a public folder. This same feature is also available in the Office products as well.

To access a public folder using OWA, simply type in the URL **http://servername/public** (Figure 6-10), where *servername* is the placeholder for the HTTP virtual server hosted by the Exchange 2000 Server. In most cases, it will be a normal domain name, such as **http://www.networkknowledge.com/public**. This URL accesses only the default public folder tree.

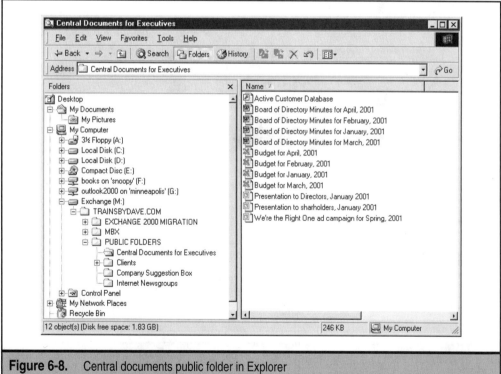

Figure 6-8.   Central documents public folder in Explorer

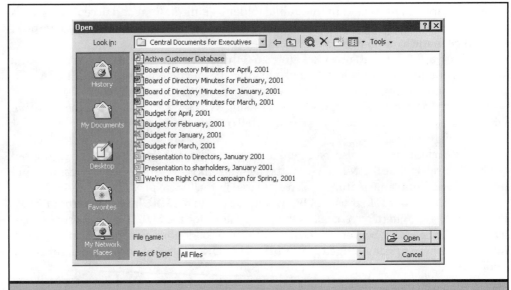

Figure 6-9. Central documents public folder in Word Open file utility

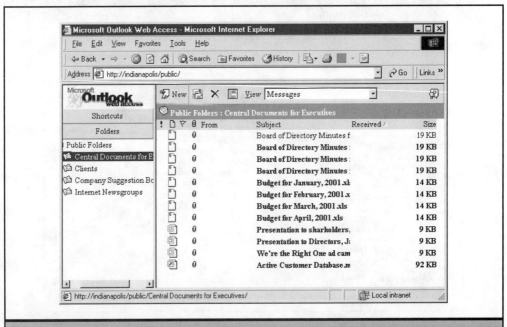

Figure 6-10. Central documents public folder in OWA

Through Outlook, public folders can be accessed by navigating to the public folders section of the utility, and clicking on the desired public folder, as shown in Figure 6-11. Remember that Outlook can only access the default public folder tree, it cannot access other public folder trees, which are available only to HTTP and NNTP clients.

Figures 6-8 through 6-11 illustrate the genius of the ExIFS. Even though this information is being held in a database, the ExIFS driver exposes the contents of the database as a file system to the network. And this information can be accessed over the Internet or over your local network, given the proper permissions. Hence, the advantages of a database are coupled with the advantages of a file system, allowing Exchange to act as a document management solution that is totally customizable to meet your needs.

In addition, there are different administrative actions that you can conduct on a public folder, depending on which utility is being used to view the folder. For instance, viewing a public folder through the M: drive in Explorer allows you to share the folder on your LAN. In so doing, you'll be able to make a public folder act like a file share to which users can map drives and write new documents. Figure 6-12 shows the properties of a public folder when viewed using Explorer.

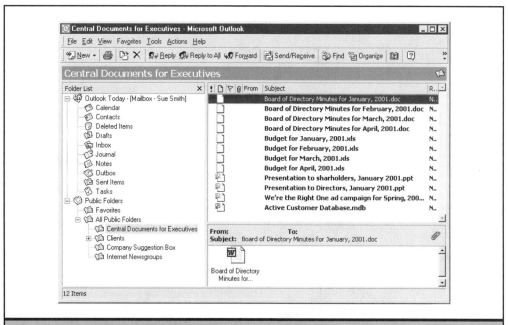

Figure 6-11.   Central documents public folder in Outlook

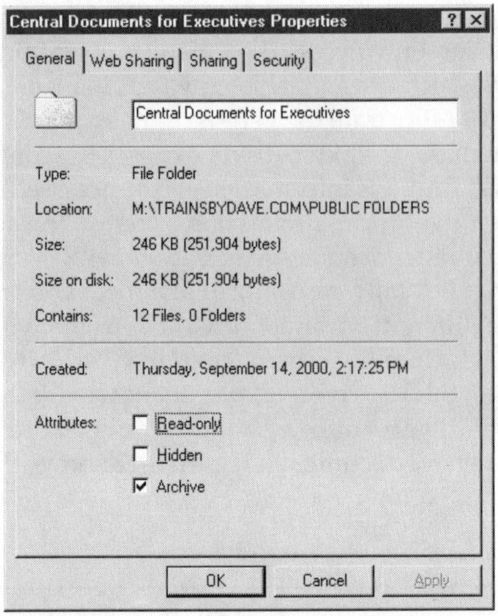

Figure 6-12.   Central Documents folder properties in Explorer

Also, through Explorer, you can make certain public folders available on a Web site, as shown in Figure 6-13, by using the Web Sharing tab in the folder's properties. Choose the Web site to be associated with the shared folder, and then type in the alias for the URL. Once you click OK, a virtual directory will be created with the folder's alias in the specified Web site. Then you can treat this folder like any other virtual directory, such as specifying a default document the user will receive when connecting to this directory. This is an excellent method for using a customized HTML or ASP page to present to the user that will front-end a customized program and database. With the assistance of WebDAV or Extensible Markup Language (XML), information can be written to these pages through the browser from the Internet and recorded in a back-end database.

Web sharing allows the public folder to act as the end-point virtual directory for a Web site. The sharing tab is for the LAN users who wish to access the folder's contents through normal LAN utilities, such as drive mappings or browsing for the folder. Once shared, the folder can also be published in AD so users can access its contents by navigating the directory. Moreover, the share can be included in any Directory File System (DFS) hierarchy in AD.

In addition, when users access information, you can force that information to be cached on their local hard drive and then made available offline. This allows remote users

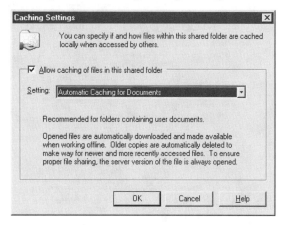

Figure 6-13. Web Sharing tab for the Central Documents public folder

the opportunity to download files from a public folder and then have them available for offline viewing. To configure this option, click the Caching button on the Share tab in the folder's properties, and configure the Caching Settings dialog box accordingly, shown here:

When accessing a public folder's properties through Outlook, there will be three tabs available: General, Home Page, and Summary. However, all configuration options will be grayed out, because users are not allowed to configure a folder's properties—unless the user has been given the appropriate permissions, or has the folder and thus is, by default, the folder's owner. On the Summary tab (Figure 6-14), most users will be able to see what permission levels they have to the folder. If the user has appropriate permissions, the user will have this information grayed in and available for configuration.

A folder's properties are available in neither the document's application, such as Word or Excel, nor in OWA. The place where most configuration options are available is through the System Manager.

Figure 6-15 shows the Central Documents For Executives folder's properties. On the General tab, you can input a description for the folder that will help with administrative duties. You can also choose to have the folder's name act as its Address Book name, or input a different name by selecting the Use This Name radio button and typing in an alias for the address book.

On the Exchange General tab, you can configure delivery restrictions to the folder by clicking the Delivery Restrictions button. Here, content can be restricted by Outgoing and Incoming message size, as well as on a user-by-user basis. When the Delivery Options button is selected, as shown in Figure 6-16, a user can be given Send On Behalf Of permissions if the folder is mail-enabled, and messages sent to the folder can also be forwarded

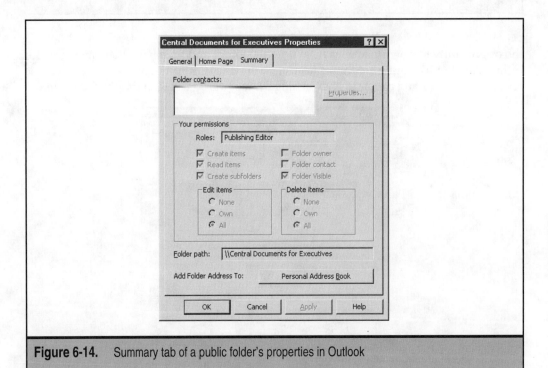

Figure 6-14.   Summary tab of a public folder's properties in Outlook

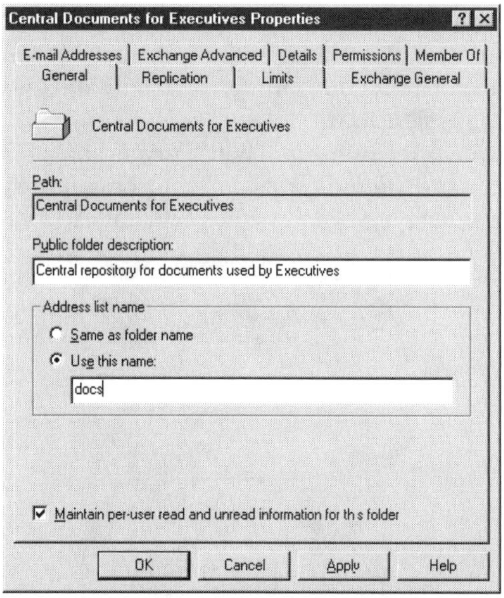

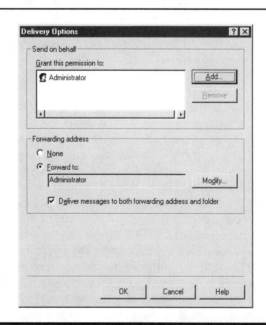

Figure 6-15. Central Documents folder's properties in System Manager

Figure 6-16. Delivery Options tab in a folder's properties

to another address for review. This is a good security and administrative feature for folders that might hold sensitive, confidential, or widely disseminated information.

If you want to hide or unhide a public folder from the address book, this can be done on the Exchange Advanced tab. If you want to work with the folder's permissions, this is accomplished on the Permissions tab.

On this tab, you'll have three buttons, Client Permissions, Directory Rights, and Administrative Rights. When the Client Permissions button is selected, you can specify who can access the folder and what type of access they will have to its contents, as shown here:

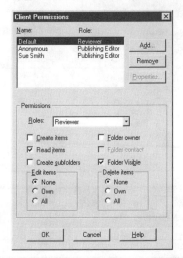

This list of permissions uses the old Exchange 5.5 permission types. You should remember that there is no one-to-one correlation between these permissions and the 13 basic permissions in NTFS (New Technology File System).

The Directory Rights button will allow you to see which rights in the directory are being inherited and which are being explicitly set. This section works the same as in AD, since the folder is considered another object in the directory. You may block inheritance and configure advanced rights on the folder as you would any other directory object.

The Administrative Rights button allows you to set who can administer the folder. This is another directory rights issue. By default, the Administrator user account—along with the Domain Admins, Enterprise Admins, and Exchange Domain Servers security groups—have full control of administrative permissions on the folder. Block inheritance and reconfigure the permissions if you need something other than the default configuration.

On the Member Of tab, you can make the folder a member of a distribution or security group. Sometimes, this will be necessary if you want to create a copy of all messages to a distribution group that is sent to the public folder. Specialized applications that are presented in a public folder might also need security permissions to other files or folders, and this feature allows for programmers to account for this folder's access to other folders. Remember: when a folder is mail-enabled, the folder acts as another recipient that can be used to assign permissions to objects and resources in the directory.

MOVING A PUBLIC FOLDER TREE

Public folder trees can be moved from one store to another. Such action will necessarily disconnect users from all the folders in the tree, so be sure to inform your users that the tree will be moved before actually doing it.

To move a public folder tree, right-click the public folder tree and select Cut. Then, expand a different Administrative Group, right-click the Folder container in this group, and select Paste.

More than likely, this action will disconnect the tree from the store that it is associated with, because moving a tree changes its directory path. To reconnect the tree with its store, right-click the tree and select Connect To. In the Select A Public Store dialog box, select the store that the tree should be connected to, and click OK.

TROUBLESHOOTING PUBLIC FOLDERS

There are common problems that many will encounter with public folders. In this section, I'll take a brief look at these problems and offer some ideas on how to troubleshoot and solve them.

No Replication Between Organizations

If replication is not taking place between organizations using the InterOrg utility, then check the Ex00yymmdd.log and Ex01yymmdd.log log files for error messages. These log files were created when you added a session to the configuration file, and they can be viewed using any text editor, such as Notepad. You might also verify that you have been granted the correct permissions on the root folders and the ExchsyncSecurity folder. If you don't have the correct permissions, you'll receive an event ID 116 error from the Exchsync source, indicating that read and write access is not available to you.

Cannot Publish Forms in Organizational Forms Library

If you cannot publish a form in the Organizational Forms Library due to a Message Application Programming Interface (MAPI) error, be sure that you have All Folder and All Message rights on the EForm folder.

Mixed Mode AD Users Denied Access to Public Folders

You might recall that Exchange 5.5 used Exchange mailboxes and distribution lists to manage access control to public folders. In Exchange 2000, this function is handled by AD. When Exchange 5.5 distribution lists are synchronized into AD, they become Universal Distribution Groups (UDGs). When the first client attempts to access the folder after this synchronization, the UDG is converted to a Universal Security Group (USG); and if the client doesn't have the Log On Locally permission to the server, the user will receive an access denied error message. The way to work around this is to grant all users Log On Locally permissions in the Local Policies security settings on the local Exchange Server.

Profile Error When Accessing a Public Folder's Properties

If you are trying to view the Client Permissions on a folder and receive an error that indicates your profile is not configured, then you are likely trying to view these permissions on an Exchange 2000 public folder on a server that has no private information store. You'll need to reconfigure the Exchange 2000 Server in order to view these permissions.

SUMMARY

In this chapter, we outlined, briefly, how public folders trees and folders are created and managed. We also discussed how to replicate information between organizations using the InterOrg utility. As you can see, administration of public folders is a huge area and one that in large organizations could easily be a full-time job.

Another full-time job in large organizations could be the creation, management, and recovery of storage groups and stores. Since Exchange holds many organizations' mission-critical information, it is essential to understand how storage groups and stores work, and how to recover in the event of a disaster.

In the next chapter, we'll look at how to create and manage storage groups and their stores. In Chapter 14, we'll look at how to perform recovery of these databases in the event of a disaster.

CHAPTER 7

Administering Storage Groups

One of the most prominent features of Exchange 5.5 Server is its ability to use a database in the multiple-gigabyte range. It is not uncommon for some environments to be managing priv.edb databases in the 40–60GB range. While databases of this size are not terribly difficult to back up, they still represent significant challenges.

One of the main challenges of managing large databases is the time needed to restore them. Long restore times often mean that many, if not all, of a company's users were less productive because they didn't have access to e-mail and public folders. In addition, most deployments don't have enough free disk space to manage a defragmentation of the database, which means that unused, but corrupted, pages could continue to cause problems for the administrator.

Microsoft has addressed this problem by implementing storage groups and stores. In short, the private information store in Exchange 5.5 now is called the *Mailbox Store* in Exchange 2000. Likewise, the Exchange 5.5 public information store is now called the *Public Store*. Each store, as we explain in Chapter 11, is comprised of two database files, an *.edb rich text file and a *.stm streaming file that holds raw data bits.

Each store must be created inside a storage group, which is a container that can hold up to five stores, each using the same set of transaction logs. Each Exchange 2000 Server can have up to four storage groups, giving you up to 20 stores that can be created on each server. There is no hard-coded size limit for each store, but the intention of giving you the ability to create multiple stores is that no one store will become so large that it creates the same challenges that existed in Exchange 5.5.

NOTE: The standard version of Exchange 2000 will only allow one Mailbox Store to be created on the server that has a 16GB limit; hence, if you need more space, be sure to purchase the Exchange 2000 Enterprise Server.

BENEFITS OF USING STORAGE GROUPS

Smart use of storage groups will give you the ability to accomplish three very important design goals:

▼ Host more users per server than was reasonably possible in Exchange 5.5

■ Quicken recovery time of damaged databases than was possible in Exchange 5.5

▲ Minimize the number of users that are affected by a database disaster

Let's look at each of these design goals individually.

Hosting More Users

Let's do a comparison. We'll assume you have 300 users that need e-mail services, and you're not sure whether you should use Exchange 5.5 or Exchange 2000 Server. One way to look at this is to determine how many users you'd like to have housed in a single database. In both platforms, all 300 users could be hosted by one database. If each user has 50MB of information in his or her mailbox, this means that a total of 15GB of information needs to be hosted. Now, in Exchange 5.5, you have no choice but to host all this information in one database; however, in Exchange 2000, this information could be spread over multiple databases. For instance, you could host 15 1GB databases on the same server.

If we continue with the same numbers, we could host 300 more users just by having 2GB databases rather than 1GB databases; however, to add an additional 300 users in Exchange 5.5, our database size would grow to 30GB, which would represent an unmanageable-sized database for most deployments.

By spreading users across multiple databases, each server can host more users and still maintain reasonable database sizes.

Quickening Recovery Time

Continuing with the same scenario, it is now easy to understand that restoring a 1GB database is faster than restoring a 15GB database. And restoring a 2GB database is much faster than restoring a 30GB database. Again, spreading users across multiple databases means that the restoration of one database need not consume large amounts of time.

Minimizing Effected Users

Finally, when a 1GB database needs to be restored, the other 14 databases can continue to operate. One of the prominent features of Exchange 2000 Server's storage architecture is that databases can be mounted or dismounted simultaneously. This means that if a storage group has four databases in it, three can be mounted and running while the fourth is dismounted and being restored from backup.

Hence, when any one particular database in Exchange 2000 Server is unavailable, only a subset of your users will lose productivity due to loss of messaging functionality. For instance, if you have four departments in your company, you could set up four databases—one for each department. If one of the databases becomes corrupted, you can restore that database from backup while the other three databases continue to operate; thus, only one department will lose messaging functionality while the other three continue to operate.

In a mission-critical environment, such as a Web-based order center where messaging is the sales lifeline of an organization, consider spreading mission-critical mailboxes across multiple, independent databases for fault-tolerance purposes.

PLANNING FOR MULTIPLE STORAGE GROUPS

Now that you've seen how using multiple storage groups can be of benefit, the question is this: how many storage groups do we need? The answer involves several factors, including

▼ Time required to restore a database

■ Need to defragment individual stores

▲ Overall amount of information that needs to be managed

Let's take a look at how this would work.

Required Restore Time

In many organizations, the loss of messaging means the loss of productivity. Such productivity loss directly impacts the bottom line of most companies. So, Exchange administrators are sometimes given maximum time periods in which to recover from a disaster so as to minimize a company's loss of productivity. These agreed upon time periods are often known as *Service Level Agreements* (*SLAs*). SLAs can be executed within a company between the IT department and other departments; outside vendors may offer an SLA to replace hardware or recover from a disaster within a given time frame.

The way to figure restore time is to figure out how large your databases will become based on average usage and then look at how fast your hardware will restore databases. Once you know this information, you can start to decrease the theoretical size of each database until the end result of the formula indicates that the restore time is within an acceptable range.

Let's assume that you have 1,000 users, each of whom, on average, will have 30 messages per day of an average size of 2KB per message. So, in an average day, messaging traffic will consist of 60,000KB of information, or 60MB ($2 \times 30 \times 1,000 = 60,000$). Since all of this information is also recorded in the transaction logs at some point during the day, we can safely assume that it will take 120MB per day of disk space to handle the message traffic for these 1,000 users. If the transaction logs are purged on a weekly basis as a result of performing a full backup, then each week (assuming a five-day work week) will require 600MB of disk space to hold messaging for these users in both the database and the transaction logs ($5 \times 120 = 600$).

Continuing on with this scenario, in one month (23 business days × 60MB), 1.38GB of messaging information will be generated. Add to that the disk space needed for transaction logs (5 days × 60MB = 300MB), and you'll need about 1.68GB of disk space per month for messaging traffic. On an annual basis, you'll need 16.46GB of disk space for messages and another 300MB for transaction logs. Since many deployments allow users to keep messages for up to 12 months, this is a common scenario to work with.

All we've done so far is to show how to figure how much messaging traffic will be incurred over the next year. The next step is to discern what the current throughput is for your backup hardware when restoring information. Let's assume your hardware will do 150MB/min for a restore operation. To restore a 16.46GB database will require approximately 1,097 minutes, or 18.2 hours. In many deployments, a restore time this long is unacceptable.

Finally, all we need to do is to find out what an acceptable time is for your users to be without Exchange. In most environments, two to four hours is sufficient; however, in some locations, one hour would be way too long. You'll need to discuss this with your supervisor in order to find out what would be acceptable. Let's assume in our scenario that two hours is the maximum acceptable time for users to be without messaging services.

Given the numbers in our scenario along with the two-hour, service-level agreement we just mentioned, the minimum number of databases that would be necessary is ten (18.2/2 = 9.1), since we really can't create 9.1 databases. Since it generally takes time to diagnose a failed database and then find the backup tape from which to do the restore and catalog the tape, it is a good idea to include some troubleshooting time in the window of acceptable time to be down. In this scenario, we would recommend no less than 19 databases with a limit of 1GB per database, which would allow for one hour to troubleshoot and another hour to do the restore of the database.

Defragmentation Considerations

From time to time, you might want to defragment your databases. There are different ways and reasons to defragment a database, and they are outlined in Chapter 15. For purposes of our discussion here, we need to remember that each storage group can hold up to five databases; however, if you ever need to restore one of those databases or conduct a defragmentation of a database, Exchange will need another database to use. So, if you place five active databases in one storage group and you need to restore one of the databases from tape backup, you'll need to dismount a second store in the storage group in order to perform a restore of the damaged database. Hence, the best practice is to put no more than four databases in each storage group so that you can conduct database administrative actions, such as defragmentation or restore, in the same storage group without having to dismount another working database.

Given that we need 19 databases in our scenario and that we are now going to limit ourselves to four databases per storage group, we'll find that we'll need at least five storage groups ($5 \times 4 = 20$) to hold our 19 databases. Since there is a hard-coded limit of four storage groups per server, we'll need to deploy at least two Exchange 2000 Messaging Servers.

Amount of Information to Be Managed

So far, we've looked at how many databases and storage groups we'll need to ensure we can recover within our two-hour time window, and we've allowed for room to perform database administrative functions within each storage group. However, we have not discussed how to structure these databases for future growth of our company. This part gets to be a bit more complicated since it is often difficult to predict what the future will hold.

We can make some educated estimates and then adjust them as time goes by. In our scenario, it is very likely that some databases may grow to be larger than our allowable limit of 1GB. This being the case, there will be times when mailboxes will need to be moved to a new database within the same storage group, or to another database that can accommodate the additional information.

Since we can move mailboxes between storage groups and even between servers, we can structure our storage groups to give us maximum opportunity for growth. For instance, creating two Exchange 2000 Messaging Servers, with one server hosting two storage groups of four databases and the other hosting three storage groups of four databases, gives us room to add an additional 12 databases, or 12GB of information to the Exchange organization before the purchase of a new server is required.

What we have not mentioned thus far is the need to have a message-retention policy in place. The development of such a policy should involve legal counsel since the discovery process in a legal proceeding can involve producing old messages. Having such a policy in place not only provides a level of legal protection, but it also provides a way of keeping your databases from growing out of control. The best practice is to develop a strong message-retention policy in conjunction with your legal counsel and then follow it without deviation.

CREATING AND ADMINISTERING STORAGE GROUPS

You'll recall that each server can host up to four storage groups. A storage group, in and of itself, is pretty useless unless it is populated with at least one store. The storage group provides the transaction logs for the stores, as well as a shell within which the databases can run. You can create a new storage group by right-clicking the Exchange Server you want to manage, clicking New, and selecting Storage Group. You should see the Properties dialog box shown in Figure 7-1. Use this dialog box to name the storage group and to determine where its files are to be stored.

In the Name field, type the descriptive name you want for this storage group. Use the Browse button to the right of the Transaction Log Location And System Path Location

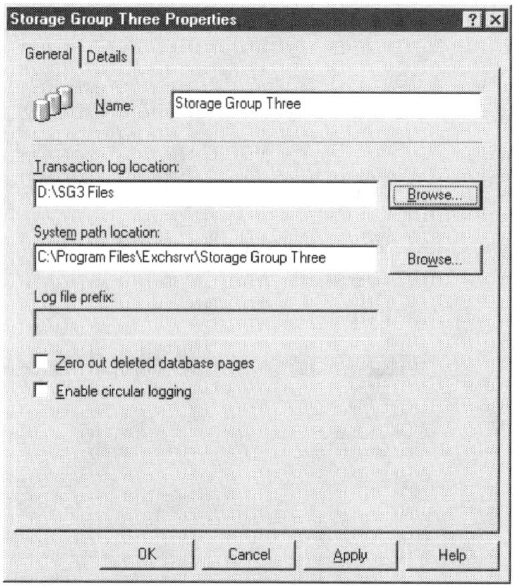

Figure 7-1.   Use this tab to name storage groups and choose files to store

fields to select a location for these files. You'll notice that we chose to place the transaction logs on the D: drive and to leave the system files in their default location on the C: drive. The folder location you select must already exist. If it does not, use Explorer to create the folder in the desired location and then return to the Browse button and select it there.

Remember that the transaction logs should be placed on a physically separate drive than the stores that will use them. Not only does this increase recoverability of data in the event of a disaster, but it also can improve performance if the logs are placed on a physical drive that is doing nothing other than hosting these files. A drive (or preferably, a mirrored pair) dedicated to transaction logging will increase Exchange's performance and response time to the end user.

Once you have chosen your file locations, click OK, and the storage group will be created. It is important to note that if, at this point, you were to look inside your folder for the transaction logs associated with the storage group, you would not find any. This is because the transaction logs are actually created when the first store is created within the storage group.

The Zero Out Deleted Database Pages check box is there to ensure that data deleted in the database is unreadable after it is deleted. This is an advanced security measure. Databases read and write information in 4KB pages. Zeroing out deleted database pages means that the deleted information is overwritten using all 0s and makes the deleted information unrecoverable.

Moving File Locations for a Storage Group

Sometimes, after the storage group is created, you'll want to change the location of the files. This may occur when a new drive is installed into the server, or if a current drive goes bad and you need to move the files to a reliable, working physical drive. You can change the transaction log location and system path for an existing storage group by first opening up the storage group's properties, clicking the Browse button, selecting a new location for the files (the new folder must already exist), and then clicking OK. Once you do this, you'll find that a message pop-up box will appear giving you the warning, shown next. Click Yes to continue, and the stores will be dismounted, the files moved, and the stores mounted, all without your intervention.

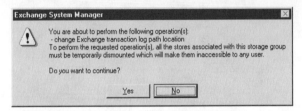

Enabling and Disabling Circular Logging

Circular logging allows Exchange 2000 Server to overwrite previously created transaction log files after the data they contain has been written to the database on the disk. This feature is commonly used in environments in which the Exchange Server needs to conserve disk space or in situations where recovery of data is not important, such as when Exchange is acting solely as an SMTP relay server. With circular logging enabled, you can only recover to the last full backup, and incremental and differential backups are not available.

Disabling circular logging allows for recovery of all your Exchange data up to the point when the disaster occurred. To learn more about backup and recovery procedures, refer to Chapter 15. The best practice is to disable circular logging when creating the storage group unless you know, for sure, that you won't need to recover any of the data that might be lost in a disaster since the last full backup. In most scenarios, nonrecovery of data will not be acceptable.

Renaming Storage Groups

Storage groups can be renamed by right-clicking the storage group, selecting Rename from the context menu, and entering a new name for the storage group. Renaming a storage group will mean that the X.500 directory path, more commonly known as the Distinguished Name (DN), will change for each object inside the storage group, including mailboxes and public folders. If you are running customized software that uses the DN of objects inside a storage group to run properly, make sure you understand the ramifications of changing the name on your third-party application.

Deleting Storage Groups

Storage groups can be deleted, but all the data inside the group must first be moved or deleted. Exchange 2000 Server only allows storage groups to be deleted when they are empty (that is, when they contain no stores).

CREATING AND ADMINISTERING STORES

New stores can be generated once the storage group is created by right-clicking the storage group, pointing to New, and then selecting either Public Store or Mailbox Store. Once you have selected which store you wish to create, fill in the new store's name and click OK. The store will be created along with its database files.

You'll recall that when a storage group is created, no transaction logs are created until the first store is made. Figure 7-2 illustrates the default files that are created when the first store is instantiated inside a storage group.

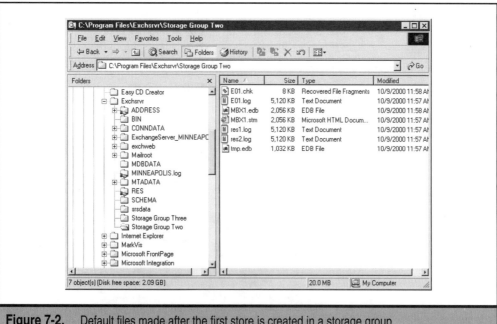

Figure 7-2. Default files made after the first store is created in a storage group

In Figure 7-2, you'll notice that we created a new mailbox store in Storage Group Two. The following explains each of the files:

▼ **E01.chk**   Checkpoint file used to track which transactions in the transaction logs have been written to disk and which have not.

■ **E01.log**   First generation of the transaction logs

■ **MBX1.edb**   Rich-text database for the MBX1 mailbox store

■ **MBX1.stm**   Streaming file databases for the MBX1 mailbox store

■ **res1.log/res2.log**   Space holders for future transaction logs if the disk should run out of space. In this event, these two files will be converted to actual transaction logs, the transactions will be recorded, and the information store service will be shut down. These are files used only in low—disk-space situations, and the best practice is not to delete them.

▲ **tmp.edb**   Transaction log to record transactions while a new log is being created.

Administering Mailbox Stores

After creating a store, the General tab (Figure 7-3) will show you a number of different configuration options. The Default Public Store box will display the default Public Store with which the Mailbox Store is associated. Click Browse to change stores.

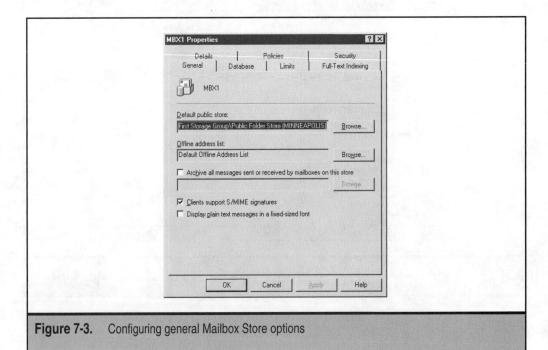

Figure 7-3.   Configuring general Mailbox Store options

The Offline Address List box will indicate which offline address book is receiving updates from this store. Each Mailbox Store exports address list information to an offline address list, which allows users to browse the Exchange organization address list when they are offline or offsite. By default, the Default Offline Address List is selected for this box.

The Archive All Messages Sent Or Received By Mailboxes On This Store allows for messages to or from a user or distribution group to be archived. Click the Browse button to select a mailbox or distribution group to archive. Notice that this is not the place to enable archiving for all the mail-enabled users and groups for archiving to one location, but, rather, a place to archive messages to or from an individual user or a distribution group.

If you want all messages to be displayed in 10 pt Courier, click the Display Plain Text Messages In A Fixed-Sized Font check box. And if you want users and groups homed on this store to support S/MIME (Secure MIME) signatures, select that check box as well.

On the Database tab, see Figure 7-4, you'll find the location where the store's databases are currently located for both the rich-text and streaming databases. To change this location, simply click the Browse button, select a new location, and click OK. The store will automatically dismount, the databases will be moved, and the store will be remounted. Remember that users homed on this store will be disconnected during the move and may need to restart Outlook in order to reconnect.

You can schedule maintenance to run on this database at a time that makes sense. For instance, it is unwise to have the daily maintenance and backup processes running on a database at the same time. The maintenance routine performs such tasks as reindexing the database and cleaning up items that have passed the deleted-items retention time. It is best to have these routines run at different times.

The Do Not Mount This Store At Start-Up will keep the store from mounting when Exchange Server is booted or when the store.exe process is started. The This Database Can Be Overwritten By A Restore check box is cleared by default, but it can be selected if you want to restore an older version of the store over the current version. This can sometimes be the case when the current store has become corrupted and a clean, but older, copy of the store needs to be restored. Note that any e-mails that were sent or received since the restored version will be lost and will not be recoverable.

Use the Limits tab to configure both storage limits and deletion settings (Figure 7-5). The Storage Limits configurations can be set in several different ways:

▼   **Issue Warning At (KB)**   Sets the size limit, in kilobytes, that a mailbox can reach before a warning is issued to the user. The warning tells the user to clear out the mailbox.

■   **Prohibit Send At (KB)**   Sets the size limit, in kilobytes, that a mailbox can reach before losing its privilege to send messages. Once the mailbox is cleared, the restriction is automatically lifted. The number used is the total mailbox size.

■   **Prohibit Send And Receive At (KB)**   Sets the size limit, in kilobytes, that a mailbox can reach before losing its privilege to both send and receive messages. Once the mailbox is cleared, the restriction is automatically lifted. The number used is the total mailbox size.

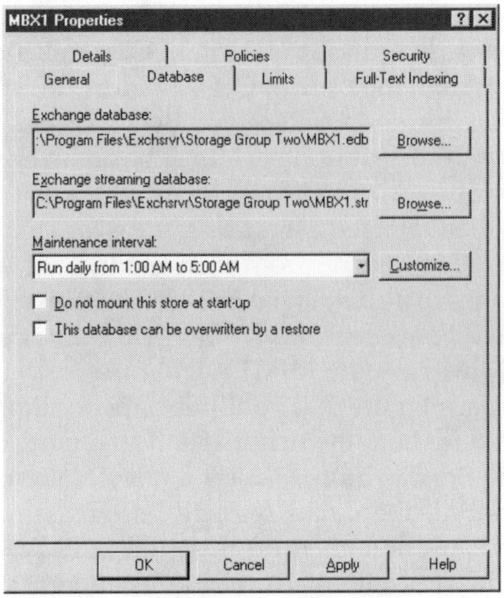

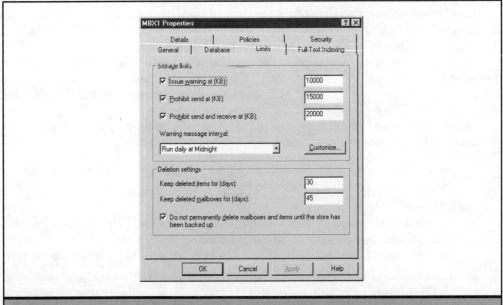

Figure 7-4.   Configuring MBX1 options using the Database tab

Figure 7-5.   Configuring MBX1 storage limits and deletion settings using the Limits tab

▲   **Warning Message Interval**   Sets the interval for sending warning messages to users whose mailboxes exceed the designated limits. The default is once per day at midnight. In large environments, these messages should be generated several times per day.

In the Deletion Settings area, you can set three different configuration options:

▼   **Keep Deleted Items For (Days)**   This value sets the number of days to retain a deleted item. The default setting is 0 days, and this means that deleted messages are not retained in the database and are, therefore, not recoverable. When the value is set to something other than 0, an item that is deleted is marked as hidden and stripped of its permissions, but retained in the database with a future date and time stamp that indicates when the item should be removed. If needed, the item can be recovered using the Recover Deleted Items option in the Outlook client.

■   **Keep Deleted Mailboxes For (Days)**   This value sets the number of days to retain a deleted mailbox. The default setting is 30 days. The best practice is to leave this at the default or increase the value. Only in rare circumstances should the value be set to 0 days. The default setting will give you 30 days to recover a deleted mailbox, if needed.

▲   **Do Not Permanently Delete Mailboxes And Items Until The Store Has Been Backed Up**   This check box ensures that deleted mailboxes and items are archived into at least one backup set before they are removed from the database.

Mailbox Store limits are designed to help you control the size of your databases; therefore, it is not uncommon to enforce size restrictions on individual mailboxes. Users who exceed these limits receive warning messages and, if they are excessive enough, lose privileges in sending and receiving e-mail. Now, this loss of privilege might make some users angry, so be sure to work with your managers to obtain consensus and approval before implementing limits on user's mailboxes.

The Details tab is a location where you can input details about the database. This box is particularly helpful if you are hosting multiple companies on the same server and need to remind yourself which database belongs to which company. The Policies tab will indicate which Exchange policies are being enforced on this database (Figure 7-6). Policies are created under the system policy container in an administrative group. For more information on creating system policies, see Chapter 8.

Recovering Deleted Items

Once an item has been deleted, it can be recovered if the deleted-items retention time has been set on the user's mailbox store. This value only refers to items that have been emptied out of the deleted items folder in Outlook. Once a user empties his or her deleted-items folder, the value you set for deleted-items retention will be enforced.

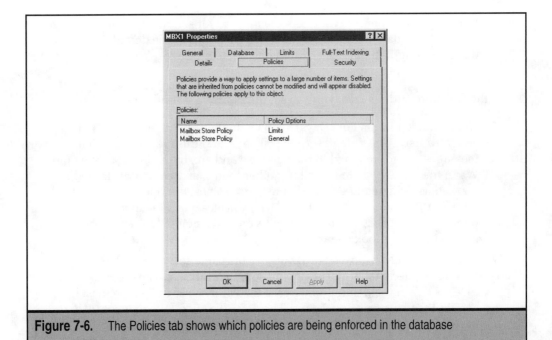

Figure 7-6.   The Policies tab shows which policies are being enforced in the database

For instance, let's assume that Bill English sent Bob Pepper an e-mail about the new ad campaign. Bob accidentally deleted it and then emptied his deleted items folder. Now, he needs to recover this e-mail. What Bob should do is navigate to the Tools menu in his Outlook client, click Recover Deleted Items, select the item he wishes to recover, and click Recover Selected Items. This action will make these items appear in the Deleted Items folder in the Outlook client, at which point Bob can move these items to any folder he desires.

Recovering Deleted Mailboxes

Once you've set the mailbox-retention interval, you can recover a deleted mailbox as long as you're within the interval. To recover a mailbox, select the Exchange Server in System Manager and navigate to the storage group you wish to work with. Inside the storage group, find the Mailbox Store and expand the store to show the Mailboxes icon. Highlight the Mailboxes icon. In the right pane, you should see a listing of all the mailboxes homed in the store. If you know you've deleted a mailbox and that mailbox does not show an X over the mailbox's icon, then right-click the Mailbox Store and select Run Cleanup Agent. This will cause the X to appear over the deleted mailbox (Figure 7-7).

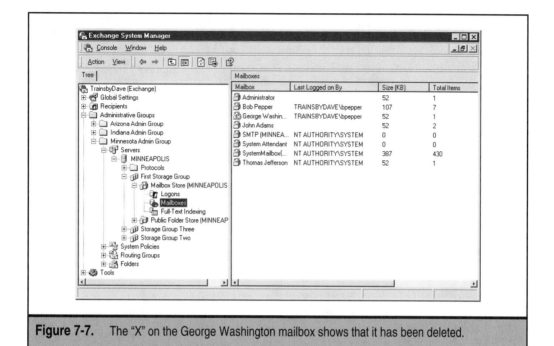

Figure 7-7. The "X" on the George Washington mailbox shows that it has been deleted.

Now, you'd think you could right-click the mailbox and find a menu choice to recover the mailbox. Not so. Instead, you need to right-click the mailbox and select Reconnect. Once you do this, a listing of the users in the Entire Directory will appear, as shown here:

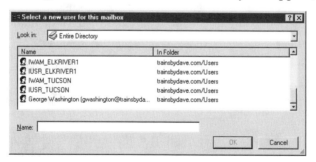

Use this Select A New User For This Mailbox dialog box to assign a user to this mailbox. Once you click OK, the mailbox is recovered and assigned to the user. If you run the Cleanup Agent again, you'll find that the X disappears over the Mailboxes icon and the user is free to use the mailbox again. This is also the method you would use if you wish to assign a mailbox to a different user, such as when one user leaves and another one is hired in her place.

Deleting a User's Mailbox Permanently

If you've set a deleted mailbox retention time but would like to manually purge a mailbox from a Mailbox Store, you can do this by performing the following steps. First, navigate to the Mailbox Store you wish to work with and highlight the Mailboxes icon inside the store. Find the deleted mailbox you wish to purge (it should have an X over its icon), right-click the Mailbox, and select Purge. Confirm your action, and the mailbox will be permanently removed from the Mailbox Store and its items will not be recoverable, unless the store is recovered from tape backup.

Reading Mailbox Summaries

A mailbox summary appears in the Exchange System Manager (Figure 7-8) and displays the following:

▼ The mailbox name
■ Who the last user to log on to the mailbox was
■ The number of messages stored in each mailbox
■ The total size of each mailbox
■ The last logon time for each mailbox
▲ The last logoff time for each mailbox

Additional items can be displayed by using the View menu to select Choose Columns. In the Modify Columns dialog box, you can select which columns to display. By default, these columns are hidden:

▼ **Deleted Items (KB)** This is the total amount of disk space, in kilobytes, occupied by deleted items that are being retained in the mailbox.
■ **Full Mailbox Directory Name** This is the full X.500 DN of the mailbox.
■ **Storage Limits** These are the limits that are being enforced on the mailbox.
■ **Total Associated Messages** This represents the total number of messages in the mailbox that represent hidden system information, such as forms, rules, views, or deferred action messages.
▲ **User Deleted Time** This is the date and time that Exchange detected the deletion of a user.

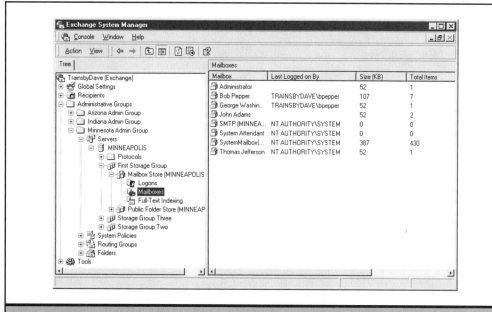

Figure 7-8.   Using the mailbox summary in the Exchange System Manager

CREATING PUBLIC FOLDER STORES

Public Stores are created and managed in the same manner as Mailbox Stores, but with some key differences. For instance, each Public Store can only be associated with one public folder tree. In addition, replication configurations are available in the store's properties, requiring more effort to administrate a Public Store.

If you would like more information on how to create and manage Public Stores and public folders, refer to Chapter 6.

SUMMARY

In this chapter, you have seen how to create and manage both storage groups and individual stores. You have also seen how to move databases for both a storage group and an individual store. Finally, you've learned how to delete and recover individual items in a Mailbox Store, as well as an individual store through the use of System Manager.

In the next chapter, we'll look more closely at how to create and manage administration and routing groups.

CHAPTER 8

Managing Administration and Routing Groups

In a matter of just a few years, many organizations have gone from no e-mail to e-mail being mission-critical system number one. When e-mail systems first became a part of the corporate world, a single administrator was all that may have been needed. In today's corporate world, organizations are spread across the globe, having many physical locations and requiring many administrators to keep their messaging up and running. Microsoft has adjusted with each messaging paradigm shift by developing a messaging platform that meets an organization's needs. Microsoft Exchange 2000 is no exception. Exchange 2000 introduces a new type of administrative model by using the concepts of administrative groups and routing groups. These two types of groups will allow flexibility in your delegation of administration and routing of messages.

A BRIEF LOOK BACK: EXCHANGE 5.x SITES

In order to understand the benefits of administrative and routing groups in Exchange 2000, let's first take a look at where these concepts evolved. Exchange 5.x used the concept of a site to define boundaries. It was used both to define the administrative separation of the Exchange organization and to represent a single physical location. This meant you would create additional Exchange 5.x sites if you needed to delegate full administrative abilities or if two Exchange Servers were not well connected with a high-speed link (10 Mbps, for example).

Administration Within Exchange 5.x Sites

As previously mentioned, a site would define the boundaries of your administrative abilities. That is to say, if you had Admin rights in one Exchange 5.x site, you did not necessarily have any privileges in another site. If you wanted to delegate authority, Exchange 5.x did provide you with some levels of permissions granularity (Permissions Admin, Admin, and View Only Admin), but these did not give you the ability to grant permissions to specific tasks within the site. For example, if you wanted to give someone the ability to modify the Internet Mail Service object, you had to grant that user View Only Admin rights at the site level (allowing him or her to navigate the Exchange Directory) and then Permissions Admin rights to either the Connections container or the Internet Mail Service object. The basic concept here is that you *could* do it, but it was neither easy nor intuitive.

Routing Using Exchange 5.x Sites

The existence of each Exchange 5.x site denotes two things: that the servers within a single site are well connected, and that they will have to route to servers in another site using some sort of connector between the two sites. This means that when you are planning your Exchange 5.*x* environment, if two servers are not well connected (perhaps they are connected using a Fractional T1), you have to create two sites.

Exchange 5.*x* Sites: The Problem

Since an Exchange site has to meet both the administrative and message routing needs of an organization, it does not provide a great level of granularity within the Exchange organization. This is why Microsoft separated these two needs and created the concepts of administrative groups and routing groups.

ADMINISTRATIVE GROUPS

An administrative group in Exchange 2000 is a logical definition of the boundaries of administration within an Exchange organization. Unlike Exchange 5.*x* sites, there is no association of an administrative group to a specific physical location. There are several objects that can be managed within an administrative group. These objects include the following:

▼   Routing groups

■   Servers

■   Public folder trees

■   Policies

■   Conferencing services

▲   Chat communities

ROUTING GROUPS

A routing group defines groupings of servers that are well connected. You will use routing groups to define how messages are routed through your Exchange organization. For example, by default, if any two Exchange 2000 Servers in a single routing group need to transmit messages to one another, because they exist within the same routing group, they can do so directly. This is called *intragroup routing* communication. However, if two Exchange 2000 Servers that exist in separate routing groups need to transmit messages to one another, they may need to route the message via other Exchange 2000 Servers that connect the two routing groups. This is called *intergroup routing* communication. (Management of routing groups will be discussed in the next chapter.)

Routing Groups Versus Exchange 5.*x* Sites

Of the two new concepts presented here, the routing group concept is closest to the Exchange 5.*x* site concept. In both cases, the concepts represent a group of servers that enjoy high-bandwidth connectivity. Also, in both cases, you would need to create connectors to establish message connectivity between the two sites or routing groups. For more information on connectors, see Chapter 9.

The major difference between a site and a routing group is that the routing group does not define any administrative boundary, it only focuses on the message routing boundary aspects of Exchange.

Administrative Models

Administration of your Exchange organization can take on one of several models. Which model is used really depends on the specific needs of the company. There are three administrative models you can choose from: centralized, decentralized, and mixed. The model you choose will most likely mirror your IT department's model. Using TrainsbyDave, let's look at each model and show how a growing company might use each.

Centralized Administrative Model

In a centralized administrative model, one or perhaps a few administrative groups would exist to divide the administration of Exchange 2000. Ideally, in concept, only one would exist. A company having a centralized IT department would use a centralized administrative model. The IT department using a centralized administrative model could consist of a single network administrator who handles everything IT for the entire company, or a team of IT individuals who focus on Exchange Administration. This is the model originally used by TrainsbyDave.

The TrainsbyDave company began as a single manufacturing and operations plant in Minneapolis, Minnesota. It also had several regional-area sales offices throughout the state (see Figure 8-1). Because a single IT department administered the entire TrainsbyDave network (including their Exchange environment), a centralized administrative model was used for Exchange Administration. A single administrative group will exist (Figure 8-2) to reflect the single IT department doing the administration of Exchange, with a routing group for each of the remote sales offices, each having its own Exchange Server.

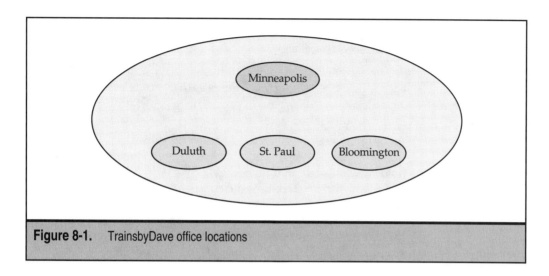

Figure 8-1.   TrainsbyDave office locations

Decentralized Administrative Model

In a decentralized administrative model, several administrative groups are utilized for administrative activities. The groups could be based on different company factors, for example, geographic division, company division, or administrative division. Table 8-1 describes when you would use each division model.

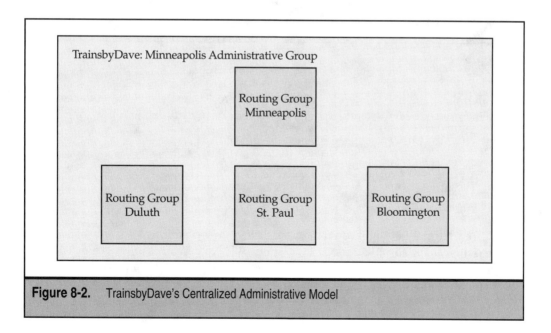

Figure 8-2.   TrainsbyDave's Centralized Administrative Model

Division Factor	Explanation/Application
Geographic	A company with several locations may have administrators at each location. Creating an administrative group for each location would allow you to properly delegate authority to the local administrator.
Company	A company may be comprised of several subsidiary entities (for example, a company that makes widgets that also owns a holdings company that invests using the earnings from the widgets). Since each part of the company has its own IT staff, and yet at the same time the company wants to maintain a unified messaging platform, an administrative group would be created for each company so they could manage their own environment within one Exchange environment.
Administrative	A company could be so large that the need for administrators to focus on specific aspects of Exchange becomes necessary. One administrative group could be created just for the routing groups, another for public folders, and yet another for chat and conferencing administration. This use of administrative groups would allow administrators to only manage their portion of the Exchange environment.

Table 8-1. Decentralized Administrative Model Divisions

With trains being the tremendous fad that they are, TrainsbyDave experiences an immense increase of business and expands its operations to include the following cities:

▼ Minneapolis, Minnesota

■ Sacramento, California

■ Tucson, Arizona

▲ Indianapolis, Indiana

With each office having its own manufacturing and operations staff, a local IT staff is required. Just as the administration of the TrainsbyDave networks moves from a centralized to a decentralized administration staff, the Exchange environments administrative model must change as well. Now it makes more sense for the Exchange environment to have one administrative group for each location (see Figure 8-3), with a routing group for each remote office that has an Exchange Server.

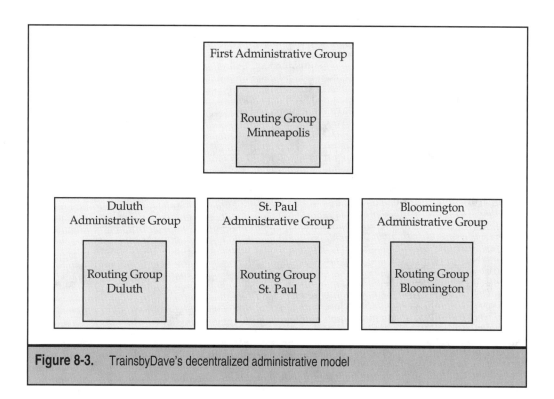

Figure 8-3.   TrainsbyDave's decentralized administrative model

Mixed Administrative Model

A mixed administrative model would most likely be used by a large, enterprise-wide Exchange environment. The term describes how this model uses parts of both the centralized and decentralized models. In an enterprise environment, a company may want to govern how some aspects of Exchange are implemented (like routing or policies), and allow other aspects (like servers and public folder trees) to be controlled by regional or local offices.

Let's suppose our company, TrainsbyDave, was to expand its operations to three geographical areas across the globe (trains are very popular overseas!), with operations in North America, Europe, and Asia. Let's also suppose that the IT departments for each of those operation regions are centralized, with their main offices in Minneapolis, London, and Tokyo, respectively. The folks at corporate IT have decided that all Exchange Policies will be dictated and administered by corporate IT in Minneapolis. It has also been decided that routing will be managed at each of the main offices, with all other administration handled at each of the company's locations throughout the world. Figure 8-4 shows you what the administrative group structure might look like. Notice that not all administrative groups contain routing groups (like the policy administrative group and each of the branch administrative groups). Only those administrative groups that are created to specifically control routing will contain routing groups.

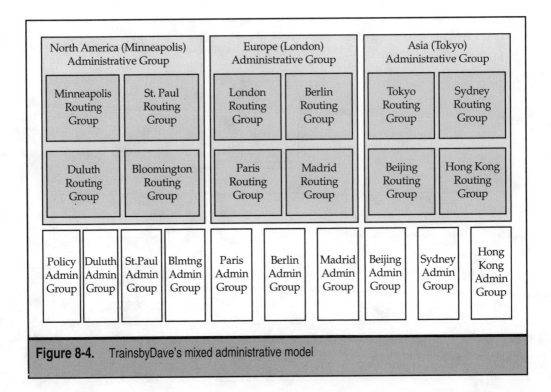

Figure 8-4. TrainsbyDave's mixed administrative model

Table 8-2 shows you how this example constitutes a mixed administrative model.

Exchange Object	Manager	Centralized or Decentralized?
Policies	Corporate office	Centralized
Message routing	Regional headquarters	Depending on how you look at it, it could be considered centralized (from a regional perspective). It also could be considered decentralized (from a corporate perspective).
Servers, public folder trees, chat and conferencing services	Branch offices	Decentralized

Table 8-2. TrainsbyDave Mixed Administrative Model Dissection

Hopefully, you now understand the basic concepts behind administrative and routing groups, and when each type is appropriate. Now let's take a look at how to implement and work with each one.

CREATING AND MANAGING A SINGLE ADMINISTRATIVE GROUP

When you first install Exchange 2000, you already have one administrative group containing one routing group. If you think about it, it makes sense: as far as Exchange knows, there is only one server after the initial install. Based on that belief, there is no need for multiple routing groups (you would need more than one Exchange Server for that) and no need for multiple administrative groups (until you tell Exchange otherwise).

Hey! Where's My Administrative and Routing Groups?

By default, the System Manager snap-in does not display either type of group, as shown here:

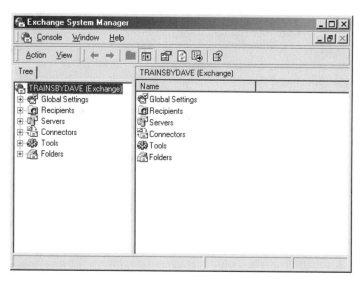

Remember, if you only have one server in the Exchange environment, you probably won't need more than one administrative group and definitely won't need more than one routing group.

To have System Manager display both groups, right-click the organization and select Properties. On the organization's General tab, you can choose to display administrative and routing groups separately, as shown next.

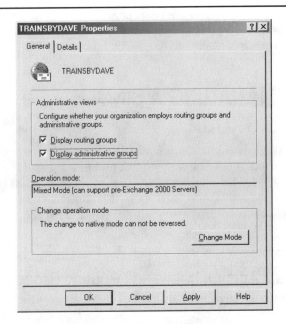

The following illustration shows that, within an administrative group, you can administer containers for servers, routing groups, and public folders. Other containers that can exist here are chat communities and system policies. A chat community's container will exist only if you have chat services installed in your Exchange organization. If you need to implement and administer policies, you will have to create at least one policy to see the system policy container under an administrative group. (See "Creating and Managing Exchange 2000 Policies," later in this chapter, for more information on policies.)

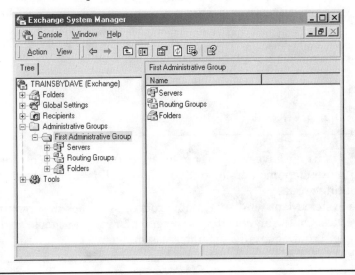

CREATING AND MANAGING MULTIPLE ADMINISTRATIVE GROUPS

Before you go off and start creating multiple administrative groups, you should plan out the use of each one and include in your plan what the contents of each group will be. This way you won't spend time after the implementation trying to clean up any unforeseen messes you've created.

After you have finished your plan, to create an administrative group, right-click the Administrative Group container, select New, and choose Administrative Group (Figure 8-5).

In the resulting Properties dialog box, give the Administrative Group a descriptive title (Figure 8-6), fill in any details you desire on the Details tab, and click OK.

If you click your new administrative group, you'll find that there are no contents. To populate your administrative group, simply right-click it, point to New, and choose Public Folders container or System Policy container. A few other container types do not appear for various reasons. Table 8-3 lists those containers and why they are not listed.

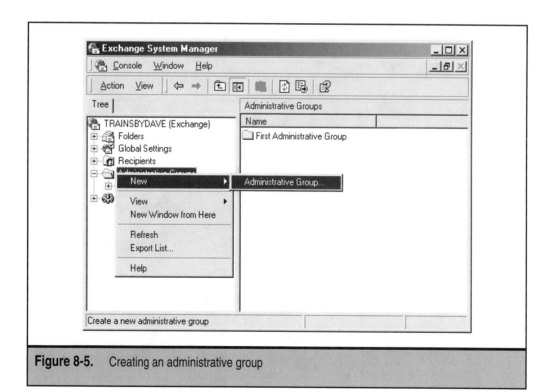

Figure 8-5. Creating an administrative group

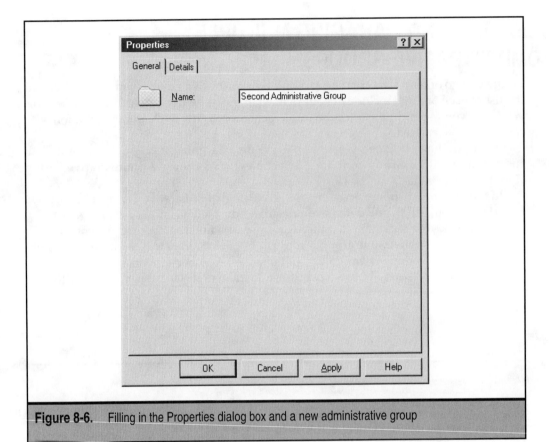

Figure 8-6.   Filling in the Properties dialog box and a new administrative group

Container Type	Reason Why It Is Not Displayed
Servers	While created in Active Directory (AD) when the administrative group is created, the servers container will be displayed after the installation of an Exchange 2000 Server in that administrative group.
Chat communities	Will be created during the installation of the chat services component.
Routing group	While created in AD when the administrative group is created, the routing group will only be displayed when an Exchange 2000 Server is installed in the administrative group.

Table 8-3.   Containers Not Shown By Default

Populating Server Containers

Even though it's neither recommended nor supported by Microsoft, you still are able to move a server from one administrative group to another. You can do so using Active Directory Sites and Services (ADS&S), using the Show Services Node option. If you scroll down to the server in question under the Services node, you can drag and drop it into the other administrative group. You can also use this mode of ADS&S to view the servers and routing group containers that do not initially show up in System Manager.

The next section, "Delegating Control Within Administrative Groups," discusses the other way—one that is supported—to place servers in separate administrative groups. You should create the administrative group that will contain the server to be installed *before* you actually install the server. One of the options during an installation of Exchange 2000 is the choice of which administrative group in the Exchange organization to place the server inside.

Delegating Control Within Administrative Groups

Whether you have a single administrative group or several, you may want to further define the administrative granularity by delegating control. Exchange 2000 provides a simple wizard that walks you through this process. To delegate control, right-click the administrative group, choose Delegate Control, and the Exchange Administration Delegation Wizard will start (see Figure 8-7).

Clicking Next will bring you to the users or groups selection page of the wizard, shown next. Click Add to select the users or groups you wish to delegate authority to.

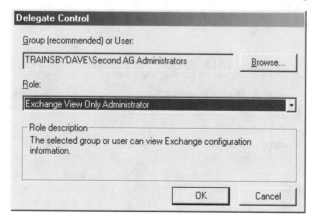

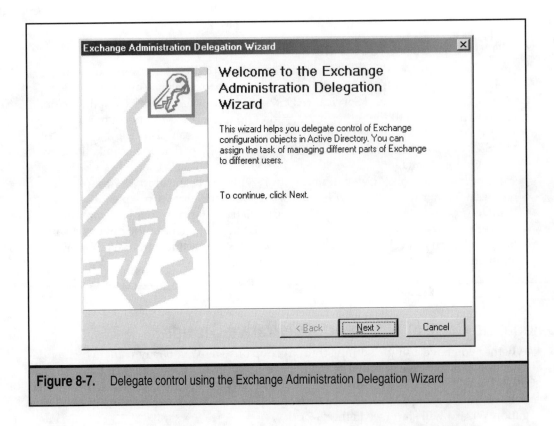

Figure 8-7. Delegate control using the Exchange Administration Delegation Wizard

Choose the Role you wish the selected user or group to have. Table 8-4 lists the roles and their privileges. Click Next and then Finish to complete the wizard. You have successfully delegated control of your administrative group.

CREATING AND MANAGING EXCHANGE 2000 POLICIES

Now that you have created your administrative groups and delegated proper authority to each, let's take a look at how you can simplify the administration of objects you will be adding to your administrative groups. Exchange 2000 has a new concept called *policies*. Policies will define a set of parameters to be applied to Exchange objects of the same class (servers, public folders, and others). The use of policies not only simplifies your administrative work in the beginning (because you establish the settings one time for many Exchange objects), but they also make it easier when a parameter has to be modified. If you need to change a value across your administrative group, simply make the change in the policy, and all objects that the policy affects will be updated with the new value.

Exchange Role	Administrative Ability	Who Should Get This Role
Exchange Full Administrator	This role can fully administer Exchange, as well as modify permissions.	Apply this role to users or groups who will completely administer the Exchange environment.
Exchange Administrator	This role can fully administer Exchange but cannot modify permissions.	Apply this role to users or groups who manage day-to-day operations.
Exchange View Only Administrator	This role can only view Exchange configuration information. Apply this role to users or groups who need to see your configuration, for example, administrators of other administrative groups who need to see the configuration of your part of the Exchange environment.	

Table 8-4.   Exchange Delegation Roles

Two types of policies can be created: system and recipient. System policies will exist within the administrative group (Figure 8-8) and will apply to mailbox stores, public stores, and servers.

Recipient policies establish e-mail addresses and will apply to mail-enabled objects. They can be found under the Recipients container, as shown in Figure 8-9.

System Policies

To create a system policy container, right-click an administrative group, point to New, and select System Policy Container (Figure 8-10). There are three types of system polices that can be created: server, public store, and mailbox store. The idea behind each of these policies is that once the policy is established, objects within the administrative group that the policy applies to will adopt the policy. It cannot be overridden at the level of the individual object.

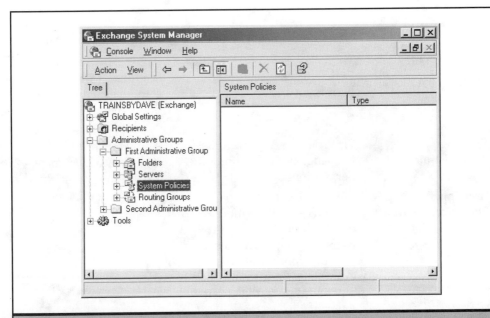

Figure 8-8. The System Policies container exists within the administrative group

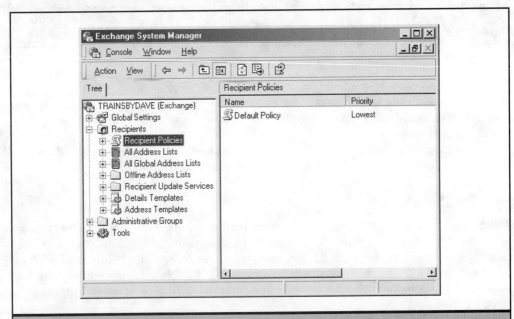

Figure 8-9. The Recipient Policies container holds recipient policies that establish e-mail addresses and apply to mail-enabled objects.

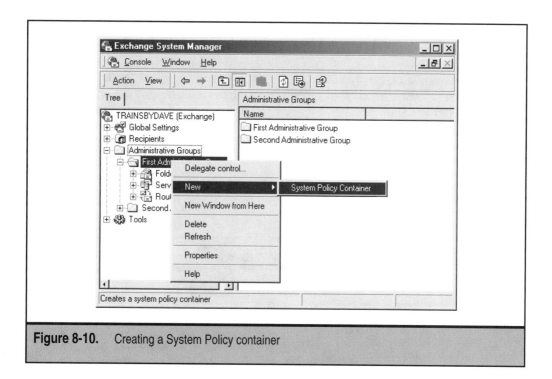

Figure 8-10.   Creating a System Policy container

Server Policies

A server policy will govern the same settings that you would find on the General tab of any Exchange Server in your organization. These settings include logging and tracking of messages, as well as the maintenance of your log files. To create a new server policy, right-click the System Policy container, point to New, and select Server Policy. The New Policy dialog box, shown next, will appear.

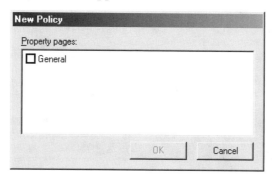

You will need to select the policy tabs you will be establishing. The server policy only has the General tab; however, other policies may have several tabs that you can choose. Select the General check box to display the policy's General tab, and click OK to see the Server Policy Properties dialog box (see Figure 8-11). Notice the General (Policy) tab is displayed. If you had not selected the General check box earlier, this would not appear.

Click the General (Policy) tab to establish the policy settings you wish to implement. To specify which servers are subject to this policy, right-click the policy you just created, and select Add Server (Figure 8-12). Figure 8-13 shows the selection dialog box where you choose the server or servers that will be placed under the control of this policy. Select the server(s), click Add, and OK.

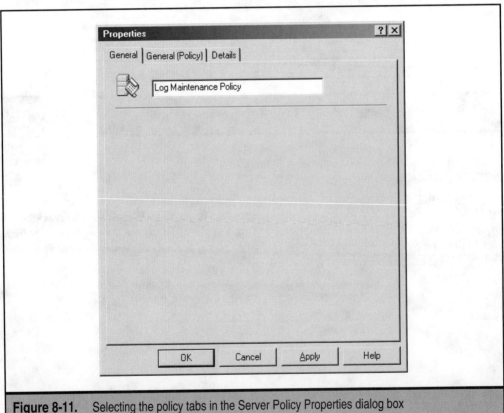

Figure 8-11.   Selecting the policy tabs in the Server Policy Properties dialog box

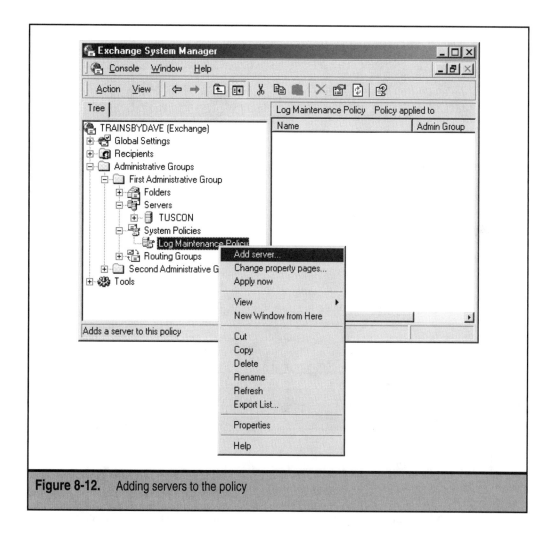

Figure 8-12.   Adding servers to the policy

As mentioned before, these settings override any settings on each server object. Figure 8-14 shows you the result of the policy being applied to a server object. Notice the options specified in the policy are grayed out and are not allowed to be modified.

Public Store Policies

Public Store Policies manage many aspects of a public folder, including indexing, maintenance, and limits. Each Public Store Policy you create will be applied on a per-store basis

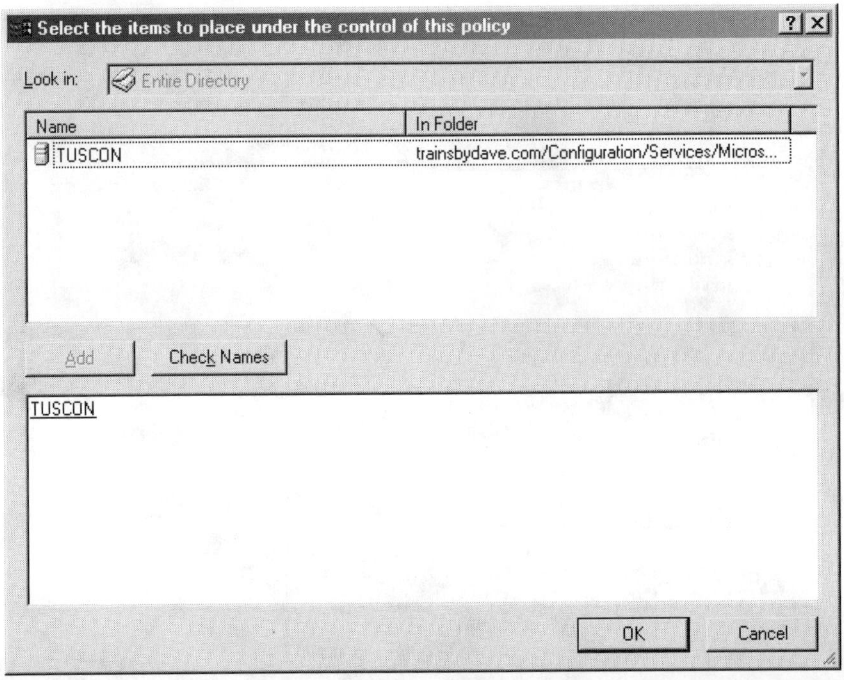

Figure 8-13. Selecting the servers to fall under the policy

and will apply across public folder trees. To create a Public Store Policy, you will follow much of the same procedure as a server policy. Begin by right-clicking the System Policy container, point to New, and select Public Store Policy. The New Policy dialog box, shown next, has several more policy tabs to choose from than a server policy.

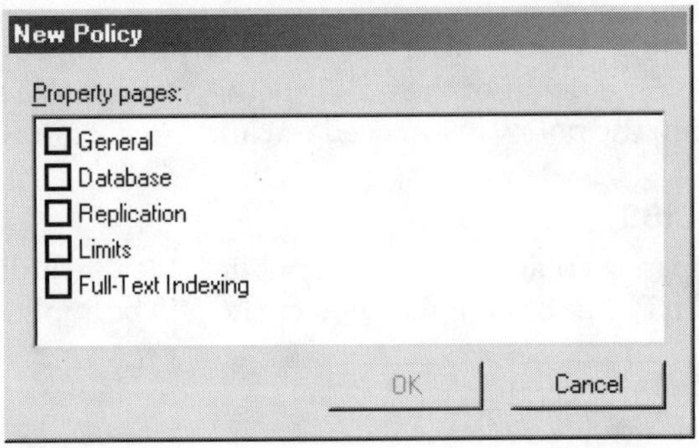

Table 8-5 lists the tabs and the settings that you can set within the policy.

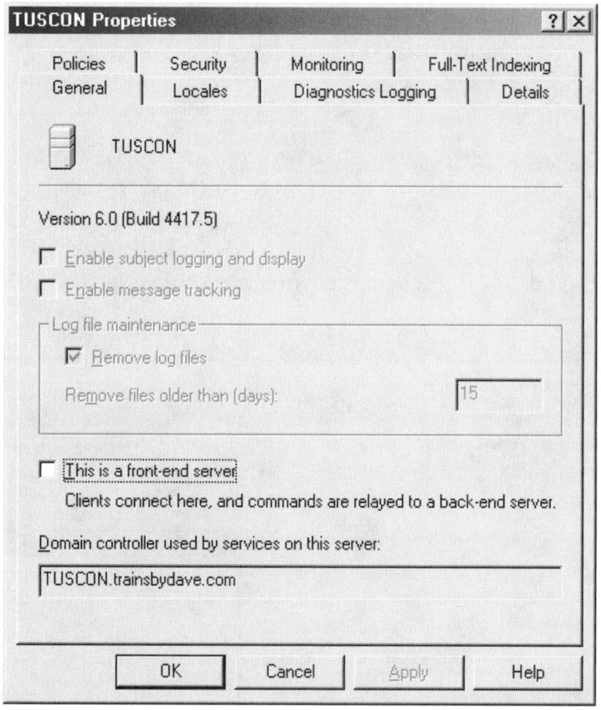

Figure 8-14.   The General tab of a server object with the server policy applied

Policy Tab	Policy Settings
General	Secure Multipurpose Internet Mail Extensions (S/MIME) signature support Fixed-font conversion for inbound Internet messages
Database	Daily maintenance run time
Replication	Replication schedule Replication limits
Limits	Storage limits Deletion settings Message age limits
Full-Text Indexing	Index update intervals Index rebuild intervals

Table 8-5.   Public Store Policy Settings

To specify which Public Stores are subject to this policy, the procedure is much the same as a server policy. Right-click the policy, select Add Public Store (Figure 8-15), and choose the public store or stores that will be affected.

Mailbox Store Policy

Mailbox Store Policies establish virtually every parameter of a Mailbox Store. Like the Public Store Policy, a Mailbox Store Policy is applied on a per-store basis. To create a Mailbox Store, right-click the System Policies container, point to New and select Mailbox Store Policy. The New Policy dialog box shows the four Mailbox Store Policy tabs.

Table 8-6 lists the tabs and the settings you can set within the policy.

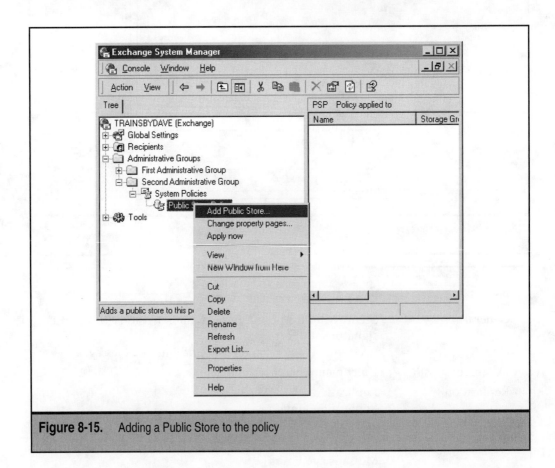

Figure 8-15.   Adding a Public Store to the policy

Policy Tab	Policy Settings
General	Default public store
	Offline address list
	Message archival
	Client support of S/MIME signatures
	Display of fixed-sized font for text messages
Database	Database maintenance interval
Limits	Storage limits
	Deletion settings
Full-Text Indexing	Index update interval
	Index rebuild interval

Table 8-6.   Mailbox Store Policy Settings

SUMMARY

From a single Exchange Server and a single administrator to a worldwide Exchange environment, Exchange 2000 administrative groups and routing groups allow your administrative structure to be both flexible and scalable. As your Exchange environment grows, policies can be utilized to mandate administrative standards without having to repeat the implementation of that policy for each Exchange Server in your organization.

In the next chapter, we will move our focus onto routing groups. We will look at the three types of connectors that can be used to connect Exchange 2000 to both Exchange 2000 and foreign e-mail systems.

CHAPTER 9

Administering Routing Group Connectors

Connectors in Exchange 2000 play a major role in providing messaging connectivity. Without them, there would be no way to communicate outside of your routing group. That means no Internet e-mail and no connectivity with any foreign messaging systems or with Exchange Servers in other routing groups. In order to avoid the painful memories of the messaging systems we supported eight years ago, Exchange 2000 supports three connectors that can be used to connect your Exchange routing groups, and that connect your Exchange organization to the foreign message systems and to the Internet: the Routing Group connector (RGC), the Simple Mail Transport Protocol (SMTP) connector, and the X.400 connector. Let's take a look at each connector, see how it is configured, and explore its benefits.

RGCs

The connector you will most likely use to get two Exchange routing groups talking is an RGC—a Routing Group Connector. An RGC is the simplest connector to set up of the three connectors described in this chapter, and is similar in nature to the Site Connector in Exchange 5.5. The RGC is basically a definition of the existence of the remote routing group and also defines which servers in the local routing group can communicate across it. Each RGC is a unidirectional connector, which means that if you wish to have two-way communication between routing groups, you will need to create two RGCs: one for each direction of communication. Not to worry, when you finish creating the RGC to handle communication in one direction, you will be prompted to automatically create the RGC for the other direction. The one main architectural difference is that the RGC will use SMTP as its transport protocol, whereas the Site Connector uses Remote Procedure Calls (RPCs). RPCs require permanent, high-bandwidth connectivity, whereas SMTP is much more tolerant of low-bandwidth, high-latency environments. Let's begin by creating and configuring an RGC.

Creating and Configuring an RGC

To create an RGC in System Manager, navigate to and right-click the Connectors container under the routing group that you want the connector to be created in, point to New, and select Routing Group Connector (Figure 9-1). If you were to provide a name for the connector and select the remote routing group that this RGC will connect to, you could press OK and be done creating the RGC. It is that simple.

You could leave your RGC as is with no additional configuration, but let's take a look at each of the parameters available by walking through each of the properties tabs.

General Tab

The General tab (shown next) lists the most basic parameters you need to specify in order to create the RGC. Table 9-1 lists each of the General tab's options, with a description of each.

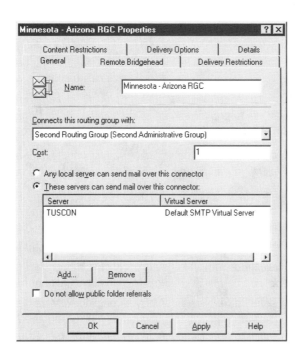

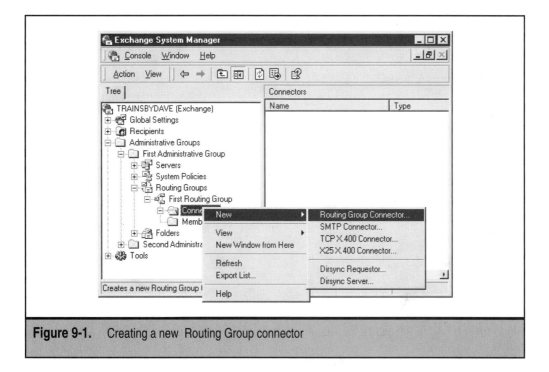

Figure 9-1. Creating a new Routing Group connector

Option	Description
Name	Provides a unique name for this connector. It should be descriptive so you know what the connector is used for.
Connects this routing group with	Specifies the remote Exchange 2000 routing group that you are connecting with.
Cost	Associates a routing cost with this connector. If you have two connectors existing between the same two routing groups, Exchange will use the connector with the lowest cost. The range is from 1 to 100.
Any local server can send mail over this connector	Allows all Exchange servers in your local routing group to utilize this connector.
These servers can send mail over this connector	Allows specific servers to utilize this connector. You will have to press the Add button and select the server or servers from a list.
Do not allow public folder referrals	Disallows users in the remote routing group to locate or use public folders on servers in the local routing group.

Table 9-1.   General Tab Options

Remote Bridgehead Tab

The Remote Bridgehead tab, shown next, is used to designate which server or servers the local servers are able to communicate with across the RGC.

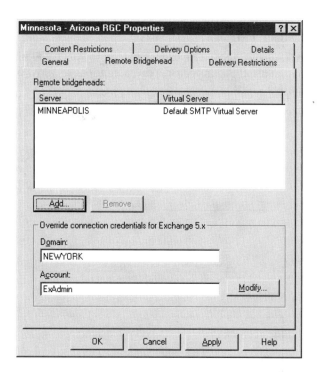

These remote servers are considered Bridgehead Servers (BHSs) because they are the points of access to that RGC. This is similar to the BHS you would specify in an Exchange 5.*x* Site Connector. The major difference between the Exchange 5.*x* BHSs and those in Exchange 2000 is that in Exchange 5.*x*, you can specify a cost to each BHS; whereas in Exchange 2000, each BHS will be contacted in sequential order in the list.

In Exchange environments running in mixed mode that still have Exchange 5.*x* sites, the connection to a remote routing group that is actually a remote Exchange 5.*x* site may require you to specify override credentials. The account specified should have Service Account Admin rights in the remote Exchange 5.*x* site.

Delivery Restrictions Tab

The Delivery Restrictions tab, shown next, allows you to specify which users in your Exchange environment can use this connector. You can choose to allow or deny all users and then establish exceptions to that rule.

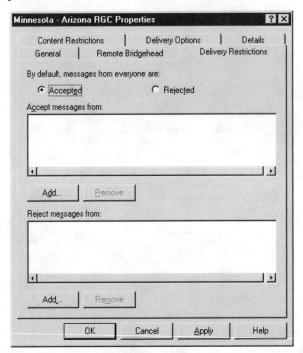

For example, if you only want one user to utilize this connector, you need to set By Default, Messages From Everyone Are to Rejected and then add the single user to the Accept Messages From field by clicking the Add button immediately under that field and selecting the Active Directory (AD) user in question.

If you want to do the exact opposite and allow everyone but one user, set the default to Accepted and add the user in question to the Reject Messages From field.

Content Restrictions Tab

The Content Restrictions tab, shown next, allows you to apply certain basic filters on the messages passing (or attempting to pass) across the connector.

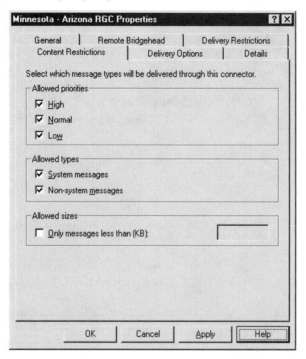

Messages can be restricted using three factors: message priority, message type, and message size. Each of the three priorities available to messages is listed within the Allowed Priorities area. You can choose messages with any and all priority levels to be allowed across the connector by selecting the appropriate priority level. Message types are broken down into two basic types: system and non-system messages. System messages are messages that are sent by Exchange 2000 itself. Examples of system messages would be delivery reports, public folder replication messages, and nondelivery reports. Non-system messages are messages sent by users. Finally, on this tab you can specify a message size limit. If a message that is larger than the limit attempts to pass across the connector, it will be rejected. Note that the default setting is to allow messages of any size to pass.

Delivery Options Tab

The Delivery Options tab, shown next, allows you to specify when the connector is available for use.

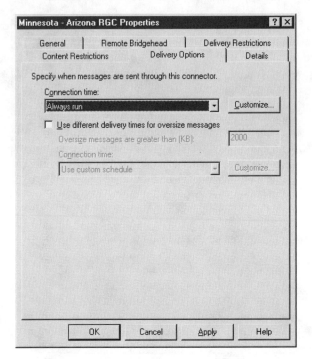

By default, all connectors are set to Always Run. You can also specify a certain time to have the connector run. The values for the Connection time are

- ▼ Always run
- ■ Run daily at 11:00 PM
- ■ Run daily at midnight
- ■ Run daily at 1:00 AM
- ■ Run daily at 2:00 AM
- ■ Run every hour
- ■ Run every 2 hours
- ■ Run every 4 hours
- ■ Never run
- ▲ Custom schedule

The Custom Schedule option allows you to specify the times of day you want your connector to be available for use. Set the Connection Time to Use Custom Schedule and press the Customize button. You can set the times for the connector to run in the Schedule dialog box and then press OK:

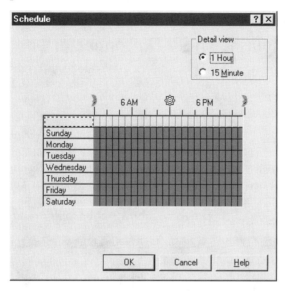

One of the greatest features is the ability to have messages over certain sizes be sent at different times. For instance, if your company is very conscious about available bandwidth throughout the business day, rather than set an upper message-size limit on the Delivery Options tab and have some messages not go through to their intended recipient, you can simply set a threshold for larger messages (the default is just under 2MB) and have the messages that are larger than that threshold be sent at a different time. The Connection Time settings for oversized messages are identical to the settings for regular messages.

SMTP CONNECTORS

You may be surprised to find out that both RGCs and SMTP connectors run over SMTP. Although it may seem redundant to have both connectors since they seem, at first glance, to provide the same connectivity, as we take a look at the SMTP connector, you will see that it has a very different purpose than the RGC.

An RGC is used specifically to connect Exchange 2000 Servers within the same forest or to Exchange 5.5 Servers within the same Exchange organization. An SMTP connector can be used to connect in the following circumstances:

▼ Connect Exchange 2000 to other SMTP-compliant e-mail systems or the Internet. (In this respect, think of the SMTP connector as analogous to the Internet Mail connector in Exchange 5.*x*.)

■ Connect Exchange 2000 to another Exchange 2000 environment running independently (that is, not in the same AD forest) within your organization.

▲ Connect Exchange 2000 to another routing group or Exchange 5.5 site using additional connection criteria such as the time of day, namespace supported, and ability to queue mail for remotely triggered delivery.

Creating and Configuring an SMTP Connector

Just like the RGC, to create an SMTP connector, navigate to and right-click the Connectors container under the routing group that you want the connector to be created in, point to New, and select SMTP Connector.

General Tab

The General tab of the SMTP Connector properties, shown next, allows you to specify a Name for the connector; choose either to Use DNS To Route To Each Address Space On This Connector or to Forward All Mail Through This Connector To The Following Smart Hosts; choose the Exchange Servers that will act as local bridgeheads to send messages through this connector; and choose to not allow public folder referrals.

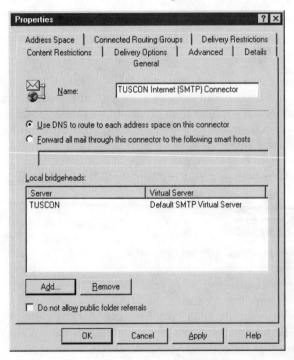

Using Smart Hosts

If you choose to use a smart host, all messages will simply be passed to the specified server. No DNS name resolution is performed since the server running the SMTP connector will not be responsible for sending messages to the recipient's e-mail server. The following table lists the kinds of smart hosts you may use and the reasons you may use them to send your SMTP messages

Smart Host	Reason for Use
Internet Service Provider's (ISP's) SMTP Server	If you are running Exchange in a small company, the Exchange Server may have a dynamically assigned IP address. Some domains will not allow e-mail from servers with dynamically assigned addresses. This is done to prevent spammers from setting up their own e-mail server at home and sending e-mail to everyone at, for example, aol.com. Using your ISP's SMTP server (that has a statically assigned IP address) will overcome this problem.
Virus Scanner	You may desire to have all inbound and outbound e-mail pass through a virus scanner that scans not only the e-mail, but also the attachments. With up-to-date virus signatures, this is useful protection against attacks like the I Love You virus.
Content Checker	Your company may want to check the content of every e-mail coming and going. Companies may look for specific words like "résumé," look for adult content, or even scan for company secrets being leaked via e-mail.

Content Restrictions and Delivery Restrictions Tabs

These tabs provide the same information as their counterparts in the RGC. (See "Creating and Configuring an RGC," earlier in this chapter for more information.)

Delivery Options Tab

At first, this tab, shown next, appears to be the same as its counterpart in an RGC. But a closer look shows one additional field at the bottom of the dialog box: the Queue Mail For Remote Triggered Delivery option allows outbound messages to be queued up locally and only be transmitted when a specific account connects and issues an ATRN or TURN command. At that point the SMTP connector will dequeue all messages to the client domain.

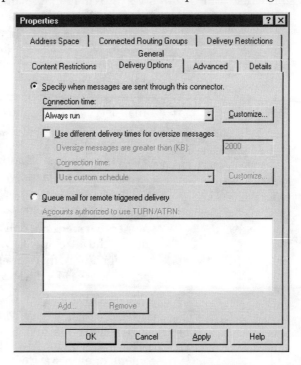

Connected Routing Groups Tab

The Connected Routing Groups tab, shown next, specifies all other routing groups within your Exchange organization that will communicate over this connector. In this specific case, the remote server *must* be an Exchange Server.

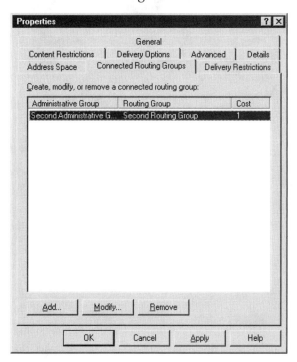

Address Space Tab

The Address Space tab, shown next, specifies the type and format of addresses that can be used across this connector. You can add a supported namespace by clicking the Add button, selecting an address space type, and specifying any Internet Address Space Properties.

Most of the time, an SMTP connector will only be supporting an SMTP address space, but you could use other address spaces and use SMTP as the transport between two routing groups.

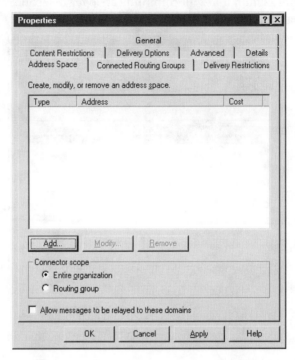

The E-mail Domain field on the Internet Address Space Properties dialog box is of significant importance. This field alone determines which domain names can be accessed by this connector. The default is an asterisk, which means all domain names are supported. But if you wanted to only support a single domain name, such as the name of a vendor who has a virtual private network (VPN) established between your company and theirs, you would put that vendor's domain name (DavesVendors.com, for example) in this field. With this value in place, the SMTP connector would only route messages that were destined for DavesVendors.com.

Two other options exist on the Address Space tab, shown in the previous illustration. You can allow this connector to be used by only the Routing Group in which it exists or the Entire Organization. You can also allow messages to be relayed through your Exchange environment and sent out this connector to the domain names that meet the address space restrictions. (The default does not allow relaying of any kind.) For example, if you were using a specific alphanumeric pager provider (PagersByDave.com, for example) and wanted outside users to send you alpha pages via e-mail, you could utilize the Allow Messages To Be Relayed To These Domains option to automatically forward your pages to your pager by doing the following:

1. Set up a mail-enabled contact pointing to your PagersByDave.com address that represents your pager.

2. Give the mail-enabled contact a second e-mail address that matches your company's domain name (for example, DavesPager@TrainsByDave.com). If you were to set up an SMTP connector that only supported the PagersByDave.com address space and allowed relaying, an e-mail could be sent destined for DavesPager@TrainsByDave.com, and Exchange would automatically route the e-mail to the PagersByDave.com domain (because it resolves the name to a mail-enabled contact and will forward it to the primary address of that contact at PagersByDave.com) by way of this SMTP connector.

3. Add the domain PagersByDave.com to the address spaces supported by the connector.

Advanced Tab

The Advanced tab, shown next, gives the SMTP connector the ability to utilize ETRN.

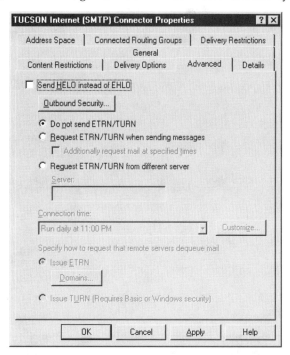

ETRN is an extension to the SMTP standards that allows the Exchange Server running this connector to, for example, communicate with an ISP queuing your company's messages and request to download them all at once. Table 9-2 lists and describes the Advanced tab options.

Option	Description
Send HELO instead of EHLO	Usually, the EHLO command is used to begin the ETRN process. Some mail servers use the default HELO instead.
Outbound Security	Your mail server may require some form of security to connect. Exchange 2000 supports the following security methods: anonymous access, basic (clear text) authentication, integrated Windows authentication, and Transport Layer Security (TLS) encryption.
Do not send ETRN/TURN	This is the default setting. The setting disables the ETRN functionality.
Request ETRN/TURN when sending messages	This will cause dequeuing messages to be sent. You can also specify times to send this command by selecting the Additionally Request Mail at Specified Times check box and specifying the times in the Connection Time field.
Request ETRN/TURN from different server	Use this option if the server you would dequeue messages from, for a certain domain name, is not the same as the one you would send to. You can specify an IP address here of a fully qualified domain name (FQDN).
Connection time	Specify the times when the ETRN command will be issued.
Issue ETRN	This connector will issue the ETRN command.
Domains	This lists the various domains that will be issued an ETRN command.
Issue TURN	This specifies that the connector will issue only TURN commands.

Table 9-2.   Advanced Tab Options

X.400 CONNECTORS

An X.400 connector is used to connect Exchange 2000 to any compliant messaging system. Because Exchange 2000 is X.400 compliant, you can use the X.400 connector to connect two Exchange 2000 routing groups. While the RGC is usually the best and simplest choice, we think you should be familiar with the X.400 connector and its options in case you need it. Before we jump into setting up X.400 connectors, let's first review X.400 addressing.

X.400 Addressing Basics

An X.400 address follows the messaging hierarchy of the e-mail system. Use the following address example and the descriptions of each part of the X.400 address in Table 9-4 to understand both the hierarchy that an X.400 address depicts and the overall X.400 address. Let's suppose that TrainsByDave has a new employee at their Tucson, Arizona, office by the name of John A. Smith. John's X.400 address might look something like the following:

c=US;a= ;p=TrainsByDave;o=Tucson;s=Smith;i=A;g=John

Table 9-3 lists and describes each field in the X.400 address space.

X.400 Component	Description
c=	Country
a=	Administrative Management Domain (not normally used by Exchange)
p=	Private Management Domain (equivalent to the name of the Exchange organization)
ou=	Organizational Unit (not normally needed in Exchange; X.400; supports 4 levels of OUs)
o=	Organization
cn=	Common Name
q=	Generation Qualifier (Jr., Sr., II, and so on)
i=	Initials
s=	Surname (the user's last name)
g=	Given Name (the user's first name)

Table 9-3.   X.400 Address Components

Service Transport Stacks

Before you can create an X.400 connector, you must first create a message transfer agent (MTA) service transport stack. The transport stack defines the details about the underlying network that the X.400 connector will travel on. Transport stacks exist on a per-server basis, as they define how X.400 traffic would travel on that particular server. There are two types of transport stacks available to you:

▼ **TCP/IP X.400 Transport Stack**   You will use this transport stack type if you plan to run your X.400 connector over a TCP/IP-based network, such as the Internet or your corporate intranet.

▲ **X.25 X.400 Transport Stack**   You will use this type of transport stack if you will be utilizing an X.25-based network. X.25 is a packet-switched network protocol.

Creating the Transport Stack

As we walk through the steps to create a transport stack, we will focus our attention on the more common of the two stack types: the TCP/IP X.400 Transport Stack. The installation process for an X.25 X.400 Transport Stack is almost identical. To begin installing the TCP/IP X.400 Transport Stack in System Manager, navigate to and right-click the X.400 container, found under the Protocols container for your server; point to New; and select TCP/IP X.400 Service Transport Stack, as shown in Figure 9-2.

On the General tab, shown next, you can change the display name of the stack, as well as specify any Open System Interconnection (OSI) address information.

Blueprints

Table of Contents

Migration Paths

In-Place Domain Upgrade

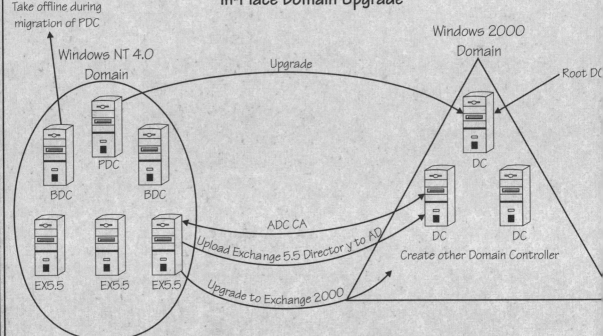

An In-Place Domain Upgrade means that the current Windows NT 4.0 Primary Domain Controller (PDC) will be upgraded to be the root Domain Controller (DC) in your new Windows 2000 forest.

Step 1: Upgrade the Windows NT 4.0 PDC to Windows 2000, and create the Active Directory (AD). The advantage of doing this is that the NT SIDs will be placed in the SIDHistory attribute of the new object in AD. Thus, even if users authenticate in the AD, they can still access resources in the NT domain.

Step 2: Install additional DCs in the Windows domain for redundancy.

Step 3: Install the Active Directory Connector Service on one of the DCs in the Windows 2000 domain.

Step 4: Create a Connection Agreement (CA) to one of the Exchange 5.5 Servers.

Step 5: Upload the Exchange 5.5 directory information to AD.

Step 6: Upgrade one Exchange 5.5 Server to Exchange 2000 Server, which installs the Site Replication Services (SRSs) and automatically creates a Configuration CA (ConfigCA). If possible, upgrade a Directory Replication Bridgehead Server (DRBHS) first.

Step 7: Upgrade the remaining Exchange 5.5 Servers to Exchange 2000 Servers, or create new Exchange 2000 Servers to meet user need and decommission the old 5.5 Servers.

Migration Paths

Exchange First Upgrade

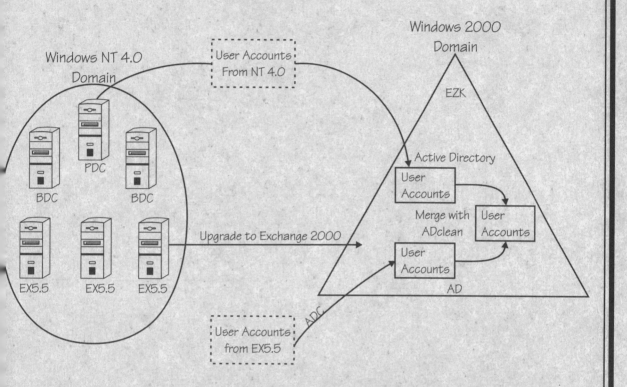

In this method, your Exchange 5.5 Servers are upgraded to Exchange 2000 Servers before your PDC is upgraded to a Windows 2000 DC. This upgrade requires the use of ADCLEAN.

Step 1: Install a new AD domain.

Step 2: Use ADC to upload Exchange 5.5 directory information to AD. User accounts will migrate as disabled accounts; users still authenticate in the NT 4.0 domain.

Step 3: Install new Exchange 2000 Servers and move the mailboxes from the Exchange 5.5 Servers to the new Exchange 2000 Servers, or upgrade the existing Exchange 5.5 Server to a Exchange 2000 Server.

Step 4: Upgrade existing NT 4.0 accounts to AD using the Active Directory Migration Tool (ADMT), which produces duplicate accounts in the Windows 2000 AD.

Step 5: Use ADCLEAN to merge duplicate accounts into one account in AD.

Migration Paths

Migrate Users with SIDHistory

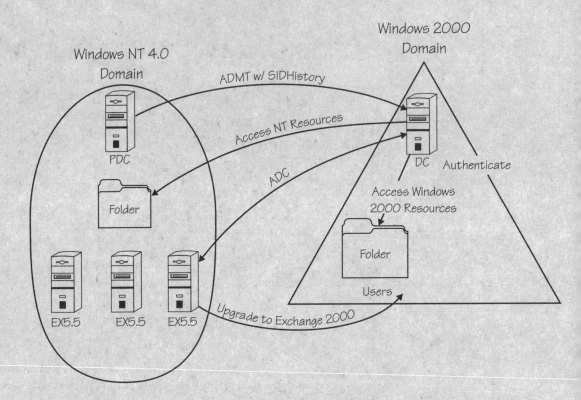

In this method, user accounts are copied out of the Windows NT 4.0 security accounts database into Active Directory with their NT 4.0 SID included in the SIDHistory attribute. This gives users instant access to resources in both domains.

Step 1: Create a new Windows 2000 AD.

Step 2: Migrate user accounts from NT 4.0 to AD retaining their old SIDs. The advantage to this is that users can then authenticate in AD and still get immediate access to NT resources that might still be on the network

Step 3: Run the ADC and upload Exchange 5.5 directory information to AD. It will recognize the SIDHistory and match the Exchange 5.5 mailbox's primary Windows NT 4.0 account to the old primary SID, which is now in the SIDHistory.

Step 4: Install new Exchange 2000 Servers and move the mailboxes from the Exchange 5.5 Servers to the new 200 Servers, or upgrade the existing Exchange 5.5 Server to a 2000 Server.

4

Migration Paths

Migrate Users without SIDHistory

User accounts are copied out of the Windows NT 4.0 security accounts database to Active Directory without their Windows NT 4.0 SID included in the SIDHistory attribute. Their new Windows 2000 user accounts must be reapplied to resources in the NT 4.0 domain before users can gain access to these resources. Also a trust relationship must be established between these two domains.

Step 1: Create a new Windows 2000 AD, and establish a manual trust relationship between the AD and the Windows NT 4.0 domain.

Step 2: Migrate all user accounts to AD using ADMT, but do not include their SIDHistory.

Step 3: Rest all the Access Control Lists (ACLs) on NT 4.0 resources to include new user accounts from AD.

Step 4: Update permissions on Exchange 5.5 mailboxes to include new AD primary user accounts.

Step 5: Run ADC to migrate the Exchange 5.5 directory information to AD.

Step 6: Install new Exchange 2000 Servers and move the mailboxes from the Exchange 5.5 Servers to the new 2000 Servers, or upgrade the existing Exchange 5.5 Server to Exchange 2000 Server.

Step 7: Run ADCLEAN to merge duplicate accounts into single accounts in AD.

Core Service and Protocol Changes in Exchange 2000

This is an illustration showing how these protocols and services are managed in Exchange 5.5 compared to how they are managed in Exchange 2000 Server.

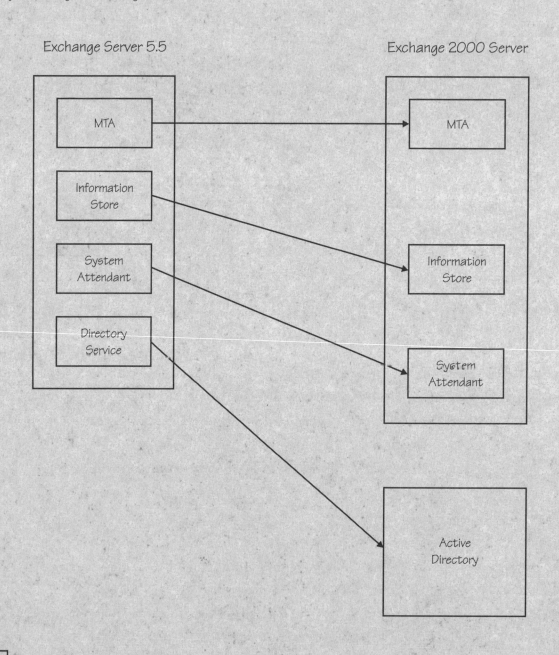

Internet Protocol Changes in Exchange 2000

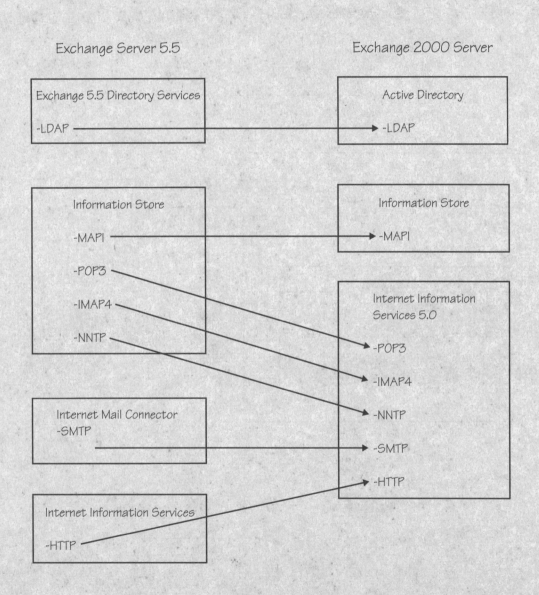

Exchange Server 5.5

Exchange 2000 Server

Exchange 5.5 Directory Services

-LDAP

Active Directory

-LDAP

Information Store

-MAPI

-POP3

-IMAP4

-NNTP

Information Store

-MAPI

Internet Information Services 5.0

-POP3

-IMAP4

-NNTP

Internet Mail Connector
-SMTP

-SMTP

-HTTP

Internet Information Services

-HTTP

Exchange 5.5 Sites
Vs.
Exchange 2000 Namespace Administrative Groups & Routing Groups

This graphic illustrates how these functions are handled in Exchange 5.5 and Exchange Server.

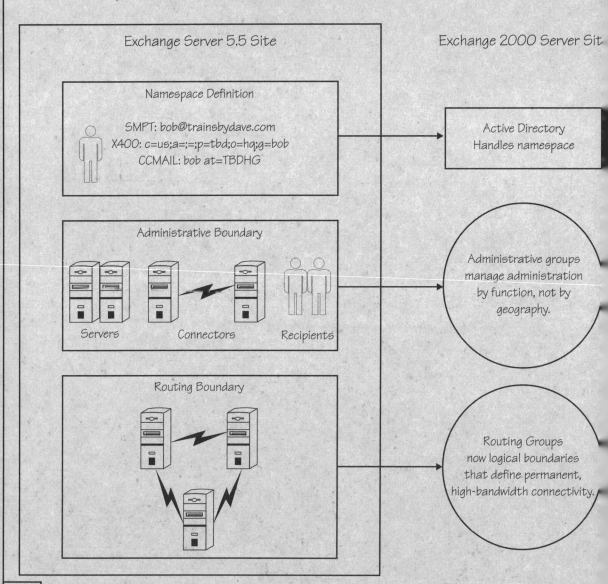

Exchange Server 5.5 Site

Exchange 2000 Server Sit

Namespace Definition

SMPT: bob@trainsbydave.com
X400: c=us;a=;=;p=tbd;o=hq;g=bob
CCMAIL: bob at=TBDHG

Active Directory
Handles namespace

Administrative Boundary

Servers   Connectors   Recipients

Administrative groups
manage administration
by function, not by
geography.

Routing Boundary

Routing Groups
now logical boundaries
that define permanent,
high-bandwidth connectivity.

The OSI address information is not required for use with another Exchange 2000 server. However, if you will be connecting to a foreign messaging system, you may need to provide specific values here. The Connectors tab will be filled in automatically once we have created an X.400 connector that utilizes this stack, and you can put in any other information on the Details tab that you see fit. To sum this procedure up, you simply need to create the stack and, optionally, modify the stack name. That's it!

Creating and Configuring X.400 Connectors

We're finally here! While it seems there is so much to do just to get to the creation of the TCP X.400 connector, once you have done it a few times, you will find it quite simple to master. To create a TCP X.400 connector in System Manager, navigate to and right-click the Connectors container, as shown in Figure 9-3, and point to New | TCP X.400 Connector.

General Tab

On the General tab, shown next, provide a display Name for the connector.

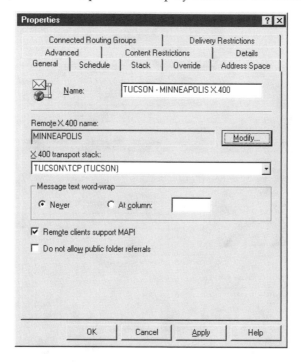

As with previous connectors, use a descriptive name that defines the path the connector travels. Next, choose the Remote X.400 Name. This is the name of the remote server for this connector. Choose the X.400 Transport Stack that you previously created. These are the most important configuration options on this tab. In addition, you can also specify whether or not to enable word wrap on outgoing messages, choose whether or not remote clients

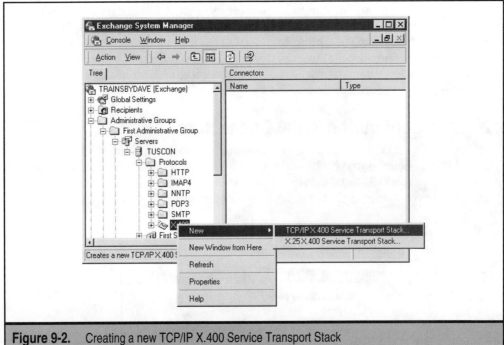

Figure 9-2.   Creating a new TCP/IP X.400 Service Transport Stack

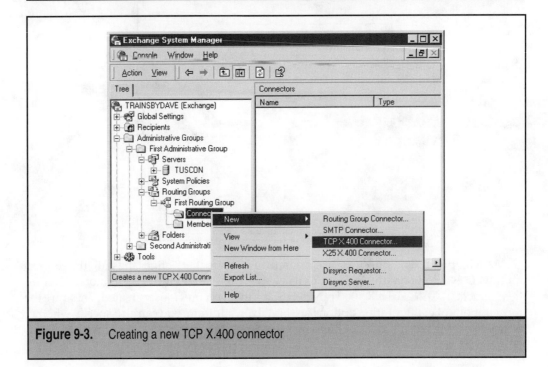

Figure 9-3.   Creating a new TCP X.400 connector

support Message Application Programming Interface (MAPI) (which enables the transmission of rich text and other MAPI information with the messages), and choose whether or not public folder referrals will be accepted across this connector.

Schedule Tab

The Schedule tab, shown next, is used to do something the RGC can't do: schedule the use of this connector.

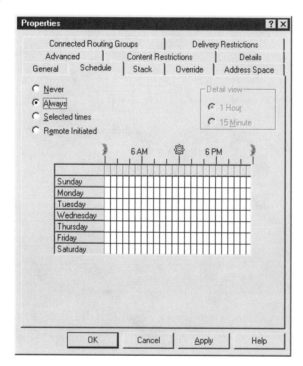

You can leave the default of Always so the connector is constantly running. If bandwidth availability between your offices is an issue, perhaps you may choose to limit the use of the connector between those offices by selecting the times the connector is available. Also note the ability to allow only one side to establish communications by using the Remote Initiated option.

Stack Tab

Use the Stack tab to specify either the name or IP address of the remote host. You can also specify optional OSI information.

Override Tab

The Override tab, shown next, is used to provide security credentials for the local MTA and to specify local MTA settings used for sending messages across the connector.

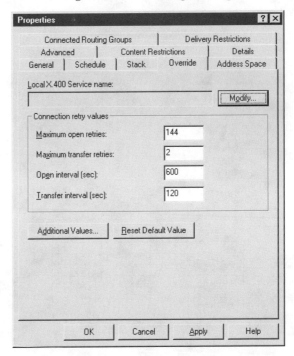

Do not change the Connection retry values unless the foreign messaging system you connect to requires values different than the defaults.

Address Space Tab

The Address Space tab, shown next, defines the scope of the recipient addresses across this connector. When you press the Add button to add an address space, you are given the ability to support a number of address spaces. However, since the intent of using this connector is to connect two X.400-compliant messaging systems, it would be best to pick the X400 address type and press OK.

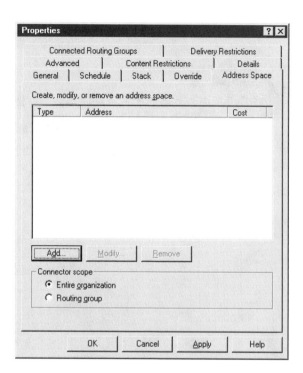

Once you've chosen to add the X400 address type, you are prompted to fill in the X.400 address of the remote system. One of the easiest ways to get this information is to ask the remote system's administrator for their X.400 addressing information. Usually, in an Exchange environment, you only need to specify the country (for example, c=US), the administrative management domain is always a space (that is, a=), and the private management domain is the name of the Exchange organization (for example, p=TrainsByDave), and the default organization is Exchange.

Other Tabs

There are four additional tabs that exist for an X.400 connector. The options found on the Content Restrictions, Delivery Restrictions, and Connected Routing Groups tabs are identical to those found on an SMTP connector (See "Creating and Configuring an SMTP Connector," earlier in this chapter). The Advanced tab lists options that you will only need to take advantage of if you are connecting to a foreign (non-Exchange) system *and* if that system requires you to modify any of these parameters. For this reason, we will not dive into a deeper discussion of those options and their values.

SUMMARY

In this chapter, we have looked at the three connectors you can use to interconnect your Exchange 2000 environment with either other Exchange environments or foreign messaging systems. From the ease of configuration of the RGC, to the necessity of the SMTP connector to interoperate with Internet-based systems, to the complexity you can take advantage of with the X.400 connector, each one has its place and its benefits in Exchange.

In the next chapter, we'll move into a new section on architecture and take a closer look at the Exchange 2000 Storage Architecture.

PART III

Exchange 2000 Server Architecture

CHAPTER 10

Exchange 2000 Storage Architecture

So far, we've taken a look at how to migrate from Exchange 5.5 to Exchange 2000 and how to perform some basic administrative tasks, such as creating user accounts and managing public folders. However, in order to understand why we do what we do, we need to learn about the architecture of Exchange 2000. This chapter will focus on the overall architecture of Exchange 2000, the storage architecture, and the Extensible Storage Engine (ESE).

EXCHANGE 2000 ARCHITECTURE

There are two main processes upon which Exchange 2000 Server relies: store.exe and inetinfo.exe, as shown in Figure 10-1.

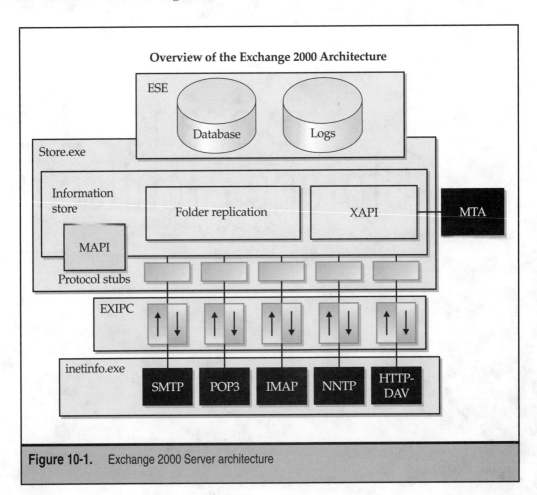

Figure 10-1.   Exchange 2000 Server architecture

The Store Process

The store process manages several important components of Exchange 2000 Server. The core of Exchange services, such as messaging and Outlook client access, are managed by the store process; however, the way that Exchange 2000 Server communicates with the outside world is through the protocol stacks housed inside Internet Information Services (IIS). The protocol stubs are managed by the store process and talk to the protocol stacks, such as SMTP, POP3, Internet Message Access Programming version 4 (IMAP4), Network News Transfer Protocol (NNTP), and Hypertext Transfer Protocol Development and Authoring Version (HTTP-DAV), which run inside IIS. The shared queues that are used to pass messages back and forth between IIS and Exchange are called the Exchange Interprocess Communications (EXIPC) layer. Another name for EXIPC is Epoxy.

The Message Application Programming Interface (MAPI) protocol is still hosted by the information store in Exchange 2000 and allows Outlook clients to communicate directly with the store, rather than having to go through the IIS and over the Epoxy layer. All other protocols that were hosted by the information store in Exchange 5.5 have been decoupled from it and installed as independent protocol stacks that run inside IIS. This is a major improvement and allows for Exchange 2000 to scale into the largest of installations.

Public folder replication continues to be the responsibility of the information store, as it was in Exchange 5.5; however, there are some significant improvements that, if you've been administering an Exchange 5.5 network, you'll find refreshing and welcome. Refer to Chapter 6 for more information on these innovations.

In order to read from or write to the Exchange databases, messages and attachments must first pass through the store process, which is responsible for managing all of the Exchange databases and storage groups.

The generic Exchange API (XAPI) is still available to work with the X.400 connector. This connector, which was so prominent in Exchange 5.5, has been significantly diminished in Exchange 2000 in favor of the SMTP connector. Refer to Chapter 9 for more information.

The inetinfo.exe Process

The inetinfo.exe process, as mentioned previously, is now doing much more work than simply hosting Web and File Transfer Protocol (FTP) sites. It now manages the messaging protocol stacks for both Windows and Exchange 2000. Since these protocols run independently of the Exchange information store, it is possible to have one or more servers manage the front-end protocols and pass user requests to a bank of Exchange Servers hosting the user's public and private information. This is known as a front end/back end (FE/BE) architecture, and we discuss this in the section "FE/BE Architecture," later in this chapter.

IIS is automatically installed as the messaging protocol engine for Windows 2000 Server. When Exchange 2000 Server is installed, it updates the SMTP protocol to include several new features, which we will discuss in Chapter 12. Hence, both Exchange and Windows 2000 use SMTP as their primary messaging protocol.

Using SMTP ensures better interoperability among Exchange 2000, the Internet, and other messaging systems. This is because SMTP is more tolerant of low-bandwidth, high-latency environments than a Remote Procedure Call (RPC), which has been the workhorse of Exchange 5.5 and Windows NT 4.0. Thus, network topologies do not need to be designed to accommodate the limitations of RPC.

STORAGE TECHNOLOGIES IN EXCHANGE 2000 SERVER

In Exchange 5.5, we were working with two databases, the priv.edb and the pub.edb, that were managed by one service, the information store service. Information written to the databases could only be written in Microsoft Database Encapsulated Format (MDBEF), so any information that was not natively in MDBEF format, such as video, graphics, or audio attachments, needed to be converted by the Internet Mail (IMAIL) process before it could be written to or read from the database. MAPI clients, such Outlook clients, will natively write in MDBEF.

Needless to say, e-mail is much more than text these days, and the number of users who routinely send graphics, video, or audio attached to their messages has risen dramatically. This has placed an ever-increasing load on the Exchange 5.5 Servers in many organizations, since such attachments consume large amounts of disk space, leading to databases that often exceed 30GB in size.

The problem with large databases is not really the time required to back them up. Most administrators back up their databases during off hours and have tended not to care a great deal whether the backups took three or ten hours. As long as the backups were done before the start of business the next day, the time required to perform the backups wasn't seen as important.

However, what administrators have discovered is that a large database that takes five hours to back up takes even longer to restore. In many environments, the increased time to restore a database from tape has become a source of concern, since many users are significantly less productive without e-mail. (Keep in mind that the database is not mounted during a restore operation.) Exchange customers have increasingly been asking for a way to both manage larger amounts of information and have shorter restore times. The lack of an ability to restore a subset of the information in the database was also disconcerting to those who wished to restore only one mailbox or public folder, and not an entire database. While third-party utilities offered these services, experiences were mixed as to how effective they were.

Moreover, companies that required absolute minimum downtime found that they couldn't host more than a certain number of users on any given Exchange 5.5 Server, which forced them to purchase additional servers to load-balance their users across multiple databases.

These factors led Microsoft to develop a better database system for Exchange 2000 Server. This database system meets several important criteria. First, it accommodates the increasing complexity of the type of information users want to store. Second, it significantly reduces the amount of information conversion that must occur. Third, it allows for information to be accessed through many clients. Fourth, it allows you, the administrator, to build databases that can be restored much more quickly, thus lowering the amount of unproductive time your users will experience. And finally, the architecture will work on most systems, whether you're running a large-capacity service with fast SCSI disks or a small server with EIDE disks.

MULTIPLE-DATABASE SUPPORT

Exchange 2000 Server overcomes all of these limitations by creating additional databases on the same Exchange Server. In fact, you can have up to 20 databases simultaneously running on one Exchange 2000 Server. These databases run inside a *storage group*, which groups no more than five databases together to utilize a common set of transaction logs. All of these databases run under a single process, store.exe, and can be individually started (mounted) or stopped (dismounted). In addition, a single database can be restored from backup while the other databases are mounted. This can significantly reduce lost productivity for your users if an Exchange database malfunctions.

Through the implementation of multiple databases, load balancing can be achieved for faster restore times. For instance, it's easy to see how it's faster to restore one database hosting 1,000 users than one database hosting 6,000 users. So, if your company has 6,000 users in Exchange 5.5, and if you only had one server (we know—this is a bit unrealistic, but we're being a bit absurd to make a point), all 6,000 will be hosted in a single database. To load-balance these users across multiple databases in Exchange 5.5, you would have needed to purchase additional servers and then move the user's mailboxes. However, with Exchange 2000 Server, you can create six databases to host 1,000 users each, or you could create 12 databases to host 500 users each, all on a single server! This can represent significant cost savings for many companies.

It should be noted that this database design is not intended to have a single mailbox hosted in a single database, since this would represent a significant overhead cost to maintain only one mailbox.

MOVING STORES AND TRANSACTION LOGS

If you want to move your stores, all you need to do is dismount the store, select a new location for the databases using the Databases tab, and click OK. The databases will be moved to their new location. It should be noted that you cannot used a mapped drive to store databases on a different server.

If you want to move the location of your transaction logs, use the General tab of the Storage Group's properties and click OK. You'll be presented with a message indicating what you are about to do and informing you that all the stores in the storage group will be dismounted while the transaction logs are moved and that users will not be able to access their information during the move. Click Yes, and the transaction logs will be moved.

PLANNING FOR MULTIPLE STORES

Now, before you dive head first into creating 20 databases, you should stop and consider the following questions. Your answers to the questions will help you decide how many databases you really need.

▼   Are multiple departments, divisions, or groups that require different backup and restore policies going to be hosted on the same server? If so, create multiple databases to accommodate these requirements. (We'll cover how this works with storage groups later in this chapter.)

■   Are certain user's activities mission critical, and do they represent a significant loss of income if the user loses e-mail capabilities? If so, consider load balancing this user group over several different databases to eliminate a single point of failure for this group. For instance, if you have a team of ten people who process Web-based orders, consider placing them in two different databases—five users per database. This will load-balance them so that if one of the databases experiences a malfunction, the other five can continue to work.

■   Do you have a time limit within which your restores must be completed, as would be the case with a Service Level Agreement (SLA)? If so, then you'll need to make sure that your database sizes can be restored within that period of time. Spreading users across multiple databases will help you achieve this goal.

■   Do you need to host multiple, independent companies on a single Exchange Server? If so, use a separate database for each company. This is most often the case for ISPs hosting e-mail for smaller companies.

■   Are you running custom software that requires its data to be hosted by an independent database? If so, create a new database for your customized software.

▲   Are your database sizes just too monstrous? If so, divide them up into smaller databases for manageability.

STORAGE GROUPS

As you can see in Figure 10-2, databases reside inside storage groups. And the first storage group that is installed, by default, is called the First Storage Group. Also, by default, within the First Storage Group, there is a Mailbox Store and a Public Store. These stores correspond to the old priv.edb and pub.edb that were used in Exchange 5.5 Server more in concept that in practice.

The storage groups are written to utilize the ESE database technology. You can have up to four storage groups per server holding a maximum of five databases per storage group. All storage groups run under the store.exe process. The storage group hosts all the databases that will utilize a common set of transaction logs. For more information, refer

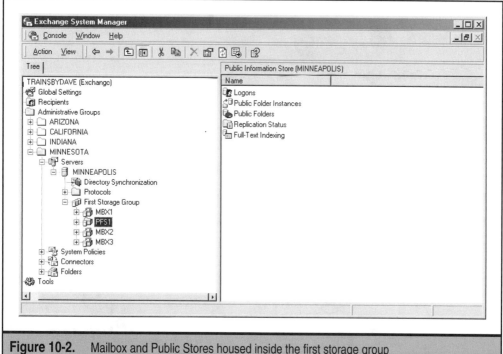

Figure 10-2.   Mailbox and Public Stores housed inside the first storage group

to the section, "Transaction Logs," later in the chapter. In terms of overhead, you should plan on at least 10MB of memory being utilized to sustain each storage group.

Storage groups are easy to set up. Simply right-click the server object in the System Manager, point to New, and select Storage Group. Figure 10-3 shows that you'll need to enter a descriptive name for this group along with the location for the transaction logs and databases. The default is c:\program files\exchsrvr, but it can be easily changed by either typing in the directory path or browsing to the location where you want the files to be held. The Log File Prefix specifies the beginning portion of each transaction log file name. This name is automatically generated and is helpful in identifying the differences between different sets of log files if all your log files are in the same directory location.

Select the Zero Out Deleted Database Pages check box if you wish for pages that hold deleted information to have zeros overwrite the deleted information. This is a good way to make sure that deleted information is not recoverable.

The Details tab is simply a place where you can enter administrative notes about the storage group you have just created. It is helpful if you are hosting multiple companies and need to remember which database belongs to which customer.

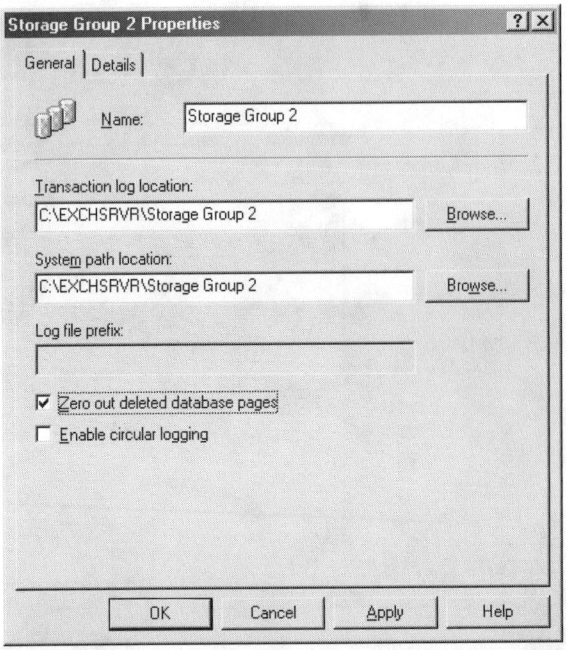

Figure 10-3. New storage group General properties tab

ESE DATABASES AND TRANSACTION LOGS

Now that you've had an introduction to the Exchange databases, transaction logs, and storage groups, its time to go one level deeper. Even though this is an introductory book on Exchange 2000 Administration, all of this information is important for you to under-stand if you are going to do a good job of managing your Exchange databases. Please do not skim this section, because even though it is detailed, it can save you hours of frustra-tion during a disaster.

ESE Databases

The ESE databases in Exchange 2000 Server are comprised of two files, the *.edb file, which we will refer to as the *rich text* file, and the *.stm file, which really has two names in the Exchange literature: the *streaming* file or the *native content store*. We'll use these names interchangeably since most of the documentation coming from Microsoft today references both of these names. And even though they are called files, they are really databases built on the B-Tree structure.

Rich Text File

The rich text file is the same database that we used in Exchange 5.5. There are few modifications to this file in Exchange 2000. It still holds information only in MDBEF format, and non-MDBEF information must still be converted before being written into the database. Consistent with ESE standards, information is held in 4KB pages inside the database. Each page will have a page number, version number, checksum, and other information that aids in ESE's ability to make sure that information is written to and read from the disk in a reliable fashion.

Streaming File

Non-MDBEF information—which, frankly, is the majority of the information that is contained these days in e-mails—will be held in the streaming file. This includes information formatted in HTTP and IMAP4. There are a couple of characteristics of this file that are important to understand. First, it is only the information that is held in this file. Overhead information for each page in the database, such as the page number and checksums, are held in the rich text file; hence, only the raw bits that represent the information are held in the streaming file. This is why any type of information can be held in this file: all it holds are the raw bits. If you know something about raw writes to RAM in UNIX, then this will make some sense for you.

Second, as part of the database overhead, each piece of information, such as a Word document or a graphics file, is assigned a unique URL. In addition, as we will learn later in this chapter, the Exchange Installable File System (ExIFS) is able to access each object as if it were a share on your LAN. This means that all the information in the file can be accessed either on the Web or on your LAN, which is very cool.

How Streaming Works

The reason this file is called a "streaming" file is due to the presence of ExIFS, which is a Win32 kernel mode driver. This driver is able to access the raw information in the streaming file and, in conjunction with the protocol stacks in IIS, streams the information to the requesting client. Hence, the information is taken directly out of the streaming file by ExIFS and passed to another kernel mode component—the Auxiliary Function Driver (AFD), which acts as a winsock driver—that then passes the information to the NT Cache Manager and out to the protocol in IIS. At no time does the streaming data enter user mode, which makes this architecture very fast and reliable. The streaming file architecture is shown here:

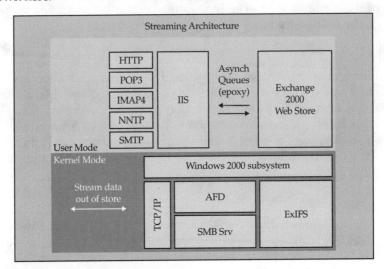

On-Demand Content Conversion

You'll recall that we discussed how Exchange 5.5 incurred a great amount of processing overhead to convert non-MDBEF formatted information before writing it to the database. In Exchange 2000, content conversion is greatly reduced, but it is still a possibility.

Recall that MAPI clients, such as those using Outlook 2000, write in MDBEF to the rich text file. If a MAPI client attempts to read a message out of the rich text file, no conversion is necessary because the MAPI client is reading information in its native format. But what happens when a MAPI client wishes to view a graphic file that is stored in the streaming file? The graphics image will be loaded into memory and presented to the client. The file is converted in the memory of the server before being presented to the client, but it is not moved from the streaming file to the rich text file. If the client makes no changes to the file and closes it, the converted information in memory is dumped and the file on disk is not changed. However, if the MAPI client decides to save the graphics file, then the converted file is moved from the streaming file to the rich text file.

This conversion of a file in the memory of the server is called *on-demand content conversion* and only occurs when a client requests non-native information from the Exchange store process.

Single-Instance Message Store

Exchange 2000 Server continues to support Single Instance Storage (SIS). What this means is that a message sent to multiple recipients will be stored only once instead of creating one copy per recipient. The goal of this architecture is to ensure that your databases remain as small as reasonably possible.

The way to understand SIS is on a one-message-per-store basis. Please refer to Figure 10-4 while reading this example. If Judy has 20 users all homed on the same database, to

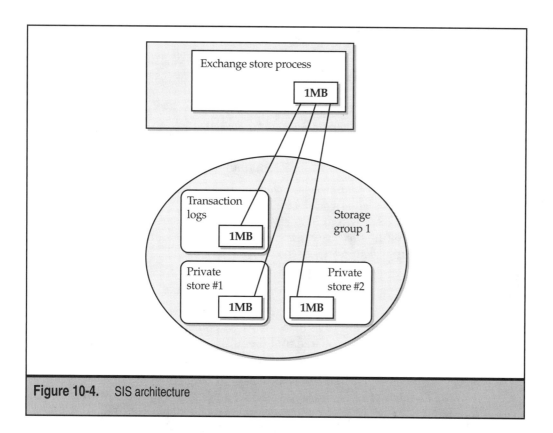

Figure 10-4.   SIS architecture

whom she wishes to send a 1MB message, without SIS, sending that message would consume 22MB of disk space: 1MB for each of the 20 recipients, 1MB for the transaction log, and 1MB for Judy's sent-items folder. However, with SIS, only 2MB of disk space is consumed: 1MB for the transaction log and 1MB for one copy to be stored in the database. Judy and her 20 recipients will simply get a handle in their in boxes pointing to the one copy of the message.

If those 20 recipients are homed on two different databases (ten in each database) in the same storage group, then a total of 3MB of disk space will be consumed: 1MB for each database and 1MB for the transaction logs. Remember that all the databases in a storage group use the same set of transaction logs.

Finally, if those 20 users are homed on two different databases, and each database is homed in a different storage group, then a total of 4MB of disk space will be needed to send the message: 1MB for each database and 1MB for each set of transaction logs.

Both of these scenarios assume that the sender is homed on at least one of the databases that is also home to some of the recipients. If the sender is homed on a different database than any of the recipients, a copy of the sender's message will be retained in the sender's home database and the message will appear under the Sent Items folder in the sender's Outlook interface.

Transaction Logs

Transaction logs are the lifeblood of your Exchange 2000 Server. Transaction logs provide the fault tolerance necessary to recover from a disaster. We can't emphasize enough that guarding and managing your transaction logs is one of the most important administrative functions you will perform. So, before we dive into transaction logs, let's lay down several administrative no-no's about managing transaction logs and their corresponding databases.

▼ **Never delete a transaction log.**   If you do, you could logically corrupt your databases but not experience a problem until days or weeks later.

■ **Never run antivirus scanning software on your transaction logs or databases**. Because antivirus software looks for a set of patterns of 1s and 0s, it is possible that a certain pattern will exist in an innocent log or page of the database. When the antivirus software attempts to fix this "problem," it will corrupt the entries in the transaction logs or the databases.

■ **Never compress your transaction logs or databases**.   You will corrupt your databases by doing so and will be forced to recover those databases from tape.

■ **Never move your databases manually**.   The transaction logs know where the databases reside on your hard disk, and if you move them manually, the transaction logs won't be able to find them. Use the methods described later in this chapter if you need to move your databases to a new location.

▲ **Never use a controller that has write-back caching enabled unless you can pull the memory chip off the controller and put it in a new controller**. Information that is written to the controller's memory but not to the disk is always subject to being lost if the controller should malfunction.

Now, in theory, the transaction log could be one giant ever-expanding file that held transactions for the ESE database; however, this file would grow to the point of running out of disk space, and that would not be a good thing.

So Microsoft has divided the transaction activities into multiple files known as *generations*. Each new transaction log is a new generation and is always 5MB in size. Transaction logs are numbered sequentially in hexadecimal, starting with E0000001.log and incrementing from there. The current generation is always named E00.log.

NOTE: The default log file prefix can be viewed on the General tab of the storage group's properties.

When the current generation becomes full, it is renamed to the next hexadecimal number and a new E00.log file is created. While this is happening, a temporary log file is created to hold transactions that occur while the new E00.log file is being generated.

Each log file consists of two parts: a header and the data. The header contains vital information for the log file to operate properly, such as the path to the databases that it references. This is why you can't start a database if you manually move the database to another location but don't change the header information in the transaction logs.

Since the same set of transaction logs are used to hold transactions for all the databases in a storage group, the administration of recovering a database is simplified because you don't have to go searching for just the right set of transaction logs to recover a database. Moreover, having multiple databases use the same set of transaction logs explains why some databases can be running while you restore another database from tape. The transaction logs can be used to perform multiple types of activities on multiple databases at the same time.

The header of a log file can be dumped using the Eseutil /ml command, as shown in Figure 10-5. The dump shows the generation number of the transaction log, the path to the database it references, and the unique signatures for the transaction log set. The data portion of the log file shows the data and where it was (or will be) inserted into the database on the disk.

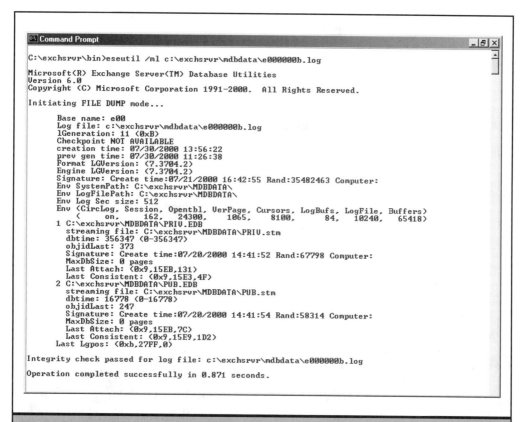

Figure 10-5.   Log file header dumped using the Eseutil /ml command

How Do Transaction Logs Work?

The main function of transaction logs is to ensure the integrity of changes to the database. Four tests are applied to each change in the database to ensure this integrity. The following list includes the four tests, which are sometimes referred to as ACID.

▼ **Atomic** Either all of the operations performed are completed or none of them are completed.

■ **Consistent** The database must be in a consistent state before and after the changes.

■ **Isolated** Changes to the database are not visible to the user until all of the operations have been performed and completed.

▲ **Durable** Changes to the databases must be preserved in the event of a system or database malfunction.

Now, we've used a couple of terms that need to be defined. An *operation* is the smallest unit of change that can be made to a database. A series of operations, when completed, comprise a *transaction*; and a transaction, once written to the transaction log, is said to have been *committed*.

So let's walk though an example of how these concepts work together, and, hopefully, you'll understand the role of transaction logs. Let's assume that John wants to move a piece of e-mail from his in box to a folder he created, called "Important." From John's perspective, this is little more than a drag-and-drop activity; however, from an ESE perspective, this represents a number of important changes to the database.

▼ The message needs to be deleted from the in box.

■ The message needs to be inserted into the Important folder.

▲ The item number for each folder needs to be updated.

Each change represents an operation. All three operations represent a single transaction. Once these operations have been completed and recorded in the transaction log, the transaction is considered committed. Because these operations are performed in a single transaction, all or none of the operations will be performed. If, during the performance of these operations, the server were to lose power, ESE will remember that this series of operations was not completed. When the store.exe process is started on reboot, ESE will roll back these operations so that the Atomic test is passed: none of the operations were performed.

Notice that in this example, we were not concerned about writing this information to the database itself. Instead, our focus was on writing information to the transaction log. This illustrates the *write-ahead* logging architecture of ESE: before we write new information or changes to the ESE database, we first write it to a transaction log. Because we are not constantly writing to the database on disk in real time, but instead use a type of *lazy write* to flush changes from memory to the ESE database at a later time, Exchange 2000 Server operates much faster and more efficiently.

Data Storage in an ESE Database

As we mentioned earlier, data is stored in 4KB pages inside the ESE database. When a change to a page in the database needs to be performed, and before the page is read into memory, the page number and checksum are verified to ensure the data is the same that was written to the disk.

NOTE: You might be wondering how large an ESE database can get in Exchange 2000 Server. An ESE database can contain up to 2^{32} or 4,292,967,296 pages. At 4KB per page, each ESE database can hold up to 16 terabytes or 17,583,994,044,416 bytes. It's safe to say that your database size limitations will be enforced by hardware limitations or corporate policy, rather than by ESE design.

Once the page is read into memory, it is considered clean. When operations are performed on the data in the page, it is marked as dirty. One transaction may require changes to many pages. Dirty pages are not written back to the ESE database in any particular order; so if your server loses power while the transaction is being written to disk, and some of the pages have been written and some have not, you need not worry. When the store.exe process is started again, those pages that were not yet written to disk from memory will be written from the transaction log to your database and your database will be updated.

When you start the information store service in the Services utility, the majority of the activity is comparing the transactions in the logs to the database and making sure that all such transactions have been flushed to the database, and that the database is in a consistent state. Should there be a failure in this process, you will receive an error message and the database will not be able to start.

There is no one way to know when committed transactions in the log files are written to the database; however, there are some guidelines. Committed transactions in the log file are written to disk when one of the following occurs:

▼   The checkpoint falls too far behind in a pervious log file. If the number of committed transactions in the log file reaches a certain threshold, ESE will flush these changes to disk.

■   If the number of free pages in memory becomes too low and affects overall system performance, ESE will flush committed transactions in memory to the disk in an effort to free up pages for system use.

■   If another application or service starts and needs additional memory, ESE will flush committed transactions to the disk to free up pages in memory for that application.

■   When the store.exe process is shut down, all committed transactions in memory are written to the disk before the process can shut down cleanly.

▲   Whenever a full backup is run on the databases with software that is specifically written to flush committed transactions from memory to the database. Examples of such software include Legato, ArcServe, Backup Exec, and Windows 2000 Backup.

ESE and Memory Management

Before a page can be loaded into memory, that area of memory must first be allocated by ESE for its own use. It would be terribly inefficient to allocate memory in 4KB blocks on demand. This would slow down Exchange services considerably. Thus, ESE takes care of this by allocating memory for itself in advance of when the memory is needed.

NOTE: In Exchange 4.0 and 5.0, the cache was set by the Performance Optimizer, and in Exchange 5.5, it is dynamically managed by ESE.

The process that is used by ESE to allocate memory to itself is called *Dynamic Buffer Allocation (DBA)*. Many Exchange Administrators report that their store.exe process eats up all the available RAM on their Exchange Servers. They are surprised to learn that this is by design.

You see, when ESE allocates memory to itself, it takes into consideration the other applications that are running on the same server, as well as its own anticipated needs. It will not allocate memory to the point of hurting the performance of other applications, and it won't consume all available RAM unless it feels that it is necessary to do so. In either event, if another application should start and that application requires memory that is currently being held by ESE, it will release the memory for the other application on demand so that it can run efficiently.

Hence, if you go into Task Manager and see that the store.exe process is consuming two to three times the amount of RAM above the other processes, don't be alarmed. This is by design and your Exchange Server is not experiencing a memory leak.

Circular Logging

There needs to be a way to ensure that the transaction logs representing transactions that have been committed to the database are eventually deleted. Usually, the way to manage this process is to allow your backup software to accomplish this activity. When the Exchange databases are backed up properly but before the process starts, the transactions in the transaction logs are flushed to the database and verified for integrity. Then the backup software purges the unneeded logs.

There might be situations, however, when recovery of information is not important, such as when your Exchange Server is active as a smarthost or relay server. In this situation, you could consider implementing Circular Logging.

Circular Logging means that ESE will not continue to create new transaction logs, but will recycle its use of logs through the same five log files; thus, when log number five becomes full, instead of creating a sixth log, the first log will be used as the E00.log and transactions in that log file will be overwritten. Of course, the original transactions are first flushed to the database on the disk before they are overwritten.

Since transactions in the log files are overwritten, you will not be able to utilize the write-ahead features of ESE during a recovery operation. Hence, when Circular Logging is enabled, you can only recover to the last full backup. Therefore, only enable circular logging when recovery of data is not important.

Real World

To illustrate, a client called one day to complain that the disk on their Exchange Server was running out of room because of "all these log files." That seemed a bit strange since they were running a very popular backup software program and doing a full backup of their Exchange databases each night. After arriving on site, it was discovered that they had close to 200 transaction logs sitting in the transaction log folder. Fortunately, the main contact there did not delete any of these log files. The backup software was not reporting any error messages in the logs of the backup program or in the Event Viewer. However, the backup job itself had been sitting on hold since August of the previous year. In other words, none of their Exchange information had been backed up in over six months! Changing the job to active and letting it immediately run was the fix. The next day, there was only one transaction log. The backup software had purged the other unneeded 199 logs.

It's important to note in this story that all 200 transaction logs were vital to their operation until they had been backed up. If any of these transaction logs had been deleted before the backup program was run, they would have certainly lost some information and probably would have corrupted their database the next time the store.exe process was started.

To enable Circular Logging, open the Storage Group Properties (Figure 10-6) and select the Enable Circular Logging check box.

Data Reliability: –1018 errors

Some people believe that the ESE database design is inherently less reliable than database designs used by other groupware vendors. This is not true, though one can understand why some people come to this conclusion.

The ESE development team made a conscious choice to check the physical bits on the disk to ensure the integrity of the data at the application layer. It is of utmost importance that you can trust the data written to the disk. This will give you confidence that what is read from the disk is the same data that was written to the disk.

A –1018 error occurs when Exchange is given a page with an incorrect page number or an incorrect checksum. Each time Exchange writes a data page to disk, it includes the page number and checksum in the page header. When the page is later read from the disk, the checksum is recalculated and the page number is verified to ensure it matches what was requested. If either of these verifications fail, meaning that the checksums don't match or the page number doesn't match, then a –1018 error is generated. You should interpret a –1018 error message as indicating that at least one page in your database is damaged. Do not ignore this error message since doing so will likely lead to further corruption.

Notice that Exchange only detects the damaged page, it doesn't cause the damage. Injury to the data is always caused by a lower subsystem failure. If an underlying device

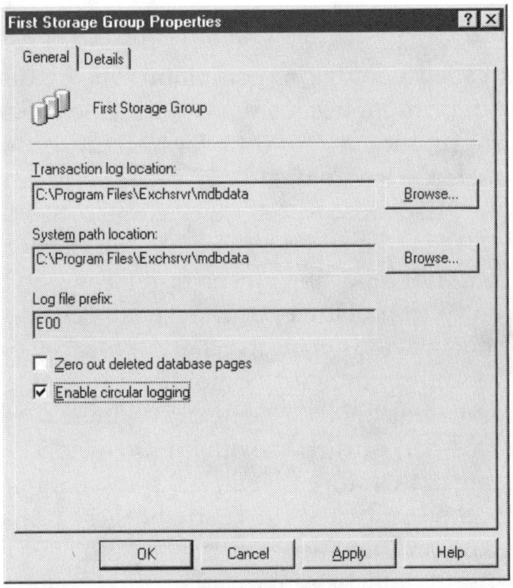

Figure 10-6. Enable Circular Logging check box in First Storage Group Properties

goes bad or malfunctions, it will return bad data to the operating system. When Exchange detects that the data is bad, it will issue a –1018 error.

The causes of –1018 errors are hardware related and can include an improperly terminated SCSI bus or other types of SCSI equipment failures. Also, if your server loses power during a write operation, the information may be corrupted while it's being written to the disk.

In addition, if you have a controller with a cache chip that has write-back caching enabled, it is possible for information to be written to its cache, but not to disk, and then have the controller malfunction. In this case, if the cache is not transferable to the replacement controller, then its information will be lost and this will corrupt the database. This is because the controller reported back to the Exchange operating system that the information was written to disk when, in fact, it was not; hence, Exchange will think there is information inserted into the database that doesn't exist. When it calls for that information, the checksums and page numbers won't match and a –1018 error will be generated.

Some software-related activities that can generate a –1018 error include running an antivirus software package that is not Exchange aware. In fact, any software that directly manipulates the database file will corrupt the file and result in a host of errors, including a –1018 error. Compression utilities will have the same effect.

Hardware origins of this type of error message are the most difficult to troubleshoot because they are the least obvious. If you thought you had a hardware problem, you'd fix it, right? Well, if you get some –1018 errors, then consider contacting your hardware vendor to make sure you have the latest firmware and device driver. If possible, have them run some detailed diagnostics on your hardware to see if it is working properly. And remember that you can contact Microsoft Technical Support, and they will work in tandem with your hardware vendor to help solve your problem. They are keenly interested in making sure they know about all the hardware bugs out there that negatively affect Exchange performance.

These –1018 errors are often detected during the backup process. This is because, during a full backup, each page is read from the disk and its checksums and page numbers are verified before being written to the tape. This design ensures that the database being written to the tape is without errors and that your backup integrity is preserved. When the backup process encounters a mismatch on a page in the database, the backup will not continue and you will be notified. Microsoft decided to always check for data integrity and to tell you if there is a problem, even if they don't have a solution.

If you receive a –1018 error during the backup, you might find that everything runs just fine and you'll be lulled into a false sense that you don't need to solve this problem right away. However, the longer you run, the higher the number of log files that will need to be replayed during recovery, and this will increase the opportunities for further corruption. Exchange 2000 will not allow a new, full backup to complete until this problem is fixed.

There are several items you should check when you receive a –1018 error:

▼ The event logs for hardware errors

■ SCSI errors and proper termination

■ Software that might directly modify the data files

■ Recent operations procedures that might cause the error

▲ High levels of recovered errors on your hard drives, which might indicate that one of your drives is malfunctioning with I/O errors

You should also ask your hardware vendor to run low-level diagnostics on your hardware.

ExIFS

The ExIFS represents a major shift in how you'll think about document management. Until the release of Exchange 2000 Server, you needed several different types of servers to manage your documents: file server for files, a Web Server for Web pages, and a messaging server for e-mail messages. With the advent of the ExIFS, which is also known as the *Web store*, all this changes. You can now host all types of documents in the streaming file in Exchange 2000 Server and access them from anywhere, given that you have the proper permissions. Let's take a look at this exciting development more closely.

The ExIFS exposes each folder and object in the store as file shares. This means that a client can map a drive directly to a folder inside an Exchange database using the normal methods we are accustomed to in Microsoft products. For instance, a user can assign a drive letter to a mapped resource and use standard applications, such as Explorer or Word, to read and write data directly in or out of the store. By default, the M: drive letter is automatically mapped to the share name of *backofficestorage*. However, you cannot map a drive to this share. Instead, you can use Explorer to share folders inside this drive letter and then map drives to the shared folder.

As shown in Figure 10-7, there are two default folders, the MBX folder and the Public Folders folder. The MBX folder is the root folder for all mailboxes on the server. When you attempt to access the mailboxes through this folder, however, the mailbox names will be invisible unless you have permissions to view the names, as shown in Figure 10-8. Once you have navigated to this point, all the items in the in box will respond to normal DOS commands, such as DIR, COPY, and DELETE. Messages will have an *.eml extension, as shown here:

```
Command Prompt                                                              _ □ ×

M:\MINNESOTA.TRAINSBYDAVE.com\MBX\SJones\inbox>dir
 Volume in drive M is Exchange
 Volume Serial Number is 00A9-8AC7

 Directory of M:\MINNESOTA.TRAINSBYDAVE.com\MBX\SJones\inbox

07/30/2000  04:38p    <DIR>          .
07/30/2000  04:38p    <DIR>          ..
07/21/2000  08:58a             629 Meeting on Monday-c6a98d81-5e75-11d4-a141-00a0c9101658-1
715-M.EML
07/21/2000  08:59a          41,236 RE%3A Meeting on Monday-c6a98d81-5e75-11d4-a141-00a0c910
1658-1716-M.EML
              2 File(s)        41,865 bytes
              2 Dir(s)   2,383,415,808 bytes free

M:\MINNESOTA.TRAINSBYDAVE.com\MBX\SJones\inbox>_
```

If you want to see a message's content, use the TYPE command, which is illustrated in Figure 10-9.

When accessing a Public Store though the M: drive, the public folders are visible inside the command prompt, as shown here:

```
Command Prompt                                                              _ □ ×

M:\MINNESOTA.TRAINSBYDAVE.com>cd public folders

M:\MINNESOTA.TRAINSBYDAVE.com\public folders>dir
 Volume in drive M is Exchange
 Volume Serial Number is 00A9-8AC7

 Directory of M:\MINNESOTA.TRAINSBYDAVE.com\public folders

07/30/2000  04:46p    <DIR>          .
07/30/2000  04:46p    <DIR>          ..
07/21/2000  04:44p    <DIR>          Internet Newsgroups
07/29/2000  04:19p    <DIR>          Company Suggestion Box
07/29/2000  04:20p    <DIR>          Company Classifieds
              0 File(s)             0 bytes
              5 Dir(s)   2,381,049,856 bytes free

M:\MINNESOTA.TRAINSBYDAVE.com\public folders>
```

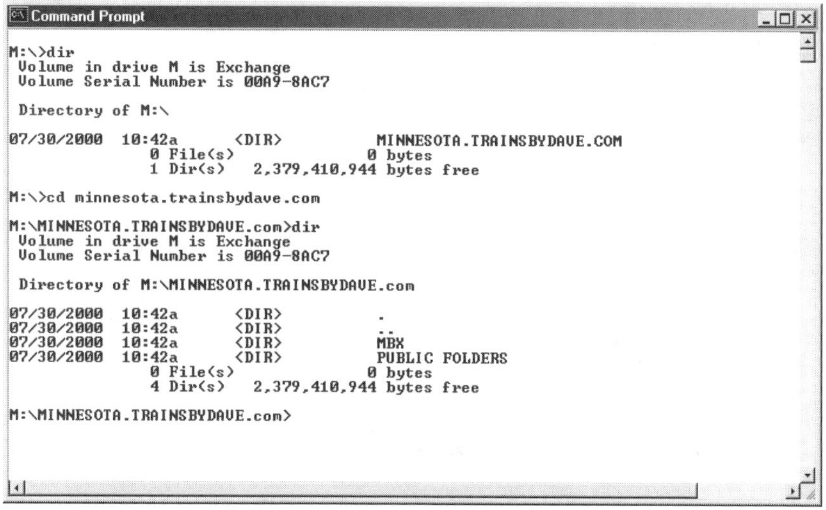

```
Command Prompt                                                      _ □ ×
M:\>dir
 Volume in drive M is Exchange
 Volume Serial Number is 00A9-8AC7

 Directory of M:\

07/30/2000  10:42a    <DIR>          MINNESOTA.TRAINSBYDAVE.COM
                0 File(s)            0 bytes
                1 Dir(s)   2,379,410,944 bytes free

M:\>cd minnesota.trainsbydave.com

M:\MINNESOTA.TRAINSBYDAVE.com>dir
 Volume in drive M is Exchange
 Volume Serial Number is 00A9-8AC7

 Directory of M:\MINNESOTA.TRAINSBYDAVE.com

07/30/2000  10:42a    <DIR>          .
07/30/2000  10:42a    <DIR>          ..
07/30/2000  10:42a    <DIR>          MBX
07/30/2000  10:42a    <DIR>          PUBLIC FOLDERS
                0 File(s)            0 bytes
                4 Dir(s)   2,379,410,944 bytes free

M:\MINNESOTA.TRAINSBYDAVE.com>
```

Figure 10-7. MBX and public folders in the M: drive

```
Command Prompt                                                      _ □ ×
07/30/2000  10:42a    <DIR>          MINNESOTA.TRAINSBYDAVE.COM
                0 File(s)            0 bytes
                1 Dir(s)   2,379,410,944 bytes free

M:\>cd minnesota.trainsbydave.com

M:\MINNESOTA.TRAINSBYDAVE.com>dir
 Volume in drive M is Exchange
 Volume Serial Number is 00A9-8AC7

 Directory of M:\MINNESOTA.TRAINSBYDAVE.com

07/30/2000  10:42a    <DIR>          .
07/30/2000  10:42a    <DIR>          ..
07/30/2000  10:42a    <DIR>          MBX
07/30/2000  10:42a    <DIR>          PUBLIC FOLDERS
                0 File(s)            0 bytes
                4 Dir(s)   2,379,410,944 bytes free

M:\MINNESOTA.TRAINSBYDAVE.com>cd MBX

M:\MINNESOTA.TRAINSBYDAVE.com\MBX>dir
 Volume in drive M is Exchange
 Volume Serial Number is 00A9-8AC7

 Directory of M:\MINNESOTA.TRAINSBYDAVE.com\MBX

07/30/2000  10:42a    <DIR>          .
07/30/2000  10:42a    <DIR>          ..
07/30/2000  10:42a    <DIR>          MINNEAPOLIS-SA
07/30/2000  10:42a    <DIR>          SJones
07/30/2000  10:42a    <DIR>          SystemMailbox{54E0FDB3-E9B3-48EA-964F-B2168FA
07/30/2000  10:42a    <DIR>          MINNEAPOLIS-SRS
07/30/2000  10:42a    <DIR>          SystemMailbox{89BDAA99-EFE0-4EA0-A7E8-B8417DD
07/30/2000  10:42a    <DIR>          SystemMailbox{9EC84862-5666-4EA2-91F5-9A0F470
                0 File(s)            0 bytes
                8 Dir(s)   2,379,402,752 bytes free

M:\MINNESOTA.TRAINSBYDAVE.com\MBX>
```

Figure 10-8. Showing the names of the mailboxes in the MBX folder

```
Command Prompt                                                                    _ |8|X|
07/30/2000  04:38p    <DIR>         .
07/30/2000  04:38p    <DIR>         ..
07/21/2000  08:58a              629 Meeting on Monday-c6a98d81-5e75-11d4-a141-00a0c9101658-1
715-M.EML
07/21/2000  08:59a           41,236 RE%3A Meeting on Monday-c6a98d81-5e75-11d4-a141-00a0c910
1658-1716-M.EML
07/30/2000  04:45p            1,115 Type.EML
                  3 File(s)      42,980 bytes
                  2 Dir(s)   2,381,025,280 bytes free

M:\MINNESOTA.TRAINSBYDAVE.com\MBX\SJones\inbox>Type type.eml
Received: by minneapolis.trainsbydave.com
         id <01BFFA6F.691D2AE0@minneapolis.trainsbydave.com>; Sun, 30 Jul 2000 16:45:00 -0500
content-class: urn:content-classes:message
Subject: Type
Date: Sun, 30 Jul 2000 16:44:59 -0500
Message-ID: <818DA9C6755ED411A14100A0C91016581B1C@minneapolis.trainsbydave.com>
X-MS-Has-Attach:
MIME-Version: 1.0
Content-Type: text/html;
        charset="iso-8859-1"
Content-Transfer-Encoding: binary
X-MS-TNEF-Correlator:
Thread-Topic: Type
Thread-Index: Ab/6b2jettvkppRbQmmCHvNniiOh0Q==
From: "Jones, Sam" <SJones@MINNESOTA.TRAINSBYDAVE.com>
X-MimeOLE: Produced By Microsoft Exchange V6.0.4368.4
To: "Jones, Sam" <SJones@MINNESOTA.TRAINSBYDAVE.com>

<!DOCTYPE HTML PUBLIC "-//W3C//DTD HTML 3.2//EN">
<HTML>
<HEAD>
<META HTTP-EQUIV="Content-Type" CONTENT="text/html; charset=iso-8859-1">
<META NAME="Generator" CONTENT="MS Exchange Server version 6.0.4368.4">
<TITLE>Type</TITLE>
</HEAD>
<BODY>
<!-- Converted from text/rtf format -->

<P><FONT SIZE=2 FACE="Arial">I can use the TYPE command to read a message in the command prompt
.</FONT>
</P>

</BODY>
</HTML>
M:\MINNESOTA.TRAINSBYDAVE.com\MBX\SJones\inbox>_
```

Figure 10-9.   Use of the TYPE command to read the contents of a message in Sue Smith's mailbox

Items in the Exchange database can also be accessed through a URL. For instance, a public folder named Company Documents that is housed on the server Minneapolis would have as its URL **http://minneapolis/public/company documents**.

Items inside the public folders, such as networkdiagram.doc, would simply append the URL with the item name, making the entire URL **http://minneapolis/public/company documents/networkdiagram.doc**.

Messages in the in box of SJones on the Minneapolis server would have the URL **http://minneapolis.trainsbydave.com/exchange/sjones/inbox/type.eml**, as shown in Figure 10-10. The default item URL generated is based on the subject of the message and the display name of the folder, not the alias. An item URL is an attribute of the item object and is, therefore, customizable should an application need to do so.

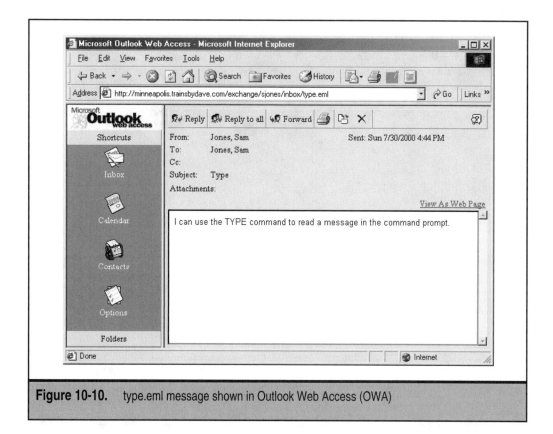

Figure 10-10.   type.eml message shown in Outlook Web Access (OWA)

If you want to find these documents through Explorer, our third method of accessing data in the store, you can do so by navigating the M: drive. Figure 10-11 illustrates how to do this.

And if you want to use Word or Excel to access an Office document in a public or private folder, then use the M: drive as illustrated in Figure 10-12. Once this is accomplished, all you'll need to do is open the document with its native program. Even though we have illustrated how to use Word to find and open a document, you are not required to do so. You can also open the document by double-clicking it either from Explorer or through OWA. When double-clicking the document in OWA, the program will open inside the browser, which will require that the program be loaded locally on the browser's machine.

Once opened inside the browser, modifications cannot be saved back to the public folder unless a Web folder was used to open the document in the first place. Now, you might be wondering, what is a Web folder? Well, a Web folder is a type of connection created on the client in My Network Places that routes traffic between an application and a

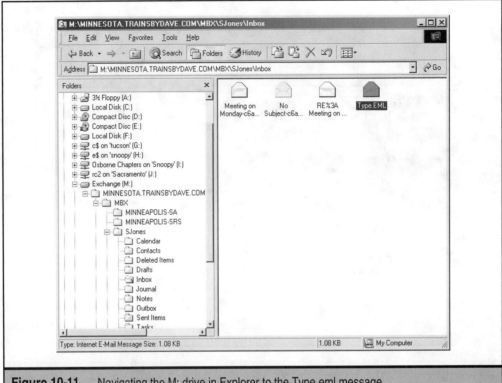

Figure 10-11.   Navigating the M: drive in Explorer to the Type.eml message

document over port 80. This allows a user to open a document from the Web store over the Internet, modify that document, and save it back to the store. All this traffic will occur over port 80. Writes to the document in the Web store will use XML. Take a look at how this works.

First, to create a Web folder, double-click the My Network Places icon on the desktop, and then double-click the Add Network Place icon. This will invoke the Welcome to the Add Network Place Wizard, as illustrated in Figure 10-13. Input the location of the network place you want to add. For purposes of our present discussion, you'll want to add a URL, such as **http://www.trainsbydave.com/public**.

When you click Next, if the location you are attempting to reach requires a username and password to log on, you'll then receive the Enter Network Password dialog box. Enter your username and password, and click OK. Once you do this, you'll receive the Completing the Add Network Place Wizard screen, where you'll be able to click Finish and the Web folder will be created, as illustrated in Figure 10-14. In this instance, we've created two

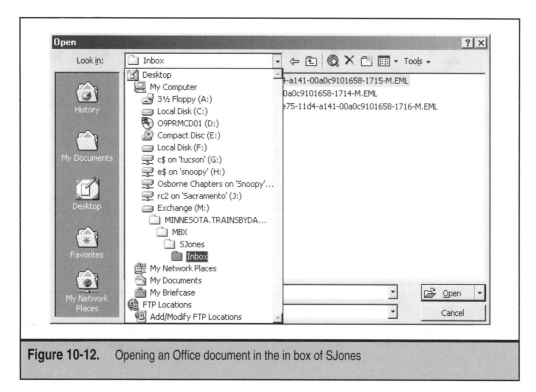

Figure 10-12.   Opening an Office document in the in box of SJones

Figure 10-13.   Welcome to the Add Network Place Wizard

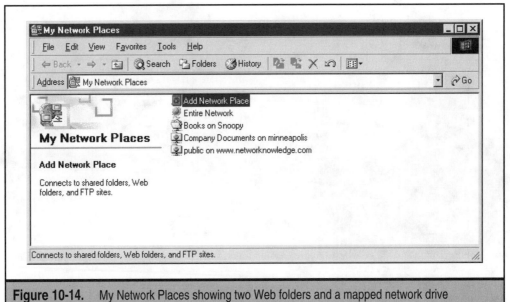

Figure 10-14.   My Network Places showing two Web folders and a mapped network drive

Web folders, one to the Company Documents public folder in the trainsbydave.com (shown as Company Documents on Minneapolis) and the other to the public folder hierarchy at **http://www.networknowledge.com**. You'll also notice that there is a mapped network drive to the Books share on the server Snoopy. Notice the difference in the icons.

Once a Web folder is created, it is treated as another location from which files may be opened and to which files may be saved. The beauty of this technology is that you no longer need to worry about using Briefcase or the Synchonrization Manager in Windows 2000. Instead, your users, when traveling, can simply connect to the Internet, open and modify files over port 80, and then save them back to your Exchange Server. And they can use the Office suite to work with these files.

In our illustration, we will open Word locally, create a new word document (illustration1.doc), and save it to a public folder at **www.networknowledge.com** using the Web folder we just created. Figure 10-15 shows the new document that has been created in Word 2000. Figure 10-16 shows how the Save As dialog box will look when the file is saved using a Web folder.

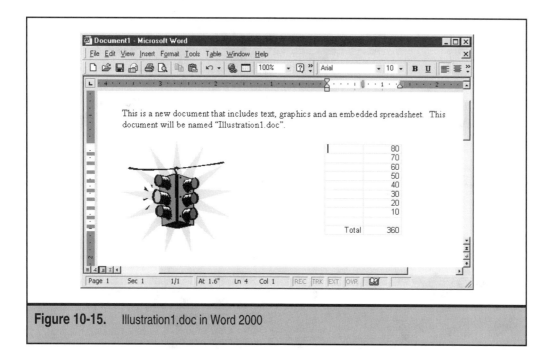

Figure 10-15.   Illustration1.doc in Word 2000

As the file is being saved, you'll see a box pop up indicating that the file is being transferred out of the memory space of the client to the memory space of the server using the Web folder to route this traffic over port 80, as shown here:

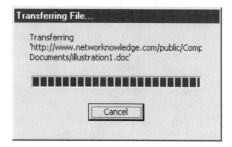

Once you've played around with this a bit, you'll want your traveling users to use Web folders. In fact, users who work from home will want to use this feature, too. We

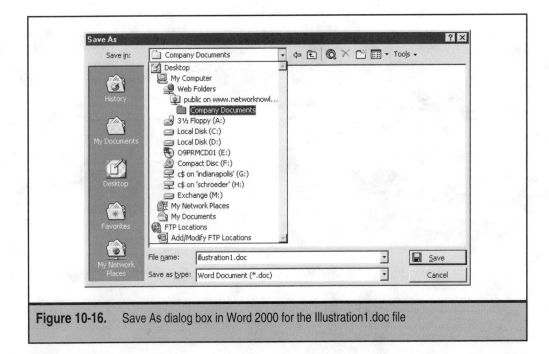

Figure 10-16. Save As dialog box in Word 2000 for the Illustration1.doc file

think this is one of the strongest selling points for Exchange 2000 Server and is one of the new features that will drive this product's sales.

There are several miscellaneous items to remember about the IFS. First, only Win32 properties are exposed to the user. If there are items saved in the streaming file that have properties other than what the Win32 Application Programming Interface (API) will recognize, then the properties won't be available for property promotion.

Second, at the time of this writing, most virus software performs its scanning on data after it has been committed to the disk. Microsoft has written APIs for virus scanning that use event sinks to scan messages before the message is committed to the database. Scanning can be performed in the precategorizer, the categorizer, or the postcategorizer queue. Since all messages are passed though these three queues before being written to disk or sent to another server, this is obviously the recommended way to perform antivirus scanning in Exchange 2000. For more information on these queues and the transport core, see Chapter 11.

INDEXING SERVICES

The indexing services in Exchange 2000 Server are written to index selected stores, which you can configure, in advance of a user's query. This proactive approach means that

MAPI text searches return results much more quickly to the end user. In addition, attachments can be indexed to allow a user's query results to include these attachments. This leads to better information being returned to the user.

Content indexing is fully integrated with the Exchange setup and is easily implemented in the Exchange System Manager utility. You configure indexing on a per-store basis and have the option of either enabling or disabling indexing as needed for each store. In addition, you can manually trigger an indexing operation on a given store or you can schedule the indexes to update automatically.

The type of documents that are indexed include

▼ Embedded Multipurpose Internet Mail Extensions (MIME) messages (.eml)

■ HTML (.html, .htm, and .asp)

■ Microsoft Excel (.xls)

■ Microsoft PowerPoint (.ppt)

■ Microsoft Word (.doc)

▲ Text files (.txt)

Full-text indexing searches for words found within messages and attachments, and uses a word-based approach. If a search for a word is performed and the search results include both a message and an attachment, the return set will only identify the messages, not the specific attachments within the message.

The service under which indexing runs is the MSSearch service. Since all searches occur within the Exchange program, it is responsible for all security enforcement. The Exchange Query Processor (QP) handles query splitting and result merging for the users. In addition, Exchange 2000 supports notification-based indexing, allowing notifications to be sent given the occurrence of predetermined events.

Let's take a look at the Search architecture by illustrating how Search works. First, using the Outlook Advanced Find dialog box, a user issues a search request for a file named networkdiagram and a document size of less than 2MB, as shown in Figure 10-17. (Use the More Choices tab to specify the document size.) In order to accomplish this, the user will first need to specify Files in the Look For drop-down list box, since it defaults to messages instead of files. Also, by clicking the Browse button, the user can select folders on which to perform the search.

The QP determines that the search should be evaluated using a free-text query and sends this part of the search to MSSearch. MSSearch then generates the results, categorizes the results to that of the query, and returns the matches to the QP.

At this point, because the query has two parts, the QP evaluates the size of the items in the result set and weeds out those that exceed 2MB. Then Exchange enforces the security settings on the items, and those left in the result set are returned to the user (Figure 10-18).

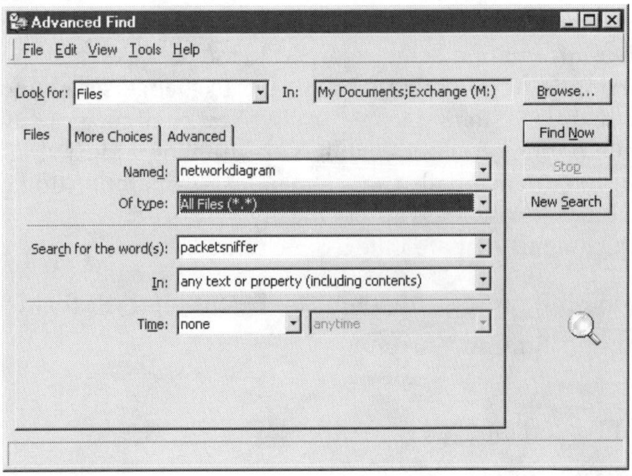

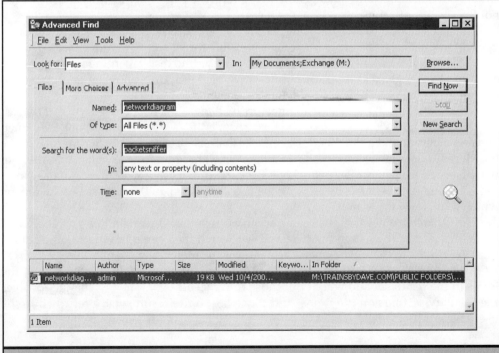

Figure 10-17. Performing an Advanced Find in Outlook 2000 for the file networkdiagram with the search word packetsniffer

Figure 10-18. Results of Advanced Search on Company Document public folder

To set up Indexing on a store, right-click the store and select Create Full-Text Index. Once you do this, you'll be asked for a location to store the catalog; then the index objects will be created under the Full-Text Indexing container. However, at this point, you have not started the indexing process.

To start the indexing process, right-click the store object again and select Start Full Population. Depending on the size of your store, this process could take from several minutes to several hours. When it is finished (refer to Figure 10-19) the indexing objects will indicate this by having definite values for the indexing objects, such as a definite last build time and an index size. There is also a feature called *Property Promotion,* with which searches can be performed against one or more properties of an object class. And since MSSearch doesn't index all the possible properties of each object, when a nonindexed property is queried, that property is said to be *promoted* so that it can be used in the search process.

To illustrate, we made *migration* a keyword for the file Exchange 2000 Migration Issues, a document held in the Company Documents public folder. By using the Advanced Find feature in Outlook 2000, we were able to navigate to the Advanced tab, use the Field drop-down list to point to Files, and then select Keyword. Thereafter, we entered "migration" and added it to the Find items that match this criteria pane (Figure 10-20).

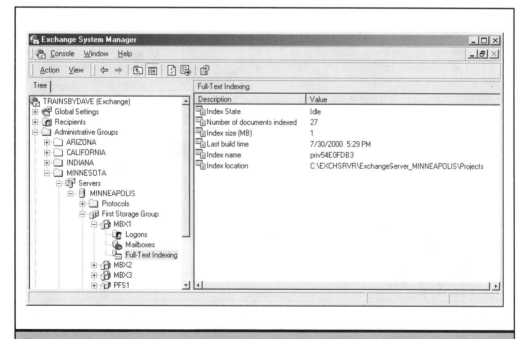

Figure 10-19.   Full-Text Indexing objects created for MBX1 on the Minneapolis server

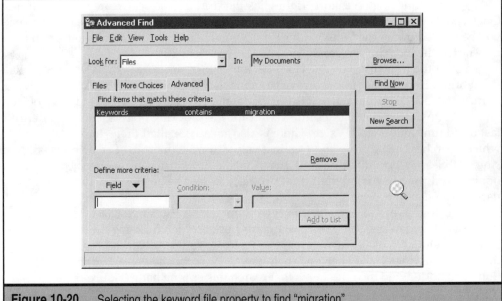

Figure 10-20.   Selecting the keyword file property to find "migration"

After making our selections, we were able to perform the search, and MSSearch returned the results we were looking for.

Now, you might be wondering how often the index is built. Happily, Microsoft has given us flexibility in the area by allowing us to choose when the index is built. This is accomplished by navigating to the store's properties and customizing the index schedule on the Full-Text Indexing tab.

And since the building of the index is an intensive task, you can set the system resource usage level on the Full-Text Indexing tab of the server's properties. Your choices are minimum, low, high, or maximum.

FE/BE ARCHITECTURE

As we stated previously, an FE/BE architecture will have a bank of front-end servers providing protocol access to a bank of back-end servers hosting Exchange 2000 databases. For instance, if you have a large base of OWA users, you might want to have several servers providing HTTP protocol access to a bank of servers that host these user's mailboxes.

Using an FE/BE architecture has several advantages, which are explained in the following list:

▼   Multiple servers can be deployed inside a single namespace. For instance, you can define a single namespace for OWA users to access their mailboxes, such as **http:// www.trainsbydave.com/mail**. Without an FE/BE architecture, each user must know the name of the server that is storing his or her mailbox. This can be an inflexible arrangement if your users move around often or if you are required to move their mailboxes, because you must inform them of their new server's name in order for them to open their mailboxes.

■ If you need or want to run Secure Sockets Layer (SSL), then the FE/BE architecture might be a good solution for you because the FE Servers handle all encryption and decryption processing, which improves performance on the BE Servers.

▲ If you are using a firewall, the FE Server can be positioned as the single point of access on or behind the firewall. Since the FE Server has no critical information on it, an additional layer of security is provided.

FE/BE architecture works differently with each protocol, so we'll need to discuss each protocol independently as it relates to this architecture.

HTTP and OWA

When an FE Server receives an HTTP request, it first uses AD to determine which BE Server the request should be proxied to. Specifically, it is looking to see which server is the home server for the requested mailbox or public folder. The FE Server uses LDAP to contact AD.

Traffic between the FE and BE Servers is always handled over port 80, which means that SSL is not available for use in this transaction, though clients can use SSL to communicate with an FE Server. Also, any virtual servers on the back-end that differentiate themselves only by port number, and not by port number and Internet Protocol (IP) address, are not supported in this topology. Therefore, if your BE Servers need to host multiple virtual servers for a particular protocol, then you should plan on using a separate IP address for each virtual server.

Now, there are two ways for a user to access his or her mailbox when using OWA. The first method is known as the *implicit* logon, which means that the username being requested is not specified in the URL. For instance, **http://www.trainsbydave.com/ exchange** is an implicit logon.

Implicit logons require authentication at the FE Server. Once the user is authenticated, then his or her security token is associated with the user's account in AD and mailbox in the Exchange store. Then the FE Server updates the URL and passes it on to the BE Server.

Not surprisingly, an *explicit* logon occurs when the username is specified in the URL. For instance, **http://www.trainsbydave.com/exchange/benglish** is an explicit URL. In this scenario, the FE Server does not perform authentication—that is left to the BE Server. The FE Server still conducts an AD lookup, associates the URL with the mailbox, and forwards the request on to the BE Server.

For public folders (PF), the virtual directory in IIS is public, by default; and for those hosting applications, their directory must be set up in the System Manager snap-in. (To learn how to do this, consult Chapter 6.) As with a user's LAN connection, when an OWA user is authenticated in the domain, the user's default public folder tree is also obtained from AD by the FE Server, and the request is then forwarded to the appropriate Exchange 2000 Server. This consistency ensures that a user will see the same data whether connecting from Outlook or from a browser.

If the user is attempting to connect to a PF tree that hosts a specialized application, the FE Server will forward this request to the BE Server because there is no corresponding information about the application in AD. The BE Server will perform the authentication of the user.

Speaking of authentication, this topology only supports Basic authentication. SSL can be combined with Basic to achieve a higher degree of security. This also means that Windows Integrated Security (WIS), Windows Challenge/Response (NTLM), Kerberos, and Digest authentication methods are not supported by Exchange 2000 HTTP FE Servers.

To set up pass-through authentication to the BE Server, set up the FE Server for anonymous authentication so that it does not challenge the user for authorization. Then, set up the BE Server for Basic authentication, and it will perform the challenge to the user. Remember that SSL is not available in this topology.

POP3 and IMAP4 Protocols

The architecture here is similar for both protocols. When a user issues a logon request to the FE Server, it will contain the name of the mailbox to be accessed. The FE Server will not authenticate the user and will use AD to determine which BE Server the user's request should be proxied to. The BE Server will perform the logon request and then send commands back and forth to the user via the FE Server.

Deployment Considerations

While there are no hard-and-fast numbers from Microsoft or anyone else, it is recommended that you deploy one FE Server for every four BE Servers. If this doesn't work for you, don't worry about it. Deploy the number of FE and BE Servers you need, and perform consistent monitoring to determine if a different ratio is best for you.

Keep in mind that you should have two or more GC Servers available to the FE Servers for fast lookups. If possible, check whether you can make your FE Servers DCs, unless they are sitting outside your firewall. This would reduce network traffic for directory lookups. Of course, this would also mean that your FE Servers would be engaged in regular directory replication traffic, something that you may not want your FE Servers to be doing.

Setting Up Different Scenarios

To set up an FE/BE topology, first you must set up a single Exchange 2000 Server as an FE Server. To do this, navigate to the server's properties in the System Manager snap-in, and on the General tab, select the This Is a Front End Server check box. Be sure that all virtual directories in IIS point to this server and that any alias names in the DNS, such as WWW, are resolved to this server as well.

Next, you should move all mailboxes and public folders off the FE Server, stop and dismount all the Exchange stores and delete them, and then stop and restart all the protocol services.

Now, by default, the IMAP4 and POP3 protocol services are dependent on the MSExchangeIS service running. This is not needed on the FE Server, so, if you'd like, you can remove this dependency by editing the following registry key:

HEKY_LOCAL_MACHINE\System\CurrentControlSet\Services\IMAP4SVC or POP3SVC\DependOnService

Remove the entry for MSExchangeIS in the MultiString editor and this will remove this dependency.

If you want to install a bank of FE Servers, then you'll need to make sure that the Windows Network Load Balancing (WNLB) service or another round-robin solution, such as DNS round robin or a hardware load-balancing solution, is installed. The WNLB is only useful if you're going to have multiple FE Servers.

WNLB ensures high availability of the FE Servers. This service spreads across multiple servers user requests over the same or multiple protocols. You can scale up to 32 hosts in a single deployment using WNLB. You will assign a virtual IP address to the cluster (no, this is not Cluster Server, but the FE Servers are said to be in a *cluster* when discussing WNLB concepts), and this presents a unified system to the users. When you install either Windows 2000 Advanced Server or Windows 2000 DataCenter, WNLB is automatically installed. All that needs to be done is to check the box in network properties (Figure 10-21) and then configure the service.

Architecturally, WNLB is implemented as an intermediate driver above the Network Interface Card (NIC) driver at the Data Link Layer but below the IP at the network layer. WNLB runs in Unicast mode, which means that the Media Access Control (MAC) address is set to the same value for all the hosts in the cluster. This way, packets are delivered in parallel to each host and those that are not intended for a particular host are filtered out. In other words, all traffic is sent to all the servers in the cluster, but one host decides to accept the

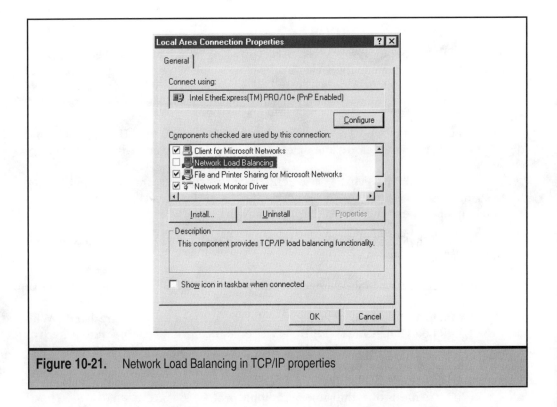

Figure 10-21.   Network Load Balancing in TCP/IP properties

packet. Algorithms run on each server to determine which server will accept which packet; furthermore, subsequent client requests are load balanced as well.

To learn more about how to configure WNLB, consult the *Windows 2000 Server Resource Kit* by Microsoft Press.

To configure the BE Server for HTTP access, open the System Manager snap-in, navigate to the HTTP folder under the server object, right-click the folder, and select New Virtual Server (Figure 10-22).

Give the server a unique name that will help you identify its use, and then click the Advanced button and add an identity for the virtual server that defines, via the hostname, the front-end namespace. The TCP port must be port 80, and the SSL port may be left at the default of 443 or another port may be chosen. Once the virtual server is created, you'll need to add virtual directories on the FE Servers to match. To learn more about configuring FE/BE topologies, consult the *Exchange 2000 Server Resource Kit* by MSPRESS.

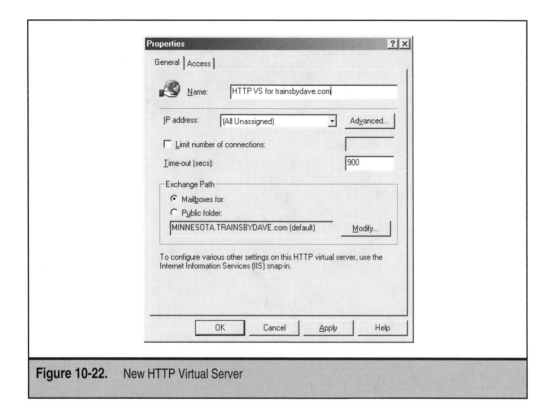

Figure 10-22.   New HTTP Virtual Server

SUMMARY

Whew! This chapter was full of concepts and ideas. Architecture is always a bit difficult to learn but, once mastered, makes a world of difference in your administrative activities. In this chapter, we covered how the ESE databases work, how to set up FE/BE topologies, and how Exchange 2000 Server is structured overall.

In the next chapter, we'll focus on the routing architecture, something that you'll be especially interested in if you have a multisite environment.

CHAPTER 11

Exchange 2000 Server Routing Architecture

In Exchange 5.*x*, the routing architecture was based on the concept of *sites*. A site, in Exchange 5.*x*, defines the administrative and routing boundary for servers that have a high-bandwidth connection between them. A site also defined the namespace boundary within the Exchange organization. In Exchange 2000, these concepts that were all based on the definition of a site are now separated into two new and distinct concepts: administrative groups and routing groups. In Chapter 8, we described the need to have multiple administrative groups and routing groups to facilitate delegated administration, as well as structured communication between Exchange Servers that were not well connected. In this chapter, we will focus on the concept of routing groups, but we will go a bit deeper by looking at several aspects of message routing within Exchange 2000. Let's start by reviewing some basic information about routing groups.

ROUTING GROUPS: A PRIMER

An Exchange 2000 routing group represents a collection of Exchange Servers that share permanent, high-bandwidth connectivity between them (for example, servers in the same office on a 100MB hub). Each of these servers can communicate directly with any other server in the routing group via the Simple Mail Transfer Protocol (SMTP), rather than the Exchange 5.*x* method of using Remote Procedure Calls (RPCs) to communicate.

Microsoft's Well-Connected Rule of Thumb

Microsoft constantly uses the term "well connected" when referring to both Exchange 2000 routing groups and Active Directory (AD) sites. Microsoft's minimum standard for being well connected is 10Mbps. Their standard is not hard and fast. It's left up to the individual administrator to determine what is well connected. I've read some documents from Microsoft that assert 64*Kbps* (!) could be construed to mean well connected.

MESSAGE ROUTING IN A PURE EXCHANGE 2000 ENVIRONMENT

All message routing within Exchange 2000 can be categorized into four types:

▼ Messages sent within the same server

■ Messages sent within the same routing group

■ Messages sent to another routing group

▲ Messages sent to a foreign e-mail system

Messages Sent Within the Same Server

When a message is sent from one mailbox to another where both mailboxes reside on the same server, that server does all handling of that message. Refer to Figure 11-1 and follow these steps through the handling of a message on the same server.

1. The message is sent by the client and is held by the information store.

2. The information store process places the message in a precategorization queue. This queue is used to process the addresses and apply any restrictions (size limits, delivery restrictions, and so on) to the message.

3. Exchange's routing engine picks up the message from the queue and maps the destination address against the domain-mapping table. Since the recipient's mailbox exists on the same server, the message is placed in the local delivery queue.

4. The information store process takes the message and places it in the recipient's mailbox. When online, the recipient is notified.

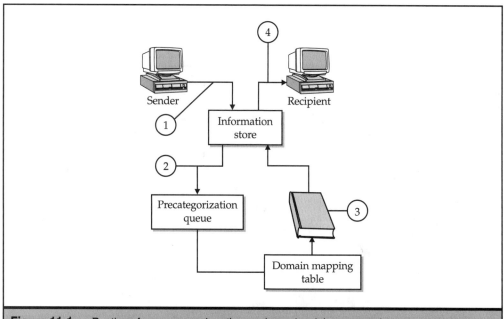

Figure 11-1.   Routing of a message when the sender and recipient are on the same server

Messages Sent Within the Same Routing Group

Messages sent within a routing group can be sent from any server within that routing group to any other server within that routing group. The servers use SMTP as their method of transport. The path a message takes (see Figure 11-2) as it is sent from one server to another in the same routing group is as follows:

1. Like the single server process, the message is sent by the client and is held by the information store. It is placed in the precategorization queue and processed.

2. When the routing engine maps the destination address against the domain-mapping table, it places the message in a dynamically created outgoing SMTP message queue bearing the name of the recipients domain. In this case, it's the local domain.

3. AD is queried for the recipient's home server, the MX record for the destination server is queried on DNS, and an SMTP session (over TCP port 25) is established between the sending and destination servers. Once received, the message is placed in a local queue (called the NTFS queue) and the Advanced Queuing Engine (AQE) (a component of the SMTP service) processes the message much in the same way as steps 3 and 4 in the preceding section.

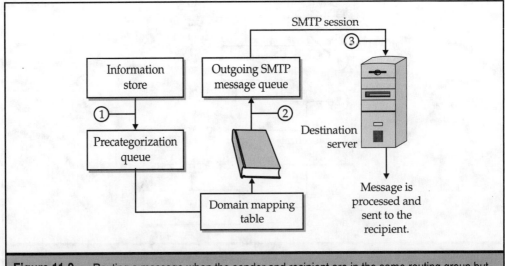

Figure 11-2.   Routing a message when the sender and recipient are in the same routing group but on two different servers

Messages Sent to Another Routing Group

When messages are sent to a server in a different routing group, we need to introduce a new concept: the routing group *Bridgehead Server*. A Bridgehead Server (BHS) is an Exchange 2000 Server designated to *receive* messages from another routing group. When a routing group connector is initially set up between two routing groups (see Figure 11-3), any server in the sending routing group can send mail to a designated BHS in the destination routing group (see Figure 11-4). Figure 11-5 shows the path a message will take using the default connector configuration.

If you wish to better control the path the messages will take between connectors, you can specify which server or servers in the sending routing group are able to use the connector. Often, the configuration of a two-routing-group environment has the BHS (for messages received from one direction) also as the only server allowed to send messages in the other direction, as shown in Figure 11-6. All messages sent between the routing groups will pass to the BHS in the local routing group, pass to the remote BHS, and then be sent to the recipient's home server.

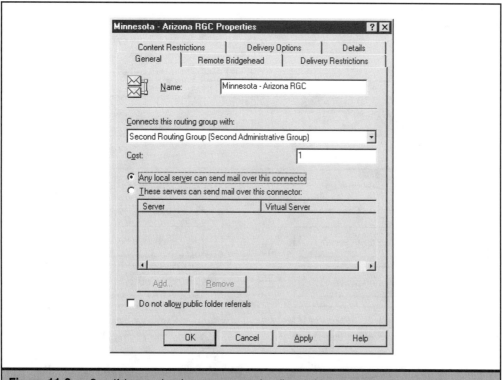

Figure 11-3.   Specifying any local server can send mail over this connector using the default setting

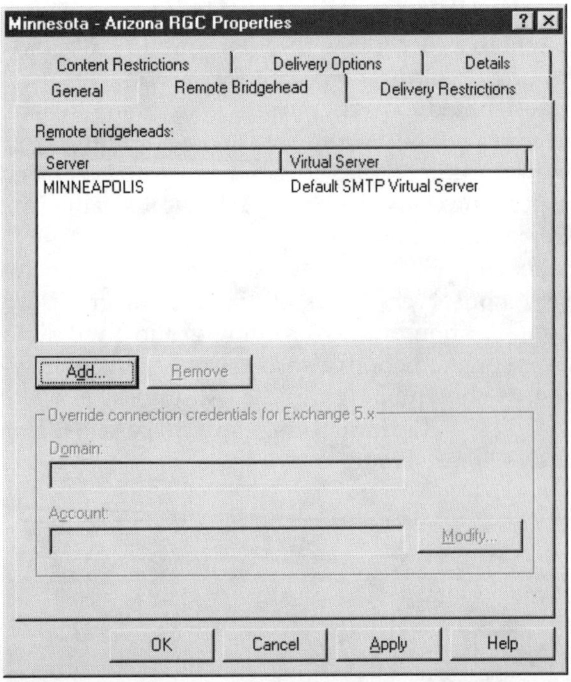

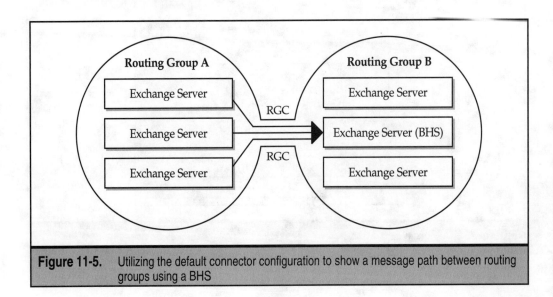

Figure 11-4. Specifying the initial Remote BHS

Figure 11-5. Utilizing the default connector configuration to show a message path between routing groups using a BHS

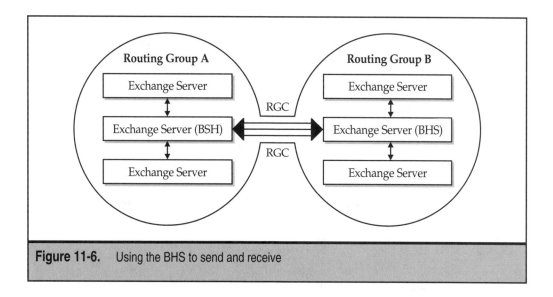

Figure 11-6.   Using the BHS to send and receive

Remember, you have a good amount of design flexibility with respect to BHS usage. You can use a number of servers on each side of the connector to pass messages across and maintain fault tolerance of the message path (see Figure 11-7). It is important to note that when multiple servers are configured at both ends, the message is always sent to the first server in the list, and only when that server is unavailable are the other servers in the list used. While this will look similar to the Site Connector's ability to have multiple target servers, there is no weighted average algorithm that is used to choose between the target servers.

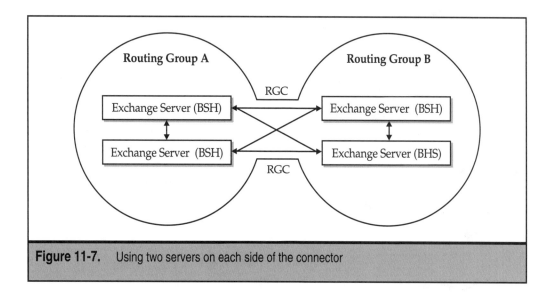

Figure 11-7.   Using two servers on each side of the connector

No matter which scenario you use to send messages to another routing group, the process is similar. In the following steps, we'll show the path of a message using the default configuration (see Figure 11-8).

1. The message is sent by the client and is held by the information store.

2. After processing the message, it is placed in the outbound SMTP message queue.

3. Routing group info is retrieved from AD, and link state information is used to determine the best path, see "Link State Information," later in this chapter.

4. An SMTP session is established with the BHS in the remote routing group, and the message is sent.

5. The remote BHS passes the message to the recipient's home server.

Messages Sent to a Foreign E-mail System

When a message is destined for a foreign message system (such as X.400, SMTP, cc:Mail, and MS Mail, among others), the message needs to be handed off to the server with the appropriate connector. The general process of sending a message to a foreign e-mail system (shown in Figure 11-9) is described using a scenario where the sender's home server is different from the server with the connector to the foreign e-mail system.

1. The message is sent by the client and is held by the information store.

2. After processing the message, it is placed in the outbound SMTP message queue.

3. Routing group info is retrieved from AD and link state information (See "Link State Information," later in this chapter) is used to determine the best path to the foreign e-mail system.

4. An SMTP session is established with the server housing the connector, and the message is sent.

5. The message is placed in an outbound queue for the connector, and the message is sent to the foreign e-mail system

Message Routing in a Mixed Exchange 2000/5.x Environment

Some of you are reading this chapter and are saying to yourself, "What about the Exchange 5.x Servers I still have?" Since many companies will have the two systems coexist for some period of time, it is important to understand how Exchange 2000 interacts with Exchange 5.x. Let's start with a recap from Chapter 9 of the routing differences between Exchange 5.x and 2000.

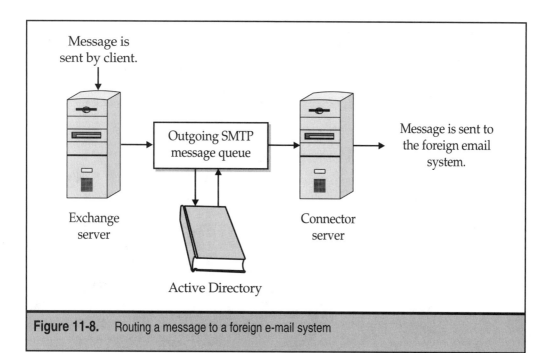

Figure 11-8. Routing a message to a foreign e-mail system

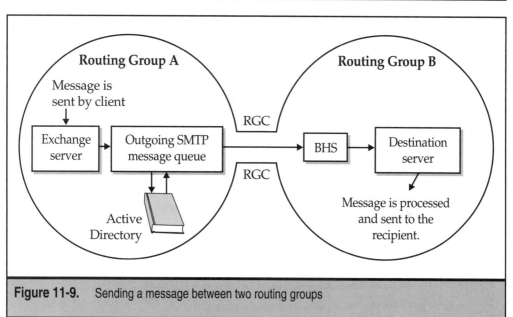

Figure 11-9. Sending a message between two routing groups

Sites Versus Routing Groups

In Exchange 5.*x*, the administrative and routing boundary was defined as a site. If you had Exchange 5.*x* Servers that were not well connected, they would be placed in separate sites with an Exchange site connector between them to facilitate the passing of messages. With regard to message routing only, sites in Exchange 5.*x* roughly translate to routing groups in Exchange 2000.

How Does Exchange 2000 Interact with Exchange 5.*x*?

Unlike the SMTP-based communication between Exchange 2000 Servers, Exchange 5.*x* Servers utilize Remote Procedure Calls (RPCs) to communicate. Therefore, in order for Exchange 2000 to effectively communicate with Exchange 5.*x*, it also uses RPCs when dealing with an Exchange 5.*x* Server. Also, since an Exchange 5.*x* site defines the administrative boundary, and not just the routing boundary, Exchange 2000 sees Exchange 5.*x* sites as administrative groups that already contain a routing group. Because of the interpretation of Exchange 5.*x* sites in Exchange 2000, as long as you are running Exchange 2000 in mixed mode, the Exchange 5.*x* Servers are locked into the routing groups that correspond to the Exchange 5.*x* site. In addition, Exchange 5.*x* sites will appear as transparent Exchange 2000 administrative groups in the Exchange System Manager snap-in.

Moreover, Exchange 5.*x* Servers will see Exchange 2000 administrative groups as sites in the Exchange Administrator. And if you have multiple Exchange 2000 Servers in multiple routing groups within the same administrative group, Exchange 5.*x* Servers will not recognize the routing groups and will place all the Exchange 2000 Servers in the same site in the Exchange Administrator. Multiple routing groups are not translated to the Exchange Administrator utility.

Messages Routed from Exchange 2000 to Exchange 5.*x*

When a message is being sent from an Exchange 2000 client to one on an Exchange 5.*x* Server, the process (see Figure 11-10) is as follows:

1. The message is sent by the client and is held by the information store.
2. After processing the message, it is placed in the local delivery queue.
3. The message is routed to the information store and then to the MTS Out folder, an outbound queue for the message transfer agent (MTA), and the MTA sends the message to the Exchange 5.*x* Server via RPC.

Messages Routed from Exchange 5.*x* to Exchange 2000

From an Exchange 5.*x* Server's perspective, the process of sending a message from an Exchange 5.*x* Server into an Exchange 2000 environment is much the same as sending a message to a native Exchange 5.*x* environment. Remember, to Exchange 5.*x*, Exchange 2000 *is* Exchange 5.*x*. The MTA on the Exchange 5.*x* Server will directly contact the target Exchange 2000 Server (except in the case that the target Exchange 2000 Server is in another

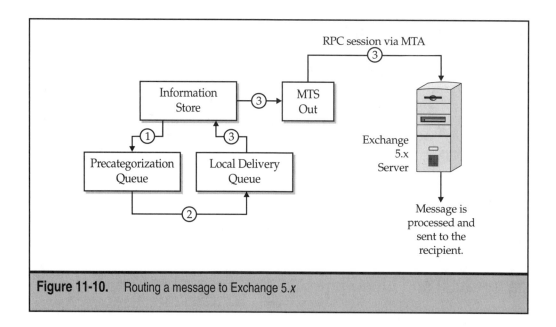

Figure 11-10.   Routing a message to Exchange 5.x

site/routing group, then the BHS of that site/routing group would be contacted directly) via RPCs to send the message.

LINK STATE INFORMATION

When messages need to be routed to other routing groups or to a foreign e-mail system via a specific server with a connector installed, there has to be a way for Exchange to know about all the possible ways to get a message from here to there. Exchange 2000 uses the link state protocol to find out that information. The link state protocol is based on the Open Shortest Path First (OSPF) routing protocol. It provides Exchange 2000 a way to ensure the integrity of message routing in the following ways:

▼   It helps Exchange 2000 Servers make the best choice about the path a message should travel based on cost and state of that route (both discussed in "Exchange 2000 and Link State Information," later in this chapter).

■   It eliminates what is commonly known as message ping-pong. This is where a message bounces between two Exchange Servers because the path to the final destination is unavailable. This no longer happens because servers are aware of unusable paths and alternate routes.

▲   It eliminates message looping. This is where a message continually hops from one Exchange Server to the next and to the next and to the . . . .

Let's first take a look back and see where message routing information came from in order to truly see and appreciate the advances we get with the link state protocol.

Exchange 5.x and the GWART

In Exchange 5.x, the Gateway Address Routing Table (GWART) was replicated to each Exchange 5.x Server used to determine the best route to be taken by a message. Each server looks to see if a path exists for a particular namespace and chooses the path with the lowest cost. Two problems exist using the GWART. The GWART only defines the next hop in the path to get a message, and it doesn't contain any status information as to whether or not that path is viable. For example, if ServerX (see Figure 11-11) in Exchange 5.x Site A wants to send a message to ServerZ in Site C, the path is obvious: through Site B using ServerY. The GWART entry on ServerX for anything targeted in Site C would point to a connector on ServerY. Note there is no information in ServerX's GWART about whether the connector on ServerY is up and running, nor is there any information about the connectors used on the other side of ServerY. In addition, your only way of determining which route to use—if more than one exists for the same recipient namespace—is the cost of the connector, see "Connector Costs," later in this chapter.

Exchange 2000 and Link State Information

Hopefully, you can see that while the GWART is a functional method of finding out message routing information, it is not entirely useful, because it does not provide real-time status information about a message path. Link state information is just what it sounds like: it is real-time information about the state (up or down) of a link (a connector). Since the focus is on the state of each of the links in your Exchange 2000 environment, your

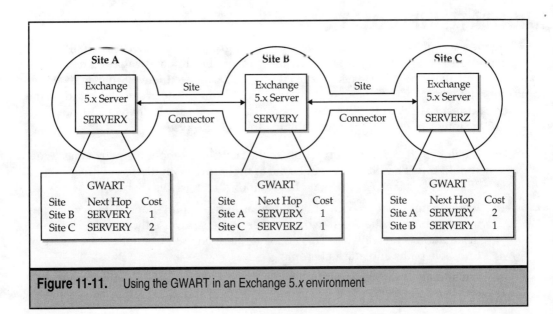

Figure 11-11.   Using the GWART in an Exchange 5.x environment

server now can more intelligently select the path for messages to take, while being well aware if a downstream link is up or not.

Updating the Link State Information

In Exchange 5.x, the GWART was updated by any server within the Exchange 5.x site. In Exchange 2000, more thought has gone into the updating of the link state information. Each routing group has one Exchange 2000 Server designated as a *Routing Group Master* (RGM). This server will receive and update all link state information within the routing group. It is also responsible for propagating that information to all servers within the routing group over TCP port 3044. Each Exchange 2000 Server maintains its own link state information. The RGM will also update RGMs in other routing groups via SMTP. It's my understanding that the RGMs are only responsible for their own group and that it is the BHSs that will pass the updated information to the other routing groups. The receiving BHS then passes the update to its RGM, which in turn floods all the servers, including the BHS, with the updated information.

Connector Costs

Like in Exchange 5.x, a cost is associated with each connector/link in Exchange 2000. This cost is used to determine the cheapest route to pass a message. The cost a route is given (ranging from 1 to 100) could be based on one or more of the following criteria about the physical link the connector(s) logically run over:

▼ Lowest monetary cost

■ Fastest throughput

■ Highest availability

▲ Preferred path

To clarify the concept of cost, let's use an example of a basic Exchange 2000 organization that has three routing groups, as shown here:

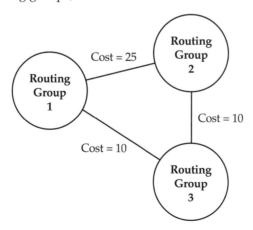

Let's first assume that all connectors are up and running. If a message was to be sent from Routing Group 1 to Routing Group 2, notice that there are two different paths the message can take: from Routing Group 1 to Routing Group 2 directly, and from Routing Group 1 to Routing Group 2 via Routing Group 3. Since all connectors are running, Exchange 2000 will decide which route to take based on lowest cost. Exchange 2000 looks at the number of routes involved (one if it goes straight to Routing Group 2, and two if it goes via Routing Group 3) and adds the costs to get a total. While you and I can see that it may be shorter to go directly to Routing Group 2, because the cost associated with that connector (25) is higher than the sum of the other two connectors (20), Exchange 2000 will send the message via Routing Group 3.

SUMMARY

This chapter has covered the concepts behind the message routing architecture of Exchange 2000. We looked at how Exchange 2000 sends messages between two servers within the Exchange organization, as well as how Exchange 2000 routes messages to foreign messaging systems. We also looked at how routing groups define the routing boundaries, with connectors providing the bridge between them, and how Exchange 2000 uses the link state information to make intelligent decisions about the routes it should take.

In the next chapter, we will focus on advanced administration of Exchange 2000, beginning with configuring security.

PART IV

Advanced Administration

CHAPTER 12

Configuring Security for Exchange 2000 Server

Messaging is rapidly becoming the medium of choice for business communication. Along with the enjoyment of instant communication across the Internet comes the concern that messages with sensitive information will be secure. With nothing more than a Simple Mail Transport Protocol (SMTP)–compliant messaging system, this concern is far from satisfied; SMTP messages are sent in plain text (no encryption) and can be read by any packet-sniffer application, such as Microsoft's Network Monitor. This chapter will focus on how you can make your messaging environment secure.

MESSAGE SECURITY BASICS

There are two facets of message security utilized by many messaging systems: *message encryption* and *digital signatures*. Message encryption allows a message to be encrypted by the sender, securely transmitted in its encrypted format across a potentially shared network (such as the Internet), and decrypted only by the intended recipient. Digital signatures allow a recipient to verify, from a trusted source, that a given message actually came from the listed sender. Exchange 2000 supports the use of both of these types of message security. Let's look at each in more detail.

Message Encryption

Message encryption is the process of taking readable text and scrambling it using a predefined algorithm or, as we'll call it, a *key*. The result is a data set that is unreadable. Once unreadable, it would be safe to send the message across an unsecured medium, such as the Internet, to the intended recipient without fear that someone else will read its contents. The only way to make the data readable again is for the recipient to have the appropriate key that will decrypt the message. Once decrypted, the message is returned to its original state and is read by the intended recipient.

To demonstrate encryption, take the following example of a simple phrase such as "I Love Exchange," and let's encrypt it by using a simple key: replacing each letter with the one just after it in the alphabet. The result of the encryption is "J Mpwf Fvdibohf"—a completely unreadable piece of text. If you know the encryption key, you can easily reverse the process. This is similar to what happens when a message is encrypted.

The preceding example was accomplished using *symmetric keys*, one of two types of encryption keys. Symmetric keys are identical. That means you use the same key to both encrypt and decrypt the message. The preceding example used the same key to both encrypt and decrypt the text message. This type of key is not very secure; once someone knows your key from interacting with you initially, they can access information not intended for them. The other key type is an *asymmetric key*. Asymmetric keys are far more secure because they use two keys, a public encryption key and a private encryption key, to handle the encryption. Only the owner of the key pair knows the private key, while the public key is available to anyone. These two keys are the only two keys that will work with each other. The use of this key pair makes up the Public Key Infrastructure (PKI), used to either encrypt or digitally sign. Let's look at how these two keys are used in implementing message encryption, and we'll discuss just how both the sender and recipient retrieve these keys in the "Digital Signatures" section in this chapter.

The Message Encryption Process

When encrypting a message, as shown in Figure 12-1, the sender needs to know the recipient's public key. (Don't be the least bit worried that senders need to know your public key; all they can do with it is encrypt messages. On top of that, they would only be readable by you!) The sender uses the recipient's public key so that the recipient can use his own private key to decrypt the message. Since only the recipient knows his own private key, only the intended recipient can decrypt the message. Think about it: if the keys were used in reverse where the sender uses his own private key to encrypt and the recipient used the sender's public key to decrypt, because the public key is available to everyone, *anyone* could decrypt the sender's message! Also, if the sender used his own public key (and not the recipient's), how would the recipient decrypt the message? Only the sender can know his own private key, and that private key is the only other half of the key pair that can decrypt a message.

Digital Signatures

Because it is possible for someone to send a message claiming to be someone else, a digital signature is used to allow the recipient of a message to verify that the message actually came from the sender. The signature is only considered valid because the signature is validated by a trusted source: a certificate authority. You can't just create your own digital signatures; they have to be created by a certificate authority and then assigned to your messaging client. It is this third party, trusted by both parties, which ensures you that senders are really who they say they are. For instance, if a close friend introduced you to someone you had never met before and said the stranger's name was Bob Johnson, would you believe your friend? Of course you would, because the source of that information is trusted. In a similar way, a digital signature is valid because the recipient trusts the source of the digital signature.

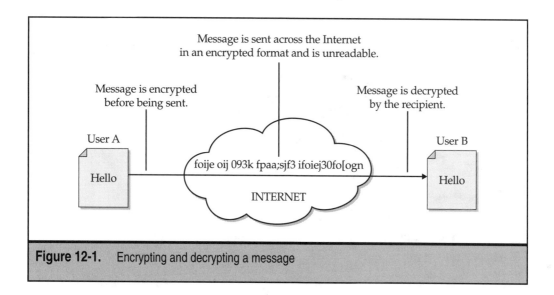

Figure 12-1.   Encrypting and decrypting a message

The sender uses his private *signing key* (different from his private key) to sign the message. The recipient uses the sender's public signing key to validate the signature. The following table summarizes the use of keys when encrypting or digitally signing.

Process	Encryption and Decryption	Digital Signatures
Sending a message	The sender uses the recipient's public key to encrypt the message.	The sender uses his private signing key to apply a digital signature to the message.
Receiving a message	The recipient uses his own private key to decrypt the message.	The recipient uses the sender's public signing key to verify the digital signature.

Now that we have a basic understanding of message security, let's look at how it is implemented in Exchange 2000.

WINDOWS 2000 CERTIFICATE SERVICES AND THE KEY MANAGEMENT SERVER

In order for both encryption and digital signatures to work within a messaging system, including Exchange 2000, you need a trusted source of the keys. This is handled by not one, but two services: Exchange 2000 Key Management Server and Windows 2000 Certificate Services. These two services work closely together to provide the PKI described previously. Let's look at each service and the role it plays.

Certificate Services

Windows 2000 Certificate Services serves as a *Certification Authority* by creating and managing certificates. These certificates are a digital statement vouching for the authenticity of a certificate holder's identity. Because we trust the Certification Authority, we implicitly trust the certificate used to either encrypt or digitally sign a message.

Certificate Services supports certificates that adhere to the X.509 standard. This standard provides two types of authentication. The first is simple authentication, which uses a password to verify the authenticity of the claimed identity (for example, a logon ID). The second type of authentication is strong authentication, which uses the PKI as its means to verify identity. An X.509 certificate includes the following information:

▼ Version number

■ Serial number

■ Signature algorithm ID

■ Certificate issuer

■ Validity dates

- Subject (who the certificate was issued to)
▲ Public key type

Keep in mind, we are only covering those portions of Certificate Services that directly apply to Exchange 2000. Certificate Services also can provide certificates to a number of other network functions, including

▼ Encrypting File System
- IPSec authentication
- Smart Card usage
▲ Secure Sockets Layer (SSL) on Web pages

NOTE: Both Connection Agrement and Certification Authority have the abbreviation CA.

Key Management Server

The Key Management Server (KMS) is a component of Exchange 2000 that acts as a Cryptographic Service Provider (CSP) to Exchange clients. It maintains its own Extensible Storage Engine (ESE) database of the Exchange users' private keys. You may be thinking, "Wait a minute! I thought Certificate Services gives out the keys." Certificate Services and KMS work in conjunction in this manner: Certificate Services generates the certificates vouching for the users' identities, and KMS installs these certificates on all the clients that enroll to use message security.

Now that we've covered some of the basics of message security and the main players who will maintain it, let's start implementing message security by first seeing how to install Certificate Services.

INSTALLING WINDOWS 2000 CERTIFICATE SERVICES

Certificate Services is an optional component of Windows 2000. Before you install it, you need to decide on which machine it should be installed. Since Certificate Services can be used by services other than Exchange, you probably won't want to install it on your Exchange server. You can install Certificate Services on a domain controller or a member server.

You can add it at any time using the Add/Remove Programs applet in the Control Panel and choose to Add/Remove Windows Components. The Windows Component Wizard starts (Figure 12-2). When you choose to add Certificate Services, a warning dialog box appears, letting you know you will not be able to rename the computer or move it into or out of a domain.

The next screen in the wizard, shown in Figure 12-3, requires you to select a Certification Authority type. There are four Certification Authority types you can choose from. Table 12-1 lists your choices and a description of each.

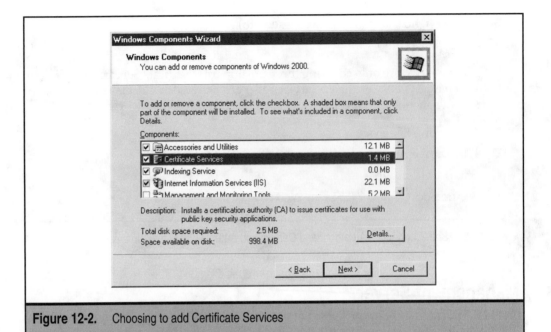

Figure 12-2. Choosing to add Certificate Services

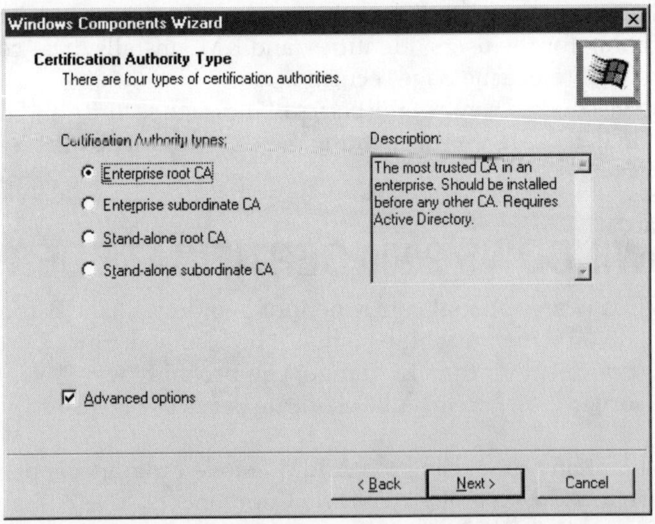

Figure 12-3. Use to select a Certification Authority type

Certification Authority Type	Description	Requirements
Enterprise Root	This is the most trusted type of Certification Authority in an organization. It will not only issue certificates, but it also serves as the root of a Certification Authority hierarchy throughout your organization.	This Certification Authority type requires that Active Directory (AD) be installed.
Enterprise Subordinate	This standard type in your organization logically exists below your Enterprise Root.	Requires AD and a certificate from another Certification Authority.
Stand-Alone Root	The most trusted in a hierarchy	Does not require AD.
Stand-Alone Subordinate	This standard type issues certificates.	Does not require AD, but does require a certificate from another Certification Authority

Table 12-1.   Certification Authority Types

If you choose the Advanced options check box, you will see an additional screen and will be able to select options about your encryption settings. As this book is a beginner's guide, we will accept the defaults. The next screen (Figure 12-4) prompts you to provide identifying information about the Certification Authority.

Table 12-2 lists the fields and describes the appropriate value for each.

The next screen (Figure 12-5) shows the default locations for the certificate database. You have the option of sharing a folder for the purpose of making Certification Authority information available to users on your network. You would only select this option if you did not have AD installed.

You will be prompted to stop Internet Information Services (IIS). Because IIS can utilize Certification Services to establish SSL browser connections, the IIS configuration needs to be made aware of Certificate Services. Once you press OK, the necessary files are copied from the Windows 2000 CD-ROM, and Certificate Services is configured.

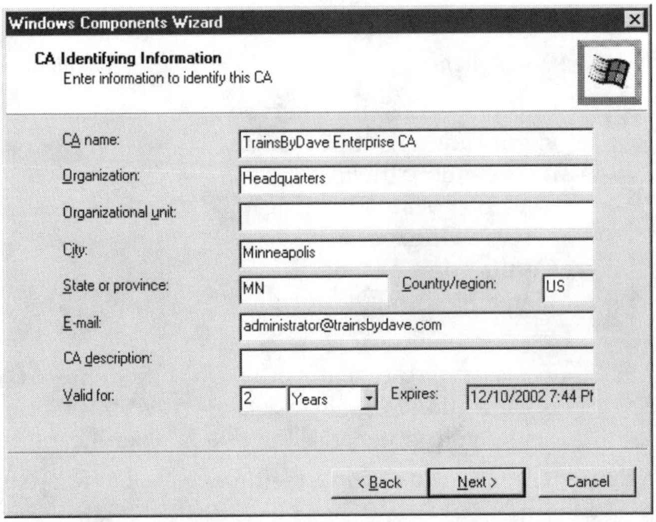

Figure 12-4. Certification Authority Identifying Information

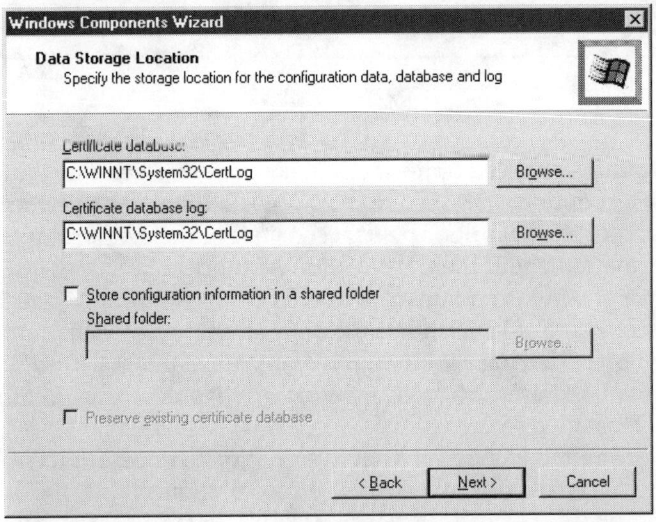

Figure 12-5. Selecting the Data Storage Location of your Certification Authority database

Once the Add/Remove Wizard is finished, you will see a new Certification Authority shortcut in Administrative Tools. You can use this tool to accomplish the following tasks:

▼   Stop and start the Certification Authority service

■   Back up and restore the Certification Authority

■   Publish revoked certificate lists

■   View issued certificates, pending requests for certificates, and failed requests for certificates

▲   Set up policy settings for the Certification Authority

Fields	Value
Certification Authority name	A unique name for the Certification Authority. (Remember, this is the name of the Certification Authority and the services it provides, not the name of a certificate.)
Organization; Organizational Unit; City; State or Province; Country/Region; and E-mail	Information that appropriately denotes the location of the Certification Authority, as well as where it fits in the hierarchy of the organization.
Certification Authority description	An optional field for a description.
Valid For	Denotes the period of time the certificate is valid for. The default is two years. Subordinate Certification Authority's are not allowed to enter a value here, as they get this from their root Certification Authority.
Expires	Shows the calculated expiration date based on the Valid For value.

Table 12-2.   Certification Authority Identifying Fields

Postinstallation Tasks

Once Certificate Services is installed, you cannot just go ahead and install KMS. The reason is that the policy of the Certification Authority you just set up has to support the needs of KMS. KMS requires that you have at least one enterprise Certification Authority that issues, in addition to the defaults, the following certificates:

▼   Enrollment Agent (Computer)

■   Exchange User

▲   Exchange Signature Only

The policy can be updated by opening the Certification Authority snap-in: right-click Policy Settings, point to New, and choose Certificate to Issue. The resulting dialog box, shown next, lists the various certificate types that the Certification Authority can issue. Select the three certificate types just listed by holding down the CTRL key and clicking OK. You should then see them listed at the bottom.

Okay—*now* you can install KMS!

INSTALLING KEY MANAGEMENT SERVICES

We're going to walk through the installation of KMS, assuming you have already installed your Exchange 2000 Server and are adding the KMS. We're also not going to walk through each step of the Exchange 2000 Installation Wizard—only the screens pertinent to the installation of KMS.

As you can probably guess by now, you install KMS by running the Exchange 2000 Installation Wizard (start it by running SETUP.EXE in the \SETUP\I386 folder on the Exchange 2000 CD-ROM). We begin the specifics of the KMS installation on the Component Selection screen of the wizard (Figure 12-6). You'll see Microsoft Exchange Key Management Service listed under the Microsoft Exchange Messaging and Collaboration Services

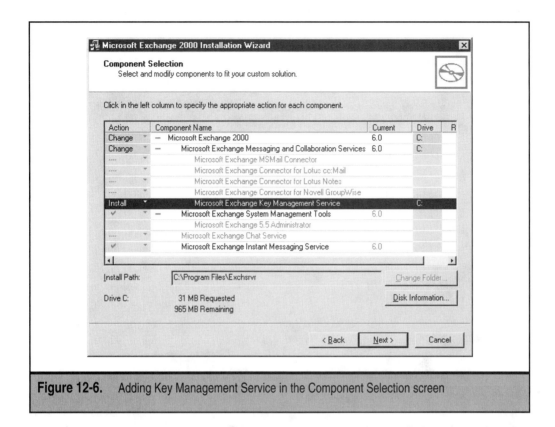

Figure 12-6. Adding Key Management Service in the Component Selection screen

component; however, if you try to select the Action column next to Microsoft Exchange Key Management Service, you'll be prompted to first modify parent components.

You need to select Change next to the Microsoft Exchange 2000 and the Microsoft Exchange Messaging and Collaboration Services components. Then you can select Install in the Action column next to Microsoft Exchange Key Management Service.

The next screen in the wizard asks you to select an administrative group. This administrative group will contain the advanced security container that you will use later to manage your KMS settings. Make certain that you have authority to administer the administrative group you choose here.

The next screen is a *very* important one. Pay attention here! The next screen allows you to choose the KMS password location (Figure 12-7). KMS requires a password at startup. It is one that is created for you and is *not* easily remembered. Without this password, you *will not* be able to get your KMS started.

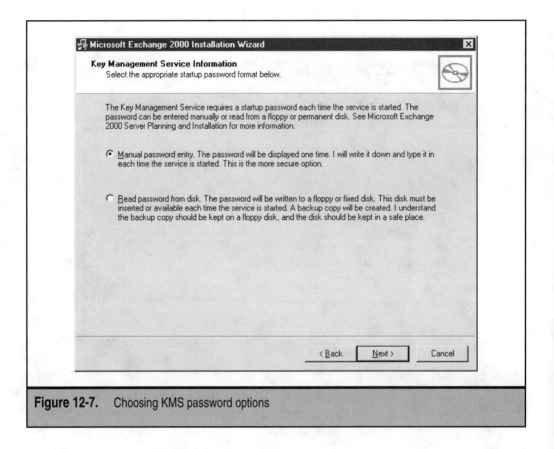

Figure 12-7. Choosing KMS password options

Let's examine this screen by selecting both options and seeing what the repercussions are of each choice. First, we'll select Manual Password Entry. After you choose this option, the wizard will present you with the startup password, shown next, that must be used to start the KMS.

Starting the KMS Using Manual Password Entry

If you choose this option, KMS will require the password to be manually entered each and every time the KMS service is started. To do this, open the Services tool in Administrative Tools. Go to the properties of the Microsoft Exchange Key Management Service, and choose the General tab. As the next illustration shows, you need to type in the startup password in the Start parameters field, and click the Start button to start the service.

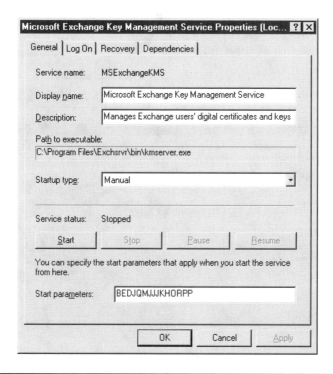

Now let's select the second option, Read Password from Disk. If you do, KMS will read the password from a file named Kmserver.pwd. The default location, as shown in Figure 12-8, is the a: drive. You can change this to a location on the Exchange Server itself. We recommend putting the master copy on the Exchange Server's hard drive, ensuring the directory is secure with NT File System (NTFS) permissions, and placing the backup copy on a floppy that is put in a secure place. You will also want to change the KMS service's startup type to Automatic; the default is Manual.

The last screen of the installation wizard summarizes your choices made during the installation. Clicking Next will finish the installation, and you'll be ready to start the service.

What If I Want to Change My Password Location?

So you don't like the current location of your password file (you may have accepted the defaults, and KMS is always looking at the a: drive). There's a simple trick to change the location: stop KMS using the Services tool in Administrative Tools. Using the Registry Editor (Regedt32.exe), navigate to the following subkey:

HKEY_LOCAL_MACHINE\Software\Microsoft\Exchange\KMServer

Find the registry entry "MasterPasswordPath," and change the value to the location where you want your Kmserver.pwd file to exist. If you chose Manual password entry during the KMS install, this value will be blank.

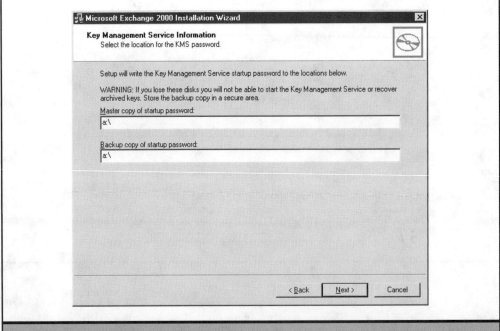

Figure 12-8.   Selecting where your Key Management Service startup password will be written to

MANAGING KMS

Once the service is started, don't just head off and begin enrolling users to use the advanced security of KMS; you must first concern yourself with the security of the KMS environment. Let's look at a few administrative tasks you need to handle before you begin rolling out KMS to your clients. To begin managing your KMS configuration, navigate to the Advanced Security container in the administrative group you chose during installation, right-click it, and choose Properties. You are prompted to log on, as shown here:

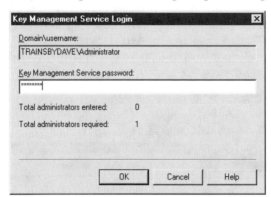

Don't be fooled by the look of this dialog box: It shows a simple username/password combination. You would think that with your user account listed, you should put in your password. Not true! The account listed is yours, but the password is specific to KMS. Put in the default password of *password*, and we'll show you later in the chapter how to change it. As you navigate to each tab of the Key Manager Properties dialog box, you'll be asked for the same password time and time again. This is a required security measure to ensure that only authorized persons can manage KMS.

Managing KMS Administrators

The first task to complete is to set who has the ability to manage KMS. If too few people are chosen, you may run into the problem where the only administrator who knew the KMS password left (on bad terms, of course!), and now you're up a creek without a paddle! If too many are chosen, you run the risk of a security breach. You will want to create additional KMS administrators for at least one of the following reasons:

▼ You want a back door in case you forget the initial KMS password assigned to the administrator account.

▲ You want to require more than one KMS administrator to perform KMS duties.

In the Key Manager Properties dialog box, navigate to the Administrators tab. Here you will add the user accounts that will manage KMS. Add a user by clicking Add, and select the account from the standard Active Directory Select dialog box. Once you choose a user account, you will need to set the password, as shown next. Like the password you used to access these property pages, the password you are about to set for the specified user account has nothing to do with his or her user account password used at log on.

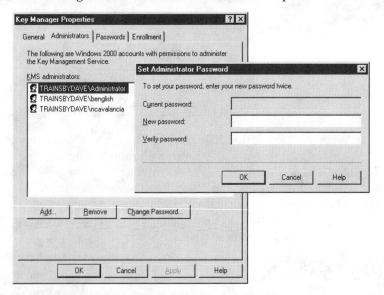

Changing a KMS Administrator's Password

To change a KMS password, simply select the administrator in question on the Administrators tab, and click the Change Password button. You will be prompted with a dialog box. Like the initial setting of a password for a new KMS administrator, the password you are about to specify as the new password has no effect on the users log-on password.

Requiring Multiple KMS Administrators

Initially, if you wish to change any of the KMS parameters within the Key Manager Properties dialog box, you only need a single KMS administrator password, as shown in Figure 12-9. You should consider changing these values to reflect the level of security you wish to put on KMS management. If a user is a KMS administrator, it would be possible for that user to reissue another user's key, reestablish that user's security settings in Outlook, and send mail out with a digital signature as that user. Anyone receiving this spoofed message would have no reason to doubt that it came from the original user.

So, to avoid this awful scenario, we recommend that you take proactive measures by requiring multiple passwords for at least the following options:

▼ Add/delete administrators, edit multiple password policies

■ Recover a user's keys

▲ Import/export user records

The other two options are not as critical, as they do not allow the KMS administrator the ability to eventually impersonate another user on Exchange.

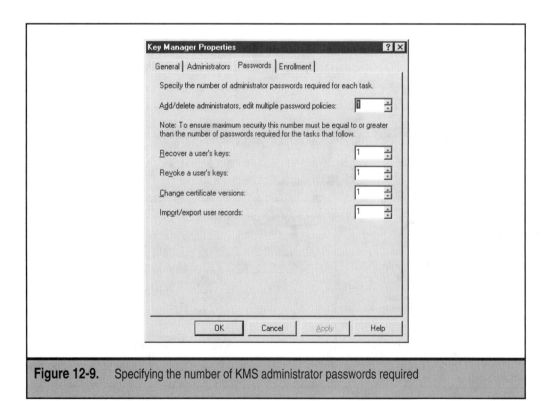

Figure 12-9. Specifying the number of KMS administrator passwords required

Changing the KMS Startup Password

What's this I hear? You can't seem to remember the KMS startup password? What's so difficult in remembering a string of 15 consonants that don't spell much of anything? We realize that most of us have a hard time remembering anything beyond telephone numbers.

Should you forget the startup password, Microsoft does allow you a way to change it. Navigate to and right-click the Key Manager object, as shown in Figure 12-10, point to All Tasks, and choose Change Startup Password. The only downside to changing the KMS startup password is that Exchange itself sets the password to another 15-character incomprehensible password. One note to remember: you have to have the KMS service running in order to even get to the point to where you can change the startup password!

KMS USER ENROLLMENT

In order for a user to utilize KMS to encrypt or digitally sign messages, they must first enroll with KMS. This process essentially begins with the user asking to enroll, with the KMS requesting a certificate from Certificate Services to create the two key pairs necessary (one pair for encryption and one for digitally signing). The part of the process involving an administrator or user is broken into two parts: the first part requires an administrator to request a security token from KMS, and the second part requires the user (or administrator) using that token to complete the enrollment process at the user's workstation within Outlook 2000.

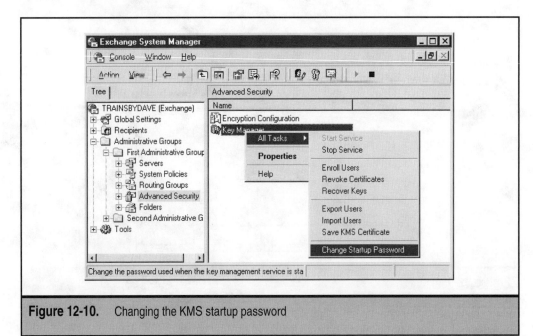

Figure 12-10. Changing the KMS startup password

Enrolling Users

KMS allows you to automatically enroll users individually or as a group. To begin the process, right-click the Key Manager object, point to All Tasks, and choose Enroll Users. The initial choice you need to make is shown here:

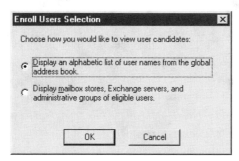

Choosing the first option will show you an alphabetic global address list, as shown in Figure 12-11. Choose the users you wish to enroll, and click the Add button. When you have finished, click the Enroll button.

You can instead choose to enroll not by individual user, but by mailbox store, server, or administrative group, which will give you the dialog box shown in Figure 12-12. You

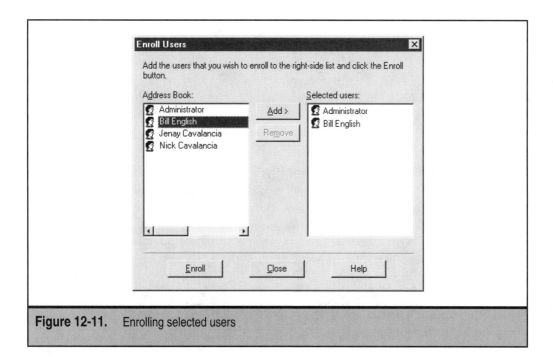

Figure 12-11. Enrolling selected users

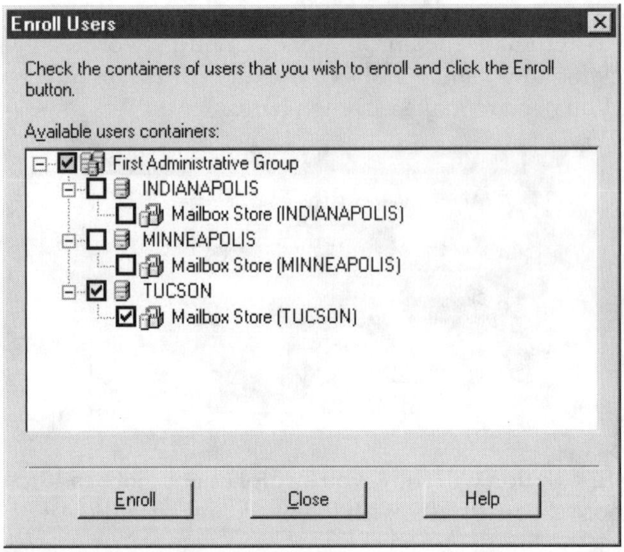

Figure 12-12.   Enrolling users by Mailbox Store, Server, or Administrative Group

can select the appropriate check box to have all mailboxes from the selected check box and logically within it be enrolled.

No matter which method you use to bulk enroll users, the users enrolled will be sent an e-mail containing their security tokens (a 12-character string of letters much like the KMS startup password).

Keeping the Security Token Secure

The one downside to enrolling users in a bulk fashion is that the messages containing the security token are not sent in a secure manner. That means that if someone other than you were to read your e-mail (perhaps they are sitting at your desk during your lunch break) and were to use the token to enroll you, they could impersonate you and send e-mail out as you with a digital signature to vouch for their identity!

While improbable, it is still possible. A more secure method of enrolling users would be one by one. In Active Directory Users and Computers, go to the properties dialog box of the user you wish to enroll, shown next. Select the Exchange Features tab, E-mail Security, and click Properties. Type in your KMS Administrator password, and you will see the E-mail Security Properties dialog box.

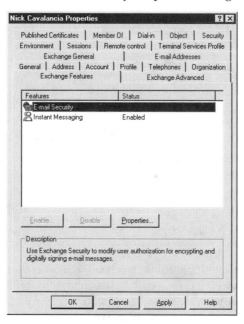

By clicking the Enroll button, you will be presented with the user's security token that will be used to complete the enrollment process, shown next. You will need to write this token down so you can use it later at the user's workstation.

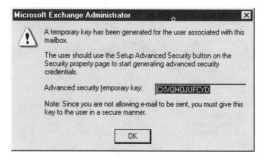

Finishing the Enrollment

Whether you used the insecure method of bulk enrollment or enrolled a single user and wrote down the security token, the second half of the process is the same: use the token to obtain the keys needed to encrypt and digitally sign messages. The process we outline in this book assumes you are using Outlook 2000 as your Exchange client. If you are using Outlook 97 or 98, the process will differ slightly.

Open Outlook, and choose Options from the Tools menu. Navigate to the Security tab, and click Get a Digital ID. Figure 12-13 shows the dialog box users see when they start the second half of their enrollment.

Choose Set Up Security For Me On The Exchange Server and click OK. The Setup Advanced Security dialog box, shown next, appears. Enter the security token you either received as a result of a bulk enrollment or that you wrote down when manually enrolling a single user.

Once you've used the security token to enroll, KMS needs some way to ensure that you are actually the person the user account is associated with. It does this by requiring a security password separate from your user account (Figure 12-14). This security password assures that someone else cannot sit down at your workstation and begin impersonating you. Remember, KMS is going to vouch for your identity; therefore, it has the need to validate your identity first.

After the security password is entered, Outlook informs you that your request to enable security has been sent to the KMS server. Now you can sit back, relax, and wait for the KMS

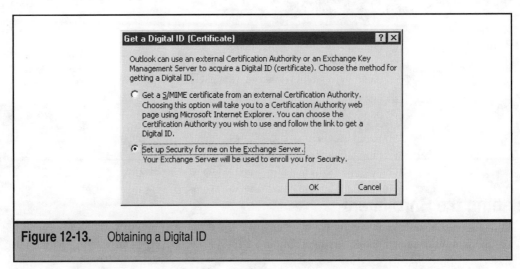

Figure 12-13.   Obtaining a Digital ID

Microsoft Outlook Security Password   [?][X]

Every Digital ID must be protected by a password.
Enter a new password for your new Digital ID.

Digital ID Name: Administrator

Password:

Confirm:

To protect your Digital ID, Microsoft Outlook will not
remember your password.

[ ] Remember password for [   ] minutes

[OK]   [Cancel]

Figure 12-14.   Entering an Outlook Security Password

to process your request and send you an enrollment e-mail. When the message arrives and
you double-click it to read it (you'll have to, because the message preview feature doesn't
work on encrypted messages), you'll be prompted to enter the password you just specified
so that KMS knows it's you sitting there and not some hacker. Once you've entered your security password, a dialog box (shown next) asking whether you want to add a certificate
to the root store appears. The root store is part of Internet Explorer, and it lists the Certification Authorities you explicitly trust. Click Yes. You will receive a message from Exchange stating that you have successfully enrolled and that security is enabled.

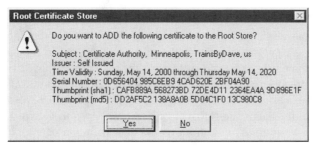

Root Certificate Store   [X]

Do you want to ADD the following certificate to the Root Store?

Subject : Certificate Authority, Minneapolis, TrainsByDave, us
Issuer : Self Issued
Time Validity : Sunday, May 14, 2000 through Thursday May 14, 2020
Serial Number : 0D656404 985C6EB9 4CAD620E 2BF04A90
Thumbprint (sha1) : CAFB889A 568273BD 72DE4D11 2364EA4A 9D896E1F
Thumbprint (md5) : DD2AF5C2 138A8A0B 5D04C1F0 13C980C8

[Yes]   [No]

Recovering Keys

In the event you lose the user's private key (which is stored on the workstation), you will
need to recover it from KMS. A good example is when a user's computer crashes and has
to be completely reinstalled. Rather than start over and re-enroll the user, it is better to recover the key so that the user can still open previously encrypted messages sent to them.

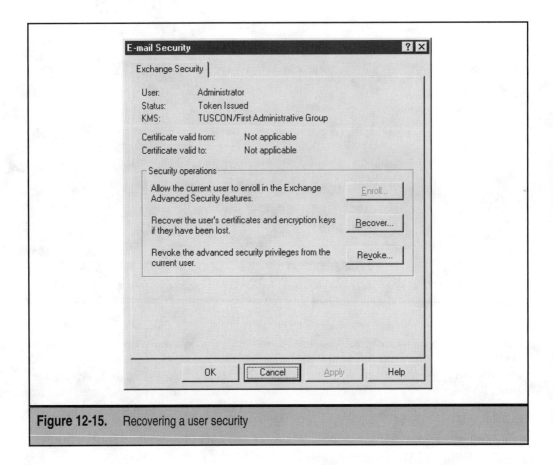

Figure 12-15. Recovering a user security

(Remember another user uses your public encryption key to encrypt a message sent to you, and you use your private encryption key to decrypt the message. If you're re-enrolled, you'd have a new private key and could not decrypt old messages.)

To recover a key, navigate to and right-click the user account in Active Directory Users and Computers, and choose Properties. Select the Exchange Features tab, choose E-mail Security, and click the Properties button. You'll be prompted for the KMS administrator password for your account. Click the Recover button, as shown in Figure 12-15, and you'll be given a new security token to begin the process of enrolling a user all over again.

SUMMARY

In this chapter, we looked at the concepts surrounding e-mail security. You learned how to install and configure both Certificate Services and KMS. You also saw the process of establishing security for a user, as well as some administrative tasks to manage KMS. In the next chapter, we'll focus on monitoring your Exchange environment using native Windows 2000 and Exchange 2000 tools.

CHAPTER 13

Monitoring Exchange 2000 Server

Like any product Microsoft creates, Exchange 2000 Server is designed to run continuously with minimal downtime. But like any software product on the market, problems will most likely arise (otherwise, you and I wouldn't have a job, right?). Since we all know that we can expect to have troubles with our Exchange Servers from time to time, and because most companies now consider their e-mail platform to be a mission-critical application, it would be beneficial for you (not to mention your job security!) to be proactively monitoring your Exchange Servers. This chapter will focus on how you can monitor your Exchange environment in an effort to be as proactive as possible in dealing with those problems. We will take a look at several monitoring functionalities that are built into Exchange 2000 using System Manager, as well as Event Viewer.

USING EXCHANGE 2000 MONITORS

Monitoring within Exchange 2000 can be broken down into two parts: monitoring servers and connections for problems, and the notification of those problems. You will first configure the objects being monitored to establish thresholds for various resources and then configure the notifications to establish the appropriate actions to be taken. All Exchange 2000–specific monitoring is configured in System Manager. As shown in Figure 13-1, all configuration and use of monitoring is completed within the Monitoring And Status container under the Tools container.

Monitoring States

Each object being monitored can be placed into one of four states: available, unreachable, warning, and critical. The granularity of a problem with a server or connection will be revealed in the latter three states. This means that you will only be notified that the server (or a connection) is in an unreachable, warning, or critical state, and not what the specific problem is. This lack of problem granularity will become clearer once you have a better understanding of notifications. See the section "Notifications," later in this chapter.

Server Monitors

Server Monitors are configured to give you an overview of the health of the server. By default, each server is configured, as shown in Figure 13-1, to monitor six Exchange-related services. The When Service Is Not Running Change State To field establishes the state the server will be placed in should one or more of these services stop.

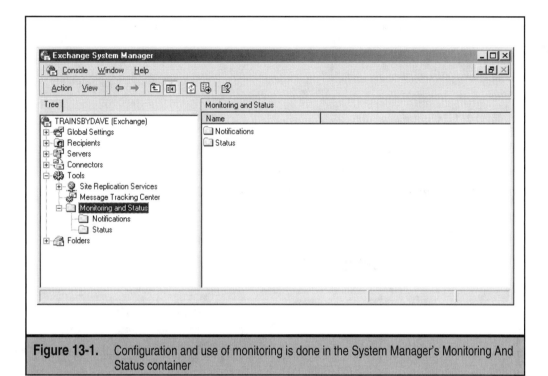

Figure 13-1. Configuration and use of monitoring is done in the System Manager's Monitoring And Status container

In Exchange 5.5, you had to manually create Server Monitors. Exchange 2000 automatically has a Server Monitor created for each Exchange 2000 server that monitors the following six Windows 2000 Services with the server set to be in a critical state should one of these services stop:

▼ Microsoft Exchange Information Store

■ Microsoft Exchange MTA Stacks

■ Microsoft Exchange Routing Engine

■ Microsoft Exchange System Attendant

■ Simple Mail Transport Protocol (SMTP)

▲ World Wide Web Publishing Service

Also, a Connection Status monitor is created for each connection.

The following six resources can be monitored within a Server Monitor:

▼ Available virtual memory

■ CPU utilization

■ Free disk space

■ SMTP Queue growth

■ Windows 2000 Service

▲ X.400 Queue growth

To add a resource to be monitored to a Server Monitor, navigate to the Status container, select the server in question, right-click the server object, and select Properties. To view the Add Resource dialog box, shown next, go to Server Monitor | Properties and click Add. Next, select the resource to be added, and click OK (see Figure 13-2).

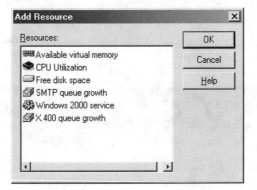

NOTE: You can also configure a Server Monitor by navigating to the Servers container, right-clicking the server in question, choosing Properties, and selecting the Monitoring tab.

Let's take a look at adding each resource to a Server Monitor and how to configure it.

Available Virtual Memory

Because Exchange 2000, like any other application or service running on Windows 2000, thrives on RAM, it is important to be able to see how much memory is available. Remember that in Windows 2000, virtual memory is considered to be the sum of the size of your physical RAM and the size of your paging file. You can establish warning and critical thresholds for the amount of available virtual memory, as shown next. If the server goes below these thresholds (entered in MBs), the server is changed to the appropriate state.

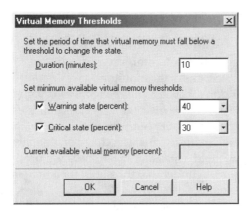

You must also specify a Duration that the server must stay below the established thresholds in order to be changed to that state.

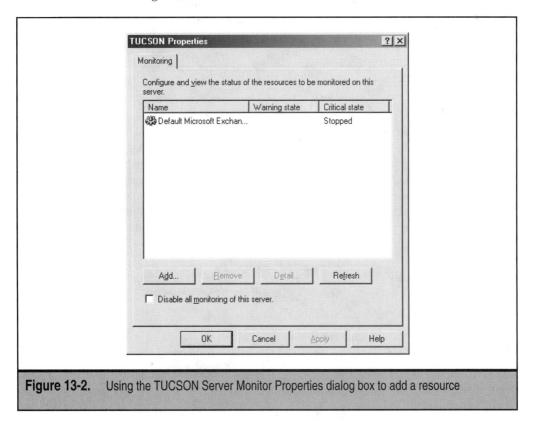

Figure 13-2.   Using the TUCSON Server Monitor Properties dialog box to add a resource

Server Monitor Durations: Getting Valid Data

In Exchange 5.5, if you were to monitor a resource like virtual memory using NT's Performance Monitor, the focus of the monitoring was the value of the available memory at the time of monitoring. While that type of monitoring yields valid data, it is not truly good data. Take this scenario, for example: It is entirely possible that the server could experience a temporary but significant increase in work to be done, which would require additional memory, making the available memory dip momentarily below a predefined threshold. Does that mean there is a problem? Certainly not. The server would need to remain under that threshold for a predetermined period of time to truly indicate a problem.

In Exchange 2000, all Server Monitor resources (with the exception of Windows 2000 services and Free Disk Space) include a Duration value (specified in minutes). This lets you establish how long the server needs to remain above (or below) the threshold in order for the server to be placed in the appropriate state. This method of monitoring gives you a validity test to determine that your server is continuing to experience problems, rather than experiencing the problem once and only for a brief time.

CPU Utilization

Because every action performed on a server involves the CPU, CPU utilization is a great general health check for your server. That is why it is important to monitor its usage. A high-running CPU can indicate several problems with your Exchange Server. You could have an overworked server due to either too many users or too many services on it. You could also have a processor that is simply not powerful enough to handle its load.

The CPU Utilization resource, shown next, allows you to establish both Warning and Critical thresholds and the duration for which the server must maintain those levels to be set in the appropriate state.

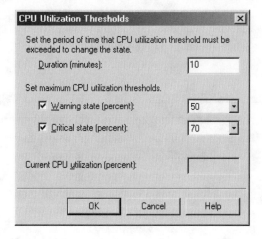

Free Disk Space

We cannot count how many companies have called asking for help with their Exchange Server whose services have stopped and won't restart. The first thing to check for is disk space. Simply put—no disk space means no Exchange! Exchange needs ample space for its various public folder and mailbox stores, the transaction logs, and the page file.

You will add a Free Disk Space resource for each logical disk on your Exchange Server. In the dialog box, shown in the next illustration, specify a disk space threshold (in MBs) for the warning and critical states.

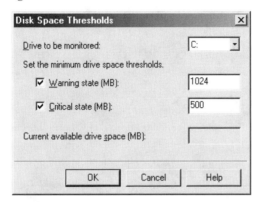

SMTP and X.400 Queue Growth

Most every Exchange 2000 server in production will utilize at least SMTP for connectivity to the Internet or another Exchange Server. In previous versions of Exchange, you could only monitor for a particular number of messages in the queue. This is not a true measure of a problem. If you just happened to have all of your users submit e-mails to external Internet addresses at the same time, you could have a large number of entries in the queue, but things would quickly return to normal once the messages are processed. This is why Exchange 2000 now monitors for continual queue growth rather than a specific number of entries. Continual growth of a queue indicates a real problem and should be considered good data. Like previous resources, this is accomplished using the Duration field.

Both the SMTP and X.400 Queue resources, shown next, allow you to specify the durations of growth for both the warning and critical states.

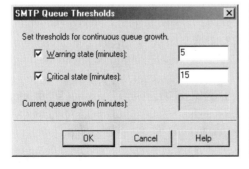
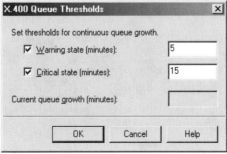

Windows 2000 Services

Although each Server Monitor already has the basic Exchange-related services being monitored, you may still want to monitor other supporting services, such as backup software agents, remote control software, or any other third-party services that extend Exchange's functionality. When adding a Windows 2000 Service, you have to first create a service group that shares a common state for the server to change to should any service within the service group stop. Then you will need to add individual Windows 2000 Services to that service group by clicking the Add button, as shown here:

The following illustration shows you a completely configured Server Monitor. Notice that each resource being monitored has both a warning and a critical level specified.

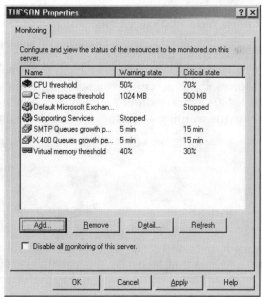

Automatically Restarting Services

When configuring a Server Monitor in Exchange 5.5 to handle a stopped service, you could set the Server Monitor to restart the service or reboot the server. This functionality is now embedded within Windows 2000 and has enhanced functionality. By running Services from within the Administrative tools menu, you can select the properties of a particular service and, on the Recovery tab, establish the appropriate response (which now includes running a file, in addition to restarting the service or computer), as shown here:

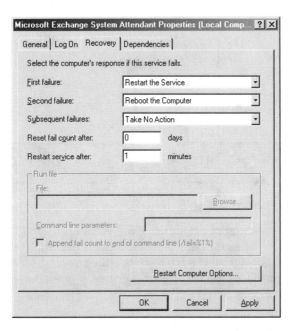

Connection Status

Monitoring Exchange 2000 Servers is like monitoring only half of your Exchange environment. An Exchange Server doesn't exist within a void; it is connected to other Exchange Servers, messaging platforms, and the Internet. A connector can exist between Exchange 2000 routing groups or between Exchange 2000 and a foreign messaging

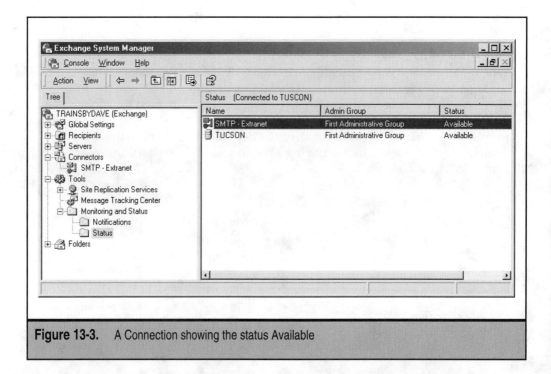

Figure 13-3. A Connection showing the status Available

system. A Connection Status object is used for monitoring each connector within the Exchange organization. The good news is that there is nothing to configure. The status of each connector, as shown in Figure 13-3, is either available or unreachable. Since a downed connector should be taken very seriously, the connector is placed in the critical state.

Notifications

Even after you configure Server Monitors for all of your Exchange Servers by specifying the appropriate thresholds for the warning and critical states, if one of those Exchange Servers had a problem, you would have no idea the problem occurred. You need to establish a method of notifying the appropriate administrative staff of the problem.

Exchange 2000 provides two types of notifications: e-mail and script. Let's look at each and see the uses and benefits of each.

E-mail Notifications

An E-mail Notification is just what it sounds like: a notification of a problem sent via e-mail. The purpose of an E-mail Notification is to provide a basic report of the status of the connections or the six Server Monitor resources. As shown in Figure 13-4, you'll find that the message sent does not contain any specific data about the Server Monitor or connection being reported on, it only give a status of OK or Error. Getting a status would only be useful to make you aware of a problem. In addition, if you know the thresholds you set for the warning and critical states, you should have an idea of what condition the server is in.

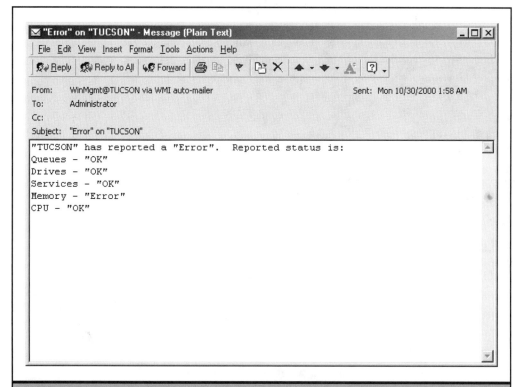

Figure 13-4.   Reporting the status of connections in an E-mail Notification message

Creating and Configuring an E-mail Notification

Before you create an E-mail Notification, I recommend that you first configure your Server Monitors, and establish thresholds for both warning and critical monitoring levels. Assuming you've already done so, as shown in Figure 13-5, navigate to and right-click the Notifications container, and select New | E-mail Notification.

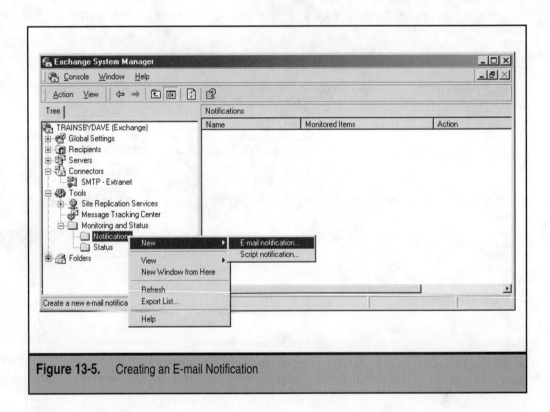

Figure 13-5. Creating an E-mail Notification

You are presented with the Properties dialog box (Figure 13-6) for a new E-mail Notification.

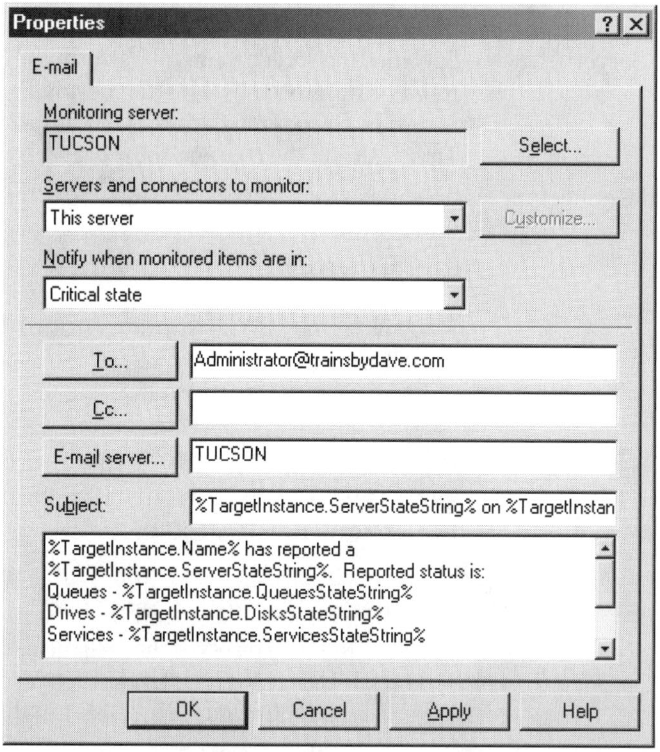

Figure 13-6.   Using the E-mail Notification Properties dialog box

Table 13-1 explains each field of the E-mail Notification Properties dialog box, as well as its use and possible values.

Parameter	Use
Monitoring Server	Specifies the server that will perform the actual monitoring processes. This can be any Exchange Server in your organization. (See "E-mail Notification Tips," later in the chapter, for more on this parameter.)
Servers And Connectors To Monitor	Specifies what servers or connectors this notification will report on: This Server All Servers Any Server In The Routing Group All Connectors Any Connector In The Routing Group Custom List Of Servers Custom List Of Connectors
Notify When Monitored Items Are In	Specifies which state (warning or critical) the notification will report on.
To / Cc	Specifies the recipients for the notification message. (See "E-mail Notification Tips," later in the chapter.)
E-mail Server	Specifies the SMTP server that will be used to actually send the message to the intended recipient(s). (See "E-mail Notification Tips" later in the chapter.)
Subject	A default subject is already provided using Windows Management Instrumentation (WMI) variables. When received, it would read something like "Error on Server X," where the status would be the appropriate status of the Exchange Server, and the server name would be the name of the server that is experiencing the error.
Message	A default message using WMI variables is provided to give the recipient a quick status of the connector (in the case of a Connection Status) or each of the six resources (in the case of a Server Monitor).

Table 13-1.   E-mail Notification Parameters

E-mail Notification Tips

In a single-server environment, the values for each of these fields would most likely be a simple choice. But in a large enterprise, the values chosen here should be considered wisely first. Let's walk down the list in Table 13-1 and go over a few real-world considerations.

▼   A server should never monitor itself. If a critical problem arose, the server might not be able to send a notification. Thus, the monitoring server field should be a different server from the one being monitored.

■   Notice that you'll have to create separate E-mail Notifications for servers and connectors (that is, you cannot choose to have one E-mail Notification sent for both types). If you have a large enterprise, you probably will further subdivide your E-mail Notifications, sending out notifications for warning and critical states separately.

■   Recipients selected for E-mail Notifications should meet one of two requirements: either the recipient provides for immediate notification or it provides for historical record. Using a mail-enabled contact that points to an alphanumeric pager or the mailbox of the current technology shift staff would meet the first recipient requirement. Using a public folder would meet the second. Bring all of these recipients into the fold by using a Distribution Group.

▲   The server specified in the E-mail Server field must not only be an SMTP server (for example, Internet Information Services (IIS), a UNIX host with an SMTP daemon running, and so on), but it must also support anonymous relaying. If you are specifying an SMTP server outside of your network, it is advisable that you use the Fully Qualified Domain Name (FQDN) for the server (for example, smtp.trainsbydave.com).

Script Notifications

A Script Notification is your best effort at initially taking care of a problem that arises with your Exchange Server. You may be able to resolve that problem, but you also may only be able to take care of the symptom. In either case, a Script Notification runs the script, batch file, or executable of your choice rather than sending an e-mail. An example of when a Script Notification might be appropriate is if the server is experiencing memory leaks. A memory leak is when an application (like Exchange) is finished and does not relinquish the memory it had been using. The end result would be a server with little or no memory left. The only recourse is a reboot to reestablish proper memory allocation. You might say, "Why do I need Script Notifications? I can reboot the server myself!" Valid point, but do you want to drive into work at 2 A.M. to do it? Probably not. In this example, the Relative Server Monitor resource to use would be available virtual memory. If the threshold is low enough to warrant a restart of the server, even if it is still providing services (however badly), Exchange can do it automatically. Also, remember that you've already set up E-mail Notifications (right?), so you will also be sent an e-mail letting you know the problem occurred.

Now that you have the big picture about Script Notifications, let's look at how to create and configure them.

Creating and Configuring a Script Notification

Before you create a Script Notification, as with E-mail Notifications, you should already have the Server Monitor(s) configured. To create a new Script Notification, in System Manager, navigate to and right-click the Notifications container, and select New | Script Notification.

You are presented with a Properties dialog box, similar to the one shown previously in Figure 13-6, for a new E-mail Notification. Table 13-2 explains each parameter, as well as its use and possible values.

Parameter	Use
Monitoring Server	Specifies the server that will perform the actual monitoring processes. This can be any Exchange Server in your organization.
Servers And Connectors To Monitor	Specifies what servers or connectors this notification will report on: This Server All Servers Any Server In The Routing Group All Connectors Any Connector In The Routing Group Custom List Of Servers Custom List Of Connectors
Notify When Monitored Items Are In	Specifies which state (warning or critical) the notification will report on.
Path To Executable	Specifies the script, batch file, or executable you wish to run.
Command Line Options	Specifies optional parameters to be fed to the executable when run.

Table 13-2.   Script Notification Parameters

Script Notification Tips

There are a few considerations to ponder when creating Script Notifications in the real world. Let's walk down Table 13-2 and cover them.

▼   Just like for the E-mail Notifications, you don't want a server monitoring itself.

■   Use separate warning and critical notifications to start different executables. For example, if a server was to be in the warning state, you may want to restart all of the Exchange Services; however, when in a critical state, you may choose to restart the server.

▲   Be sure to use a combination of Script and E-mail Notifications in order to not only make an attempt at fixing the symptom or problem, but to also make the appropriate people aware of the occurrence of the problem.

USING THE MESSAGE TRACKING CENTER

We've heard our clients tell us that when in a dispute in corporate America, the person with the most documentation wins. It would be nice to prove you did actually send that critical report to your boss on time, wouldn't it? Exchange has the ability to keep a record of each and every message it sends and receives. Your access to that information is the Message Tracking Center (MTC). Now don't go running to your boss claiming to have a way to monitor all messages; this is not an e-mail monitoring application, this simply keeps track of all messages sent and received. If you are looking for message monitoring software that looks for keywords or keeps copies of messages sent to the Internet, you will need a third-party product.

Message tracking is enabled on a per-server basis. To enable message tracking on an Exchange 2000 Server, navigate to and right-click the server object in System Manager and select Properties. On the General tab (Figure 13-7), select the Enable Message Tracking check box.

To access the MTC, go to the tools container, navigate to and right-click the MTC container, and select Track Message. Figure 13-8 shows the MTC search dialog box. A simple search can be accomplished with nothing more than filling in who the message was from, using the From field; to whom it was sent, using the Sent To field; and what server should be searched.

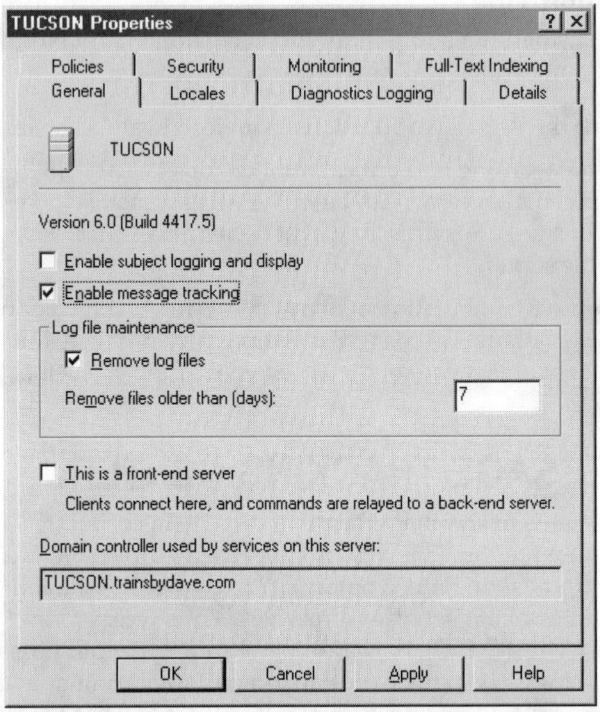

Figure 13-7.   Enabling message tracking

If you want to perform a more detailed search, you can use the Date & Time tab or the Advanced tab. The Date & Time tab (Figure 13-9) allows you to further drill your message search by specifying a period of time (by a specific day, a specific number of previous days, or a date/time range) during which the message was sent. The Advanced tab (Figure 13-10) allows you to specify a message to search for by message ID.

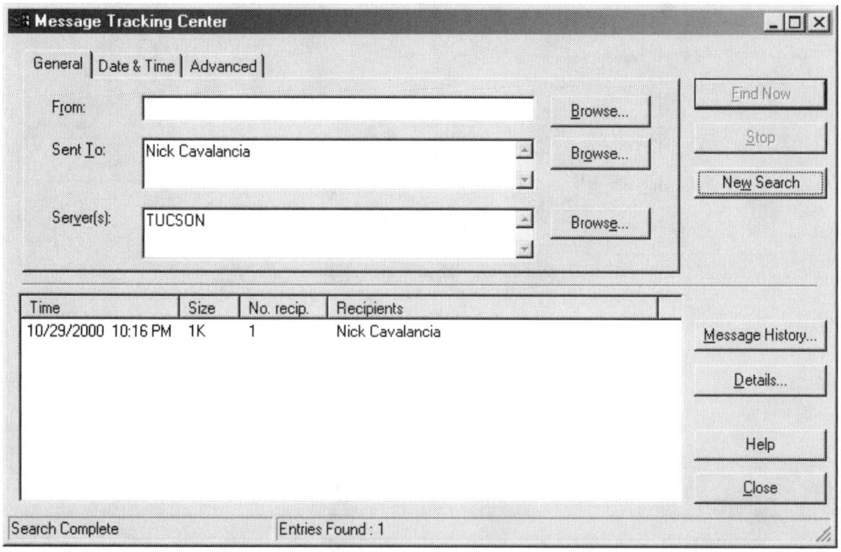

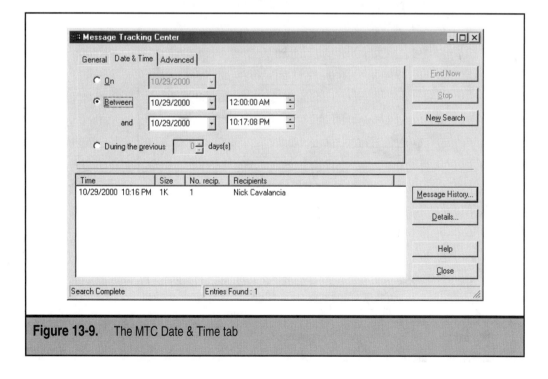

Figure 13-8.   Searching with the MTC

Figure 13-9.   The MTC Date & Time tab

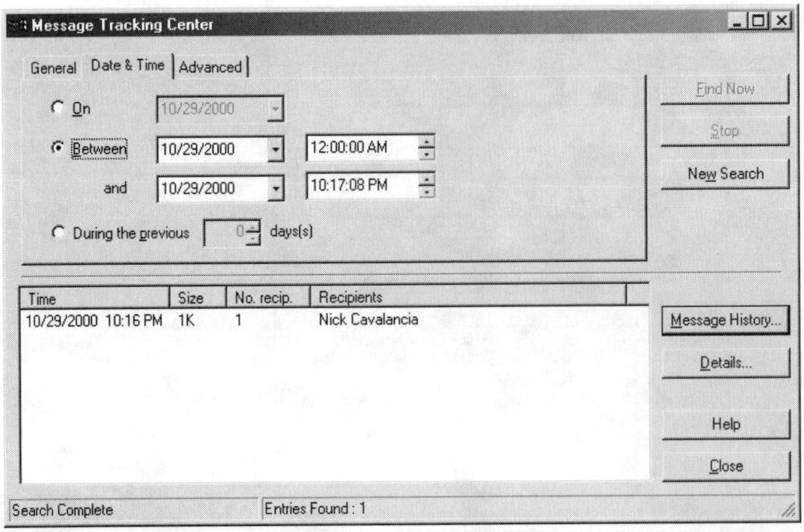

Figure 13-10. The MTC Advanced tab

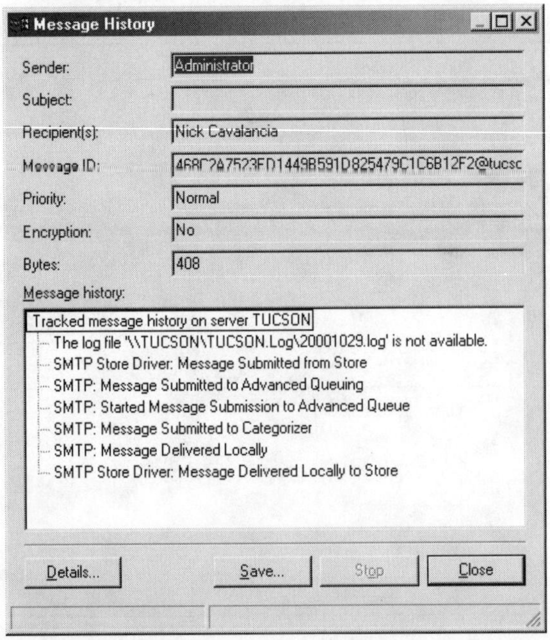

Figure 13-11. The Message History dialog box

The message ID can be found by looking at the properties of the message within your e-mail client.

Once you have specified your search criteria, clicking Find Now will yield your search results. If you would like to see the details about a certain message, single-clicking it from the results list will give you a message history (Figure 13-11).

Using Diagnostics Logging and Event Viewer

Out of the box, Exchange is configured to log major events in the Application Log. But when you are experiencing problems and wish to get a more detailed look into what is (or is not) happening with your Exchange environment, you can selectively have Exchange log more and more detailed information into the Application Log. This is accomplished with Diagnostics Logging. The basic premise behind Diagnostics Logging is that Exchange inherently has the ability to give you a play-by-play record of just about each and every thing it is doing. If Exchange were to report all that it did in the Application Log, you would have thousands upon thousands of entries to sort through—not a good thing when you are looking for a problem entry within the thousands of healthy entries. So Microsoft only has major system events (or major problems) recorded in the Application Log.

Should you find yourself needing to get more detail about a specific process, you can configure Diagnostics Logging by navigating to and right clicking the server object representing the Exchange Server you wish to investigate, choosing Properties, and choosing the Diagnostics Logging tab (Figure 13-12).

Notice in Figure 13-12 that you see the many services (and subcomponents of those services) within Exchange. Each of these components has a service-specific list of categories about which you can log entries. Each category represents a process handled by the service. To enable Diagnostics Logging, select the service and then the appropriate category, and choose the logging level. The logging level values of None, Minimum, Medium, and Maximum simply denote a general sense of how granular the logged events will be. For example, a logging level of Minimum may only log high-level entries (for example, the process starting/stopping), while a logging level of Maximum may give you a much deeper level of detail (for example, each step of the process would receive an entry in the Application Log). Technically, each event in Exchange is given an event level. The logging levels of

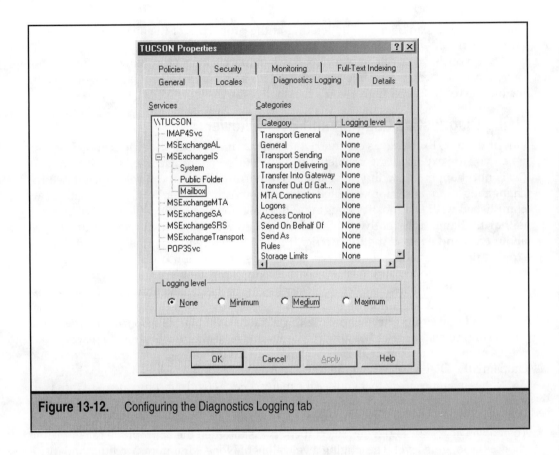

Figure 13-12.   Configuring the Diagnostics Logging tab

None, Minimum, Medium, and Maximum correspond to event levels 0, 1, 3, and 5, respectively. As you set the diagnostics level to a higher level (with None being lowest and Maximum being highest), Exchange will log events with that level value or lower.

No matter what logging level you choose, all the entries are placed in the Application Log. You can view this via Administrative Tools | Event Viewer | Application Log (Figure 13-13).

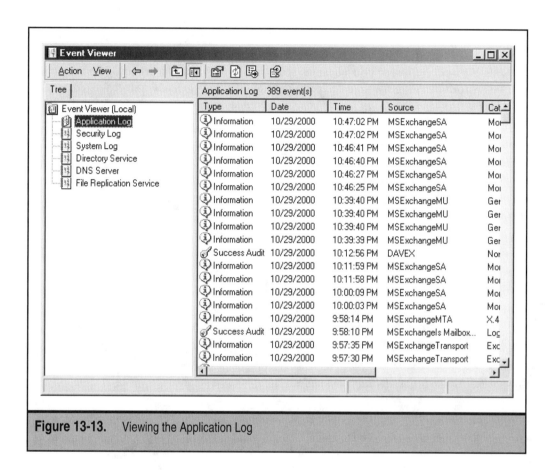

Figure 13-13. Viewing the Application Log

When Your Event Log Runneth Over

If you change the Diagnostics Logging levels on several Exchange components, you will naturally see more and more events logged in the Application Log. Since the default size for the Application Log is 512K and, by default, the system will only overwrite events that are older than seven days, it is reasonable to expect that you will fill up the Application Log. If it fills up, you may miss the opportunity to have that specific event you've been looking for to get logged. It would be wise for you to both increase the size of your Application Log (I usually start with 8192K) and, if need be, set the log to overwrite events as needed by right-clicking the log and choosing Properties, as shown here:

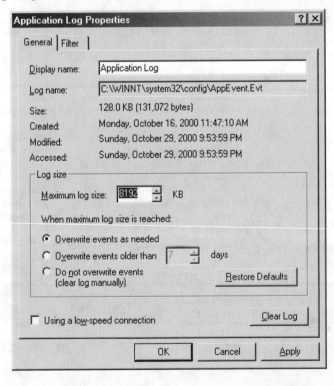

SUMMARY

In this chapter, you learned about tools you can use to monitor your Exchange environment. The Server Monitors, Connection Status, and E-mail and Script notifications help keep the watch over your Exchange Servers as proactive as possible. The MTC gives you a window into the comings and goings of messages on your server. The Diagnostics Logging and Event Viewer allow you to troubleshoot problems with pinpoint accuracy. All of these tools together will empower your efforts toward keeping your Exchange environment up and running.

In the next chapter, we'll look at not only how to properly back up your Exchange environment, but also how to ensure a good restore. We will also discuss backup terminology and possible errors you may see with the databases when backing up and restoring.

CHAPTER 14

Backup and Recovery

Y ou may or may not be surprised to learn that 24 percent of all the calls received by Microsoft Product Support involve the backup or restoration of an Exchange database. This means that there must be a sizable number of Exchange administrators who don't understand databases or how they are backed up and restored.

However, we bet that you would agree that the prospect of having to restore an Exchange database represents one of the most feared administrative duties for any Exchange administrator, including yourself.

As you read through this chapter, you might think that this chapter provides more information than you need, especially as someone who is new to Exchange 2000. Well, the reason this is a detailed chapter is that we want you to have the information necessary to ensure proper backup and recovery of your Exchange 2000 databases. This is a tricky area and one with which you should be very familiar. Following the principles and suggestions in this chapter will enable you to avoid loss of data and ensure your data's integrity in the event a disaster occurs.

In this chapter, we'll look at several areas. First, we'll look at how the transaction logs are used in both the backup and the restore processes. Then we'll learn how to use the backup program that ships with Windows 2000 to perform backups of your Exchange data. Then we'll look at how to restore the data; and, finally, we'll discuss advanced techniques to ensure that your data is there after a disaster.

NOTE: It is important to understand that your data can be lost, not only due to a disaster, but because you ran the wrong commands at the wrong time. We will show you when and how to use the recovery commands so that you don't unwittingly create problems for yourself.

TRANSACTION LOGS IN BACKUP AND RECOVERY

You'll recall from Chapter 11 that Exchange uses the Extensible Storage Engine (ESE) database structure. This means that information is written to the database in 4KB chunks called *pages*. Each page contains a time stamp, page number, and checksum information. The checksum represents the results of an algorithm that is calculated on the data in the page. The page number is just that, the number of page, and the time stamp represents the last time the page was modified.

During the backup process, each page in the database is loaded into Random Access Memory (RAM) in sequential order. After being loaded into RAM, each page will have its checksum recalculated by the backup process. The results of the recalculation of the checksum is compared to the checksum recorded on the page, and, if they match, the page is then copied to tape. If the checksums do not match, this means that the page is most likely corrupted. In this case, the backup process will record an error message in the Event Viewer and stop backing up the database.

While the process of checksumming each page represents significant overhead during the backup process, it also represents a high commitment to quality on the part of Microsoft. They would rather that you knew about a corrupted page—even if that page contained no data—than to allow you to back it up and not tell you about it. In addition, the earlier you can catch page-level corruptions in your database, the better your chances of full recovery.

During the recovery process, after you have restored your databases from tape to disk, the log files will be replayed. This will occur when you start the store.exe process. Replaying the logs constitutes the start point of starting the store process and consumes most of the time required to actually start the information store.

Replaying the transaction log files means that for each log record in each transaction log, the corresponding page in the database on disk is read into RAM, and the time stamp on the page read out of the database is compared to the time stamp of the log record that references that page. If the log record has a later time stamp than the time stamp on the page, the page is modified in RAM with the log record information. If the time stamp on the page is equal to or more recent than the time stamp on the log record, the log record is ignored and the process moves to the next log record in the transaction log.

To illustrate this, let's assume a log entry has a time stamp of 40 and the page read from the database has a time stamp of 39. ESE will see this and know that the modification to this page in the transaction log (as represented in the actual log entry) is more recent than the page held in the database, so it will write the log entry to the page in RAM. Later, that page will be flushed to disk to update the actual database on the disk. However, if the page's time stamp was 44, then the log entry would be ignored because the page in the database has a more recent modification than the log entry, and ESE would move onto the next log record in the transaction log. Therefore, it stands to reason that the more transaction logs that exist when you start the store.exe process, the longer it will take to start the store.exe process.

Modifications to the database that are held in RAM can be manually flushed to the database by one of two actions: performing a full backup of your Exchange databases or performing a graceful shutdown of the store.exe process. Either action will force all the changes in RAM to be written to the database. Transactions are only read out of the transaction logs to the database when the store process is started. Stopping the store.exe process may consume a considerable amount of time, depending on how many transactions in RAM need to be written to the database.

You might have noticed that there is a checkpoint file that accompanies your databases. This file is used to mark which log entries in the transaction logs have been written to the database and which have not. However, the writing of the new information to the database is not done from the transaction logs, but from the pages in RAM. Hence, on an Exchange 2000 Server, there are always two copies of each change to the database: the change written to the page (or series of pages) in RAM, and the log record of those changes in the transaction logs.

When a change is made to a page in RAM, that change is recorded to the transaction log (E00.log) that has also been loaded into RAM; and a connection is created between them such that if the change to the page needs to be written to the disk, then the log entry will be flushed to the transaction log first. This ensures that in the event of a system crash, we can recover our information.

There is a third element here that we have not mentioned: the version store. As changes are being made to the page in RAM, they are being recorded in the version store. Once the set of changes meets the ACID tests (see the four Atomic, Consistent, Isolated, Durable tests in Chapter 11 to learn more about committed transactions), these changes constitute a committed transaction, and it is the entire transaction that is written to the transaction log and the information is erased from the version store. The version store's purpose is to keep track of operations (changes to the database) that have not been committed to a transaction log in the form of a transaction. Near the end of the time required to start the store process, the version store will be consulted to see if there are any operations that were performed but that didn't constitute a full, committed transaction. If there are such operations in the version store, those operations will be *rolled back*: a message transferred will be untransferred, or a counter updated on a folder will be reverted to the former number. This action is called *physical redo, logical undo*.

One author had personal experience with many transactions in the transaction logs not being flushed to disk. One company thought they were getting good backups of their Exchange database until their transaction logs consumed so much disk space that they ran out of disk space. When they called for help, the author was able to help them move their databases and then start the store.exe process. It took 30 minutes for the store process to start because they had 427 transaction logs, containing many entries that had not been written to disk. They were running a very popular third-party backup software that indicated the Exchange databases were being successfully backed up when, in fact, they were not. But this illustrates the value of transaction logs. Even if the information is lost in RAM, if it has been written to a transaction log, it can be recovered and written to the database.

BACKUP OF EXCHANGE 2000 SERVER

It might seem that as long as you have all the files on the disk backed up, you'll be okay. However, when it comes to Exchange 2000 Server, this is not the case. There are more than a few things to which you'll need to pay attention; and in this section, we'll outline what some of those things are.

In Exchange 2000 Server, one storage group can hold up to five stores. Each store can be either mounted (started) or dismounted (stopped) individually within the store. All stores and storage groups run inside the store.exe process, which must be running before any of the stores or databases can be mounted. In addition, you can have concurrent backup and restore procedures running on different databases, regardless in which storage group the databases reside.

Unlike Exchange 5.5, in which the store.exe process needed to be stopped before a restore process could run, in Exchange 2000, the store.exe process must be running to restore a database from backup—though the database must be dismounted. In addition, unlike Exchange 5.5, the System Attendant is not used in the restore process and the Restore in Progress key is replaced with the restore.env file. Finally, hard recovery of a database is now available via the command line using the eseutil /cc command.

There are different types of backups available for Exchange 2000 Server. Table 14-1 lists these types and their functions.

NOTE: If circular logging is enabled, you cannot perform differential or incremental backups. Only copy and full backups can be performed.

Type	Copies Database	Copies Log	Purges Logs	Explanation
Full (Normal)	Yes	Yes	Yes	First copies the logs to disk and then purges the logs that are not needed. Backup marker is set on all files backed up.
Incremental	No	Yes	Yes	Backs up log files prior to the checkpoint log file and then deletes them. To restore the database, you'll need the last full backup plus all the subsequent incremental backups.
Differential	No	Yes	No	Backs up log files prior to the checkpoint log file, but does not delete them. To restore the database, you'll need the last full backup and the most recent differential backup. This is the fastest restore process.

Table 14-1. Backup Types And Their Functions Performed On Transaction Logs

Type	Copies Database	Copies Log	Purges Logs	Explanation
Offline	Yes	N/A	N/A	Offline backups mean that the store process has been shut down prior to backing up the database. This means that all the transaction logs have been flushed to the database and that the database is in a consistent state. Therefore, offline backups are always full backups, because the database must be shut down first. There are no additional transaction log files needed to complete a restore of an offline backup. Offline backups require manual selection of the database during the backup process.
Copy	Maybe	Maybe	No	Copy backs up any files that have changed since the last full backup. You must specify which files should be copied. In most scenarios, the copy backup will copy the new transaction logs and the databases since they will have most likely changed since the last full backup. However, if there are no changes, these files will not be backed up. You can manually select which files should be included in a copy backup, and we suggest that you use the copy backup to copy the transaction logs but not the databases.

Table 14-1.   Backup Types And Their Functions Performed On Transaction Logs *(continued)*

During the backup process, it is possible that changes to the database will occur in those parts of the database that have already been backed up. For instance, if there is a 10GB database, it is possible that after 7GB have been backed up, a user will modify a page that resides somewhere in those 7GB. In order to account for changes in those parts of the database that have already been backed up during the backup process, a *patch* (*.pat) file is created that copies those changes to the file. Once the backup process is completed, the total backed up database is a combination of the database plus the patch file. These two, together, will give you the snapshot of your database at that point in time. It is important to note that during a restore process, you could lose information or even corrupt your database by not having the patch file available.

The Exchange 2000 backup process begins with the backup Application Programming Interface (API) telling the store.exe process that a backup is about to begin and what type of backup will be performed. Then the store.exe process informs ESE, and ESE enters backup mode. At this point, the patch file is created for each database in all storage groups. The next step is that a new log file is created and the current log file is renamed. Then the backup agent requests pages out of the database sequentially, and the checksums are calculated as the page is read. Split pages are written to the patch file.

When the page reading is complete and all the pages have been copied to tape, the remaining log files are copied to tape along with the patch files. One patch file is created for each database that is being backed up. Unneeded transaction logs are deleted and the backup set is closed. After this point, ESE returns to normal mode and the backup is considered complete.

PERFORMING EXCHANGE BACKUPS WITH NTBACKUP

The Windows 2000 backup program (ntbackup.exe) ships with the Windows 2000 operating system. It is not our intention today to explain all the intricacies of this utility but, rather, to demonstrate how this utility is used in conjunction with backing up Exchange databases. For more information on how to use ntbackup, please consult the Windows 2000 Resource Kit.

By default, the ntbackup menu option is located under the System menu, which can be found by navigating from the Start menu to Programs, and then to Accessories. After the backup utility appears, you can click the Backup tab, as illustrated in Figure 14-1, which will expand the drives on the local server from which you are working.

You'll notice that near the bottom of this tab is a drop-down box labeled Backup destination. This is the place where you can choose to back up to tape, disk, or other supported media. It is grayed out in our example because we do not have a tape drive installed on this server. Our examples in this chapter will back up information to disk.

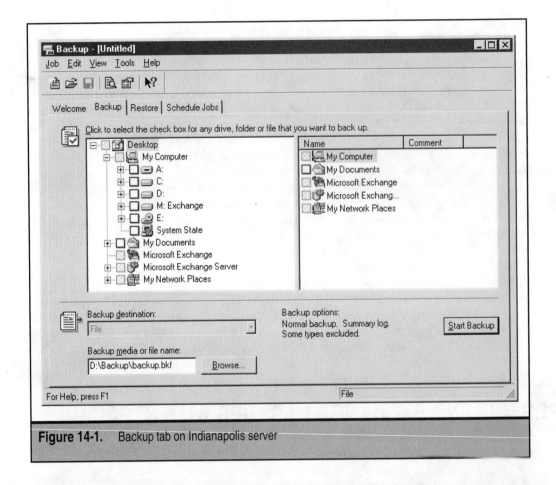

Figure 14-1.   Backup tab on Indianapolis server

Referring again to Figure 14-1, you'll also notice that there is a Microsoft Exchange Server object that can be expanded. When expanded, as illustrated in Figure 14-2, you'll see that all the Exchange 2000 Servers in the forest are listed, along with their Information Stores. If the stores are expanded, you'll find that each storage group can be individually selected for backup.

Once you've made your selections of stores to back up and the media to which they should be copied, then its time to click the Start Backup button. Once you do this, you'll see that there are more options in Figure 14-3 in the Backup Job Information dialog box. First, you can choose to either append this backup job to any backup sets that currently exist in your target tape or disk, or you can choose to replace existing backup sets with this new backup set. In our example, we'll choose to overwrite the current backup set and give the new backup set the name **Exchange Full Backup**.

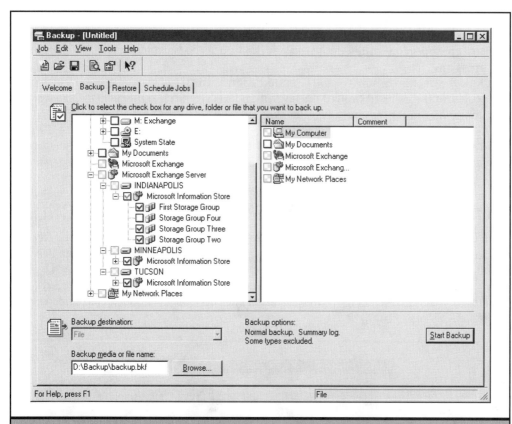

Figure 14-2.   Listing Exchange Servers and storage groups in the ntbackup utility

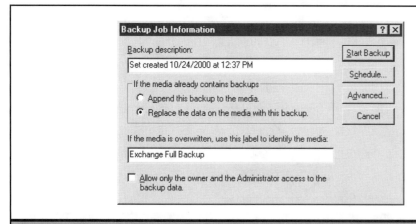

Figure 14-3.   Use the Backup Job Information dialog box for more store options

If you click the Advanced button, you can modify such settings as whether the backup is an incremental, differential, or normal backup. You can also set ntbackup to perform compression on the data being backed up if the hardware device is capable of compression.

Once the backup is started, the Backup Progress display box will appear with information about the elapsed time of the backup, which store it is currently processing, and how many files and bytes have been backed up (see Figure 14-4).

As you can see, performing a standard, basic backup using ntbackup is not a difficult activity. However, performing restores is a bit more complicated, so let's take a look at how to use ntbackup to restore our data.

PERFORMING EXCHANGE RESTORES WITH NTBACKUP

We'll use ntbackup to perform our restores as well. To perform a restore, click the Restore tab. In the left pane, you'll see a listing of the tape drives and files that have been used for backup activities. In Figure 14-5, File is listed as the source location from which to perform a backup; but you'll notice that there are three different jobs that we can select to restore. This is due to the fact that three different backup jobs were conducted and now are available for a restoration.

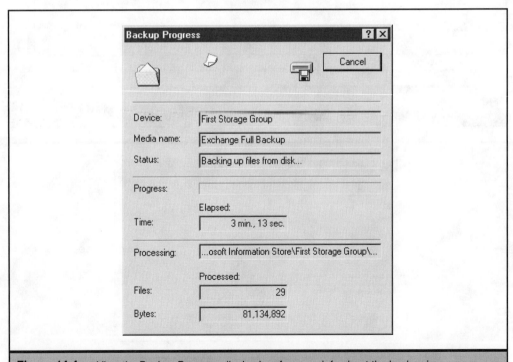

Figure 14-4.   View the Backup Progress display box for more info about the backup in progress

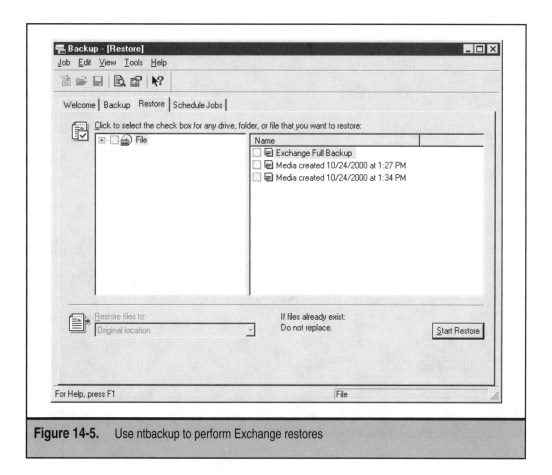

Figure 14-5.   Use ntbackup to perform Exchange restores

If we expand the File object in the left pane in Figure 14-6, we can see that under the Exchange Full Backup job, each server and information store is listed. There are several interesting things to note here. First, the third and fourth storage group on the Indianapolis server have a question mark (?) over the folder. This indicates that there were no databases inside these two storage groups during this backup job; therefore, there is nothing to restore.

Second, we can see that when the second storage group on the Indianapolis server is expanded, each store, both public and private, is listed in alphabetical order. In our example, there are five public folder stores in this storage group, PFS1 through PFS5. PFS3 is highlighted. Notice that nothing appears in the right pane for this public folder store. In fact, for all of these stores, when highlighted, nothing will appear in the right pane. This is because ntbackup operates at the store level, not the mailbox level. Restores can only be conducted on the database itself, not on individual mailboxes.

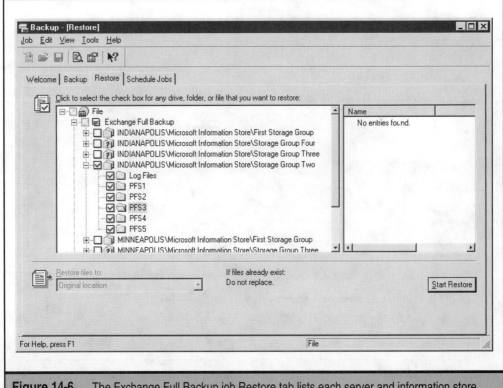

Figure 14-6. The Exchange Full Backup job Restore tab lists each server and information store.

Third, you can see that the log files are also available for restoration. If you've housed both your databases and log files on the same physical drive, then the log files can be restored along with the database.

When the Start Restore button is invoked, the Restoring Database Store dialog box appears (Figure 14-7). Select the server to which you need to restore the database and then specify the temporary location on that server for the log and patch files.

When you restore an Exchange 2000 database, you have the option to indicate that the restore procedure that you are performing is the last restore procedure you will perform before you mount the database. For instance, if you have been running incremental backups, you may need to perform several restore operations on the same database before mounting the database. To tell ntbackup that the current restore operation is the last restore operation that will be performed on this store, select the Last Backup Set check box after you click the Start Restore button on the Restore tab in ntbackup.

The Last Backup Set check box in Windows 2000 Backup determines whether hard recovery should be run after the backup completes. If you select this check box, hard recovery is run automatically after the restore procedure finishes, and then the temporary files

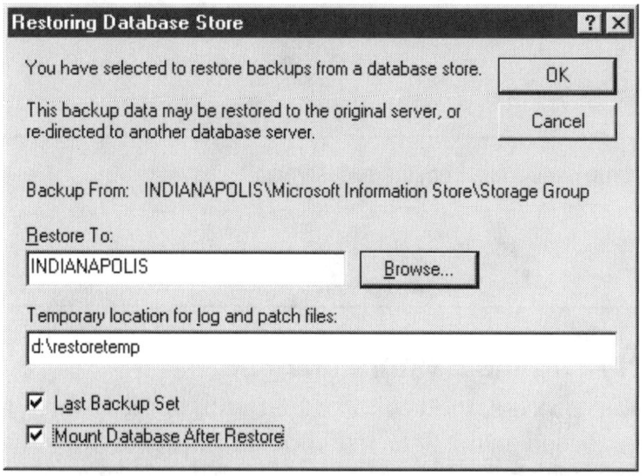

Figure 14-7. Use the Restoring Database Store dialog box to select the server to restore your database to.

are removed. At this point, you can mount the database. If you don't select this check box, hard recovery is not run. After the database files and temporary files are copied to disk, the restore procedure finishes. You *should not* attempt to mount the database at this point; doing so could cause additional corruption in the database, because, without the Last Backup Set check box selected, it is assumed that there are more restores or more transaction logs that are needed before recovery is commenced.

The purpose of not selecting the Last Backup Set option is to allow you to restore a full backup and then restore one or more incremental backups or a differential backup. You only select this check box during the last restore procedure because you do not want hard recovery to run until all the log files to be recovered are in place.

For example, if you are restoring an Exchange Server 2000 database from a full backup and two incremental backups, be sure that the Last Backup Set check box is cleared when you restore the full and the first incremental backups. Then select the Last Backup Set check box only for the last incremental backup.

There may be times when you do not want to run hard recovery immediately after the restore procedure. In addition, you may forget to select the Last Backup Set check box during the last restore procedure. For these reasons, you can manually run hard recovery using the eseutil.exe utility by typing in the following command at the command prompt:

```
eseutil /cc <path to directory containing the Restore.env file>
```

For example, if you specified in the Temporary Location For Log And Patch Files box the path of C:\Temp, then the command to run hard would be

```
eseutil /cc c:\temp
```

TIP: You must run eseutil.exe from the exchsrvr\bin folder.

Hard Recovery and the Restore.env File

During the restore process, the backup agent will ask the store process where to place the database based on the database Global Unique Identifier (GUID). The store process will instruct the backup agent to place the database from tape on top of the database on disk. In addition, during the restore process, the restore.env file is created, which holds the following necessary information for the restore process:

▼ Restore database path

■ Restore log file path

■ Correct storage group

■ System parameters for the restore storage group

■ Log file range

▲ Restore time

Remember that when you restore an online backup of an Exchange 2000 database, until the hard recovery process is completed, the database is in an inconsistent state. Bringing the database to a consistent state after a restore procedure is called *hard recovery*. During hard recovery, the ESE replays the log files and patch files to redo operations performed on the database, and then to undo any operations that belong to incomplete transactions. Unlike Exchange 5.5, where hard recovery was controlled by the Restore in Progress registry key, Exchange 2000 controls hard recovery with the restore.env file that is created in the folder you specify during the restore process in the Temporary Location for Log and Patch Files box. This folder will also contain the log files and patch (.pat) files necessary to complete recovery on the database.

During the log file replay, the log file signature is first checked to ensure that it is the correct log file for the database, the patch file is read, and then each record in the log file(s) are replayed into the database if their time stamp is later than the record in the database. If there are multiple databases in a storage group, only the log records applicable to the failed database(s) are replayed and the other records are ignored. Happily, log file replay in Exchange 2000 Server is at least three times faster than it was in Exchange 5.5.

Concurrent restores can be conducted to databases residing in the same storage group or in multiple storage groups; however, concurrent restores cannot be conducted on the same database. In addition, if you restore multiple databases in a storage group simultaneously, you'll need to restore each backup set to its own temporary log directory and ensure that you *don't* check the Last Backup Set check box so that the hard recovery process isn't run until all the restore operations are conducted.

After you've made your selections in the Restoring Database Store dialog box, you'll click OK and the restoration will begin. The Restore Progress display box will appear informing you as to the progress of the restore procedure. Thereafter, another box will inform you that the restore procedure has completed, and you'll be able to either close the box or print out a report detailing the procedure's activities.

To summarize, the flow of events for an Exhange 2000 Server is as follows:

1. The database(s) must be dismounted.

2. Verify that the This Database Can Be Overwritten By A Restore check box is selected on the Database tab in the store's properties.

3. The store process informs ESE that a restore procedure is going to be conducted, and ESE enters restore mode.

4. The backup agent copies the edb and stm database files from tape (or file, in our example) to their original location by checking the restore.env file for the database path.

5. The backup agent copies the log files and patch file to the temporary folder specified in the Temporary Location For Log And Patch Files input box.

6. If the Last Backup Set check box is selected, ESE checks the log file sequence and warns you if a log is missing or if there are log files from a different file set. (In the event that you cannot supply the missing or correct log files, ESE replays the logs from tape and brings the database to a consistent state; however, information created or modified since the last backup will be lost.) Then the patch file and log files are processed by ESE, unrecorded records are written to the database files, and unfinished transactions are rolled back. If the Last Backup Set check box is not selected, then the database, and log and patch files are copied to their original location, and the restore procedure ends.

7. ESE replays any current log files not copied from tape, and unrecorded records are written to the database files.

8. ESE enters normal mode and mounts the database(s).

9. Data is deleted from the temporary directory.

NOTE: If you did not verify that the This Database Can Be Overwritten By A Restore check box is selected in the store's properties Database tab, it may take up to 15 minutes for the databases to be mounted after the restore is finished.

ADVANCED BACKUP TECHNIQUES AND CONSIDERATIONS

There are a few techniques to consider, as well as some pitfalls to avoid. This section will outline how to restore a database to an alternate server, as well as how to use the eseutil and isinteg utilities.

Restoring to an Alternate Server

Restoring a database to an Exchange Server that is different from the one on which you performed the backup enables you to recover individual items from a backup without restoring over a server that is in use. Restoring Exchange data to a nonproduction server is the only method of recovering data that has exceeded the retention time limits. This is a last-resort method for retrieving items from individual mailboxes or public folders. This method requires an additional computer with enough hard disk space to restore the entire backup and that meets the minimum hardware requirements to run Exchange. Refer to Chapter 2 for the minimum hardware requirements for Exchange 2000 Server.

The first thing you'll need to do is to build a new Exchange 2000/Windows 2000 Server with all the latest hotfixes and service packs installed. This will require another physical box. After building this new server, you'll need to run DCPROMO to create a new forest and give it a different Domain Name System (DNS) name, such as "newdomain.mycompany.com." Install DNS as standard primary, allow dynamic updates, and point the server to itself for DNS resolution. However, when you install Exchange 2000 Server, *use the same organization name* that was used on the current installation.

In order for the databases to work in the new forest, the LegacyExchangeDNs must match. The first Exchange 2000 administrative group is always First Administrative Group in the Distinguished Name (DN). We realize that in the Exchange System Manager (ESM), the administrative group display names can be changed, but this doesn't change the LegacyExchangeDN value.

After creating the new server, be sure to use the same naming convention through the Exchange installation as was used in the original Exchange installation. Also, be sure the database paths are the same on both servers. After creating a new storage group and database with matching display names, dismount the database and select the This Database Can Be Overwritten By A Restore check box. Then restore the backup sets and mount the database.

After the database is mounted, you should run the Active Directory Account Cleanup Wizard (ADCLEAN) to ensure there is only existence for each user account in the new forest. Then, log on and extract the data that is needed for the first installation. Normally, this will be to extract a mailbox to a .pst file and then synchronize this information back to the original Exchange database.

Mailbox Reconnect and Restoring a Single Mailbox

Sometimes, you'll need to reconnect a mailbox to a user account. This is most often the case when a deleted mailbox needs to be recovered. In order to ensure you can recover a deleted mailbox, configure the Keep Deleted Mailboxes For (Days) setting on the Limits tab in the store's properties (Figure 14-8). The value configured here means that any mailbox that is deleted can be recovered up to the configured value, which, in our example, is 45 days.

When a mailbox is deleted, the icon is not removed in the ESM and a red *X* will appear over the mailbox icon. A mailbox can be deleted by using the Exchange Tasks Wizard in Active Directory Users And Computers. Once deleted, the mailbox can be recovered by reconnecting the user account to the mailbox. To learn more about how to do this, please see Chapter 7.

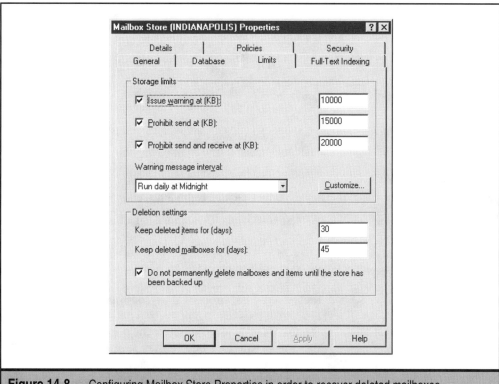

Figure 14-8.   Configuring Mailbox Store Properties in order to recover deleted mailboxes

Planning a Backup Strategy

There are three main considerations when choosing a backup and restore strategy. These three elements are as follows:

▼ **Time to restore**   Determine how long a restore should take and then plan accordingly. If your databases are too large to be restored within the desired time, then consider creating new databases to host these users.

■ **Capacity to restore**   Make sure you'll have sufficient hard disk space to complete the restore process. The more transaction logs created between each full backup, the more disk space you'll need to restore the Exchange database.

▲ **Time to backup**   If it takes too long to perform an online backup of your database, consider creating new databases and load balancing your users across these databases. Then consider running simultaneous backups or increasing the speed of your backup equipment, or both.

The more common methods of performing a backup are outlined in Table 14-2.

Type	Comment
Full Daily Backup	This is a full backup that is performed online each day. Transaction log files are deleted daily, keeping disk space free. However, if a backup set becomes corrupted for some reason, the previous backup set cannot be brought up to the current time because the transaction log files will be missing.
Daily Copy Backup Plus Incremental	A copy backup is the same as a full daily backup, except that the transaction logs are not deleted. An incremental backup, when performed with a copy backup, will save all the transaction log files in the copy process and then have those log files deleted by the incremental process. This combination of backup types resolves the problems of a bad backup set for the full daily backup because the copy backup saves the transaction logs before they are deleted by the incremental process.

Table 14-2.   Common Backup Methods

Type	Comment
Weekly Full Backup Plus Partial Backups	The main benefit of this method is that the backup processes during the week are greatly reduced in time. However, to restore the databases, you'll need enough disk space to hold all the transaction logs that were created since the last full backup. If a differential backup is selected, then the restore time will be faster because only the full and the last differential backup will be required to restore the database. However, as time passes, there will be a build up of transaction log files and the backup time will increase as the week progresses.

Table 14-2.   Common Backup Methods *(continued)*

After selecting which type of backup method meets your needs, you need to have these best practices to follow when a disaster strikes:

▼ First restore, then repair. ESE databases are designed to be recovered by restoring the database file and then replaying the transaction logs. Using the repair utilities, such as isinteg.exe or eseutil.exe, may result in some loss of data.

■ Always make copies of your current databases and transaction logs before starting a restore. This will be of help if the restore fails and you need to start over.

■ Disable circular logging.

■ Make sure all the transaction log files are in place before performing a hard recovery and attempting to replay the log files into the database. Replaying log files out of sequence will likely result in your database experiencing further corruption.

▲ Use quality hardware.

If your server fails, there could be one of several database problems:

▼ The contents in memory are lost and the database file is now in an inconsistent state. This is always a recoverable event (provided you've taken the necessary actions to plan for this).

- The database file incurs page corruption. This can occur after a power outage, because the spike or brown will hinder proper writing of information to the disk. This type of problem is dependent on having good backups.

▲ One or more transaction log files have become corrupt. Complete recovery may not be possible if a recent transaction log file is corrupt.

ESE records the state of the database file in its file header. When the database is operating, the state is always marked as inconsistent. It is only marked as consistent when the database is dismounted normally. The database header can be dumped to determine the state of the database.

During a shutdown, ESE reads the checkpoint file to determine which log file(s) need to be flushed to the database on disk. ESE writes these records to the database on disk, and then the service shuts down. If no checkpoint file exists, ESE starts from the earliest transaction log file that it can find and then attempts to write each record to the database. Those records with a time stamp equal to or older than the record in the database are not written to the database. This is the same routine that is followed when ESE performs a soft recovery. In either case, once the records have been successfully written to the database and the services have shut down, the database should be in a consistent state.

Physical Corruption of the Database

Physical corruption of the database usually occurs at the page level. Since the cause of page-level corruptions is *always* outside of ESE, you should address the causes of page corruption before restoring your Exchange databases. ESE can detect and report page-level corruptions, but ESE is never the cause of these corruptions.

Common causes of page-level corruption include

▼ **Virus protection software** Virus protection software watches for certain data patterns in order to detect a virus. It is possible for one of these patterns to appear in an innocent e-mail—especially given the number and type of e-mails being passed today. If the virus software does not recognize the presence of the Exchange Server, the software could make changes to the database file that cause physical corruption. Be sure to use virus software that recognizes and works with Exchange 2000 Server.

- **Hard disk controllers** Sometimes a controller or device driver cannot keep up with the stress ESE creates. This can lead to inaccurate read/write errors that, in turn, create page-level corruptions. Be sure you are working with the latest device driver from each hardware manufacturer. If corruption problems persist, replace the firmware or hardware device with a faster, more robust device.

▲ **Bad hard disks** These can easily cause page-level corruptions when a sector goes bad and part of the database is residing on the sector. In this case, the hard disk should be replaced.

ESE uses checksums to detect physical corruption and ESE is proactive in running these checksums. It is important to catch page-level corruptions early because once a page is corrupted, it cannot be repaired. Early detection can mean that the database can be restored with the transaction logs, and no data will be lost. Once the transaction logs are purged, if the corrupted page is not detected, then you'll probably lose data fixing the problem.

Whenever a page is written from memory to disk, ESE writes a checksum to the page. Then, when the page is read back into memory, the checksum is recalculated and compared to the first checksum written to the page. If they match, then the data is assumed to have integrity. If not, ESE will record an event in the Event Viewer. The error codes will appear as outlined in Table 14-3.

There are three things that cause ESE to generate these kinds of error codes. First, ESE asked the device driver to write the page to disk, but the device driver malfunctioned or the disk controller malfunctioned and prevented the page from ever being written to the disk. When ESE asks for this page, it's not there. So the checksum fails and the 1018 error is generated.

Second, the page was successfully written to the disk, but the device driver or disk controller malfunctioned, causing the contents of the page to change. When the page is read from disk, the checksum fails and an error message is generated.

Third, the page is successfully written to disk; but when ESE requests the page from disk, the device driver or controller malfunctions, causing the wrong page to be returned. Again, the checksums will fail and that will generate an error message in the Event Viewer.

One of the best ways for ESE to detect a page-level corruption is to have an online, full backup performed. During the process, as each page is passed from the database to tape,

Error Code	Meaning
1018(JET_errReadVerifyFailure)	The data read from the disk is not the same as the data that was written to the disk. This means that there is a page-level corruption.
1019(JET_errPageNotInitialized)	The requested page is not initialized. This can be the result of either page-level corruption or the transaction logs being replayed out of sequence.
1022(JET_errDiskI/O)	Either the page is not readable or ESE cannot open the database file. This error can be caused by page-level corruption or by transaction logs being replayed out of sequence.

Table 14-3. Page-Level Corruption Events Codes

ESE runs the checksum on each page. If the checksums do not match, then the backup process will fail and a 1018 error message will be generated in the Event Viewer. If the online backup finds a page with the first 40 bytes all zeroes, then it considers the page uninitialized. However, this may also indicate a page corruption, and an 1019 error will be generated in the Event Viewer.

If you want ESE to check for corruption of an offline backup, use the esefile utility. This utility can be used to check for corruption of the entire database file or a single page. The command line syntax is as follows:

```
esefile [/c source destination] [/x file] [/s file] [/d file pgno],
```

where

- ▼ /c copies source to destination
- ■ /s Ese.dll format checksum
- ■ /x Edb.dll format checksum
- ■ /d dumps a page from file
- ▲ pgno = page number

Figure 14-9 illustrates how to check a database for checksum errors.

Resolving Physical Corruption Errors

In theory, the solution to resolving physical corruption errors is easy: find the faulty device driver or hardware device and replace it. If this is going to be a time-consuming task, then rebuild another Exchange Server and restore the databases to that server. Restoring the database to the same computer is likely to generate the same errors unless new hardware or updated device drivers have been installed.

Troubleshooting Database Recovery

If the recovery of your database isn't successful, then you should take a moment to consider some of the more common restore problems that can occur.

First, one of the more common mistakes that administrators make during a restore process is that they have either the wrong transaction log files present or an incomplete set of transaction log files present when hard recovery is attempted. This can occur if a transaction log was renamed, if an incremental backup was not restored, or if the checkpoint file is not removed and files prior to the checkpoint file are skipped during replay.

ESE may respond in a couple of different ways. First, if it finds that a transaction log is missing, ESE will halt and log an error in the Event Viewer. However, if ESE cannot discern that the log file is incorrect or out of order, it will replay the records in the log to the database. When the database is mounted, you might experience additional errors or random freezing of the database.

```
Command Prompt                                                                    _ 8 X

D:\UTILS\I386>esefile /x d:\databases\priv1.edb

Microsoft(R) Exchange Server(TM) Database Utilities
Copyright (C) Microsoft Corporation 1999-2000.  All Rights Reserved.

ERROR: page -1 checksum failed ( 0x92d147d5 / 0x190d67e5 )
ERROR: page 0 checksum failed ( 0x92d147d5 / 0x190d67e5 )
ERROR: page 1 returned page 0
ERROR: page 1 checksum failed ( 0x6c8543da / 0x77eac7d2 )
ERROR: page 2 returned page 0
ERROR: page 2 checksum failed ( 0xaceccd30 / 0xfd3c590c )
ERROR: page 3 returned page 0
ERROR: page 3 checksum failed ( 0x2e4a98c7 / 0x63e7f619 )
ERROR: page 4 returned page 0
ERROR: page 4 checksum failed ( 0x1bd46bc3 / 0x3a369229 )
ERROR: page 5 returned page 0
ERROR: page 5 checksum failed ( 0x7f0eb76a / 0x293d98fa )
ERROR: page 6 returned page 0
ERROR: page 6 checksum failed ( 0x2e6eaf88 / 0x6353eef8 )
ERROR: page 7 returned page 0
ERROR: page 7 checksum failed ( 0x5fa1e94e / 0xb9e0dd9c )
ERROR: page 8 returned page 0
ERROR: page 8 checksum failed ( 0xd19032b3 / 0x1cfa0d09 )
ERROR: page 9 returned page 0
ERROR: page 9 checksum failed ( 0x92f8dbe / 0x8898e24e )
ERROR: page 10 returned page 0
ERROR: page 10 checksum failed ( 0x6e0aaef3 / 0x7ea411e9 )
ERROR: page 11 returned page 0
ERROR: page 11 checksum failed ( 0x89c0f272 / 0x89bac612 )
ERROR: page 12 returned page 0
ERROR: page 12 checksum failed ( 0x89ace669 / 0x89aaca63 )
ERROR: page 13 returned page 0
ERROR: page 13 checksum failed ( 0x8e430ce4 / 0x649aede6 )
ERROR: page 14 returned page 0
ERROR: page 14 checksum failed ( 0x7a8eab0f / 0xb04b5ffd )
ERROR: page 15 returned page 0
ERROR: page 15 checksum failed ( 0xf2b58e7 / 0xd98b6b03 )
ERROR: page 16 returned page 896000
ERROR: page 16 checksum failed ( 0xa4abc33a / 0x6ec3c7c )
ERROR: page 17 returned page 0
ERROR: page 17 checksum failed ( 0x8f25157 / 0x72f4fd61 )
ERROR: page 18 returned page 0
ERROR: page 18 checksum failed ( 0xd8c7431e / 0xc6296bb0 )
ERROR: page 19 returned page 386304
ERROR: page 19 checksum failed ( 0xb97b41ae / 0xe2b5bdd8 )
```

Figure 14-9.   Using esefile to diagnose checksum error for priv1.edb

The way to ensure you have the correct transaction log files during a restore is to follow these tips:

1. Always copy existing files, including transaction logs, database files, and the checkpoint file to a neutral location. If the restore doesn't go well, you can use these files to retry the restore.

2. Before performing the restore, preview the transaction log file directory to ensure that there are no gaps in the log file numbers.

3. Never rename a transaction log file

The point is that you need to ensure you have all the transaction logs in order since the last full backup for all the data to be recovered. For instance, if you experience a system crash on Wednesday at noon and your last full backup was on the previous Friday night, then here is what you'll need to recover to the point of the disaster:

▼ **Database from the full backup tape from Friday**   This will restore all the information in your Exchange database from last Friday and before.

▲ **All transaction logs from Friday to Wednesday at noon**   This will contain all the information that was entered into the Exchange system between the full backup on Friday night and the system disaster on Wednesday at noon.

NOTE: Before replaying log files, you should move the checkpoint file so that it isn't in the same directory as your transaction logs. If the checkpoint file is present, replay will begin at the location in the log file to which the checkpoint is pointing. Any log files and records previous to the checkpoint file will be ignored because ESE will assume they have already been written to the database.

Second, one of the more common mistakes Exchange administrators make is running isinteg before restarting the database. Isinteg is a utility that is used when an offline backup is restored to resynchronize the GUIDs between the information store databases and Active Directory (AD). If the GUIDs are not synchronized when the database is started, an error message will be produced instructing you to run the isinteg utility.

However, if this utility is run after the restore of an online backup, the database will become logically corrupt, though no error messages will be generated. It is unnecessary to run this utility after performing an online restore because ESE automatically runs this command when an online restore is performed; hence, you shouldn't run this command unless you are directed to do so by an error message.

Third, a common problem that Exchange Administrators run into is that their backup set is bad. Perhaps a single tape in a tape set is missing, or the tape is old and the information was not written to the tape correctly, or even the information was never written to the tape in the first place. If you're running lots of full backups between a few tapes, information could be overwritten on the tape, which would make that backup set useless.

Along the same lines, it is best to use a combination of copy and incremental backup procedures instead of using full daily backups, because full daily backups may leave a transaction log file gap. However, the disadvantage of this method is that duplicate copies of information are saved. In some environments, this could represent several hundred megabytes of information that is duplicated to tape each day.

Preventing Restore Errors

If you've skipped to this section because you're in the middle of a disaster, we would encourage you to take the time to read the balance of this chapter before implementing a restore. The information in this section, without background knowledge, will not make much sense.

If you have just restored from backup tape and are not sure that you have all the correct transaction log files, you should dump the headers of some of the key files to compare the signatures and log file generated numbers. Here are the files that you should dump:

▼ Lowest numbered transaction log

■ Highest numbered transaction log

■ One file below the highest numbered transaction log

■ E00.log

■ Database files

▲ Patch file

Compare the signatures to make sure they match. Make sure that you have all the log files by counting, manually, all the log files in order. If you're missing one or more log files, then try to recover them from tape. If you can't recover or find one of the log files, then you'll only be able to recover to the next log file previous to the one that is missing. All others should not be used during replay and this data will be lost.

The reason this data is lost can be explained with this illustration. Let's assume that in transaction log number 10, a log entry exists to modify page number 1001 in the database with "NowThen." Let's assume that in log number 15, there is a delete command that effectively deletes all the information on page 1001. Now, let's assume that in log number 20, there is a new message created with "herethere," and that this record is recorded on page number 1001.

During the restore operation, you can find logs 10 and 20, but you cannot find log number 15. If you restore the database and replay log number 10 and then log number 20, the information from log number 20 will conflict with the information from log number 10 because the entry in log number 20 assumes that page 1001 is a clean, empty page. Without the delete command being replayed into the database, the log record in log number 20 will corrupt the page with conflicting information. Moreover, the checksums won't match and the page will be corrupted because of this, too.

If you cannot locate all the transaction logs since the last full backup, only restore those transaction logs that you can find that can be replayed in order. *Do not replay out-of-order transaction logs.*

Database Restart Errors

Table 14-4 offers a list of some of the more common database restart errors and what they mean. You'll find these errors displayed in the Event Viewer.

Error Number	Explanation
528 Log File Missing	The E00.log is either missing or it's the wrong one.
530 Bad Log File Signature	One or more log files have the incorrect signature relative to the database.
550 Database Inconsistent	At least one database that you are working with was not shut down properly. At least one database is in an inconsistent state.
1011 GUID Not Synchronized	You need to run isinteg –patch.
1023 File Path Not Valid	The database files have not been placed in the correct path. Check the database locations and transaction log locations by dumping the file headers.
1201 Duplicate Database	The database has not been found in the place specified, so a new one is being created; however, there is already a database with the same name in the same place, but it is recognized as the wrong database. This is caused by wrong log file locations or wrong database locations.
1206 Database Header Corrupted	The database file header is corrupt. This can also be due to the transaction logs and database signatures not matching, or files not in the right locations
1811 File Not Found	The database is looking for transaction log files and can't find them. Examine the header of the checkpoint file and transaction logs. Do you have the correct files? Correct locations? Have the log files been moved?

Table 14-4. Common Database Error Messages

Eseutil

This utility has several important uses. First, eseutil can be used to defragment the database and reduce its physical size. When information is deleted in the database, the pages that held that information are not deleted, so the size of the database is not reduced. Each night, there is an online defragmentation that is run by ESE, and it reports the amount of free disk space that is available in each database. This is illustrated in Figure 14-10.

The only way to recover free disk space inside of an ESE database is to take the database offline and run the eseutil against it. ESE defragments, repairs, and checks the integrity of the database. When it restarts, it creates a new database and copies the records to it. It also discards unused pages, freeing up this disk space for system use. You should have free disk space equal to the size of the database you're defragmenting, plus 20 percent.

In addition, when the defragmentation is run, new database signatures are created and previous transaction logs cannot be replayed into the new database; therefore, when you defragment a database, you make the previous transaction logs useless with the new database. Except in cases in which data recovery is not important, you should not

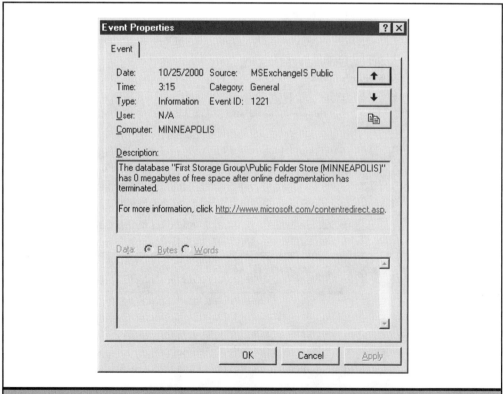

Figure 14-10.   Use exeutil for a report of free disk space on each of your databases

defragment your database as a method to repair the database and get it back online. Doing so could result in data loss.

To dump a database or transaction log file header, use the eseutil /mh command, as illustrated in Figure 14-11. Notice the /m switch is before the file specification and the /h switch is after the file specification. However, they can also be placed together, /mh, and you'll get the same results.

Figure 14-11. Using eseutil to dump the header file for priv1.edb

TIP: Be sure that there are no spaces (such as program files) in your database paths. Eseutil won't know what to do with them and the command will fail.

To run a defragmentation on the database, use the eseutil /d command, as illustrated in Figure 14-12. You can see that this utility first did the defragmentation on both database files, and then it copied each one individually back to the original location. Notice also that the command was just for the priv1.edb, but ESE also defragmented the priv1.stm file.

To check the integrity of your database, run the eseutil /g command. This command is a read-only command that does not make changes to the database. It checks the database tables, rebuilds all indexes on a temporary database, and compares the indexes to ensure integrity of the original index. This command is illustrated in Figure 14-13.

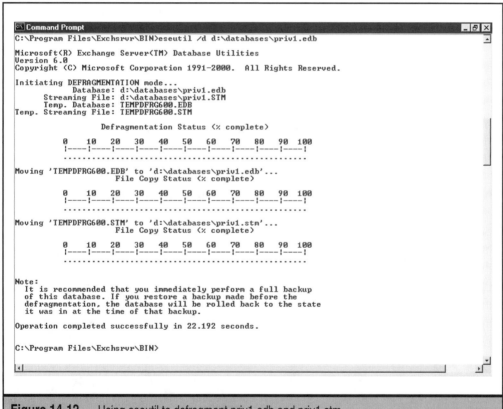

Figure 14-12.   Using eseutil to defragment priv1.edb and priv1.stm

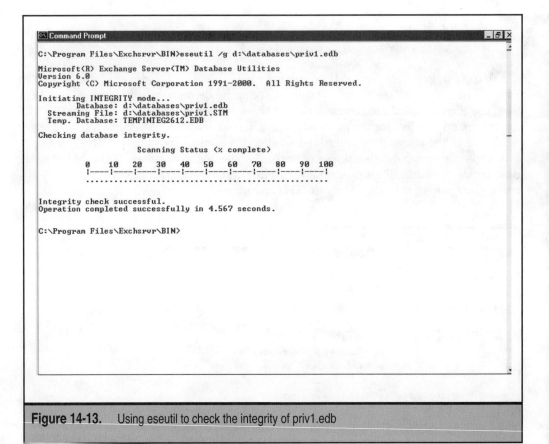

```
Command Prompt                                                              _ □ X

C:\Program Files\Exchsrvr\BIN>eseutil /g d:\databases\priv1.edb

Microsoft(R) Exchange Server(TM) Database Utilities
Version 6.0
Copyright (C) Microsoft Corporation 1991-2000.  All Rights Reserved.

Initiating INTEGRITY mode...
          Database: d:\databases\priv1.edb
     Streaming File: d:\databases\priv1.STM
     Temp. Database: TEMPINTEG2612.EDB

Checking database integrity.

               Scanning Status (% complete)

        0    10   20   30   40   50   60   70   80   90  100
        !----!----!----!----!----!----!----!----!----!----!
        ..................................................

Integrity check successful.
Operation completed successfully in 4.567 seconds.


C:\Program Files\Exchsrvr\BIN>
```

Figure 14-13. Using eseutil to check the integrity of priv1.edb

Finally, if you want to dump the header information for your transaction logs, the command to do so is eseutil /ml. In the output, you'll see the log generation number if decimal, the signature for the log file, in the log file's database location, and a reference to the log file that was E00.log the last time ESE was started. This is illustrated in Figure 14-14.

Figure 14-14. Using eseutil to dump the file header for e0000005.log

SUMMARY

Whew! Looks like backing up and restoring Exchange 2000 databases is much more complicated than it appears to be. In this chapter, you learned how to back up and restore an Exchange database using the ntbackup utility. We also discussed a number of advanced topics, including how to restore databases to an alternate server, how to plan your backup strategy, and the pitfalls to avoid when restoring a database.

In the next chapter, we'll move our focus away from disaster recovery to Exchange 2000 Server performance tuning.

CHAPTER 15

Performance Tuning Exchange 2000 Server

At this point in the book, if you were to read it from front to back and implement your environment with each chapter, you would have a completely functional, well-designed Exchange 2000 organization. Once that's accomplished, the main concern would be the performance of your Exchange Servers. Day-to-day performance of Exchange will most likely be considered good (as long as no users call complaining that their e-mail is too slow, right?). However, the question still remains: how well is your Exchange environment running? The Exchange performance litmus test previously mentioned (no complaints equals good performance) is somewhat of a commentary on the reactive method by which many administrators gauge the performance of Exchange. It would be far more advantageous to actually monitor Exchange for performance.

Performance monitoring of Exchange is not only a good idea, it can be critical for the maintenance of your environment. Let us ask a few questions about your current Exchange environment to see whether yours will be a success:

▼ When do you project your Mailbox Store drive will run out of disk space?

■ At what time of day or day of week is your Exchange server's processor busiest?

▲ How many users logged onto Outlook Web Access (OWA) yesterday?

Knowing the answers to these questions won't just help your Exchange server run more efficiently, but it can also make the difference between the life and death of an Exchange Server. This chapter will first cover some basic information of performance monitoring using the Windows 2000 System Monitor tool. Then we will look at Exchange-specific counters to monitor, as well as how to make the information gathered work for you.

PERFORMANCE MONITORING BASICS

Before you can begin monitoring your Exchange Servers, you need to know a little about performance monitoring in general. We'll begin by focusing on monitoring Windows 2000 in general. Then we'll see how we can apply what we've learned to monitor Exchange 2000.

Performance monitoring is the process of collecting performance data for the purpose of analyzing resource usage. There are four basic reasons you will want to monitor performance of your Exchange server:

▼ To Diagnose problems

■ To Test configuration changes

■ To Identify the effect the server's workload has on its resources

▲ To Forecast hardware needs

Monitoring Resources

There are four basic hardware resources you should monitor:

▼   Memory

■   Processor

■   Disk subsystem

▲   Network subsystem

Every server has a finite amount of these resources with which to work, that is, you can itemize exactly how much of each resource the server has (for example, 128MB RAM, 18GB of disk space, a 800MHz processor, and so on). With Exchange 2000 (and, therefore, Windows 2000), a delicate balance must be maintained so that you do not overconsume one resource to the detriment of another resource.

For example, if you are using up too much memory, the server will use the paging file to compensate, causing two repercussions:

▼   Additional disk space may be used if the paging file needs to grow.

▲   Disk performance suffers because your disk subsystem is spending time away from normal operations to read from and write to the paging file.

The example above demonstrates the fact that you need to watch your server's resource usage in order to keep it running at peak performance. In addition to the basic resources, you will probably want to monitor application-specific information (in our case, Exchange 2000) in order to ensure that Exchange 2000 is running at peak performance.

Performance Monitoring Concepts

In order to define what you want to monitor, you need to become familiar with a few concepts: objects, counters, and instances. These concepts will allow you a much deeper level of monitoring granularity. For example, monitoring your server's processor utilization only gives you a bird's-eye view of what your server is doing. Instead of just monitoring your server's processor utilization, you could look at a specific processor's utilization while running a specific application; then you have a better idea of what your server is actually doing.

Performance Objects

An object can represent any facet of the operating system. Objects like Memory, Physical Disk, and Processor represent hardware on your server. Objects such as Server, Domain Name System (DNS), Browser, and Redirector represent specific services running on the server. Objects such as TCP (Transmission Control Protocol), NNTP (Network News Transfer Protocol), and ICMP (Internet Control Message Protocol) represent specific protocols running on the server. When you install any Microsoft BackOffice product, such as Exchange 2000 Server, additional objects specific to that product are added in order to be monitored.

Performance Counters

A set of counters is predefined for each object. These counters are calculated values measuring some specific aspect of that counter. For instance, the % Processor Time counter of the Processor object would measure what percentage of the time the processor is busy. There are a number of counter types utilized to give you valuable (and not just raw) data. Table 15-1 lists the counter types available.

Instances

A server may have multiple objects of the same type, requiring some method to distinguish between them while monitoring. For example, if your server has multiple processors, and you wanted to see the % Processor Time for only one of those processors, you need to be able to select it to be monitored independently of the other processors. Utilizing instances allows you to accomplish this.

To summarize these three concepts, think of their relationship this way: You select an object you wish to monitor and choose the counter to report to you a specific measurement about that object. If you need more granularity, use a specific instance of that object.

Counter Type	Description
Average	The average of the measurement of the last two values sampled
Difference	The difference between the most recent measurement sampled and the one just prior to it. This only displays a number if there is a positive difference (for example, 700-500=200). If the difference is a negative number, the value shown is zero.
Instantaneous	The most recent measurement sampled
Percentage	The most recent measurement sampled shown as a percentage
Rate	The measurements sampled over time are divided by the amount of time being sampled to display a rate of activity.

Table 15-1.   Use Counter Types To Gather Valuable Data

Maintaining Your Performance Monitoring Focus

What you monitor can depend on what your monitoring focus is. If you are troubleshooting, you will look at different counters than if you are forecasting resource usage. The following table lists the aspects of performance you may want to focus on when monitoring.

Performance Aspect	Monitoring Focus
Usage	Verify resource usage is within acceptable limits
Bottleneck	Look for excessive demand on a certain resource resulting in a possible slowdown of overall performance
Throughput	Ascertain the current performance rate of a specific resource

USING SYSTEM MONITOR

Windows 2000 provides the System Monitor Microsoft Management Console (MMC) snap-in as a comprehensive performance monitoring tool. System Monitor allows you to both view real-time data and log current data for future viewing. To open System Monitor, you can use the Performance tool found in Administrative Tools. System Monitor opens with a blank chart, as shown in Figure 15-1.

In order to have System Monitor provide you with any data, you will have to add counters to the chart. You can add counters by right-clicking the chart area and selecting Add Counters. The Add Counters dialog box, shown inFigure 15-2, opens. There are a number of concepts to learn about System Monitor just from looking at this dialog box.

In Figure 15-2, which shows the Add Counters dialog box, the first option is to choose between Use Local Computer counters and Select Counters from Computer. This option allows you to monitor either the server you are logged onto or another computer. Whichever you choose, System Monitor will only display those performance objects that exist on that computer. For example, if you were to run System Monitor on a Windows 2000 member server not running Exchange 2000, the performance objects would not list any Exchange 2000–related objects. However, if you were to choose the Select Counters from Computer option and choose an Exchange 2000 Server, the performance objects listed would include Exchange 2000–related objects.

Once you've chosen which computer to monitor, you will want to focus on the objects you want to monitor. Later in this chapter, we will look at not only which generic objects you should use to monitor basic server health (such as memory, processor, disk, and network), but also objects specific to Exchange 2000 functionality. For the purposes of this topic, let's simply choose the Processor object, which is the default object selected when you open the Add Counters dialog box.

Just below the listing of objects in Figure 15-2 is the list of counters to choose from. You do have the option of choosing All Counters. We would not recommend that, unless

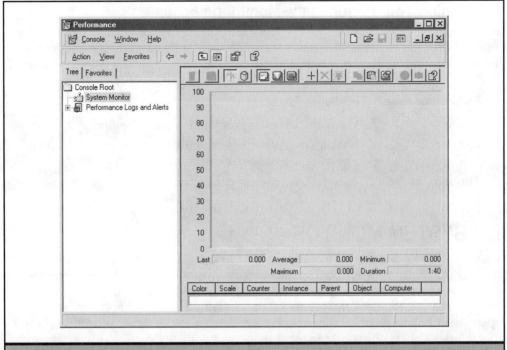

Figure 15-1.   Use System Monitor to view your system's performance

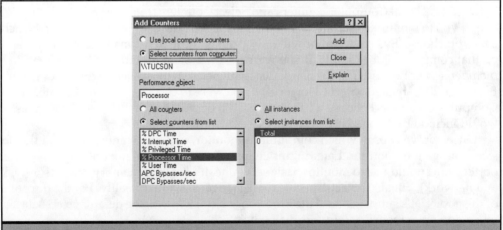

Figure 15-2.   Use the Add Counters dialog box to learn more about System Monitor

you know what information each counter provides and actually want each and every counter for that object. If you choose All Counters, System Monitor will create an entry on the chart for each one. In some cases, you will end up with a chart that looks like Figure 15-3, which was generated by selecting All Counters under the Process object (and ran the processor to 100 percent utilization we might add!). It is so confusing that you begin to realize that all of the counters aren't really necessary. Most likely, you will never need to look at all of the counters for a specific object. Each object already has a default counter selected. Microsoft usually selects one counter that provides a general feel regarding the health or performance of that object.

Last, if applicable, you need to select the instance of the object you wish to monitor in the Add Counters dialog box. This could be one of several processors on your computer or, in the case of Exchange 2000, one of many Mailbox Stores on your server.

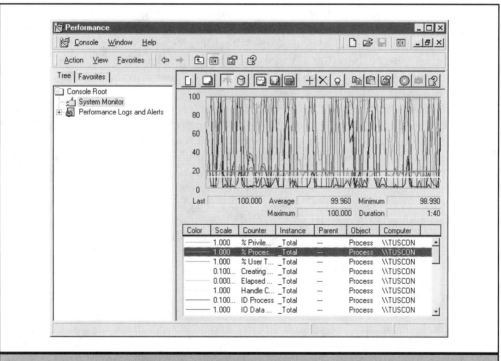

Figure 15-3. A Performance Chart using all the counters of one object (what a mess!)

MONITORING THE FOUR MAIN RESOURCES IN WINDOWS 2000

We listed the four main resources you should monitor earlier in the chapter:

- ▼ Memory
- ■ Processor
- ■ Disk Subsystem
- ▲ Network Subsystem

Let's dig a little deeper into System Monitor by learning to monitor these resources. We'll cover the preliminary counters you should use, as well as explain why you should use them.

Setting the Foundation: Create a Baseline

If someone were to tell you their server is constantly running at 75 percent utilization, would you consider that a problem? Your first reaction might be to say yes. However, if you think about it, you really do not know. What if the server is old, and running at 75 percent is considered to be within normal operating parameters? Now that we've got you thinking, it becomes more obvious that the true answer to our initial question is that we really cannot know without a baseline.

A baseline is nothing more than a point of reference for future use. You would create a baseline by monitoring certain resources on a server, and either documenting or saving the results in a log file. In baselining your server, you really aren't doing anything differently than normal monitoring; you are just going to use the results for a different purpose. We'd suggest that you create your baseline by monitoring your servers during normal business hours, over a period of several days to several weeks, to really get an idea of how a particular resource is being used throughout the workday.

Pay attention to the Average value for each counter listed just below the chart you create in System Monitor. The Minimum and Maximum values could represent as little as a single instance throughout your monitoring period (perhaps hours, days, or weeks), while the Average value yields a better idea of how the server is running overall.

Monitoring Memory

The overall reasons for monitoring memory are to see how much is in use, what it is being used for, and how much remains free. Table 15-2 lists some of the counters you will use to monitor memory use, and Figure 15-4 shows the results of adding those counters.

Object	Counter	Description
Memory	Pages/sec	This counter shows the number of times per second the server cannot find a page (which is 4KB of memory) of information in an applications working set (the applications exclusive area of physical memory) and has to search for that information on the pagefile, which resides on a disk. If this value is constantly above 20, this is an indication that your server does not have enough physical RAM to handle the applications loaded on it.
Memory	Available Bytes	This counter shows the amount of physical memory that is available for processes to utilize. This value should remain above 4000KB. Like the Pages/sec value, anything below this value would indicate too little memory on the server.
Paging File	%Usage (_Total)	This counter shows what percentage of the pagefile is in use. The _Total instance is selected so that you get an overall idea of the pagefile use, even if multiple pagefiles are in use. A high percentage (anything consistently above 75 percent) would indicate insufficient physical memory.

Table 15-2.   Memory Counters to Monitor

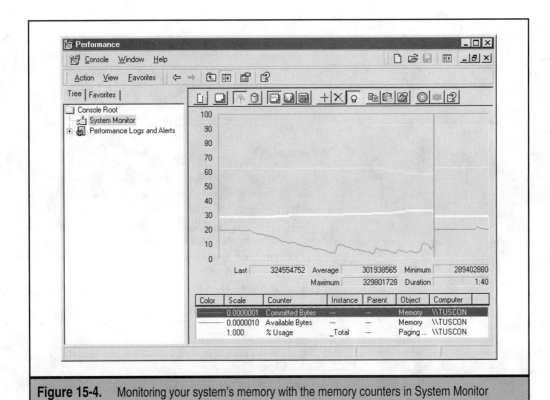

Figure 15-4. Monitoring your system's memory with the memory counters in System Monitor

One additional note about memory usage needs to be made: in Exchange 2000, the Store process will utilize as much memory as the Exchange Server has, voluntarily releasing memory to applications that need additional memory as they need it. So don't be alarmed that your Exchange Server's Available Bytes value is low. This is normal for an Exchange Server.

How Much Memory Is Exchange Using?

If you take a closer look at the Memory Performance object, you'll see that there are no instances listed. So how do you tell how much memory Exchange (or any other service) is using? Use the Task Manager, and look at the Processes tab. You can see each of Exchanges applications and memory is use under the Mem Usage column (see the next illustration). Use the following application filenames for the various Exchange processes:

▼ STORE.EXE = Information Store

■ MAD.EXE = System Attendant

■ KMSERVER.EXE = Key Management Server

■ EMSMTA.EXE = Message Transfer Agent (MTA) Stacks

■ EVENTS.EXE = Event Service

▲ SRSMAIN.EXE = Site Replication Service

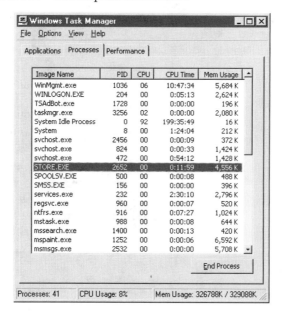

Monitoring the Processor

The processor is always busy. Even where there is nothing to do, the system gives the processor an idle thread for it to process. When the server is busy processing nonidle threads, questions remain: why is the server so busy, and what is it busy doing? Table 15-3 lists the counters you can use to monitor memory usage, and Figure 15-5 shows the results of adding those counters in System Monitor.

Object	Counter	Description
Processor	% Processor Time (_Total)	This counter shows the percentage of the time the processor is busy processing nonidle threads. You can also select specific instances of the processor object to see how busy each processor is in a multi-processor system.
Processor	Interrupts/sec	This value shows the number of times an interrupt is triggered by a peripheral (such as a disk, mouse, or network card). This will cause a rise in the % Processor Time. This rise in processor time would indicate hardware usage could be the cause of the rise in % Processor Time.
System	Processor Queue Length	This counter shows the number of threads waiting in a queue for the processor to handle. If this value is consistently above 2, your processor is most likely overburdened.

Table 15-3.   The Different Processor Counters to Monitor

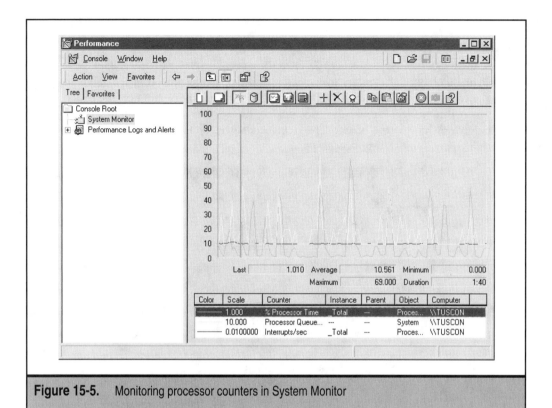

Figure 15-5. Monitoring processor counters in System Monitor

Monitoring the Disk Subsystem

Windows 2000 allows you to monitor both Logical Disk counters and Physical Disk counters. Logical Disk counters focus on each logical drive you created on the system and are disabled by default. To enable Logical Disk counters, run the command *diskperfyv* at the command prompt. Physical Disk counters focus on actual disk usage and are enabled by default. Table 15-4 lists the counters you should use to monitor disk usage, and Figure 15-6 shows the results of adding those counters in System Monitor.

How Much Processor Time Is Exchange Using?

Since the Processor object only gives you the overall use of a processor, you can use the Process object and specify instances relating to Exchange. This will give you an idea of what kind of load each Exchange-related process is putting on the processor. The next illustration shows the monitoring of each of the Exchange-related processes using the Process object. The previous section, "How Much Memory Is Exchange Using?" lists these processes.

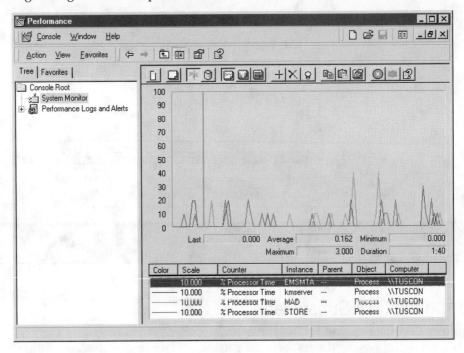

Because the counters are disk-activity specific, with System Monitor there is no way to look at Exchange-specific disk activity.

Monitoring the Network Subsystem

System Monitor's ability to monitor the network is limited to counters that inform you of general network information, such as network utilization, throughput, and transmit/receive statistics. Windows 2000 also includes the Network Monitor tool to look at your network traffic packet by packet. We will focus on System Monitor in this chapter. Table 15-5 lists the counters you should use to monitor your network subsystem.

Object	Counter	Description
PhysicalDisk	% Disk Time (_Total)	This counter shows the percentage of the time the disk subsystem is busy. You can also select each disk as a separate instance.
PhysicalDisk	Avg. Disk Queue Length	This counter shows the average number of requests (read or write) that are queued up to be handled by the disk subsystem. Anything over an average value of 2 is considered high and may indicate that the disks are too slow relative to the demands being placed on them.
PhysicalDisk	Avg. Disk sec/Transfer	This counter shows the amount of time (in seconds) it takes to complete a single transfer of data.

Table 15-4. The Different Disk Counters to Monitor

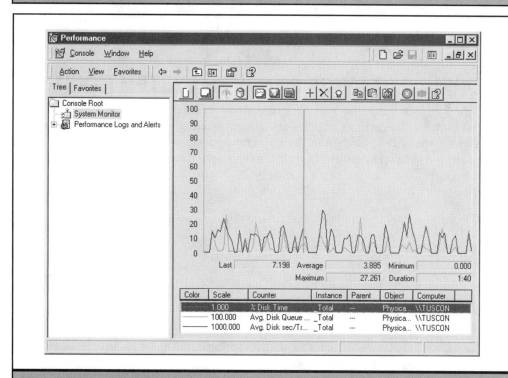

Figure 15-6. Use this screen to see what happens when you add disk counters in your System Monitor.

Object	Counter	Description
Network Segment	% Network Utilization	This counter shows the percentage of time the network is busy.
Network Interface	Output Queue Length	This counter shows the number of packets sitting in the output queue waiting to be sent. A number above 2 may indicate either that a server is servicing too many clients, or that a network interface card (NIC) needs to be upgraded.
Network Segment	Total frames received/sec	This counter shows the rate at which frames of data are being received by that NIC.

Table 15-5.   Use These Network Counters To Monitor Your Network Subsystem

MONITORING EXCHANGE 2000 WITH SYSTEM MONITOR

There are over 30 objects that are either directly or indirectly related to Exchange 2000. Each one of those objects has a number of counters associated with it. Microsoft certainly has provided you with enough granularity for monitoring Exchange 2000. It would take a book of its own to cover every object and counter, so we'll focus on a few of the important objects to begin your monitoring of Exchange 2000.

Hey! How Come I Don't Have Those Objects?

You may have noticed that you are missing both the Network Segment and any TCP/IP-related objects. This is because you need to install additional Windows components in order for those objects to be used. To use the Network Segment object and counters, install Network Monitor Tools. To use the Transmission Control Protocol/Internet Protocol (TCP/IP)–related objects and counters, install the Simple Network Management Protocol (SNMP). Both Network Monitor Tools and Simple Network Management Protocol can be found as subcomponents of Management and Monitoring Tools, as shown here:

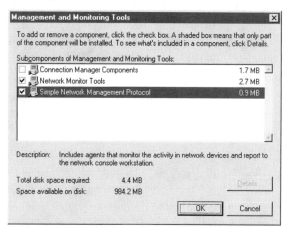

Mailbox Store Counters

Since most of your interaction with Exchange involves sending another user a message, it seems appropriate to take a look at the Mailbox Store–specific counters. There are so many viable counters with meaningful information you can use to establish a performance baseline or determine performance problems, that this object becomes very important. Table 15-6 lists the counters that you can use to monitor the Mailbox Store–specific performance.

Also note that for each Mailbox Store counter, you can choose an individual Mailbox Store in the Instance field. This will allow you to narrow the focus of your monitoring to a subset of your Exchange environment.

Object	Counter	Description
MSExchangeIS Mailbox	Average Delivery Time	This counter shows the amount of time (in seconds) it takes for a message to be delivered. This is calculated using the average of the last ten submissions. This is a great counter to watch if you are looking to see if you have been hit with a macro virus similar to the I Love You virus. You will see delivery times going from less than 1 second to (depending on the server) over 20 seconds.
MSExchangeIS Mailbox	Active Client Logons	This counter tells you how many clients are logged on and have performed any actions within the last ten minutes. The significance of this counter is that you can use this in conjunction with any other counter to see if there is a correlation between the number of users and the performance of Exchange.
MSExchangeIS Mailbox	Receive Queue Size Send Queue Size	These counters show the number of messages in each queue. Compare them against a baseline value to determine whether the Exchange Server is overburdened. A high number of messages (relative to your baseline) could mean you need to offload certain Exchange responsibilities, such as Outlook Web Access (OWA), connectors, or public folder store access to other Exchange Servers.

Table 15-6.   Use These Counters To Monitor The Mailbox Store–Specific Performance

Public Folder Store Counters

Public folder counters can be broken down into two distinct areas: client usage of public folders and public folder replication. The client usage counters will most likely be used to determine how busy the server is while servicing client requests to access public folders, as well as to see if performance degradation exists as you increase the number of users. The replication counters will most likely be useful in troubleshooting replication performance issues. Table 15-7 lists some of the counters you will use to monitor client access to public folders, and Table 15-8 lists some of the counters dealing with public folder replication.

Object	Counter	Description
MSExchangeIS Public	Active Client Logons	This counter tells you how many clients are logged on and if they have performed any actions within the last ten minutes.
MSExchangeIS Public	Folder opens/sec	This counter shows the rate at which public folders are opened. An increase above your baseline would indicate larger numbers of users traversing the tree structure.
MSExchangeIS Public	Receive Queue Size	This counter tells you how many messages are waiting to be delivered to the appropriate public folder. If this number exceeds your baseline, your server could have too many responsibilities within the Exchange organization.
MSExchangeIS Public	Single Instance Ratio	This counter shows the average number of references to a message within the public folder store. You want this value to be as low as possible. Exchange tries to store a message only once within its databases and use pointers to the same data if multiple instances of the message need to exist.

Table 15-7.   Use These Public Folder Store–Specific Counters To Monitor Client Access

Object	Counter	Description
MSExchangeIS Public	Replication Folder Changes Sent Replication Folder Changes Received	This counter tells you how many changes have been sent to and received from other servers since startup. You need to monitor how quickly the number increases, rather than look for a threshold value.
MSExchangeIS Public	Replication Receive Queue Size	This counter shows the number of replication messages waiting to be processed.
MSExchangeIS Public	Replication Backfill Requests Sent Replication Backfill Requests Received	These counters tell you how many replication backfill messages have been sent or received. An increase above your baseline would indicate a possible connectivity problem to that servers public folder replication partners. Backfill requests should only occur if normal replication is not functional. A server that has not replicated in a long time due to connectivity problems, once finally connected to another public folder replication partner, will send a backfill request to ensure all public folder changes are replicated.
MSExchangeIS Public	Single Instance Ratio	This counter shows the average number of references to a message within the public folder store. You want this value to be as low as possible. Exchange tries to store a message only once within its databases and uses pointers to the same data if multiple instances of the message need to exist.

Table 15-8.   A List Of Public Folder Store–Specific Counters Related To Public Folder Replication

Like the Mailbox Store counters, you can select an individual public folder store to monitor in the Instances field under each of these counters.

Simple Mail Transport Protocol (SMTP) Counters

Exchange 2000 heavily relies on SMTP—not just for Internet connectivity, but also for all communications between Exchange 2000 Servers. This makes the SMTP protocol far more important than other Internet protocols, such as Post Office Protocol version 3 (POP3) and Internet Message Access Protocol version 4 (IMAP4). Table 15-9 lists the SMTP counters to monitor.

Object	Counter	Description
SMTP Server	Inbound Connections Current	This counter tells you how many simultaneous connections the SMTP server has over TCP port 25.
SMTP Server	Categorizer Queue Length	This counter shows the number of messages waiting to be categorized. An increasing number more than your baseline could indicate a problem with one of the Event sinks running against a message in the queue. A value of zero could indicate that the service is either hung or stopped.
SMTP Server	Remote Queue Length	This counter shows the number of messages in a specific SMTP outbound queue waiting to be sent to another server. If one queue is increasing, it could indicate a connectivity problem with that server.
SMTP Server	Badmail Messages (six variants of this counter)	These six counters show the number of messages delivered to the badmail directory for reasons such as malformed messages, general failures, exceeding maximum hop counts, or missing recipients.

Table 15-9.   Monitor These SMTP Server–Specific Counters

OWA Counters

With the number of telecommuters, remote users, and roaming users, it is no wonder that OWA is increasing in popularity. Table 15-10 lists the counters that will be helpful in monitoring OWA use.

One interesting note is that Internet Explorer version 5 (IE5) clients interact with OWA differently from any browser below IE5; therefore, the Instances for almost every object are IE5 and Above, non-IE5, and _Total.

SUMMARY

In this chapter, we looked at the basics of monitoring Windows 2000 and Exchange 2000. We saw how to monitor the four basic resources using standard counters provided by Windows 2000. We also saw which counters to use to monitor specific aspects of Exchange 2000. In the next chapter, we will take a look at the various clients Exchange 2000 supports.

Object	Counter	Description
Web Service	Current Connections	This counter tells you how many simultaneous connections there are with the Web service. Be sure to choose the Web site containing OWA under Instances.
MSExchange Web Mail	Message Sends (Total) Message Opens (Total)	These counters show the number of messages sent or opened by the client using OWA. This would be helpful in determining OWA user trends.
MSExchange Web Mail	<Data Type> Sends, Saves, Opens, Deletes, Edits, Updates	These counters show the trend of what users are doing with messages, appointments, attachments, folders, and recipients. There are additional counters that measure the rate of performing these same tasks on the same data types.

Table 15-10.   Use These Counters To Monitor OWA Use

PART V

Client Administration

CHAPTER 16

Installing and Administering Outlook 2000

Until now, we have focused on the server side of Exchange 2000 Server, because this book is about administering Exchange. However, it would do us well to go over the various clients that exist for Exchange 2000 Server and that you might find in your environment:

▼ Microsoft Outlook 2000

■ Microsoft Outlook Express

■ Microsoft Outlook Web Access

■ Exchange Client

■ Microsoft Schedule+

■ Standard Internet mail clients

■ UNIX clients

▲ Macintosh clients

While each of these clients can be used in an Exchange 2000 environment, many of you will be using Microsoft Outlook 2000, Microsoft Outlook Web Access, or Microsoft Outlook Express. Now, there is not enough room in this book to cover each of these clients in depth; so we will merely introduce each client to you, and then focus on the Microsoft Outlook 2000 client since it is the most widely used client in today's market.

MICROSOFT OUTLOOK 2000

This is Microsoft's premier messaging client for Exchange 2000 Server. Microsoft Outlook (Outlook) was originally introduced with Exchange Server 5.0 and combined the functions of the Exchange client and the Schedule+ client into one utility.

The Outlook client also introduced the concept of an *add-in*, which is a program module that can be seamlessly added to the Outlook client. Examples of add-ins include Deleted Item Recovery, Delegate Access, and NetMeeting Extensions. Third-party software vendors can also write add-ins for the Outlook client. One example of this is a product named Pretty Good Privacy (PGP), which allows a user to send encrypted and signed messages using the PGP protocol.

Outlook 2000 is also a component of the Microsoft Office 2000 suite and is automatically installed when the Microsoft Office suite is installed. It is included in all the Microsoft Office 2000 packages:

▼ Microsoft Office 2000 Small Business

■ Microsoft Office 2000 Premium

■ Microsoft Office 2000 Standard

■ Microsoft Office 2000 Professional

▲ Microsoft Office 2000 Developer

Outlook 2000 has three different service options, each of which provide a different set of features for different circumstances. The first service option is No E-mail, which will limit you to the contact, task, and scheduling features of Outlook. In this mode, Outlook functions as a stand-alone Personal Information Manager (PIM). Information is stored in a set of personal folders that are held in a singular *.pst file. This file can be password protected.

The second option is the Internet Only option, which includes all the features of the No E-mail option plus the ability to use Internet mail. The only difference between the No E-mail option and the Internet Only option is that no mail account is set up in the No E-mail option. Otherwise, these options pretty much give you the same set of services and features. Also, in the Internet Only option, Outlook can access messages on any POP3, SMTP, or IMAP4 servers. Clients still store their information in a set of personal folders that are held in a *.pst file.

The final option is the Corporate Or Workgroup option, which allows Outlook to use a Local Area Connection (LAN) with a messaging server. In this mode, the use of a *.pst file is optional, since messages and information in any folder can be stored on the messaging server. This is the preferred mode for most corporate installations unless there is a specific reason to install Outlook using a different service mode.

Use the following criteria when selecting a service option:

▼ If the user is only planning to use the PIM features, then choose the No E-mail option.

■ If the user receives all e-mail over the Internet, then choose the Internet Only option.

▲ If the user will receive messages from a messaging server on the LAN, choose the Corporate Or Workgroup option.

By default, the Outlook Today page (see Figure 16-1) is shown first when you start the Outlook 2000 client. Outlook Today presents the highlights of your new messages, active tasks, and calendar information. The Outlook Today page can be customized to include information you desire.

What is important to understand about the Outlook Today page is that it is really just a Web page; therefore, it is possible to configure it. For instance, referring to Figure 16-1, you can see a link in the lower right-hand corner to Customize Outlook Today. If you click on the link, you'll get the configuration screen, as illustrated in Figure 16-2.

As you can see, you can configure the Outlook Today page to always appear when the Outlook client starts. You can choose which folders will appear, how many days will be shown from the calendar, and how the task lists should appear. There are also several visual styles from which to choose. But these configurations are only the tip of the iceberg.

Microsoft has introduced a new idea it calls *digital dashboards*, which is a way to highly customize the Outlook Today page to consolidate personal, team, and corporate information into a single location. It is designed to give users a single point of focus to access all the information they will need during the course of the day. If you'd like to learn more about digital dashboards, a digital dashboard starter kit is available at Microsoft's site at **http://www.microsoft.com/digitaldashboard**.

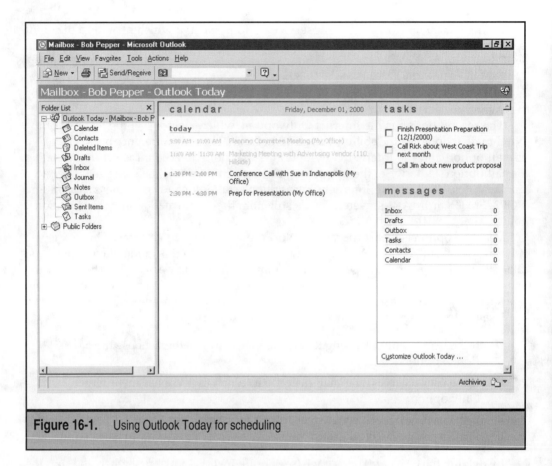

Figure 16-1.   Using Outlook Today for scheduling

MICROSOFT OUTLOOK EXPRESS

Outlook Express (OE) ships and installs with Internet Explorer. Its main advantage over Outlook 2000 is that it has an NNTP client that works well with Internet newsgroups. It also has the ability to send and retrieve e-mail, and possesses both the POP3 and IMAP4 client. OE can also query X.500-based directories over LDAP. In an Exchange environment, OE does not query a directory via Exchange. Instead, OE will query the AD directly over TCP port 389.

Where OE falls short is in its inability to connect to public folders and its lack of calendaring abilities. In our consulting experience, we have generally recommended OE primarily as a newsgroup reader and Outlook 2000 for all other functions.

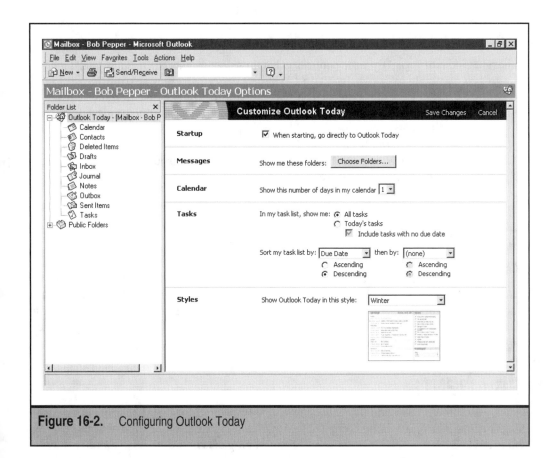

Figure 16-2.   Configuring Outlook Today

OUTLOOK WEB ACCESS

Outlook Web Access (OWA) is a browser-based method of accessing mail and scheduling information from an Exchange Server. An Outlook 2000 look and feel is created inside the browser to help make the user experience similar to using Outlook 2000. OWA uses TCP port 80, because it is really connecting to a series of Web pages that are written to look like Outlook 2000.

OWA is installed when Exchange 2000 Server is installed. This is an attractive client for those whose users are widely dispersed and lack enough bandwidth back to the Exchange Server to support the RPC necessary to run the Outlook 2000 client. Many companies find OWA to be a useful alternative, even if it is only used on their intranet. To learn more about OWA, see Chapter 3.

EXCHANGE CLIENT

Frankly, this client is hardly used anymore. In days past, it was the default client for Exchange. It is available in both a 16-bit and a 32-bit version. There is also a Microsoft Disk Operating System (MS-DOS) and Macintosh version of this client. Its main drawback was that it didn't have the scheduling capabilities built into it, so it depended on Schedule+ to provide this capability.

The 16-bit version is really not a powerful client, but it does include messaging and the ability to access public folders, task lists, and personal and group scheduling. This client will not be enhanced in the future; so if you're running it now, consider upgrading to Outlook 2000. Your users will thank you.

SCHEDULE+

Schedule+ was the main program used for scheduling and contact management until Exchange Server 5.5, when it was replaced by Outlook. Both the 1.0 and the 7.0 versions are available in both 16-bit and 32-bit Windows, and Macintosh. Data can be migrated from Schedule+ to Outlook if needed. Schedule+ will work with Exchange Server; but, like the Exchange client, it will not be enhanced in future versions. If you are running Schedule+ now, consider upgrading to Outlook 2000.

OTHER CLIENTS

Because Exchange 2000 and Windows 2000 are standards-based platforms, nearly any POP3 or IMAP4 client will be compatible. If you are running other Internet mail clients, you can use Exchange 2000 Server as your messaging server. Some functionality may be sacrificed in this situation, but it is very possible to do.

In our discussions in this book, we have readily assumed a complete Windows operating system environment. However, there are many UNIX and Macintosh deployments as well, and we need to consider how non-Windows-based clients can connect to Exchange 2000 Server.

UNIX Clients

There is no Outlook or Exchange client for the UNIX operating system, so UNIX users have one of two choices to make.

The first option is that a standards-based POP3 or IMAP4 client may be used to access messages from the Exchange 2000 Server. If access to public folders is necessary, then an IMAP4 client should be utilized because a POP3 client cannot access public folders.

The second option is to install a browser on the UNIX machine and use OWA to access e-mail. This might be a preferred method in some environments, since the same utility can be used for more than one purpose.

Macintosh Clients

There are several choices that can be made for a Macintosh client. First, there is a Macintosh version of Outlook that will work with Exchange 2000 Server. This client is being updated on a regular basis. Usually, this client lacks some of the functionality of the Windows-based version of Outlook, and consulting experience suggests that it tends to require more administrative effort to install and maintain. Like UNIX clients, a second choice would be for Mac users to install and use a generic POP3 or IMAP4 client. Finally, a third choice for Macintosh users would be to use Outlook Web Access for e-mail from a Mac-based browser.

CONFIGURING OUTLOOK 2000

Most environments will be using the Windows-based Outlook client. In this section, we'll take a look at some of the configuration features of Outlook 2000 that you might want to be aware of.

Most of the configuration options for Outlook 2000 are found in Tools | Options. You'll see a series of tabs, as shown here:

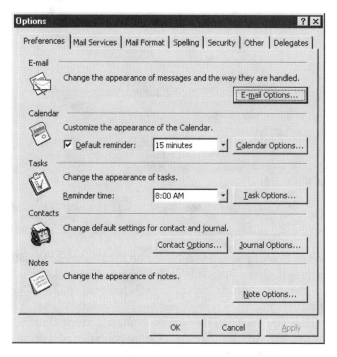

In this dialog box, you can see that preferences can be set for E-mail, Calendar, Tasks, Contacts, and Notes. Click the E-mail Options button to pull up the E-mail Options dialog box, shown in the next illustration, which offers several important configurations:

▼ Whether to close an e-mail or leave it open when replying or forwarding a message

■ Where to save copies of messages you have sent

■ Whether you want a notification displayed when new mail arrives

■ Whether you want to automatically save unsent messages

■ Whether you want the original text included and/or indented when replying or forwarding a message

▲ Whether you want your comments in a reply to be marked with a standard string of text

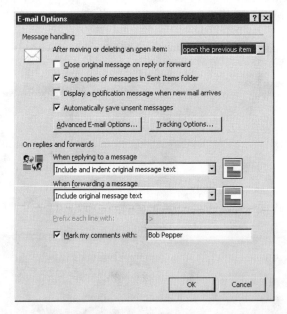

This last option is one of the more cool options that we like to use in our everyday e-mail. Let us illustrate it. Our fictitious user, Bob Pepper, has asked that his comments be marked with "Bob Pepper." Figure 16-3 illustrates how this will look to Sue Smith, who has e-mailed Bob with concerns about a proposed contract. Bob's responses will appear in blue following the bolded and italicized [Bob Pepper]. Notice that he has inserted them into the text of her message to him. Notice also that [Bob Pepper] didn't appear in his reply message at the top of the message.

Under the Advanced e-mail options, shown next, you'll have the ability to configure even more e-mail options.

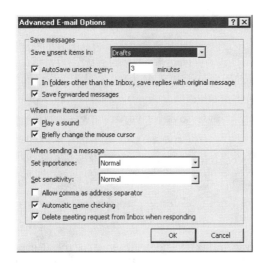

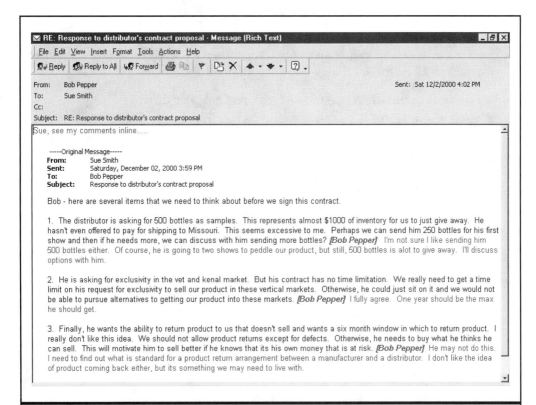

Figure 16-3.   Viewing Bob's reply to Sue

You can

▼ Specify where to save unsent items

■ Specify how often unsent items should be saved automatically

■ Specify where to save replies to messages in folders other than the Inbox folder

■ Specify whether or not to save forwarded messages

■ Play a sound or change the mouse cursor when new mail arrives

■ Set the default importance and sensitivity levels for outgoing messages

■ Specify whether to perform automatic name checking on the Exchange Server

▲ Specify whether or not to delete a meeting request from the in box when responding

Be sure to set the configuration value pretty low for the AutoSave of unsent messages. It's not uncommon for users to create e-mail that may require over 10 or 15 minutes to create. If the message is being autosaved and if the user's machine experiences a failure, the entire message will not be lost. This is very helpful to the user. Bear in mind that when a user is creating a message, the user is working in the memory space of the server, not the memory space of the client; and the unsent message is saved on the server, not the workstation.

Use the Tracking Options dialog box to configure the following:

▼ Whether or not to process requests and responses on arrival

■ Whether or not to process receipts on arrival

■ Where to move receipts after processing

■ Whether you want to delete blank voting and meeting responses after processing

▲ Whether you want to request a read and/or delivery receipt

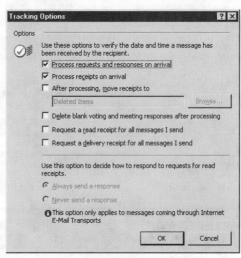

Most think that if a read or delivery receipt is requested, Outlook will automatically send the receipt; however, if the user has disabled Process Receipts On Arrival, then the requesting user will not receive a receipt even though it is requested. If you don't want people knowing when you read their messages, then you should deselect this option.

Bear in mind that if everyone in your organization enables both read and delivery receipts, that this will likely generate much unnecessary messaging overhead for your environment. The best practice is to use the receipt options on a message-by-message basis.

On the Mail Services tab, you'll have the option of always prompting for the user to choose his or her profile or always starting Outlook with the same profile. In situations in which multiple people use the same computer, such as a nurses station in a hospital, it would be wise to select the Prompt For A Profile To Be Used radio button:

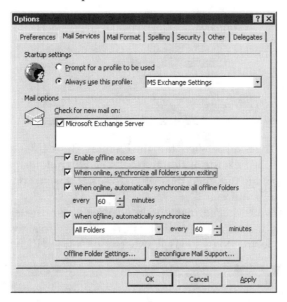

Also, you can have Outlook check for new mail on multiple services just by selecting each server in the Check For New Mail On selection box. In our example, we only have one server; but there are other scenarios when more than one server will be necessary, such as a contractor who needs to check mail on his own employer's server plus the client's messaging server.

Offline access is configured on this screen if it is enabled. When enabled, you can force synchronization at certain times or whenever the user logs off. In addition, you can force Outlook to synchronize at regular intervals even if the user is offline by selecting the When Offline, Automatically Synchronize check box. In this case, you'll need a dial-up connection to the messaging server. This is most advantageous when the user is out of the office, but has the computer regularly connected to a phone line so that Outlook can check for new messages (and send messages, too) at regular intervals.

To enable offline access, open Tools | Services. Then open the properties of the Microsoft Exchange Server service. On the Advanced tab, click the Offline Folder File Settings button and make your configurations. Once accomplished, click OK and you'll see the Enable Offline Use check box selected, shown here:

When you go back to the Mail Services tab, the Enable Offline Use check box should be selected. If you deselect the box, the option to reselect it will not disappear; however, if you have never enabled offline use, then the option to select this box on the Mail Services tab will be dimmed and unavailable.

Now to the fun tab, the Mail Format tab, shown next. This is the tab where you make can e-mail come alive—and unnecessarily fill up your mailbox stores, too. On this tab, you can select which message format to use: HTML, Microsoft Outlook Rich Text, or Plain Text.

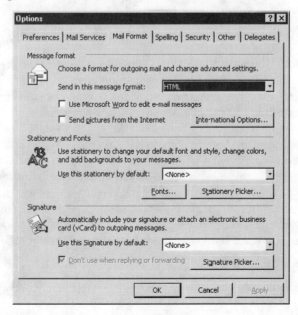

If you choose HTML or Microsoft Outlook Rich Text, then you'll be able to use the font- and style-editing choices when composing a message, such as bold or italics. If you choose the plain text format, you lose these options, since you've told Outlook to operate in plain text, which is Courier 10-pt type.

At the bottom of the Mail Format tab is the Signature section where a user can create a customized signature for e-mails. In addition, the signature can be attached to replies and forwards.

By selecting HTML you can also select a unique stationery and font to use when sending messages. This can spruce up the look of your e-mail, but it does take about 2KB of overhead for each e-mail message. Moreover, if the recipient is operating in something other than HTML or Microsoft Outlook Rich Text, the stationery will be reduced to an attachment, which can be opened and looked at by the recipient. The following illustration shows what an e-mail will look like when sent with stationery.

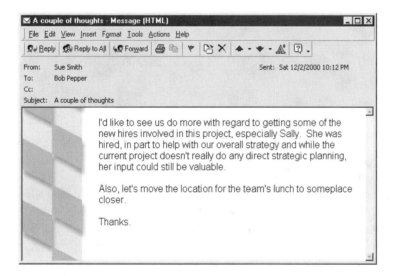

Generally, unless you have a good reason to allow widespread use of stationery, we think it is a bad idea, mainly because it consumes additional disk space on the server that isn't necessary.

You should configure the Spelling tab, shown next, for most of your users. This is the tab where you can force Outlook to check the spelling of the message before it is sent. If you need a customized dictionary (both domestic and international), you can specify that on this tab. Given the number of misspelled words, it is a good idea to enforce spelling in messages.

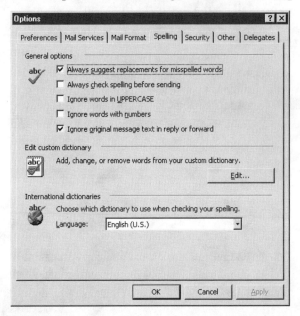

The Security tab is where you can install digital signatures and certificates for use in encrypting e-mail. This is also where you can configure security zones to decide if you want scripts and active content to run in HTML messages. Allowing scripts to run in HTML messages leaves an opening for hackers to plant programs on your network that will help them gain greater access to your network. Although there are many ways to hack a network, this is one way to help secure it.

The Delegates tab is the location where users can specify that they want another user to perform certain actions on their private folders. For instance, Sue could specify Bob as her delegate and give him permission to do the following:

▼   Read and create items in her in box

■   Read, create, and modify items in her task list

■   Read, create, and modify items in her calendar

▲   Read contact items

Once she makes these configurations, she then would select Automatically Send A Message To Delegate Summarizing These Permissions, and Bob would receive an e-mail similar to this:

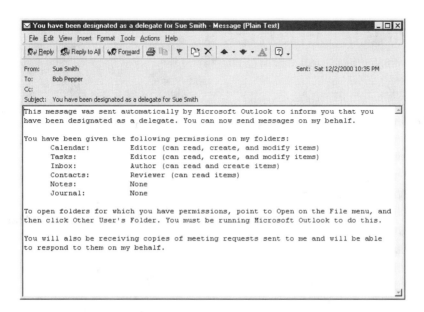

Now, if Bob needs to open her in box, he can do so by simply navigating the File menu, pointing to Open, and selecting Other User's Folder. He would then input Sue's name, and her inbox would automatically open up. Very nice.

Moreover, if we were to take a quick look at Sue's account properties in AD, we would find that Bob's name appears in Delivery Options under Grant This Permission To, shown next. Our consulting experience indicates that you can achieve a more granular level of delegated permissions by using the client to create these permissions rather than using the server-side Active Directory Users And Computers snap-in.

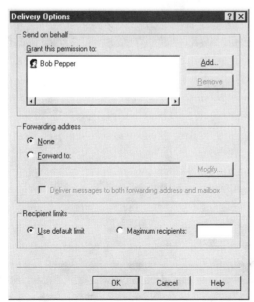

RECOVERING DELETED ITEMS

Users can recover their own deleted items if you have enabled a deleted item retention period on the server.

The deleted item retention time only starts ticking after the user has emptied out the Deleted Items folder. In our illustration, Bob has deleted four messages, which really means that the pointer for the message has changed folders from the Inbox to the Deleted Items folder. Now, if Bob were to highlight the Deleted Items folder and click the Tools menu, he would see an option to Empty Deleted Items.

What this action does is strip these items of their permissions and mark them as hidden. Then after the deleted item retention period has expired, Exchange will wipe the items from the database. Until then, however, even though the items are hidden, they can still be recovered by using the Recover Deleted Items menu choice on the Tools menu. Figure 16-4 illustrates that when Bob selects this menu choice, the Recover Deleted Items From – Deleted Items dialog box appears. All Bob needs to do is highlight one or more messages (using the CTRL key if he wants to recover multiple items) and click the Recover Selected Items button, and the messages will reappear in the Deleted Items folder of Bob's mailbox (Figure 16-5). At this point, Bob can move these messages to other folders and use them at will. They are no longer subject to the deleted items retention period configured on the Exchange Server.

Training your users how to do this will help reduce help desk calls asking you to recover an item from tape backup (if your backup software supports that feature). Consider spending time training users about this to make your and their lives easier.

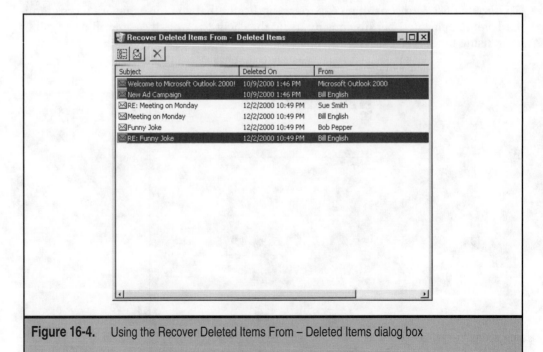

Figure 16-4. Using the Recover Deleted Items From – Deleted Items dialog box

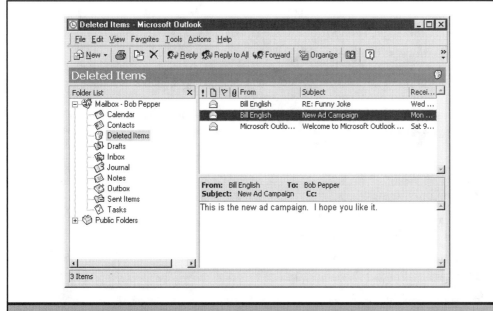

Figure 16-5.   Recovering items from Bob's Deleted Items folder

RULES WIZARD

The Rules Wizard is a handy tool designed to allow users to configure what they want to do with messages when the messages arrive. We'll run through how to set up a rule in this section and discuss some of the more important aspects to consider.

The Rules Wizard is invoked by going to the Tools menu and selecting Rules Wizard. What appears is a rather bland dialog box that offers you the ability to create a new rule. Click the New button, and the fun will begin.

First, the Office Assistant (OA) may appear asking if you would like help with the Rules Wizard. If you'd like, you can have the OA help you through this; but if you're like us, we hide this pesky thing every time it comes up. There are a number of rule types that can be created, including

▼   Check messages when they arrive

■   Check messages after sending

■   Move new messages from someone

■   Notify me when important messages arrive

■   Move messages based on content

■   Delete a conversation

■   Flag messages from someone

■   Assign categories to sent messages

- ■ Assign categories based on content
- ■ Move messages I send to someone
- ▲ Stop processing all following rules

In the lower pane, for each selection that you highlight, you'll see a brief description of what the option means, shown in Figure 16-6.

We've selected Check Messages When They Arrive and clicked Next. Figure 16-7 illustrates that the next screen will give you a number of conditions that the message needs to meet in order to be processed by the rule. These conditions are named next.

- ▼ Where my name is in the To box
- ■ Sent only to me
- ■ Where my name is in the Cc box
- ■ Where my name is in the To or Cc box
- ■ Where my name is not in the To box
- ■ From people or distribution list
- ■ Sent to people or distribution list
- ■ With specific words in the recipient's address
- ■ With specific words in the sender's address
- ■ With specific words in the subject
- ■ With specific words in the body
- ■ With specific words in the subject and body
- ■ With specific words in the message header
- ■ Flagged for action
- ■ Marked as important
- ■ Marked as sensitive
- ■ Assigned to a category
- ■ Which is an Out of Office message
- ■ Which has an attachment
- ■ With selected properties of documents or forms
- ■ With a size in a specific range
- ■ Received in a specific date span
- ■ Uses the form name form
- ■ Suspected to be junk e-mail or from Junk Senders
- ▲ Containing adult content or from Adult Content Sites

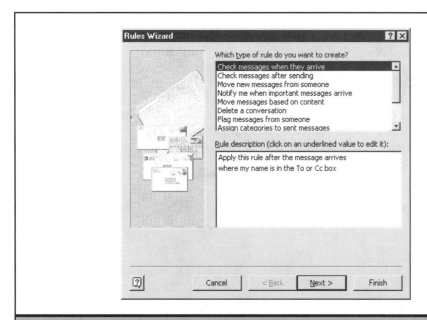

Figure 16-6.   Creating rules using the Rules Wizard

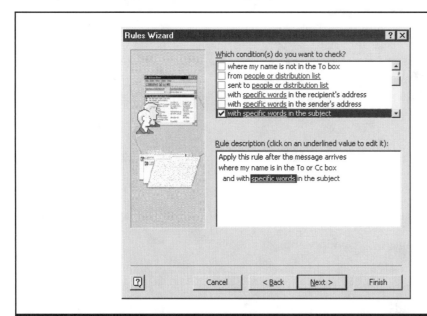

Figure 16-7.   Using the Rules Wizard conditions screen

As you can see, this is quite a list of conditions from which to choose. Happily, you can make multiple selections and combine these conditions any way you'd like to apply to those messages you're creating the rule for. In our example, we'll choose the Where My Name Is In The To Or Cc Box and the With Specific Words In The Subject conditions to illustrate what we'll do with certain messages.

As you can see, the With Specific Words In The Subject condition has a link in it, indicating that this is the place to configure those specific words. When the link is selected, the Search Text dialog box appears, shown in the next illustration; we'll enter **"Project100"** so that all messages coming in about Project100 will meet the conditions of this rule.

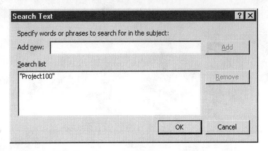

On the next screen, shown in Figure 16-8, we'll indicate what we want done with this message. You'll have many Out options to pick from:

▼ Move it to the specified folder

■ Move a copy to the specified folder

■ Delete it

■ Permanently delete it

■ Forward it to people or distribution list

■ Forward it to people or distribution list as an attachment

■ Print it

■ Redirect it to people or distribution list

■ Reply using a specific template

■ Have server reply using a specific message

■ Notify me using a specific message

■ Flag message for action in a number of days

■ Clear the Message Flag

■ Assign it to the category

■ Play a sound

■ Start application

■ Mark it as important

■ Perform a custom action

▲ Stop processing more rules

In this example, we've created a Project100 folder in Bob's private folders, so we'll select to move it to the specified folder; and you can see that in the lower pane, the Project100 folder is selected.

Notice that in this list we have some very interesting actions. One of these actions is the ability to reply to the message using a template message. This gives us the ability to create automatic replies when the message meets the conditions. Moreover, we can start a customized application that will allow scripts or other programs to run if the message meets a certain condition.

For instance, if the condition that was selected was With Selected Properties Of Documents Or Forms, then we could have a customer send us a predefined document with order information in it, including part numbers and quantity, and we could have a customized program take that information and input it into our order-entry program and/or billing program. Hence, a customer could send us orders, and that information could be entered into our system without us ever having to manually enter it. This gives you an idea of the power that exists in using the Rules Wizard.

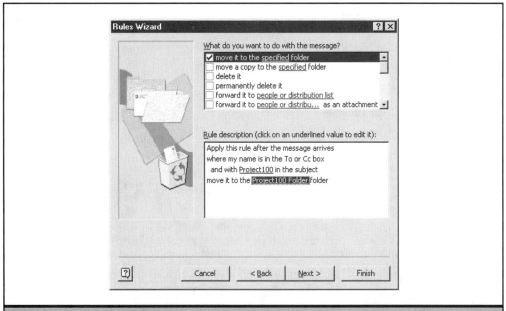

Figure 16-8.　Moving the message to a specific folder

Going back to our scenario, we've chosen the rule type, the condition, and the action we want to perform. The next screen gives us the option of creating exceptions to what we have just configured. Here are the possible exceptions:

▼ If sent directly to me
■ If sent only to me
■ Where my name is in the Cc box
■ If my name is in the Cc box
■ Where my name is not in the To box
■ If from people or distribution list
■ If sent to people or distribution list
■ With specific words in the recipient's address
■ With specific words in the sender's address
■ If the subject contains specific words
■ If the body contains specific words
■ If the subject or body contains specific words
■ If the message header contains specific words
■ If it is flagged for action
■ If it is marked as important
■ If it is marked as sensitive
■ If assigned to category
■ If it is an Out of Office message
■ If it has an attachment
■ With selected properties of documents or forms
■ With a size in a specific range
■ If received in a specific date span
▲ If it uses the form name form

In our ongoing example, we won't choose a specific exception; but as you can see, the list is extensive and gives you maximum flexibility when creating these rules.

The next screen is the final screen in the Rules Wizard, asking you to specify a name for the rule, whether or not the rule should be enabled, and whether you want to run the rule on items in your Deleted Items folder, and then giving you a brief description of the rule that was just created. Click Finish, and the rule will be created.

After creating a rule, it's a good idea to test it to ensure that the rule will do what you want it to do. Given the number of possibilities, it's easy to create a rule that you think will do one thing when, in fact, it does something else. The best practice is to test the rule before walking away from the user's desk.

These rules should enforce whether or not the Outlook client is up and running. Test your specific rule with both the Outlook client open and with the Outlook client closed. Be sure the rule runs in either case, so the user isn't confronted with unwanted messages or unprocessed messages in their in box when the Outlook client is started.

SUMMARY

In this chapter, you have learned about the various clients that are available as messaging clients for Exchange 2000 Server. Moreover, you've learned about how to configure Outlook 2000, how to recover deleted items, and how to run the Rules Wizard. We really just scratched the surface of this client. There are entire books out there that can be referenced for every detail of this powerful client.

In the next chapter, we'll switch gears and look at one of the newest features in Exchange: Instant Messaging.

CHAPTER 17

Supporting
Instant Messaging

Instant messaging (IM) is fast becoming a very popular way to communicate. IM represents the ability to have real-time communication in text form and it combines the functions of both telephone and e-mail systems. IM is a collaboration service that is designed for individual users who want to have real-time, one-to-one conversations. The benefits of using IM include the following.

▼ It reduces (and perhaps eliminates) telephone tag. Rather than leaving a voice mail message for someone who is out of the office, you can check the user's presence information to determine when the user is available and then send a message.

■ It allows users to multitask for greater productivity. For instance, a person could work on a Microsoft Word document and engage in an IM conversation from the same desktop.

▲ It breaks down traditional barriers to communication, such as geographical boundaries. Even if the person with whom you need to communicate is located in a different city, you can send an IM instead of making a telephone call. And with IM, you can have multiple, nonrelated, ongoing conversations with several different people at the same time.

INTRODUCTION TO IM

Perhaps the greatest architectural distinction between IM and e-mail is that IM messages are not retained in the Exchange 2000 Store. All IM messages are held in RAM. Once the message has been deleted or the workstation has been shut down, the message is gone forever and cannot be retrieved.

To send and receive messages, an IM client, such as MSN Messenger, must be installed. The IM client can be kept open and minimized to allow IM messages to flow throughout the day.

Presence information helps you identify when other people are online, out of the office, or just not receiving calls. When a user is online, a status notification is sent to the IM server, which passes this information to those who have subscribed to the presence information. Since a subscription list is persistent—meaning that it is retained even though the IM client might be shut down and restarted—a user logging onto the network can quickly find out who else is online. Presence information can be retrieved both internally and over the Internet for online users.

IM ARCHITECTURE

All IM occurs over the Rendezvous Protocol (RVP). RVP is an extended subset of the Web Development Authoring and Versioning (WebDAV) Protocol, which, in turn, is an extension to HTTP 1.1. RVP can work through firewalls and proxy servers because it works over port 80. IM takes place using HTTP, and the message format employed is XML.

The RVP allows for subscribers to obtain presence information for *presentities*. A presentity is the target user of whom presence information is being gathered by the watcher. The *home server* is the IM server responsible for hosting IM user accounts and their presence information. The home server is also is responsible for issuing notifications of changes in a user's status to any subscriber. The *IM router* receives instant messages, determines their destination home server, and forwards the messages to user accounts on the home server.

An *IM domain* is a grouping of IM users and servers under the same Domain Name System (DNS) namespace. Each IM server is really a virtual server, meaning that one physical server can host multiple IM servers. If there is only one home server in an IM domain, then, by default, it also functions as the IM router. In this scenario, the DNS Fully Qualified Domain Name (FQDN) of the home server is the same as the IM domain name. However, if there are going to be two or more IM home servers, then you'll need to install an IM router. In this scenario, the FQDN of the router is the same as the IM domain name.

The IM server runs as part of the inetinfo.exe process and is implemented as an *Isapi.dll*. You can choose to have IM work with parties outside your network by configuring the Firewall Topology Module. This module retains information about each computer running IM and whether it is inside or outside the firewall. We will discuss how to configure this module in "Working with Firewalls," later in this chapter.

You will use the IM client to log onto the IM server. However, RVP does not require users to authenticate to their home servers. IM uses either Windows Integrated Authentication (WIA) Challenge/Response or the Digest authentication method, which is able to pass through proxy servers. The Digest authentication method is also good to use when clients are on non-WIA platforms, such as UNIX.

IM depends on Windows 2000 for several functions. First, it needs AD to enable IM services on each user account. It is not necessary to create a separate user account for IM. IM also depends on IIS because IM clients connect to IIS using the instmsg alias when logging onto an IM server. Finally, IM depends on DNS in that you must create an A (Address) record within DNS for all IM servers. These records allow IM clients to resolve DNS names to Internet Protocol (IP) addresses in order to make network connections.

When a user logs onto IM, the following transactions occur. This list assumes both a routing and home server:

1. The user's computer queries DNS for the SRV record of the server offering RVP services on the network. DNS returns the resolution of this IP address to the user and refers the user to the routing server.

2. The user establishes a network connection to the IM router.

3. The user sends a request to the IM router indicating that the user wishes to log onto its IM home server.

4. The IM router queries AD for the user's IM home server. This query actually goes to the GC Server.

5. The IM router returns the user's home server's URL address to the user.

6. The IM user uses this address to connect to the home server.

7. The IM home server validates the user's credentials and logs the user onto IM services.

It is important to note that the IM client will use the Internet Explorer profile for the IM logon. This profile, by definition, uses NTLM (NT LAN Manager) as its authentication method. NTLM, you'll recall, cannot pass through a proxy server; thus, if a user's browser is configured to use a proxy server, you'll need to configure an exclusion for the IP address of the IM routing and home server, as illustrated here:

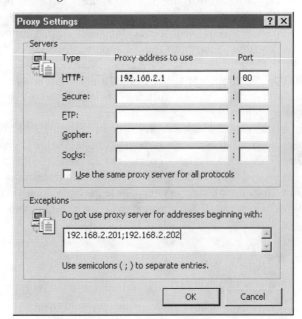

INSTALLING IM

To install IM, you'll need to rerun the Exchange setup program and select the Microsoft Exchange Instant Messaging Service component. You'll need to be sure to select the Change action on the parent Microsoft Exchange 2000 component. This is illustrated in Figure 17-1.

Next, you'll need to select which administrative group will manage the IM server, agree to the licensing agreement, and finish the installation. As you can see, the installation of IM services is not difficult. One thing to note, however, is that all Exchange services will be stopped and restarted during the install procedure. This would represent an interruption of services to your users if IM is installed during business hours.

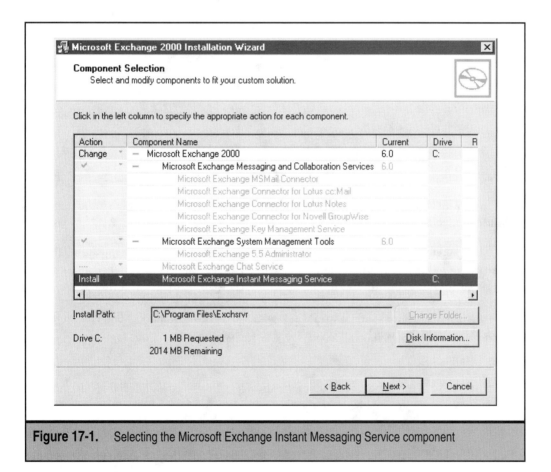

Figure 17-1. Selecting the Microsoft Exchange Instant Messaging Service component

To install the IM client, run mmssetup.exe from the Exchange Server CD-ROM, agree to the licensing agreement, and wait for the client to install. In this chapter, we'll illustrate IM using the MSN Messenger 2.2 client. Once the MSN client has installed, a configuration wizard will automatically appear that will take you through the basic setup of the client. The first screen will welcome you to the wizard; and the second screen, shown next, will ask for the e-mail address that will be used to log the user onto Exchange IM.

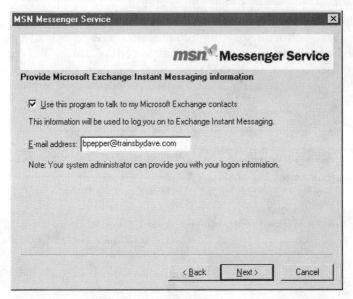

If you want to silently install the MSN client, use the /Q switch, which indicates that it should be installed in quiet mode. This is a good choice when installing MSN Messenger as part of a larger package of applications.

On the next screen, you'll select to use Exchange Instant Messaging only. Even if you're going to be using IM on the Internet, this is the correct selection because you can configure Internet Explorer and the Firewall Topology Module for Internet access. Then finish the setup program, and you're done with installing software. At this point, the MSN client will attempt to log onto IM services, but it should fail because you've just installed IM on your network. Now you need to configure it.

CONFIGURING IM

First, you'll need to navigate to the Instant Messaging (RVP) object under the protocol folder in the Exchange System Manager (see Figure 17-2).

Creating New IM Virtual Servers

From here, right-click the object and click New | Instant Messaging Virtual Server. This action will invoke the Welcome screen of the New Instant Messaging Virtual Server Wizard. You can click Next through to the Enter Display Name screen. The name that you select

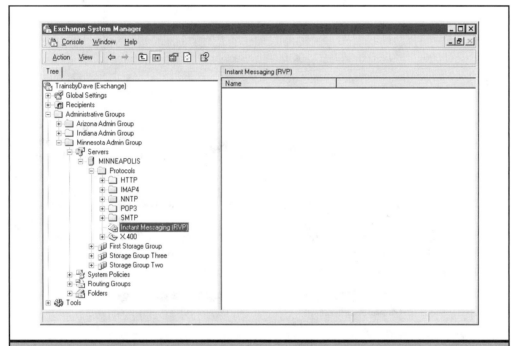

Figure 17-2.   Instant Messaging (RVP) object in the Exchange System Manager

should identify whether this is a home server or a routing server. In our example, we will create a new IM home server:

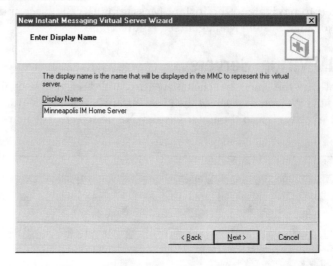

The next screen will ask which Web site you wish to associate with this IM server. This is necessary because all IM traffic is conducted over port 80. When IM server is installed, it will create a virtual directory under the default Web site that you have chosen and will name this directory *Instmsg*. It is through this directory that messages are routed.

The next screen will then ask for the DNS Domain Name and port number to which the server will respond. Even though it asks for the DNS domain name, when creating an IM home server, you must enter only the server's host name without a period: for example, "Minneapolis" instead of "Minneapolis.trainsbydave.com" or "Minneapolis." as shown next. If you place a period in the name of the server in this screen, IM will route the request to a proxy server, even if no proxy server exists.

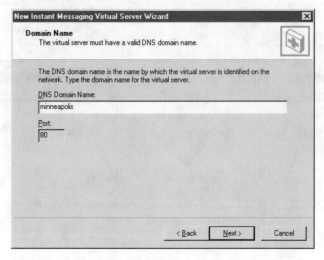

The next screen enables you to select the Allow This Server To Host User Accounts check box:

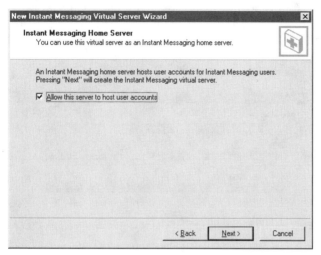

Selecting this check box will enable this IM virtual server to host user accounts. Leaving this check box unselected will make this IM virtual server a routing server. This is the only difference in the initial configuration between an IM home server and an IM routing server.

You can then finish the creation of the new IM virtual server, and it will now appear as a new virtual server beneath the Instant Messaging (RVP) container. After you've created the virtual server, it is ready to host user accounts.

To create an IM routing server, start the New Instant Messaging Virtual Server Wizard and step through its screens. When you are asked to name this server, you need to input the FQDN of the server. As illustrated next, this will be Indianapolis.trainsbydave.com. Interestingly enough, placing periods in this name will not route packets to the proxy server because this virtual server will not be hosting user accounts.

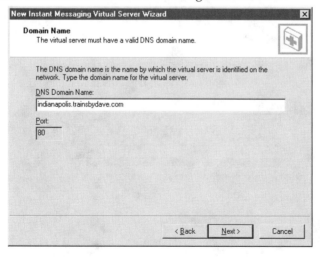

Enabling IM for User Accounts

To configure a user for instant messaging, open up Active Directory Users and Computers, navigate to the user account, and start the Exchange Task Wizard by right-clicking the user's account and selecting the wizard from the context menu. Under the Available Tasks screen, you'll find that there is an option to Enable Instant Messaging. Highlight this option and proceed to the next screen, as shown:

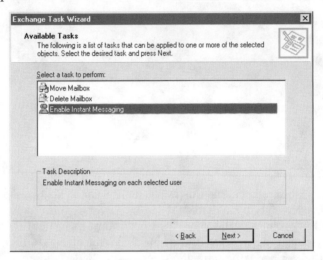

On the following screen, you're asked to select an IM home server, as well as the domain name to be used if the DNS SRV RVP record is not available or if the lookup fails. If you've installed a routing server, you'll have two choices: the home server's host name or the FQDN of the routing server. You should choose the routing server; then, the wizard will associate this information with the user's account and display the results in the Completing the Exchange Task Wizard screen (see Figure 17-3).

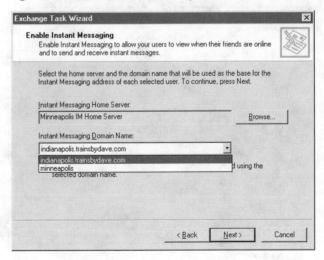

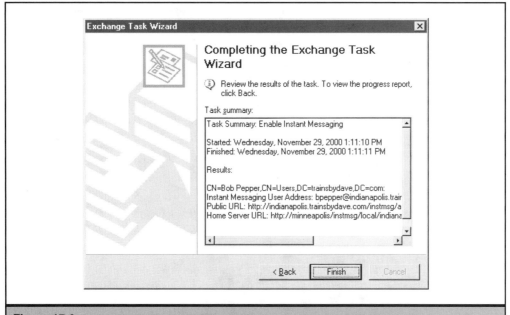

Figure 17-3. Use this screen to confirm your IM home server and domain name

Configuring DNS for the RVP

Configuring DNS for RVP should not be a big hassle. First, you should remember to enter an A (Address) record for each IM server into the DNS database. Second, if you have routing servers, consider giving them the host name of "im." While this is not required, Microsoft is pushing to use this standard so that companies with different installations of IM can still send and receive IM messages over the Internet. Users can then guess what another user's SMTP address would be in another company. For instance, if we wanted to get presence information on a friend at another company, we could guess that it would be friend@im.domainname.com.

Third, you'll need to create an _RVP SRV resource record for the RVP protocol and enable it to work over port 80. This record should map directly to the routing server. CNAME records are not necessary to configure DNS properly, though some documents early on in the Exchange 2000 development cycle indicated this.

TIP: In a single-server environment, it might be good to alias your home server with the "im" name. This will allow you to retain your internal naming convention while being compatible with other IM installations on the Internet. Be sure that your ISP's DNS records have an FQDN mapping for the IM alias to your incoming IP address over port 80. You will set up two virtual servers on your Exchange 2000 Server, one to be a home server and the other to be the routing server. If you do not want to configure a routing server, use the "im" FQDN as the host header for your default Web site to have messages routed into your server.

To create an RVP SRV record, open the DNS Manager, right-click the domain name, and select Other New Records. You'll then want to select the Service Location in the Resource Record Type selection box, and click the Create Record button, as shown here:

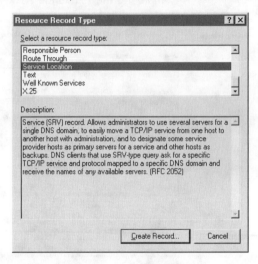

On the New Resource Record dialog box, shown next, you'll want to manually type **_rvp** in the Service input box. Your tendency will be to click the down arrow and discover that "_rvp is not a standard selection." Then you'll get all bent out of shape. Don't do that. Instead, just type it in manually and select _tcp as the protocol. Leave the Priority and Weight at 0 and type **80** as the port number. Finally, type in the FQDN of the routing server, and you should be good to go.

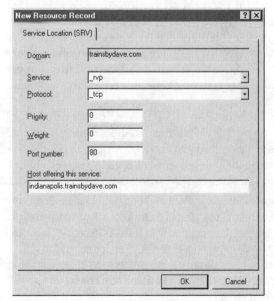

Now, if this is an Active Directory Integrated DNS implementation, then you'll need to either force replication of this new record using Active Directory Sites and Services (ADSS) or you'll need to wait for replication to complete *before* having your users attempt to use IM; otherwise, you'll just generate a bunch of unnecessary help-desk calls.

WORKING WITH FIREWALLS

Now that you've configured the client, the servers, and the DNS, let's take a look at how IM works with firewalls. If you're going to run IM behind a firewall *and* if you want to do IM over the internet, you'll need to configure the Firewall Topology tab in the Instant Messaging Settings Property Sheet.

It can be found in the Exchange System Manager under the Global Options container. Open Instant Messaging Settings | Properties | Firewall Topology tab, shown next. On this tab, you can identify which IP addresses are protected by your corporate firewall, and you can enable IM to work through the firewall by selecting the This Network Is Protected By A Firewall check box. In addition, to route outgoing IM messages through a proxy server, you'll need to enter its IP address in the HTTP Proxy Server area of the tab.

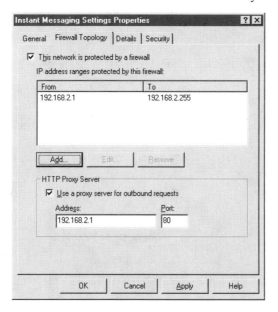

WORKING WITH THE IM CLIENT

In this section, we'll illustrate how to work with the MSN Messenger 2.2, found in the \Instmsg\i386\client\USA directory on the Exchange 2000 Server CD-ROM. To make this client available for distribution to your users, simply copy mmssetup.exe to a share point on a file server.

There are seven presence settings, shown next, that can be chosen to reflect your presence information. Here, Online is the default setting and Appear Offline means your presence information will not be displayed even though you are logged on.

▼ Online

■ Busy

■ Be Right Back

■ Away

■ On The Phone

■ Out To Lunch

▲ Appear Offline

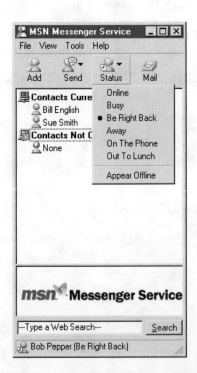

There are three other settings that are configured automatically by the IM client. The first is *idle*, which is displayed when there has been no activity at your keyboard for a given period of time, usually 15 minutes; it will switch to *online* when you touch your keyboard and initiate activity with your mouse. The third is *offline*, which reflects that you are not logged onto the IM server.

Once the client is up and running, you can send and receive instant messages. For instance, in the following two illustrations, Bill English has sent a message to Sue Smith, who replies with her own message. Notice that in the first illustration, Bill's message to Sue is about joining him and others for lunch. But notice that the Instant Message box title is "Sue Smith – Instant Message." The box title will always indicate to whom the message is being sent. Notice also that the message is typed in the lower pane and any message that will be received will be typed in the upper pane. Notice also that in Sue's IM client, Bill's message appears in the upper pane and Sue types her reply in the lower pane.

The MSN client has four main menus: Add, Send, Status, and Mail. The Add menu brings up a wizard that first asks how you would like to add a contact. This can be accomplished by either typing in the e-mail address or searching for a contact, either in the local address book or by searching IM for the user. What you are doing here is subscribing to another user's presence information. Once the contact has been added to your MSN client, the contact will appear either under the Contacts Currently Online or Contacts Not Online sections of the MSN client. Contacts added are persistent: they will reappear when the MSN client is restarted. The Send menu allows you to send a message to one of your contacts or to another person who is not presently a contact but for whom you have an e-mail address. The Status menu allows you to control what subscribers to your presence information will see. Changes in your status will be communicated immediately to your subscribers. The Mail menu option will open up your default mail client, such as Outlook 2000.

If you right-click a contact's name in the MSN Messenger client, the context menu illustrated in Figure 17-4 will appear. This context menu will allow you to make several choices. You can send an IM or invite the contact to a NetMeeting. You can also block the client from getting any presence information from you. Interestingly enough, you need to subscribe to their presence information before you can block them from getting your presence information. Figures 17-5 and 17-6 illustrate how this will appear. In Figure 17-5, Bob has blocked Sue, so now Sue's contact in Bob's MSN Messenger appears with a blocked signal over the contact icon. In Figure 17-6, in Sue's MSN Messenger client, Bob will appear as not online, even though he is.

You can also delete the contact using the context menu or obtain properties on the contact. The contact's properties will give you their logon name, status, and service, which will always be Microsoft Exchange Instant Messaging.

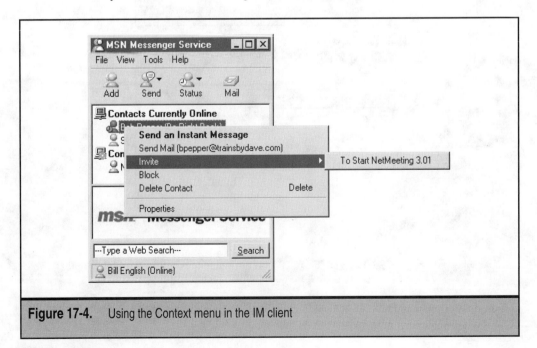

Figure 17-4.   Using the Context menu in the IM client

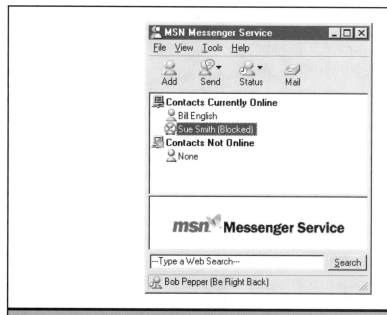

Figure 17-5.   Blocking Sue in Bob's IM client

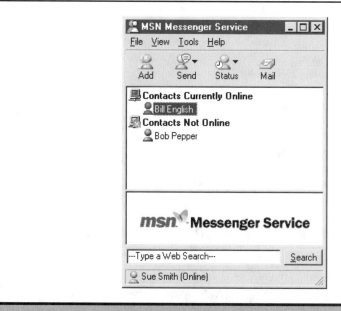

Figure 17-6.   Showing Bob offline in Sue's IM client

Click Tools | Options to find five tabs that might be of interest when configuring the MSN IM client. The first tab is the General tab, which offers several configuration choices, including the amount of time you need to be idle before automatically being shown as Away.

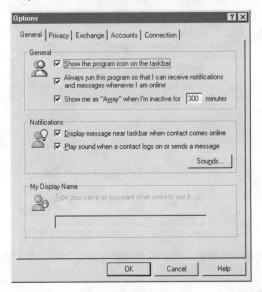

On the Privacy tab you can control who can see your online status and who can send you instant messages. The only users who will appear in this pane are those to whom you have subscribed. The reason for this is simple: given that IM works over the Internet, and hence, there is no common user databases for all users on the Internet, it is impossible to define in advance who can and cannot see your presence information unless you first know about them. So, if you want to block someone from seeing your presence information, you'll need to first subscribe to them. If you click the View button, you'll see the list of users that have added you to their list. In other words, this is the list of people currently receiving your presence information.

MANAGING IM SERVICES FROM THE SERVER

In this section, we'll take a look at how IM is managed from the server. Specifically, we'll look at the administrative actions you can perform in Active Directory Users and Computers.

Disabling IM for an Individual Account

We've already seen how to enable IM for an individual user account. But there may be times when you want to disable a user's IM account as well. You'll do this with the Exchange Task Wizard, just as you did to enable IM for the user. The only real difference is that you'll choose Disable Instant Messaging, which disassociates the user's account from the IM home server.

However, as you can see in the next illustration, you can also choose to associate the user's account with a different IM home server by selecting Change Instant Messaging Home Server and stepping through the remaining screens. Remember that if you change the home server for a user, the user will need to completely exit the IM client and reconnect to establish a new connection to the home server. This will take some patience. The next paragraph explains why.

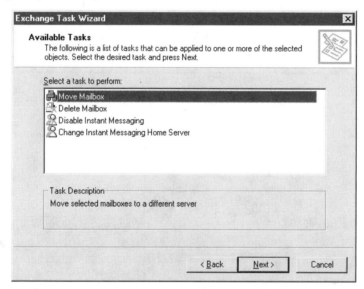

Recall that the client first connects to the routing server and then is referred to the home server. Also recall that the routing server contacts GC services to retrieve the user's home server. When you change a user's home server, you'll need to wait for this attribute change to be replicated to all the GCs before you allow the user to reconnect. Otherwise, the user may receive an error message and generate an unnecessary help desk call.

TIP: The IM-specific attributes that are replicated to the GC are *msExchIMAddress*, *msExchIMMetaPhysicalURL*, and *msExchIMPhysicalURL*. It is these attributes that the routing server uses to look up a user's home server.

Finding an IM User on Your Network

Sometimes, you'll need to find an IM user on your network. And, sometimes, this will mean that you'll need to perform an advanced search of AD, since the IM information is held as a set of attributes to the user's account. In Active Directory Users and Computers, open Action | Find | Find Users, Contacts, And Groups. Next, click the Advanced tab, select Field | User, and scroll to the IM options in the menu, shown in Figure 17-7.

ENSURING A USER'S PRIVACY

There will be some users for whom privacy is a concern. For instance, top executives may not desire to have their presence information available to just anyone in the organization. Moreover, you may find that you want to control which groups of users and servers can access an IM user's presence information for a variety of reasons. Earlier, we discussed how the user could block another user from obtaining presence information, but this is

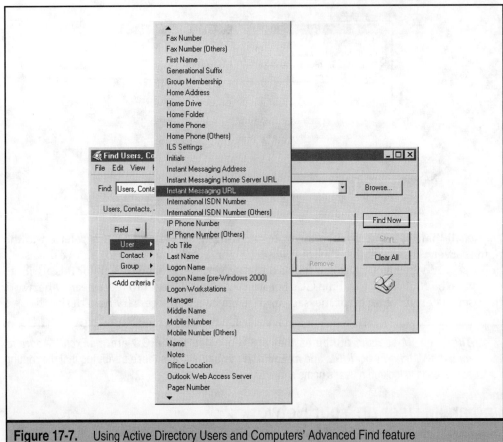

Figure 17-7.   Using Active Directory Users and Computers' Advanced Find feature

clearly not the best method to ensure privacy. Now, we'll discuss the preferred method: configuring a user's IM properties in his or her user account.

In Active Directory Users and Computers, navigate to the Exchange Features tab in the user's account properties, highlight Instant Messaging, and click the Properties button. Another box will appear, as you can see in Figure 17-8. Click the Privacy tab. This is where you can specify who can access this user's IM services. Click the Allow Access Only From These Servers And Users radio button, click the Add button, and configure as needed. If you leave the first radio button selected, which is the default, then the account has no restrictions on it (other than what the user might enforce from the IM client), and anyone can gain access to presence information. However, selecting the second radio button will limit access to this account's IM services to those in the list. Keep in mind that if there are those outside your organization who need interaction with this account's IM services, you'll need to create their account as a mail-enabled contact in your AD.

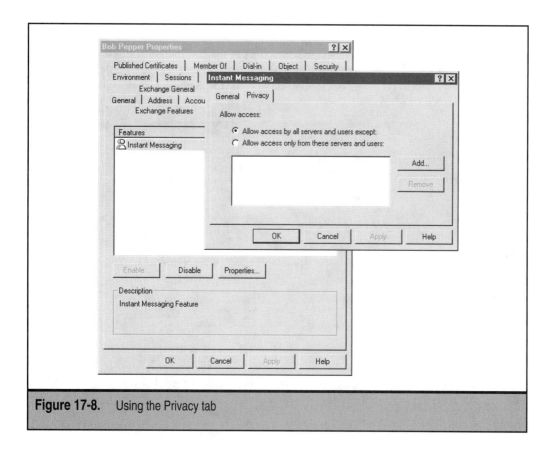

Figure 17-8.   Using the Privacy tab

MANAGING IM SERVERS

There will be times when you'll want to either remove or take an IM server offline. You also might want to move your IM databases to another location. This section describes how to perform these administrative functions.

Removing an IM Server

There are many scenarios when you'll want to remove an IM server, but the most common is if you are upgrading Exchange services to run on a faster, bigger, and better box. If you need to remove an IM server, there are a couple of ways to do this. First, you can remove the virtual server while leaving the IM service installed; or, second, you can remove the IM service, which will also require removing the IM virtual server.

If you think you'll need to create another IM virtual server at some point in the future, then leave the IM service installed. However, if you know that this server will not be used for IM services in the future, then completely remove the IM service.

To remove an IM virtual server, right-click the virtual server in the Exchange System Manager and select Delete. This action will produce the Delete Instant Messaging Virtual Server dialog box, shown next, in which you'll be asked if you'd like to move the users hosted by this virtual server to another virtual server and, if so, which one they should be sent to.

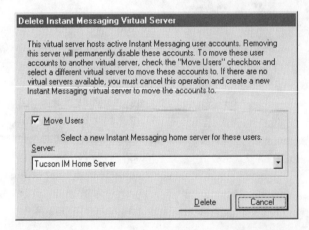

If you are deleting the last home server, the dialog box will still appear, but its configurations will be dimmed. When the last IM home server is deleted, all the user accounts are also disassociated with the server. If you then create a new IM home server, you'll need to reassociate your user accounts with the new server.

Taking an IM Server Offline Temporarily

In order to take an IM server offline, you'll need to stop the IIS virtual server. This is not accomplished in the Exchange System Manager, but instead is accomplished in IIS by stopping the virtual site that the IM server is using. Just right-click the virtual site and select Stop. Users will experience that messaging immediately stops. To place the server back online, start the virtual directory using the IIS Manager.

Moving IM Databases

Even though there are databases for the IM server, it is important to remember that these databases do not permanently store messages. You can designate a new location of IM data and its log files on the property pages of the Instant Messaging (RVP) protocol folder, shown here:

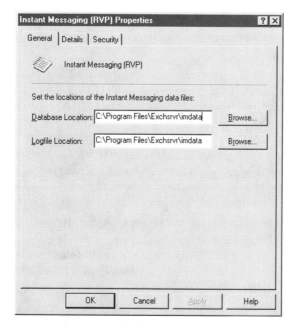

Changing the database and log file location does not move these files, but instead creates new files in the new location after the service is stopped and restarted. If you want to use the same databases and transaction logs, you'll need to manually copy the files to a new directory and then restart the virtual Web site in IIS.

TROUBLESHOOTING IM

IM is one of the most frustrating services we've ever had to troubleshoot. However, if you can understand a few important points, then troubleshooting IM isn't so bad.

First, before you start troubleshooting, you really should install Network Monitor and be able to capture packets on the network. The packets can exactly pinpoint the trouble.

Second, here is a list of things to check if IM isn't working:

▼ During the installation of the IM home virtual server, did you give the server a name that included a period (.)? If so, then all client requests will be redirected to the proxy server, even if none exists. Be sure that the home server is not created with a period in its name.

■ After making a change, did you wait long enough to allow the GC to be updated? Some IM server AD lookups are to the GC, such as a user's IM home server; and if a change has not had time to replicate, you could receive an error message when trying to log on even though the new change is a correct configuration.

■ If the client logon screen immediately reappears after clicking OK to log on to the IM server, this probably represents an HTTP 404 Server not found error. This can be the result of the DNS RVP record not being fully replicated or being incorrectly created. Ensure that you have the correct SRV record created in DNS. And if your DNS is AD integrated, then allow enough time for the directory to replicate any changes to either the DNS server, such as the addition of the _RVP protocol SRV record. This could also represent that an incorrect logon name has been input into the client. Check to make sure that the logon name matches the logon name in the user's account properties in Active Directory.

■ During the installation of the IM routing server, did you input the FQDN of the routing server in the DNS domain name box? For routing servers, this is the correct configuration. Inputting a period in this box for a routing server will not send packets to the proxy server because this virtual server is not hosting user accounts.

■ Did you check the Internet Explorer (IE) profile? Remember that the MSN client will use the IE profile for its own profile. Therefore, if you are using a proxy server, you'll need to exclude the IP addresses of both the routing and the home server in the profile in order for the MSN messenger to contact these servers. Without adding these IP addresses into the exclusion box, all the client packets will be sent to the proxy server because the profile is configured to send all port 80 packets to the proxy server.

■ If you have a routing server, then be sure that (a) there is an SRV record in DNS for this server referencing the _RVP protocol, (b) the client's logon is to the DNS domain name that the router server resides in (which is the same domain name that you selected when you created the routing server), and (c) if you are using MSN Messenger, that you are using version 2.1 or higher. Earlier versions of MSN Messenger will not work with Exchange 2000.

- It may sound silly, but be sure the client has connectivity and name resolution.

- If you need to re-create an IM server, be sure to delete the Instmsg virtual directory before re-creating the IM server. Do not re-create or create a new IM server using the same Web site without first deleting the existing Instmsg virtual directory.

- Do not use alias names in DNS for your routing server. If your routing server's host name is something other than "im," either use the real host name or add a second—a record that resolves the "im" host name to the IP address of the server. But do not attempt to use an alias, such as "im," for the host name of the server. Chances are it won't work, or if it does work, it will be unreliable.

- If you delete and then create a new routing server, this new information is not automatically updated in the user's properties. After deleting and then creating a new routing or home server, you'll need to disable and then re-enable IM services in the user's properties. Again, since the routing server and the IM client does most of their lookups to the GC, you'll need to be patient to allow the GC to update as well.

- Be sure your IM clients are using a password for their logons. Microsoft has said that the IM clients will not accept a client logon with a password, but some have been able to accomplish logon with a blank password. When in doubt, use a password.

▲ If using the MSN messenger client, be sure it's version 2.2 or higher. Older versions of MSN will not work with IM in Exchange 2000.

Overall, experience suggests that patience is the key to troubleshooting IM, because of all the replication that must occur for a configuration change to work. So, if your IM isn't working, first have a pizza delivered, get a Diet Pepsi (remember: no beer when working with the servers), and then be very methodical and patient when making changes to IM. In the end, it will work and your spouse won't have to cook you a late supper.

SUMMARY

In this chapter, you have learned how to install and configure IM. You have also seen how this service works, both from the client and the server sides. We've also supplied a list of items to check in case your installation didn't go according to plan.

Since there isn't another chapter to send you on to, we'd like to thank you for reading this book. We hope it's been helpful and that you've learned a great deal about how to get started administering Exchange 2000 Server. Be sure to check Microsoft's Web site often at **http://www.microsoft.com/exchange** for the latest information about Exchange 2000 Server. And if you see either of us at a conference, please, stop and say "Hello." We would enjoy meeting you!

INDEX

N

 O

P

S

INTERNATIONAL CONTACT INFORMATION

AUSTRALIA
McGraw-Hill Book Company Australia Pty. Ltd.
TEL +61-2-9417-9899
FAX +61-2-9417-5687
http://www.mcgraw-hill.com.au
books-it_sydney@mcgraw-hill.com

CANADA
McGraw-Hill Ryerson Ltd.
TEL +905-430-5000
FAX +905-430-5020
http://www.mcgrawhill.ca

**GREECE, MIDDLE EAST,
NORTHERN AFRICA**
McGraw-Hill Hellas
TEL +30-1-656-0990-3-4
FAX +30-1-654-5525

MEXICO (Also serving Latin America)
McGraw-Hill Interamericana Editores S.A. de C.V.
TEL +525-117-1583
FAX +525-117-1589
http://www.mcgraw-hill.com.mx
fernando_castellanos@mcgraw-hill.com

SINGAPORE (Serving Asia)
McGraw-Hill Book Company
TEL +65-863-1580
FAX +65-862-3354
http://www.mcgraw-hill.com.sg
mghasia@mcgraw-hill.com

SOUTH AFRICA
McGraw-Hill South Africa
TEL +27-11-622-7512
FAX +27-11-622-9045
robyn_swanepoel@mcgraw-hill.com

**UNITED KINGDOM & EUROPE
(Excluding Southern Europe)**
McGraw-Hill Education Europe
TEL +44-1-628-502500
FAX +44-1-628-770224
http://www.mcgraw-hill.co.uk
computing_neurope@mcgraw-hill.com

ALL OTHER INQUIRIES Contact:
Osborne/McGraw-Hill
TEL +1-510-549-6600
FAX +1-510-883-7600
http://www.osborne.com
omg_international@mcgraw-hill.com